Imagining a Renaissance in Teacher Education

Teacher Education Yearbook XVI

Edited by Cheryl J. Craig
and Louise F. Deretchin

Published in partnership with the
Association of Teacher Educators

Rowman & Littlefield Education
Lanham, Maryland • Toronto • Plymouth, UK
2008

Published in partnership with the
Association of Teacher Educators

Published in the United States of America
by Rowman & Littlefield Education
A Division of Rowman & Littlefield Publishers, Inc.
A wholly owned subsidiary of The Rowman & Littlefield Publishing Group, Inc.
4501 Forbes Boulevard, Suite 200, Lanham, Maryland 20706
www.rowmaneducation.com

Estover Road
Plymouth PL6 7PY
United Kingdom

Copyright © 2008 by Cheryl J. Craig and Louise F. Deretchin

All rights reserved. No part of this publication may be reproduced, stored in a retrieval system, or transmitted in any form or by any means, electronic, mechanical, photocopying, recording, or otherwise, without the prior permission of the publisher.

British Library Cataloguing in Publication Information Available

Library of Congress Control Number: 2006930214

ISBN-13: 978-1-57886-716-5 (cloth, alkaline paper)
ISBN-10: 1-57886-716-9 (cloth, alkaline paper)
ISBN-13: 978-1-57886-717-2 (pbk., alkaline paper)
ISBN-10: 1-57886-717-7 (pbk., alkaline paper)

∞ ™ The paper used in this publication meets the minimum requirements of American National Standard for Information Sciences—Permanence of Paper for Printed Library Materials, ANSI/NISO Z39.48–1992.
Manufactured in the United States of America.

Teacher Education Yearbook XVI

EDITORS

Cheryl J. Craig, University of Houston
Louise F. Deretchin, Educational Consultant

EDITORIAL ADVISORY BOARD

Leslie Agard-Jones, William Paterson University of New Jersey
Lillian Benavente-McEnery, University of Houston–Clear Lake
Blake R. Bickham, Mesa State College
Christa Boske, University of Houston–Clear Lake
Caroline M. Crawford, University of Houston–Clear Lake
Sarah DeHaas, Juniata College
George J. Fero, McKendree University
Andrea S. Foster, Sam Houston State University
Nancy P. Gallavan, University of Central Arkansas
Victoria Giordano, Adrian Dominican School of Education–Barry University
Linda Houser, Indiana University, Purdue University–Indianapolis
Michele Kahn, University of Houston–Clear Lake
Meng-Fen Grace Lin, University of Houston
Susan G. Magliaro, Virginia Tech
Carrie Green Markello, University of Houston
Susan McCormack, University of Houston–Clear Lake
Denise McDonald, University of Houston–Clear Lake
Angela López Pedrana, University of Houston–Downtown
Melissa E. Pierson, University of Houston
Rita Pokol Poimbeauf, University of Houston
Lilia Ruban, University of Houston
Felix Simieou III, University of Houston–Clear Lake
Alice Young, Marymount University

EDITORIAL SUPPORT BOARD

Yung-Chen Chung, University of Houston
Xiao Han, University of Houston
Trinidad R. Hernandez, University of Houston

EXECUTIVE DIRECTOR

David Ritchey, Association of Teacher Educators, Manassas Park, Virginia

Contents

List of Illustrations	ix
Foreword *Terry L. James*	xi
Introduction *Cheryl J. Craig, Louise F. Deretchin*	xv

DIVISION 1: THE ROOTS OF RENAISSANCE

Overview and Framework *Cheryl J. Craig, Louise F. Deretchin*	3
1 Schwab's Call for a Renaissance: A Teacher Education Perspective *Vicki Ross, Elaine Chan*	4
2 Preparing Urban Educators for the Twenty-First Century: What the Research Suggests *Deborah L. Voltz, Loucrecia Collins, Janice Patterson, Michele Jean Sims*	25
Summary and Implications *Cheryl J. Craig, Louise F. Deretchin*	41

DIVISION 2: SHIFTING PERSPECTIVES AND PRACTICES

Overview and Framework *Cheryl J. Craig, Louise F. Deretchin*	47
3 Daring to Care: Adding Caring to Our Vision of Teacher Education *Robin Haskell McBee, Patrick M. Westcott*	49

4	Spiritual Voices of Preservice Teachers *Shelley McIntosh, Linlin Irene Chen, Beatrice Villareal, Marion Godine*	66
5	Teachers' Thoughts about the Rewards and Joys of Teaching: A Neglected Component in Teacher Education Programs *Miriam Ben-Peretz, Gabriella Landler-Pardo*	80
6	Educating for Inquiry through a Reflective Portfolio Process: What Are the Imperatives for Teachers or Students to Think Well in Contexts? *Nona Lyons*	98
7	The Wisdom of Fifth Graders: A Voice in the Renaissance *Barbara Morgan-Fleming, Mya Kendrik-Mercer, Susan Myers, Connie Wilson Anderson*	118
8	Star Tech: The Net Generation! *Ronald A. Berk*	131

Summary and Implications 147
Cheryl J. Craig, Louise F. Deretchin

DIVISION 3: ALTERING CONTENT

Overview and Framework 155
Cheryl J. Craig, Louise F. Deretchin

9	The Reimagination of a Graduate Reading Program: Roles and Responsibilities, Themes, Reflections, and Implications *Kathleen F. Malu, Salika A. Lawrence, Geraldine Mongillo*	157
10	Preservice Teachers' Beliefs about Curriculum Theory: Is It Meaningful and/or Useful? *Elida Giraldo*	170
11	Professionalism vs. Reality: Student Awareness of Legal Rights and Responsibilities *Rita P. Poimbeauf*	185
12	Student Teachers' Diversity Rights: The Case Law *Zorka Karanxha, Perry A. Zirkel*	201

Summary and Implications 213
Cheryl J. Craig, Louise F. Deretchin

DIVISION 4: PROBLEMATIC CONDITIONS

Overview and Framework 219
Cheryl J. Craig, Louise F. Deretchin

13	Preservice Teachers Leading the Way: Improving Field Experiences by Cultivating Candidates' Voice and Agency *Wendy Burke, Ryan Cowell, Russell Olwell, David Osta*	221
14	Fence Sitting: Preservice Teachers' Agreement with Tenets of Economic Responsibilities and Social Justice *Thomas A. Lucey*	237
15	The Categories that Bind: Connecting Teacher Education to Teaching Practice *Renée T. Clift, Raúl A. Mora, Patricia Brady*	252
16	Encountering Relational Complexity: On "The Arts of the Practical" in Learning to Teach *Margaret Macintyre Latta*	271

Summary and Implications 287
Cheryl J. Craig, Louise F. Deretchin

DIVISION 5: RENAISSANCE IN ACTION

Overview and Framework 293
Cheryl J. Craig, Louise F. Deretchin

17	Calling for a Renaissance of Care *Terri Hebert, Tami Burcham, Tara Gordon*	295
18	Small Steps: Moving Toward a Renaissance in Teacher Education *Helen Freidus*	314
19	A Renaissance of the Arts in Classrooms: A Collaboration between a College, a Public School, and an Arts Institution *Abigail McNamee, Andrea Zakin, Marietta Saravia-Shore, Alexandria Lawrence Ross, Jeanne M. Peloso, Nancy E. Dubetz, Christy Folsom, Mia L. Mercurio, Juan Morales-Flores, Holly Fairbank, Jaime Porteus Iurato*	328
20	Cultivating Parent-Child Collaboration Concerning Mathematical Learning: A Necessary Objective for Teacher Preparation Programs *Regina M. Mistretta*	348
21	Minimizing Barriers in Teacher Diversity Professional Development *Earl Thomas, David Lamont Bell*	363
22	Valuing Narrative Authority, Collaboration, and Diversity in Revitalizing a Teacher Education Program *Margaret Olson*	377

Summary and Implications 395
Cheryl J. Craig, Louise F. Deretchin

DIVISION 6: LESSONS LEARNED

Overview and Framework 403
Cheryl J. Craig, Louise F. Deretchin

23 Teacher Education that Makes a Difference: Developing Foundational Principles of Practice 405
John Loughran, Fred Korthagen, Tom Russell

24 Questioning What We Know About Teacher Education 422
Stefinee Pinnegar, Lynnette B. Erickson

Summary and Implications 437
Cheryl J. Craig, Louise F. Deretchin

Afterword 441
Cheryl J. Craig, Louise F. Deretchin

Illustrations

Tables

9.1	Knowledge Activity	162
9.2	Inquiry Activity	163
9.3	Dispositions	163
9.4	Sample of Curriculum Map	165
14.1	Items Resulting in the Highest Neutrality	245
14.2	Items Resulting in the Lowest Degree of Neutrality (N = 75)	247
15.1	Crossing Contexts Participants Teaching in Same Schools since Graduation	257
15.2	Crossing Contexts Participants Who Have Changed Schools since Graduation	258
15.3	Crossing Contexts Participants Who Chose Not to Teach	259
17.1	Contact Log	308
19.1	Crossing Contexts for Participants Who Chose Not to Teach	337
19.2	Brainstorming Guide for Aesthetic Education Curriculum Plan	338
20.1	Independent Samples T-Test Results for Groups 1 and 2	357
20.2	Independent Samples T-Test Results for Groups 2 and 3	357
20.3	Mean Responses to Survey Statements (S1 to S14)	358
21.1	First Year Project Aims and Activities	369
21.3	Descriptive Statistics of Teacher Perceptions with Respect to Grade Groupings	371
21.3	Descriptive Statistics of Teacher Perceptions with Respect to Years of Experience	372

Figures

2.1	Competencies for Success	28
7.1	Student Drawings of a Good Teacher	122

20.1	Parent Survey	355
23.1	Clustering Seven Principles into Elements of Programs and Program Change	416

Foreword

Terry L. James
University of Central Arkansas

> Terry L. James, Ed.D., is professor and interim chair of the Department of Leadership Studies in the College of Education at the University of Central Arkansas. He serves as president of the Association of Teacher Educators (2007–2008), where he has been a member for thirty-six years. Dr. James is a consultant to EAST, Inc. (Environmental and Spatial Technology), a private non-profit organization that prepares teachers to function as facilitators in EAST classrooms that utilize advanced software applications as part of authentic project based learning and include a service component. Begun in 1995, the program is found in eight different states and over 200 schools with nearly 10,000 students in grades 3–12. Researching and writing in the fields of teacher education, school reform, and educational change, Dr. James' areas of teaching expertise include curriculum and issues in education.

The Association of Teacher Educators' Yearbook XVI reminds us how quickly events occur and time passes. The concept of renaissance is not a new one, but rather one we revisit periodically just as the meaning of the word conveys. For many of us, it seems only yesterday that we were reading and contemplating implications of the seminal work *Educating a Profession* (Howsam, Corrigan, Denmark, & Nash, 1976). About the time we digested the suggestions made by these distinguished authors, we were confronted by *A Nation at Risk* (1983) that provided a "new vision" for a renaissance in education. Shortly after this publication came two other seminal works that influenced our visions of powerful teacher education, *The Knowledge Base for the Beginning Teacher* (Reynolds, ed., 1989) and ATE's own first edition of *The Handbook of Research on Teacher Education* (Houston, 1990). The ATE Yearbook XVI, *Imagining a Renaissance in Teacher Education,* continues our journey exploring provocative ideas to cogitate as we contemplate the potential influence on our own programs. In the final analysis, quality *can and must* be assured at the institutional and program levels of teacher education.

The ATE Yearbook editors have selected authors whose manuscripts reflect changes for revitalization in our profession. The Yearbook is superbly organized into six divisions, with Division 1 providing the context for a renaissance. Then, in Division 2, several chapters address shifting perspectives and practices. Division 3 takes us inside programs to consider specific examples on ways content can be altered to initiate and sustain a renaissance at the local level. Division 4 provides insights on addressing these conditions. Wisdom of experience coupled with other more formal sources of information tell us that change must address the problematic conditions that accompany the change process. Exemplars that others educators can emulate are found in Division 5. Lessons learned are found in Division 6.

The authors, as a collective group, offer multiple viewpoints on the concept of renaissance applied to teacher education. Representing seven countries, found among these authors are some with international reputations, many whose names may be new to our membership, one or two who are practically household names within our association, and upstarts including classroom teachers and graduate students. As a reader, you will have the opportunity to look through the eyes and experiences of fifth-graders to get their collective vision of a good teacher. We are treated to an analysis of the challenges that must be faced when we design teacher education programs for preparing educators to teach students who are growing up in a "different" kind of world than many of us experienced as children and adolescents. And we are cautioned that a continuous revitalization of our work is dependent upon making connections to the world of practice. A true renaissance in teacher education is possible only when accompanied by systematic change in the actual education of P–12 students.

The theme for my ATE presidency, *Multiple Realities in Teacher Education: Exemplars for Addressing Dilemmas, Conundrums, and Processes*, reflects my own lifelong educational journey that began in a one-room schoolhouse. Just as many of you, I experienced teachers who possessed some, but not all, of the requisite qualities to be a highly competent teacher. They were knowledgeable of content but demonstrated little care for kids and a lack of knowledge of growth and development; some of my own teachers really cared for us, but they were not well versed in the content or how to teach it. When I reflect on the teacher educators who helped prepare me for the profession, I found a few who were also lacking in one or more ways. Fortunately, in both of those worlds, I learned from and with highly competent professionals who could both walk the walk and talk the talk. I am thankful for each one of them. They helped develop within me the qualities that put me on the pathway to become a self-motivated learner with a solid understanding of professional ethical behavior. The content of the ATE Yearbook XVI reminds me why I chose my theme. It addresses many of the realities we face as a profession. The authors provide exemplars for addressing the dilemmas and conundrums that confront us.

Congratulations to the editors and authors who made this publication possible for all teacher educators. May each of you enjoy your reading and find ideas that you can contemplate and use. Finally, let all of us heed the words of Henry Adams, "Teachers affect eternity," as we reawaken within ourselves our mission to teach those who teach the students.

References

Houston, W. R. (Ed.) (1990). *Handbook of research on teacher education. A project of the Association of Teacher Educators.* New York: MacMillan.

Howsam, R. B., Corrigan, D. C., Denmark, G. W., & Nash, R. J. (1976). *Educating a profession. Report of the Bicentennial Commission on Education for the Profession of Teaching.* Washington, DC: AACTE.

National Commission on Excellence in Education. (1983). *A nation at risk: The imperative for educational reform.* Washington, DC: U.S. Government Printing Office.

Reynolds, M. C. (Ed.) *Knowledge base for the beginning teacher.* New York: Peramon Press (1989).

Introduction

Cheryl J. Craig
University of Houston

Louise F. Deretchin
Educational Consultant

> Cheryl J. Craig, Ph.D., is a professor in the College of Education at the University of Houston and serves as the Director of Elementary Education and Coordinator of Teaching and Teacher Education. She is author of the book, *Narrative Inquiries of School Reform: Storied Lives, Storied Landscapes, Storied Metaphors* (Information Age Publishing), as well as numerous articles that appear regularly in *Teaching and Teacher Education, Journal of Teacher Education, Teachers College Record,* and *American Educational Research Journal,* among other publications.

> Louise F. Deretchin, Ph.D., is an educational consultant, former Director of Higher Education for the Houston A+ Challenge (formerly the Houston Annenberg Challenge), a fellow in the Association of Teacher Educators Leadership Academy, founding member of the Texas Higher Education Coordinating Board Houston P-16+ Council, and co-founder of the *Regional Faculty* whose purpose is to take a regional approach to directing the growth of educational systems. Her work focuses on creating collaborations among colleges, the business community, and school districts to improve teacher education, teaching, and learning.

For *ATE Yearbook XV* (Deretchin & Craig, 2007), the theme of the impact of international accountability systems was selected. The call prompted researchers from across the nation and around the world to examine issues relating to accountability and what they believed accountability systems were and were not accomplishing. For *ATE Yearbook XVI*, we decided to draw something different to the fore, something more directly linked to teacher education. At the same time, we recognized that whatever theme was chosen needed to take a markedly different direction from *Studying Teacher Education: The Report of the AERA Panel on Research and Teacher Education* (Cochran-Smith & Zeichner, 2005). While comprehensive and worthy of major attention, that volume took an eye-of-the-needle approach to sizing up the state of teacher education and, in the process, left out some promising national and international research available in the field. We knew we needed a more inclusive approach, one with a wider inquiry net.

And so, the idea of taking a positive spin on teacher education and imagining a renaissance from teacher educators' perspectives emerged. The notion of an educational renaissance, of course, was borrowed from Schwab (1969/1978) who forecasted that a renaissance in the field of curriculum would be needed to address its "moribund state" (p. 287). More recently, Hamilton and McWilliam (2001) echoed Schwab's sentiment in *The Handbook of Research on Teaching* (Richardson, 2001). To those authors, teaching and teacher education suffer from the same maladies as curriculum and therefore also are in need of rebirth.

Meanwhile, other noteworthy developments have taken shape on the teaching and teacher education front. One such development was the release of *Educating School Teachers* (Levine, 2006), the second of three reports of The Education Schools Project, a study commissioned by the Annenberg Foundation, the Ford Foundation, the Kauffman Foundation, and the Wallace Foundation. Predictably, the Levine report ruffled feathers. However, two of Levine's observations bear mentioning here. One was the appalling lack of investment in teaching and teacher education research in the richest, most powerful nation in the world—not to mention the shockingly uneven distribution of available funds. The second was the utter fallacy of equating the quality of teacher education programs with colleges' and universities' abilities to produce paper facsimile copies of students' learning and teacher educators' practices (Levine, 2006; also see Latta & Field, 2005).

Around the same time, Reading First grabbed the nation's attention. Administered by the U.S. Department of Education, the $6 billion reading program was reviewed by the Inspector General's Office (2006) and found not to be in compliance with the grant application process. This prompted at least six other investigations. Since then, other legal and ethical violations have been made public. More recently, an appointed House panel ruled "to slash Reading First aid" (*Education Week,* June 8, 2007). Readers may wonder, "What does the corruption associated with Reading First have to do teacher education?" Simply put, Reading First is the jewel in the ruling government's science-based research crown and the use of science-based research methods in the examination of teaching and teacher education practices sits alongside it—as the research parameters that were determined for *Studying Teacher Education* reflected. Of course, the question remains as to whether the reputation of narrowly defined approaches to science-based research will be tarnished by the Reading First debacle and whether a spillover effect will be felt in teaching and teacher education, most specifically with respect to how future funded research is conducted.

In the same week (June 4, 2007), yet another article, "How to Fix No Child Left Behind" (Wallis & Steptoe, 2007) appeared in *Time* magazine. In it, Wallis and Steptoe assigned the No Child Left Behind Act a lackluster grade of C. But it was the article's final recommendations that bore implications for teaching and teacher education. Among them were: (1) "Leave turnaround [solutions] . . . to the people who are closest to students . . . ," (2) fund research that works, and (3) ". . . listen hard to the people who are working in the nation's schools [and schools of education?] every day" (p. 41). "It's the only way to ensure that policies that sound great in Washington aren't leaving educational reality behind" (p. 41), Wallis and Steptoe concluded.

Yearbook XVI, in our opinion, captures teacher educators' ideas about what potentially could happen and what is working and not working in particular teaching and teacher education settings. In a nutshell, it distills changes mapped by luminaries in the national and international research communities.

Division 1: The Roots of Renaissance, which is comprised of two chapters, centers on the roots of renaissance approached from both historical and contemporary perspectives. Meanwhile, Division 2: Shifting Perspectives and Practices, spanning six chapters, focuses on changing perspectives and practices, many of which have been enacted in local sites, while Division 3: Altering Content, encompassing four chapters, dwells on desired shifts in the content of teacher education programs with those shifts including and transcending core content. Next comes Division 4: Problematic Conditions with four chapters focusing on perplexing conditions that teacher educators face. This is followed by Division 5: Renaissances in Action and its six chapter lineup. Finally, Division 6: Lessons Learned concludes the volume. It appropriately features two chapters: one, international; the other, U.S.-based.

We believe readers will be excited by the multiplicity of topics that captured authors' imaginations when they entertained the possibility of a renaissance in teaching and teacher education. Additionally, we think readers will be surprised that our contributors included teacher educators, classroom teachers, and graduate students, in addition to K–12 student informants, a principal, an educational humorist, and legal experts. We also imagine readers will be struck by the commonalities in sources, challenges, practices, and possibilities that weave throughout the pages regardless of the region within the U.S. or the country around the world from which the works emanated.

Before launching the volume, we especially wish to thank those who served as blind reviewers of the chapters, the members of the Faculty Academy who assisted in an advisory review board capacity, the research assistants who provided editorial support, and the authors who penned the chapters. Each of these individuals helped make this yearbook possible. As can be seen, many people's contributions—in addition to our own—made *Imagining a Renaissance in Teacher Education: Yearbook XVI* a reality.

References

Cochran-Smith, M., & Zeichner, K. (2005). *Studying teacher education: The report of the AERA panel on research and teacher education.* Washington, DC: American Educational Research Association.

Deretchin, L., & Craig, C. (2007). *International research on the impact of accountability systems: Teacher education yearbook XV.* Lanham, MD: Rowman & Littlefield Education.

Hamilton, D., & McWilliam, E. (2001). Ex-centric voices that frame research in teaching. In V. Richardson (Ed.), *Handbook of research on teaching* (4th ed., pp. 17–43). Washington, DC: American Educational Research Association.

Latta, M., & Field, J. (2005). The flight from experience to representation: Seeing relational complexity in teacher education. *Teaching and Teacher Education*, 649–660.

Levine, A. (2006, September). *Educating school teachers.* The Education School Project www.edschools.org/pdf/Educating_Teachers_Report.pdf, accessed June 8, 2007.

Schwab, J. J. (1969/1978). The practical: A language for curriculum. In I. Westbury & N. J. Wilkof (Eds.), *Science, curriculum, and liberal education: Selected essays* (pp. 287–321). Chicago: University of Chicago Press.

United States Department of Education (2006, September). *The Reading First Program's grant application process: Final inspection report* (ED-OLG I13–F004, pp. 1–51). Washington, DC: U.S. Department of Education.

Wallis, C., & Steptoe, S. (2007, June 4). Report on No Child Left Behind. *Time*, 34–41.

Division 1
THE ROOTS OF RENAISSANCE

Overview and Framework

Cheryl J. Craig

Louise F. Deretchin

The beauty and mystery of an open submission yearbook such as this one, is that editors never know which ideas will be generated, what chapters will be contributed, and how those chapters will cohere around the call, which, in this case, was "imagining a renaissance in teacher education."

In Division I, The Roots of Renaissance, we have chosen to feature two chapters. Both trace different, though not incongruent, roots suggesting a need for rebirth or "renascence," as Schwab once referred to it, in the field of education.

In Chapter 1, "Schwab's Call for a Renaissance: A Teacher Education Perspective," Vicki Ross and Elaine Chan reach back into Schwab's scholarship and present the context within which the esteemed scientist's appeal for a renaissance was rendered. Not only do Ross and Chan focus on teacher education along the continuum, they make connections in a point-counterpoint way between Schwab's groundbreaking, historical scholarship and the current literature on teaching and teacher education.

In Chapter 2, "Preparing Urban Educators for the Twenty-First Century: What the Research Suggests," Debora Voltz, Loucrecia Collins, Janice Patterson, and Michele Jean Sims also respond to the call for renaissance in teacher education but develop their argument from a different angle. They focus attention exclusively on urban schools and rightly argue that the need for renaissance is most urgent there. To make their case, they review the literature on urban education and, from it, distill features of teacher education programs that best address the identified concerns.

Hence, this volume begins with two literature reviews: one, historical and comprehensive; the other, contemporary and specific. Together, they provide a conceptual and practical backdrop for the yearbook divisions and chapters that follow.

CHAPTER 1

Schwab's Call for a Renaissance
A TEACHER EDUCATION PERSPECTIVE

Vicki Ross
Northern Arizona University

Elaine Chan
University of Nebraska–Lincoln

>Vicki Ross, Ph.D., is assistant professor of Elementary Education in the Department of Teaching and Learning, College of Education, Northern Arizona University. Her teaching and research interests are in the areas of curriculum, mathematics education, teacher knowledge and identity, teacher education, and narrative inquiry as the study of experience.
>
>Elaine Chan, Ph.D., is assistant professor of Diversity and Curriculum Studies in the Department of Teaching, Learning, and Teacher Education, College of Education and Human Sciences, the University of Nebraska–Lincoln. Her teaching and research interests are curriculum, multicultural education, teacher education, ethnic identity of Chinese students, and educational equity policies.

ABSTRACT

>In this chapter, we explore what would be necessary to bring about a Schwab-like renaissance in the field of teacher education. We examine the changing parameters defining what is meant by teacher education, and describe common themes before launching into a more detailed discussion of current issues facing the field of teacher education. Throughout our discussion, we intersperse Schwabian notions such as the curriculum commonplaces, the process of deliberation in education, and thoughts on the how, what, and why of inquiry extracted from his essays. We conclude by drawing attention to practices that infuse teacher education with a Schwab-like vision.

Introduction: Coffee with Schwab

The year is 1969. The setting is Judd Hall, University of Chicago. Early morning, before classes begin. There is coffee at the table and around the room conversational groups fill in background noise.

Elaine Chan, addressing a man wearing heavy, black-rimmed glasses and smoking a cigarette, begins the conversation, "Professor Schwab, my colleague and I have read many of your essays. We are especially interested in your recent publication in which you said that you felt the field of curriculum had lost its vitality. Actually the word you used to describe the field was 'moribund.'"

Schwab (1969/1978), nodding, responds, "The field of curriculum is moribund. It is unable, by its present methods and principles, to continue its work and contribute significantly to the advancement of education" (p. 287).

Vicki Ross asks, "Why do you think so?"

Professor Schwab responds, "The curriculum field has reached this unhappy state by inveterate, unexamined, and mistaken reliance on *theory*" (Schwab, 1969/1978, p. 287).

She interrupts, "I wonder how you see this reliance on theory manifested?"

Schwab considers, "On the one hand, it has adopted theories (from outside the field of education) concerning ethics, knowledge, political and social structure, learning, mind, and personality, and has used these borrowed theories theoretically, e.g., as principles from which to 'deduce' right aims and procedures for schools and classrooms." He continues, "On the other hand, it has attempted construction of educational theories, particularly theories of curriculum and instruction" (Schwab, 1969/1978, p. 287).

"Why do you think this pursuit of theoretical knowledge is wrong-headed?" Elaine Chan asks.

". . . theoretical constructions are, in the main, ill-fitted and inappropriate to problems of actual teaching and learning" (Schwab, 1969/1978, p. 287).

Puzzled, she probes, "Why?"

"Theory, by its very character, does not and cannot take account of all the matters which are crucial to questions of what, who, and how to teach; that is, theories cannot be applied, as principles, to the solution of problems concerning what to do with or for real individuals, small groups, or real institutions located in time and space—the subjects and clients of schooling and schools" (Schwab, 1969/1978, p. 287).

Warming to the why question, he continues, "Second, many of the borrowed theories, even where appropriate, are inadequate, even as theories, to their chosen subjects: Many are incomplete; some (especially of political structure and personality) are doctrinaire" (Schwab, 1969/1978, p. 287).

"We can see how inflexibility of thought would be an issue in education," Elaine agrees.

Nodding, Schwab continues, "Third, even where a borrowed theory is adequate to its own subject matter, it begs or ignores questions about other subject matters" (Schwab, 1969/1978, pp. 287–288).

"What do you mean by 'begging questions'?" we implore.

"Theories of personality, for example, beg or ignore problems of social structure and ethics or merely dictate solutions to them. Theories of knowledge usually ignore problems of personality. Yet all these matters (values, social and political structure, mind, knowledge) are involved in schools and schooling, and theories concerning them severally cannot be combined into a unified theory adequately covering all of them except by an enormous extension of the genius and assiduity which yielded the separate theories—a task which might or might not be accomplished in a hundred years" (Schwab, 1969/1978, p. 288).

"Professor Schwab," Vicki inquires, "What do you think needs to be done to correct this situation?"

"There will be a renascence of the field of curriculum, a renewed capacity to contribute to the quality of American education, only if curriculum energies are in large part diverted from theoretic pursuits (such as the pursuit of global principles and comprehensive patterns, the search for stable sequences and invariant elements, the construction of taxonomies of supposedly fixed or recurrent kinds) to three other modes of operation. These other modes, which differ radically from the theoretic, I shall call, following tradition, the *practical*, the *quasi-practical*, and the *eclectic*" (Schwab, 1969/1978, p. 288).

Organization of the Chapter

In *The Practical: A Language for Curriculum*, on which the aforementioned hypothetical interchange is built, Schwab (1969) challenges the place of theory in the field of curriculum, endeavoring to reinvigorate the field by infusing it with the practical. In this opening chapter, we take up the task of exploring what would be necessary to bring about a Schwab-like renaissance in the field of teacher education. To establish a common understanding of the current field, we first explore the changing parameters defining what is meant by teacher education. We then describe themes common to the field, followed by a more detailed discussion of four issues facing teacher education. We intersperse throughout this discussion of current issues understandings we have gleaned from Schwab's essays. Helpful among these are: the curriculum commonplaces, the process of deliberation in education, and thoughts on the how, what, and why of inquiry. After this discussion of issues facing the field of teacher education, we conclude by noting practices that promote a Schwab-like vision of teacher education and by revisiting thoughts that emerged during the writing of this chapter.

Creating a Context for Understanding Teacher Education

In describing the climate, commentary, and critique of the field of teacher education, Borko, Liston, and Whitcomb (2006) contend that major scholars, including Darling-Hammond and Bransford (2005) and Cochran-Smith and Zeichner (2005) have published "major tomes" (p. 200) setting the stage for understanding the terms, themes, and issues shaping teacher education. Our intent here is not to replicate that work, but rather, to bring that work into the scope of Schwab's perspective as a writer in the field of education. We draw upon the work of these and other writers to place before readers generally accepted views of what constitutes the field of teacher education. To this end, we explore terms, themes, and issues encountered in our review of the literature.

Current Understandings of Teacher Education

Depending upon parameters set for a definition, understandings of teacher education differ considerably. Using a broadly constructed term, "teacher development" may be construed as the wide array of learning opportunities and experiences before and during the professional career of teachers. This is the view taken in Craig and Ross's (in press) exploration of the cultivation of the teacher-as-curriculum-maker metaphor (Connelly & Clandinin, 1988). The authors reviewed the field of teacher development and its intersecting points of interest. But, such a conceptualization, linking teacher development with teacher education, may be narrowed by including only formalized educational opportunities within the teaching profession. This view includes the academic work that teachers do to continue their professional development through the course of their career. This definition may be further limited by setting boundaries to include only those prerequisites for initial licensure or certification, or even more tightly constrained, by considering only those programs offered through universities and colleges. Zeichner (2006), for example, argues persuasively that those working within teacher education "embrace the entry of new kinds of alternative teacher education programs into the field and focus on the quality of all programs, traditional and alternative" (p. 332). While focusing on the quality of preparation programs, Zeichner (2006) simultaneously decries the type of programs that "put people into classrooms without any preparation" (p. 332). At the same time, others in the field define teacher education as "those programs of instruction based at colleges and universities that are designed to prepare college students or graduate students for careers as K–12 teachers and that lead to certification as a professional teacher" (Fallon, 2006, p. 140).

Themes in Teacher Education

In considering teacher education, what story would those who work within the field tell? What themes shape the narrative of a renaissance in teacher education? In exploring the literature of teacher education, one dominant theme seems to be that teacher education is a field pressed from within and without by conflicting perspectives and agendas. Many perceive the pressure originating from outside influences. Fallon (2006) argues that teacher education "has been under attack" (p. 140) for more than fifty years. Borko, Liston, and Whitcomb (2006) argue that this "perpetual professional calamity" hearkens to the 1930s and onward. They refer to the Dean of Teachers College, William Russell, who in 1936 called for "a new charter for teacher education" (p. 199), continue to trace the historical thread of persistent criticism through the 1960s, and cite Koerner (1963) and Conant (1963) as further examples calling for change. In the 1980s, *The Nation at Risk Report* (National Commission on Excellence in Education, 1983), caused an "uproar" (p. 199) in teacher education. To Borko, Liston, and Whitcomb, these historical pieces support the argument that "teacher education has been inundated by multiple and persistent criticisms" (p. 199). Others within the field also perceive internal shaping influences. For example, Zeichner (2006) identifies three underlying tensions when considering themes or "visions" for teacher education—specifically "professionalization, deregulation, and social justice agendas" (p. 327).

Four Pressing Issues in Teacher Education

In this third section dealing with creating an understanding of the context of the field of teacher education, we explore current issues shaping the field. We frame our discussion around four issues Cochran-Smith (2006) identified as being "both promising trends and potential pitfalls for the future" (p. 98) of the field. These four issues are:

- continuing heightened attention to issues regarding teacher quality and teacher preparation;
- sophisticated new research designs and instruments to study the complexity of teacher preparation;
- growing emphasis on research and evidence as the basis for decisions; and,
- working within and against the teacher education system to expand the ways we think about teacher education's purposes in society.

HEIGHTENED ATTENTION TO ISSUES REGARDING TEACHER QUALITY AND PREPARATION

The "continuing heightened attention to issues regarding teacher quality and teacher preparation" (Cochran-Smith, 2006, p. 98) is one facet of the field of teacher education viewed with ambivalence. Seen in a providential light by teacher educators, the developing consensus underlying much current public policy that teachers' work matters to the academic success of students both gratifies and vivifies. This present-day public policymakers' occupation with issues regarding teacher quality and preparation seems, at least in some measure, to originate and to be anchored in analyses conducted by Sanders and his colleagues (Sanders & Horn, 1994; Sanders & Rivers, 1996; Wright, Horn, & Sanders, 1997). Shalock, Shalock, and Ayres (2006) present the salient findings of the Tennessee research referred to as "value-added" (p. 116). They say,

> During a multiyear period . . . Sanders focused on what happened to students whose teachers produced high achievement versus low achievement results. He found that when children, beginning in third grade, were placed with three high performing teachers in a row, they scored on average at the 96th percentile on Tennessee's statewide mathematics assessment at the end of the fifth grade. When children with comparable achievement histories in third grade were placed with three low performing teachers in a row, their average score on the same mathematics assessment in fifth grade was at the 44th percentile. (p. 116)

Fallon (2006) argues that despite the controversial nature of this genre of value-added studies, of which Sanders' work is but one example, they demonstrate "the reliable presence of a strong teacher effect" (p. 149). This demonstration of strong teacher effect fuels the current heightened attention to teacher quality and preparation alluded to by Cochran-Smith (2006).

Placing these current developments within an historical view is advantageous in examining how and why this issue shapes both the present and future of teacher education. We believe this present-day emphasis somewhat mirrors earlier perspectives emerging from the process-product studies. One of the upshots from research conducted in this vein eventually evolved into one of three themes defining teacher education, as described by Zeichner (2006)—that of the professionalization of teaching. Similar to today's value-added studies, the purposes shaping process-product research in the 1960s and 1970s as a knowledge base for teaching was structured to link teacher behaviors with student outcomes. Another similarity between these two schools of thought is that they are both entrenched within, and advance, what Schön (1983) called a "technical-rational" sense of the world. Arising subsequently were severe criticisms of the process-product studies—the methods and findings, as well as the motives. Both today's research and these aforementioned critiques serve us well as we attempt to make meaning of today's education demands and contexts.

While such an historical perspective contributes to our understanding of current policies, we find applying a Schwabian lens to this current, heightened attention on teacher quality and preparation helpful, as well. Regarding the linkages between teacher quality and student performance, we believe that Schwab, in his call for renaissance, would agree that teachers make an important contribution to student learning. Viewing teachers as the sole and critical component in a student's academic achievement, however, would be too narrow a focus. For Schwab, the curriculum commonplaces broaden our thinking about student academic achievement.

SCHWAB'S PERSPECTIVE ON THE ISSUE: CURRICULUM COMMONPLACES AND DELIBERATION

Schwab's (1973/1978) notions of the commonplaces of curriculum and the deliberative process (Schwab, 1983) are pivotal in addressing the assumed correlation between teacher quality and student outcome. Here we explore: the underlying need for commonplaces; the four commonplaces required for curriculum development; the defining qualities of these four bodies of experience; and why we feel the commonplaces address the heightened attention on teacher quality and preparation. After examining the commonplaces of curriculum in relation to this issue, we describe a commonplace Schwab argued for, and within that argument, discuss the importance of the role of deliberation.

Schwab's (1973/1978) notion of commonplaces emerges from his studies of Aristotelian thought. Based on the notion of commonplaces, Schwab argues that curriculum—what we ought to teach our students—has certain bodies of experience that need to be considered. Schwab (1973/1978) argues that "defensible educational thought must take account of four commonplaces of equal rank: the learner, the teacher, the milieu, and the subject matter" (p. 371).

In considering the subject matter commonplace, Schwab (1973/1978) forwarded the argument that it is important to have the subject matter body of experience represented, both the "scholarly materials under treatment and with the discipline from which they come, when creating curriculum. Suppose the materials under consideration are historical: then a member of the group must be familiar not only with this body of historical material but must also know what it is to be a historian" (p. 366). Continuing the articulation of the commonplaces, he explains that when creating the curriculum, a body of experience dealing with children is appropriate. This knowledge ought to be both general and intimate: this body of experience is understanding of the general knowledge of children and knowledgeable about ways in which individual children differ from the general "knowledge achieved by direct involvement with them" (p. 366). For example, this body of experience must represent what is known in an age group and what it is ready to learn. At the same time, this body of experience must represent "the present state of mind and heart treated as a stage in development toward their probable destiny . . ." (p. 366). A third body of experience, the learners' milieus, must be taken into account in the defensible educational thought. Schwab argues these milieus are "manifold" (p. 366)—the classroom, school, and community immediately come to mind, but other educational considerations such as policy and influence of government are included. Knowledge of teachers constitutes the fourth commonplace.

Schwab (1969) argued for equal representation of each of these curriculum commonplaces, stating that "coordination, not superordination-subordination is the proper relation of these four commonplaces" (p. 366). The difficulty with linking student achievement with teacher quality is that the three remaining commonplaces—learner, milieu, and subject matter—are given short shrift. Although much emphasis is placed on the learner's performance, little attention is given to the actual body of experience that would represent the learner. Likewise, the milieu and subject matter are not taken into account when the focus is concentrated on the teacher commonplace. Furthermore, there is a lack of equality in the ranking. Schwab argues for a different relationship between these commonplaces.

Schwab (1973/1978) also argued for a fifth body of knowledge, that of the curriculum maker. This body of knowledge facilitates balance of consideration for all of the commonplaces, and in some ways, represents a sense of deliberation. It is this ability to deliberate that seems to be lacking in conversations about curriculum and education in today's polemic educational debates. Schwab would argue for the acknowledgement of multiple perspectives, rather than an out-of-hand dismissal of ideas highlighted in a commonplace rightfully belonging within the deliberative process. "Each representative of a body of experience must discover the experience of the others and the relevance of these radically different experiences to curriculum making for a partial coalescence of these bodies of experience to occur" (p. 367–368), he remarked. These two points—the multiple perspectives demanding representation within the defensible educational thought and the deliberative processes through which they are given voice—hint at the next issue in the field of teacher education that Cochran-Smith (2006) raised. More specifically, Cochran-Smith emphasized the need for tools and methods to study the complexity of schooling.

SOPHISTICATED RESEARCH DESIGNS AND INSTRUMENTS TO STUDY TEACHER PREPARATION

Cochran-Smith (2006) identifies a wide array of newly available, sophisticated research methodologies to study teaching as a second issue with which the field of teacher education must grapple. Although these research practices make it much more possible to study the complexities of teacher preparation, it has also been argued that earlier studies were of "limited utility in answering questions pertaining to policy or practice concerning preparation and licensing of teachers" (Shalock, Shalock, & Ayres, 2006, p. 102). This assertion is based on, and echoes, findings from a report sponsored by the American Education Research Association Consensus Panel on Research and Teacher Education, an analysis of over "500 peer-reviewed studies of pre-service teacher education in the United States published largely between 1990 and 2003" (Schalock, Schalock, & Ayres, 2006, p. 102).

As noted in the earlier description of Sanders' (Sanders & Horn, 1994; Sanders & Rivers, 1996; Wright, Horn, & Sanders, 1997) analyses, much of today's research represents an attempt to link teacher quality with student performance in a linear way. Interesting metaphors are applied to the research in this area: Cochran-Smith (2006), for example, refers to this as the "horse race approach" (p. 98); others call this research the "black box" (Shalock, Shalock, & Ayres, 2006, p. 110), or "the positive impact mandate" (Zeichner, 2006, p. 332). While important conclusions may be drawn about the existence of teacher effect on student learning, many researchers feel that these value-added approaches—which correlate student achievement on standardized tests with teacher quality—lack complexity. For example, in discussing Sanders' Tennessee study, Shalock, Shalock, and Ayres (2006) argue that this type of research "carries no information on the knowledge, skills, or classroom performance of teachers studied and little information on the classroom and school contexts in which teaching and learning occurred" (p. 110). These researchers level the same critique—lack of appreciation for the complexity of the teaching and learning process—on other similar studies as well. They consider the lack of such "explanatory power" regarding the "why, how, or what within teaching or teacher preparation" leading to the "relationships found" render this type of research of "limited utility in guiding or refining policy, practice, research" (p. 110). We know from the studies that teachers make a difference in students' performance, but it is not specified what it is about teachers that constitutes the difference.

Yet another layer of complexity, described by Cochran-Smith (2003) as the "unforgiving complexity of teaching" (p. 3–5), is absent from this type of research. For example, "nearly overwhelming," is how Darling-Hammond (2006) describes the "realities" of what teachers attempt when "all children truly have an opportunity to learn" (p. 301). In describing the student population that creates part of the context of practice for teachers, Darling-Hammond (2006) states:

> In the classrooms most beginning teachers will enter, at least 25% of students live in poverty and many of them lack basic food, shelter, and health care; from 10% to 20% have identified learning differences; 15% speak a language other than English as their primary language (many more in urban settings); and about 40% are members of racial/ethnic "minority" groups, many of them recent immigrants from countries with different educational systems and cultural traditions. (p. 301)

Others use slightly different language to address this layer of complexity. Cochran-Smith (2006), for example, argues that the view of teachers as the "central determining factor" in the academic performance of students ignores other "complex and confounding variables" of "family structure, poverty, housing, health, and employment" (p. 98). Building upon this theme, others argue that the complexity of teaching enfolds "different kinds of learning outcomes to be accomplished by students in different subject areas, and the enormous diversity in talents, dispositions, and histories that students bring to what is to be learned within each subject studied" (Shalock, Shalock, & Ayres, 2006, p. 110).

When the context of the teaching and learning endeavor is considered and the complexity acknowledged and peeled back, the interrelationships and deepening layers become even more muddied. In addition to the differences among students and means of meeting their varying learning needs, there remains yet another complexity not accounted for in the value-added research focus: the teacher. Shalock, Shalock, and Ayres (2006) state that "teachers change with experience, and school contexts change continuously in ways that affect both teacher work and student learning" (p. 111). While it is difficult to underestimate the important ways in which teachers are shaped by their context, this comment alludes to another interconnected factor in the professional context of teachers—the growth and change of teacher development over time.

In attempting to create an understanding of the field of teacher education, we noted that a definition of teacher education is difficult to fit into a box because the size of the box determines what is defined. This issue of teacher change over time hints at an area influential in shaping teacher quality. Some feel that this needs to be looked at more closely. Zeichner (2005), for example, argues that there exists a "clear need to look more at how teachers' knowledge and practices are shaped by their preparation including after they have completed their programs" (p. 746). Seeking to illustrate his point, Zeichner (2005) notes that a major report on the field of teacher education, *The National Academy of Education Report on Preparing Teachers for a Changing World* (Hammerness, Darling-Hammond, & Bransford, 2005), for example, includes only cursory acknowledgement of the continuing professional development of teachers.

Cochran-Smith (2006) argues that "the growing acknowledgement" of the "complexity of the entire teacher education enterprise" (p. 98) and the desire to focus research on that complexity is encouraging. Others support this argument, adding that "it is the complexity of teaching that needs to drive educational research" (Shalock, Shalock, & Ayres, 2006). Cochran-Smith (2006) notes that we have at our disposal "richer data sources, more powerful analytical techniques, and increasingly sophisticated researchers" (p. 98). Her concern is whether these research methodologies and tools can be marshaled to focus on the complexity in order to break out of the black box. She warns that,

> the future of teacher education depends in part on whether we end up with increasingly sophisticated models that are still basically linear, with students' test scores the end point, or on the other hand, we end up with multifaceted studies that include a range of questions, research paradigms, and outcomes. (p. 98)

The argument seems to favor bringing all the methodological tools at our disposal to study the complexity of teaching. At the root of the complexity alluded to by the authors above is Schwab's (1969/1978) term, "particularity." Readers will recall that he stated that

> curriculum is brought to bear, not on ideal or abstract representations, but on the real thing, on the concrete case, in all its completeness and with all its differences from all other concrete cases, on a large body of fact concerning which the theoretic abstraction is silent. . . . The curriculum constructed of these particulars will be brought to bear, not in some archetypical classroom, but in a particular locus in time and space with smells, shadows, seats, and condi-

> tions outside its walls which may have much to do with what is achieved inside. Above all, the supposed beneficiary is not the generic child, not even a class or kind of child out of the psychological or sociological literature pertaining to the child. The beneficiary will consist of very local kinds of children and, within the local kinds, individual children. The same diversity holds with respect to teachers and what they do. (p. 309)

A focus on the particular within educational endeavors would lead us away from the linear connections between teacher behavior and student test scores. Focusing on the particular is also a way of redirecting attention away from theoretical use of theory, a practice at the crux of Schwab's criticism of the field of education.

SCHWAB'S PERSPECTIVE ON THE ISSUE: PARTICULARITY AND STUDYING TEACHING

As we step back from this second issue—this availability of sophisticated means of studying the complexity of teaching—we introduce two puzzles to Schwab's writings. The first is an attempt to understand this complexity. For this, we turn to Schwab's terms of the practical and the particular in teaching. We then focus on what and how to study teaching in these terms.

In considering the complexity of teaching, Schwab (1971/1978) contributes an understanding of the practical concerns of the undertaking. He holds that teaching and learning consists not of the abstract; rather teachers are concerned with the concrete and real. He argues that, "theories of curriculum and of teaching and learning cannot, alone, tell us what and how to teach, because questions of what and how to teach arise in concrete situations loaded with concrete particulars of time, place, person, and circumstance" (p. 322). Schwab goes on to state that theory is of limited help in knowing what and how to teach because of its "abstraction from . . . particulars, by omitting much of them" (p. 322). At the same time, Schwab does not dismiss the usefulness of theory—"The strength and value of theory lie in its generality, system, and economy" (p. 323). His argument is that theory is of limited usefulness in the practical work of teaching and learning. Rather, teaching and learning are fundamentally practical in nature and, therefore, concerned with the particular nature of persons, places, and curricular matters. This stance in many ways mirrors Cochran-Smith's (2006) statement, referred to earlier, about the unforgiving complexity of teaching. If, as it is assumed from existing research that teacher quality affects student outcomes, what can be learned about those teachers and their practices that are important to student learning?

We begin with an exploration of factors Schwab (1969/1978) argues are necessary to study in education to enrich our understandings of teaching and learning. He stated,

> What is wanted is a totally new and extensive pattern of *empirical* study of classroom action and reaction; a study, not a basis for theoretical concerns about the nature of the teaching or learning process, but as a basis for beginning to know what we are doing, what we are not doing, and to what effect; what changes are needed, which needed changes can be instituted with what costs or economies, and how they can be effected with minimum tearing of the remaining fabric of educational effort. (p. 313–314)

Schwab (1969/1978) made the case for this new, extensive, empirical study of classrooms, saying, "It is an effort without which we will continue largely incapable of making defensible decisions about curricular changes, largely unable to put them into effect, and ignorant of what real consequences, if any, our efforts have had" (p. 314).

EMPHASIS ON RESEARCH AND EVIDENCE AS THE BASIS FOR DECISIONS

We now return to Cochran-Smith's (2006) third pressing issue shaping the field of teacher education: the increasing role of research and evidence as a means of improving practice (p. 98–99). Cochran-Smith raises concerns and looks to the possibilities related to this renewed emphasis. On the positive end, this approach "reflects efforts to build the capacity within teacher education programs themselves to assess progress and effectiveness, to shift accountability from external policy to internal practice, and to generate knowledge that can be used in both local programs and more broadly" (p. 99). Furthermore, it "puts teacher education at the forefront of other professions in using performance evidence to assess effectiveness" (Cochran-Smith, 2006, p. 99). Zeichner (2006) counters, however, that "although professional schools in some fields are accredited in part based on the pass rates of their graduates on licensing exams, I am not aware of any other field in which professional schools are held accountable for the performance of their graduates in the field after completion of their programs" (p. 332).

On the negative end of the issue, Cochran-Smith (2006) warns of the dangers of "scientism." Some are firm supporters of the role of science in decision making in teacher education. Fallon (2006), for example, argues,

> Advocates of teacher education programs within institutions of higher education cannot promote them effectively with a predominance of logical propositions and moral argument. In the end, dependable relationships between the interventions of teacher education programs and the learning of pupils taught by teachers who have been subject to those interventions must be reliably demonstrated with convincing evidence. (p. 152)

Fallon (2006) further develops his position by stating, "A principal purpose of scientific analysis is to increase the reliability with which evidence informs our propositions and, thus, to increase our confidence" (p. 143). He supports this position with what he refers to as Dewey's (1916/1966) "famous summary conclusion"—"ultimately and philosophically, science is the organ of general social progress" (p. 230).

Fallon (2006) acknowledges that "sensitivity to the value of humanistic inquiry is important for educational research" (p. 143), but warns that it is necessary that these methods be, "at least equally informed by scientific method" (p. 143). He expounds that, "Science is, of course, not above criticism . . . This criticism is informed, however, by scholarship that is thoroughly grounded in the methods and principles of science, and it is this grounding that appears generally weak and undeveloped in educational research . . ." (p. 143).

While Fallon builds the case that decisions in education are supportable only as they are based on convincing scientific evidence, Cochran-Smith (2006) takes another view. She argues that moral and logical purposes are of no lesser value to teacher education than decisions based on scientific evidence. She states, "Teacher education will not get better simply because more people gather evidence, and decisions based on evidence will not necessarily be better than decisions based on moral purposes or experience with time" (p. 99).

As argued in relation to the first issue, an historical understanding of the origins of this debate is helpful. Again, we find these competing views of the role of scientific evidence as the basis for making decisions reminiscent of arguments shaping the earlier critiques of the process-product research.

SCHWAB RESPONDS: CAUTIONS REGARDING THE RHETORIC OF CONCLUSION AND SUGGESTIONS FOR HOW AND WHAT TO STUDY IN TEACHING AND TEACHER EDUCATION

As we reflect upon the role of evidence in decision-making to improve upon practice both in teacher education and in classroom practice, there are two cautions we extract from Schwab's essays. The first is related to the idea of "the rhetoric of conclusions" (Schwab, 1956/1978, p. 134) especially as it relates to the development of theoretical knowledge. The second understanding delineates points of scientific decision-making—at the point of stable versus fluid inquiry (Schwab, 1960/1978). Both ideas create a richer intellectual context in which to understand evidence and the role it has in decision-making regarding practice.

Related to Schwab's (1969/1978) cautions around the rhetoric of conclusions is his understanding of theoretical knowledge. Schwab states that, "all theories, even the best of them in the simplest sciences, necessarily neglect some aspects and facets of the facts of the case" (p. 309). We recognize that without knowledge of the structure on which the theory rests, the questions of inquiry are not clear. Further, the aspects and facets that are neglected are not readily apparent either. Schwab (1969/1978) continues, "A theory covers and formulates the *regularities* among the things and events it subsumes. It abstracts a general or ideal case. It leaves behind the nonuniformities, the particularities, which characterize each concrete instance of the facts subsumed" (p. 309).

In the preceding section, we discussed the centrality Schwab gives to particularity within and the concrete nature of the constituents of defensible educational thought. As a reminder to readers, for Schwab, particularity is at the heart of teaching and learning, and education is made up of concrete participants and materials. Schwab (1969/1978) details further characteristics of coming to a theoretical perspective. "Moreover, in the process of idealization, theoretical [i]nquiries may often leave out of consideration conspicuous facets of all cases because its substantive principles of [i]nquiry or its methods cannot handle them" (p. 309).

At the same time, in no way do we feel that Schwab is anti-theoretical. He, too, speaks of theory's value to human progress. However, in this instance, he is explaining the nature and characteristics of theory. He compares then, the place of theory in "the simplest sciences" within the social sciences. "And what is true of the best of theories in the simplest sciences is true *a fortiori* in the social sciences. Their subject matters are apparently so much more variable, and clearly so much more complex, that their theories encompass much less of their subjects than do the theories of the physical and biological sciences" (p. 309).

Schwab (1960/1978) argues above all for caution in the net of inquiry; it is important to understand the structure of the inquiry, to recognize questions the inquiry is framed to answer as well as those it cannot. Further, in a discussion of the six decision points of inquiry, Schwab (1960/1978) presents an important frame for us as we consider scientific evidence for making decisions regarding improving practice in teacher education. His terms are "fluid" and "static" inquiry. These two forms of inquiry involve differences in ends and means.

A stable inquiry focuses "exclusively on the subject matter itself" (Schwab, 1960/1978, p. 217). In describing the methods of stable inquiry, he says, "it lends itself to segmental structuring" (p. 217). Stable inquiries may be designed with "relatively short duration" (p. 217); they may focus on those aspects of phenomenon ". . . which will cause the least trouble. . . ." (p. 217). Schwab goes on to say, "what is required by way of data is unequivocal . . . Precision, thoroughness, and 'technique' are maximized as the criteria of excellence" (p. 217).

In contrast, fluid inquiry is focused on a "probably imperfect image or model of some supposed subject-in-fact, probably imperfect image or model of some supposed subject-of-[i]nquiry is pursued with the aim of discovering and repairing its inadequacies and limitations; whether the subject will speak to the problem as posed; whether the data required can be elicited with the necessary accuracy; whether data will be found for which the terms of the enquiry cannot give an account" (Schwab, 1960/1978, p. 217). Continuing the contrast, Schwab describes the ambiguous nature of fluid inquiry. Such research has indefinite timelines, uncertainty regarding what shall be viewed as insignificant data, and the endpoint is unknowable. He concludes by saying that fluid inquiry demands a "pleasure in the creation of new structures" (p. 218).

In cautioning comments about the ends and means of inquiry that we pursue as evidence for making decisions, Schwab (1969/1978) likewise makes suggestions regarding what we ought to pursue. Whereas the major criticism of Sanders's work does not inform us of what leads to the findings, Schwab argues that what leads to the findings is precisely what we ought to pursue. In other words, learning about *"what is and has been going on in American schools"* (p. 313) is the type of evidence we need on which to base our decision.

Expanding the means, ends, and subject addressed in education research is one approach to addressing the third issue raised by Cochran-Smith—the increasing role of research and evidence as a means of improving practice. In addition, Cochran-Smith argued that the ways in which we think about the purposes of teacher education ought to be expanded as well. It is especially encouraging, for example, to read essays written before the adoption of business metaphors in the field of education, when the purpose of education was perceived, at least by Schwab, as the nurturing of future citizens.

EXPANDING THE WAYS WE THINK ABOUT THE PURPOSES OF TEACHER EDUCATION IN SOCIETY

Cochran-Smith (2006) identifies four issues that continue to face the field of teacher education. Depending upon how these issues are addressed and resolved, they may result in positive or negative outcomes. The first three include: a refocus on teacher quality and preparation, a retooling of the research methods used to study teaching and learning, and a reinstatement of scientific evidence in decision-making regarding teacher preparation. This fourth issue facing teacher education reflects a different sort of challenge—an effort to change the underlying assumptions about the purposes of teacher education. Cochran-Smith (2006) explains that within the field, some teacher educators work "simultaneously within and against the larger educational system by critiquing prevailing views about teacher education and expanding the ways we think about its role in society and its broader goals and purposes" (p. 99). She goes on to note that these educators are "working to change the terms of the debate" (p. 99).

SCHWAB ANSWERS WITH A CALL FOR A RENAISSANCE IN THE FIELD

Schwab (1959/1978) recounts, in an essay titled "The 'Impossible' role of the teacher in a progressive school and curriculum" that Dewey sought to change the terms of the debate that swirled around his philosophy of experience in education. In expanding the role of teacher education in society, we extract two concerns with which Schwab felt teacher education programs ought to engage: first, encouraging teachers to be both learners and teachers. He believed that teachers must do more than just become proficient with accepted aspects of "acting as a teacher" (p. 182); this, he equated with becoming "a capable apprentice" (p. 182). Second, he challenged teacher educators. Teachers' knowledge must enable them to be more than just "efficient" policy executioners; they must be able to "improve a policy or change it as problems change" (p. 182). Rather than limiting teachers' knowledge or practice, Schwab's vision of a "good 'progressive' teacher" (p. 167) was one who engages in classroom inquiry, one who "uses the classroom as the occasion and the means to reflect upon education as a whole" (p. 182). These reflections are then used to inform classroom practice. However, in addition to being a learner, the teacher must teach. The teacher's goal is to guide students to their unique and full intellectual potential. Schwab links this notion to Dewey's levels and dynamics of "pragmatic intellectual space" (p. 179). Anything less, Schwab concluded, fails a democratic society. If we are to reframe the teaching and teacher education debate, these are the terms Schwab would use to do so.

Schwab-like Renaissance for Teacher Education

We believe Schwab's call for educational renewal is overarching in nature. In accepting his challenge, those who work in teacher education ought to regard, in a more inclusive way, the ongoing development of teachers and teacher educators. Bringing a Schwab-based understanding of "the particular" to teacher education, likewise, leads us to the conclusion that there are no standard practices for renaissance, but there are multiple visions of renewal emerging in different contexts, involving different actors and addressing different problems and issues, which despite commonality, are locally expressed and experienced. Teacher education and development practices that we see linked directly to Schwab's notions are, for example, action research, case study, research portfolio methods, narrative inquiry, self-study, and arts-based practices, many of which are included in this yearbook.

Returning now to the central inquiry of this chapter, would Schwab call for a renaissance in the field of teacher education? Would he consider those in the field enamored of theory? Would he see in the field of teacher education a need to embrace the practical, the quasi-practical, and the eclectic? He certainly offers strong direction in moving this way through his commonplaces of curriculum, the role of deliberation in education, the place of particularity in teaching and learning, and a framing of a productive understanding of the relationship between theory and practice. But what more would he add?

Our close reading of Schwab's arguments prompts us to advocate for deliberate change. We choose the word "deliberate" here for layered meaning. We argue for deliberate change in the sense that we begin with an informed understanding, informed through empirical classroom studies, of what is happening in classrooms. This informed understanding of the current state is vital: only then can results of change, when made, be deliberate. We speak not of deliberate in a narrow sense of the word, but rather, we have information regarding not only intended outcomes but unintended ones as well. The word 'deliberate' also recalls Schwab's (1969/1978) sense of change as consisting of small steps, such that these changes do not "tear at the . . . fabric" (p. 314) of teacher education, or more broadly, the fabric of education overall. We use the word deliberate in the sense that deliberative processes are brought into play around the means and ends of change, and we work toward "defensible educational thought" (Schwab, 1973/1978, p. 371) and policy. In each of these ways, Schwab would argue for deliberate change.

We raise a further point taken from our reading of Schwab—the centrality of the process of reflection in learning, and its presence within many teacher education practices. Reflective practices, in one form or another, reside within each of the practices reviewed for this chapter and additionally are evident in the chapters throughout this volume. Schwab's (1959/1978) views of reflection are that,

> If teachers are effectively to guide their students through and to the exercise of intelligence, they cannot, themselves, be unreflective. The

teachers college and the administrative structure of the school cannot afford, therefore, to repeat the error of the epitomists, to provide their teachers with fixed techniques, content to be learned by rote, and imposed curriculums. Teacher training ought, in some measure, to become teacher education despite the pressure of an expanding population. It ought to exhibit the material which their students will teach as matter for reflection rather than as matter for docile mastery. It ought to exhibit proposed ends and methods of instruction in some of their difficult, tangled, and doubtful connection with the imperfect and incomplete researches on society, the learning process, human personality, and similar topics, from which they stem. (p. 173–174)

In regard to this emphasis on the role of reflection, we raise one concern—that the more natural aspects of reflection, those done in solitude or in conversation with a friend, relative, or group of colleagues, are not adequately represented in research and writing on teacher education. We argue that this organic aspect of reflection is a substantial aspect of teachers' lives and work. This type of reflection is difficult to account for in that it may or may not be accessible for accountability purposes, but it is nonetheless important. The channeling of reflective work into artifacts logged to demonstrate performance either on the part of the teacher, teacher candidate, or teacher education program in some ways narrows and lessens the notion of reflection in learning and in practice (Latta, 2008).

Our final concluding thought is that more often defining our work in the broader sense, seeing teacher education as a continuum of growth is beneficial to those involved in the field. This expanded notion would benefit our students both at the undergraduate and graduate levels. Keeping in mind Dewey's intellectual space, as we enable our students to advance in intellectual development, knowing that there is a continuum along which teachers develop advances is a helpful perspective. Returning to Dewey's intellectual space, are there times in the growth of teachers when "competent hands" or "apprentices" are expected? We wonder if it might not be profitable to consider the ways in which we might support teachers as they develop their learning from and through experience to consider the "ends and means" in education, and in the setting up of experience.

References

Borko, H., Liston, D., & Whitcomb, J. A. (2006). A conversation of many voices: Critiques and visions of teacher education. *Journal of Teacher Education, 57*(3), 199–204.

Cochran-Smith, M. (2003). The unforgiving complexity of teaching: Avoiding simplicity in an age of accountability. *Journal of Teacher Education, 54*(1), 3–5.

Cochran-Smith, M. (2006). Thirty editorials later: Signing off as editor. *Journal of Teacher Education, 57*(2), 95–101.

Cochran-Smith, M., & Zeichner, K. M. (Eds.) (2005). *Studying teacher education: The report of the AERA Panel on Research and Teacher Education.* Mahwah, NJ: Lawrence Erlbaum.

Conant, J. (1963). *The education of American teachers.* New York: McGraw-Hill.

Connelly, F. M., & Clandinin, D. J. (1988). *Teachers as curriculum planners: Narratives of experience.* New York: Teachers College Press, Columbia.

Craig, C. J., & Ross, V. (in press). Cultivating the image of teachers as curriculum makers. In F. M. Connelly, M. F. He & J. Phillion (Eds.) *Handbook of curriculum and instruction.* Thousand Oaks, CA: Sage Publications.

Darling-Hammond, L. (2006). Constructing 21st century teacher education. *Journal of Teacher Education, 57*(3), 300–314.

Darling-Hammond, L., & Bransford, J. (Eds.) (2005). *Preparing teachers for a changing world.* San Francisco: Jossey-Bass.

Dewey, J. (1916/1966). *Democracy and education.* Toronto, Canada: Collier-Macmillan.

Fallon, D. (2006). The buffalo upon the chimneypiece: The value of evidence. *Journal of Teacher Education, 57*(2), 139–154.

Hammerness, K., Darling-Hammond, L., & Bransford, J. (with Berliner, D., Cochran-Smith, M., McDonald, M., & Zeichner, K.) (2005). How teachers learn and develop. In L. Darling-Hammond & J. Bransford (Eds.), *Preparing teachers for a changing world* (pp. 358–389). San Francisco: Jossey-Bass.

Koerner, J. (1963). *The miseducation of American teachers.* Boston: Houghton Mifflin.

Latta, M. M. (2008). Encountering relational complexity: On 'the arts of the practical' in learning to teach. In C. J. Craig & L. F. Deretchin (Eds.), *Imagining a renaissance in teacher education: Teacher education yearbook XVI.* Lanham, MD: Rowman & Littlefield Education.

Sanders, W. L., & Horn, S. (1994). The Tennessee value-added assessment system (TVAAS): Mixed-model methodology in educational assessment. *Journal of Personnel Evaluation in Education, 8*(3), 299–311.

Sanders, W. L., & Rivers, J. C. (1996). *Cumulative and residual effects of teachers on future academic achievement.* Knoxville: University of Tennessee Value-Added Research and Assessment Center.

Schön, D. A. (1983). *The reflective practitioner: How professionals think in action.* New York: Basic Books.

Schwab, J. J. (1956/1978). Chapter 4: Science and civil discourse: The uses of diversity. In I. Westbury & N. J. Wilkof (Eds.), *Science, curriculum, and liberal education: Selected essays* (pp. 133–148). Chicago: University of Chicago Press.

Schwab, J. J. (1959/1978). Chapter 6: The "impossible" role of the teacher in progressive education. In I. Westbury & N. J. Wilkof (Eds.), *Science, curriculum, and liberal education: Selected essays* (pp. 287–321). Chicago: University of Chicago Press.

Schwab, J. J. (1960/1978). Chapter 7: What do scientists do? In I. Westbury & N. J. Wilkof (Eds.), *Science, curriculum, and liberal education: Selected essays* (pp. 184–228). Chicago: University of Chicago Press.

Schwab, J. J. (1969/1978). Chapter 10: The practical: A language for curriculum. In I. Westbury & N. J. Wilkof (Eds.), *Science, curriculum, and liberal education: Selected essays* (pp. 287–321). Chicago: University of Chicago Press.

Schwab, J. J. (1971/1978). Chapter 11: The practical: Arts of eclectic. In I. Westbury & N. J. Wilkof (Eds.), *Science, curriculum, and liberal education: Selected essays* (pp. 322–364). Chicago: University of Chicago Press.

Schwab, J. J. (1973/1978). Chapter 12: The practical: Translation into curriculum. In I. Westbury & N. J. Wilkof (Eds.), *Science, curriculum, and liberal education: Selected essays* (pp. 365–383). Chicago: University of Chicago Press.

Schwab, J. J. (1983). The practical 4: Something for curriculum professors to do. *Curriculum Inquiry, 13*, 239–265.

Shalock, H. D., Shalock, M. D., & Ayres, R. (2006). Scaling up research in teacher education: New demands on theory, measurement, and design. *Journal of Teacher Education, 57*(2), 102–119.

Wright, S., Horn, S., & Sanders, W. L. (1997). Teacher and classroom context effects on student achievement: Implications for teacher evaluation. *Journal of Personnel Evaluation in Education, 11*, 57–67.

Zeichner, K. (2006). Reflections of a university-based teacher educator on the future of college- and university-based teacher education. *Journal of Teacher Education, 57*(3), 326–330.

CHAPTER 2

Preparing Urban Educators for the Twenty-First Century
WHAT THE RESEARCH SUGGESTS

Deborah L. Voltz
University of Alabama at Birmingham

Loucrecia Collins
University of Alabama at Birmingham

Janice Patterson
University of Alabama at Birmingham

Michele Jean Sims
University of Alabama at Birmingham

>Deborah L. Voltz, Ed.D., is an associate professor in the Department of Leadership, Special Education, and Foundations at the University of Alabama at Birmingham. Prior to teaching at the university level, Dr. Voltz taught students with learning disabilities, grades K–8, in the Birmingham City Schools. She has written and published numerous articles and book chapters related to teaching culturally and linguistically diverse populations in inclusive settings.

>Loucrecia Collins, Ed.D., is an associate professor in the Department of Leadership, Special Education, and Foundations at the University of Alabama at Birmingham. She is a veteran educator of thirty years who has taught in Mississippi, Georgia, Louisiana, and Alaska. As a principal, she was recognized for her outstanding leadership role with the Anchorage School District. Dr. Collins has researched, published, and presented extensively on proactive approaches to school violence and bullying.

>Janice Patterson, Ph.D., teaches in the Department of Curriculum and Instruction at the University of Alabama at Birmingham. She has taught at all levels from four year olds to graduate level students in urban, rural, and suburban settings. Her research focuses on resilience, teacher leaders,

educational policy and school-university partnerships. She has published widely in her field and has conducted workshops and presentations throughout the United States and in Canada, Israel, Ecuador, Spain, Australia, the United Kingdom, and the Netherlands.

Michele Jean Sims, Ed.D., teaches in the Department of Curriculum and Instruction at the University of Alabama at Birmingham. She was an elementary classroom teacher and a Chapter I/Title I teacher in the New York City Public Schools, a Title I Reading teacher at the middle/junior high school level in the Philadelphia School District, and a member of the Philadelphia Writing Project. Her publications focus on collaboration and inclusion.

ABSTRACT

This chapter provides a review of the research related to preparing teachers for urban settings. Specific competencies requisite to the successful preparation of urban teachers are presented, along with the research base supporting these competencies. The authors argue that teacher preparation program features that support the development of these competencies would contribute to a renaissance in teacher education.

Nowhere is the need for renaissance greater than in urban schools. Many unique factors exist that differentiate urban schools from suburban or rural school settings. The unique context of urban schools complicates the educational lives of many children in America's inner cities.

Obidah and Howard (2005) posit that the majority of economically disadvantaged students and families of color live in densely populated hubs. Approximately 64% of students in major cities are culturally and linguistically diverse. Of those students, 56% participate in the free lunch program (Jacob, 2007). For public schools, poverty is identified by the number of students eligible for free and reduced lunches. The financial deprivation experienced in urban centers is an integral factor embedded in urban school education.

The social, economic, and political realities of inner city living and schooling have been noted as an American crisis (Kozol, 2005; Monroe, 2005). The economic and financial neglect means that there are few banks located in urban centers. The lack of banking services needed to promote economic development has promulgated decay and decline in the infrastructure of life for urban dwellers. Often, the most successful businesses are liquor stores, funeral homes, and loan companies. Litter strewn streets from infrequent trash pick-ups, poor sewer systems, and deteriorating housing describe the environment of many urban areas. The decline in property values has led to a decrease in property taxes that has negatively impacted the development of urban schools (Jacob, 2007).

How have the results of economic deficits impacted urban education? Schools in urban areas have become racially and economically segregated. Other negative realities for urban schools include: dilapidated, overcrowded school buildings, significant teacher turnover, and community and school violence (Murnane & Steele, 2007). In addition, urban school students face (1) student achievement challenges; (2) inadequate school readiness skills; (3) low parental involvement; (4) limited access to learning resources; (5) high mobility rates; (6) linguistic challenges; and (7) inadequate student health care (Rothstein, 2004).

Why Is There a Need for a Renaissance in Teacher Education Programs?

A significant difference exists between teachers and students in urban schools where race, gender, socioeconomic status, and native language are concerned. Differences in sociocultural identities between teachers and students may affect teacher retention and student success in urban schools. Howard (2007) argues that continuing with business as usual in how teachers are prepared may lead to failure for urban students. Currently, urban districts lose nearly one half of their newly hired teachers within the first five years of classroom teaching (National Commission on Teaching and America's Future, 2003).

Ninety percent of U.S. teachers are white, middle-class women who do not reside in urban centers. In striking contrast, 37% of the students are children of color who exist in poverty (Children's Defense Fund, 2001; Young, 2002; National Center for Education Statistics, 2005). Hence, cultural incongruence may impact the instructional programs of many urban schools.

Many educators grapple with providing instruction to linguistically diverse students. Teachers are expected to instruct students who are linguistically diverse even though they speak only one language. Sachs (2004) noted that the sociocultural identities of teachers and students, and factors that differentiate urban from suburban and rural settings characterize a unique urban context for examining teacher success.

Teacher preparation programs have noted the challenges and need for preparing educators for urban schools (Jacob, 2007). In New York, more than 2,000 certified teachers turned down job offers in one year, choosing not to teach rather than be assigned to a low performing school (Grace, 2001). In a study that reviewed placement choices of teachers, Lankford, Loeb, and Wyckoff (2002) found that teachers routinely moved away from districts with low levels of academic achievement and high concentrations of minority children identified as living in poverty. The reluctance to accept teaching positions in underperforming, urban schools points to a failure of teacher preparation programs to prepare and inspire adequate numbers of teachers to teach in urban school systems.

As the faces of America's children change, so do their educational needs. A renaissance is needed in teacher preparation programs to inspire and ignite preservice and in-service teachers. The purpose of this literature review is to address salient research regarding this movement.

Competencies for Success

The competencies presented have been synthesized from research in the field and represent the value-added pieces that programs preparing urban teachers must address. As illustrated by Figure 2.1, these competencies have been organized in four strands: sociocultural competence; affirming attitude; collaborative skills; and pedagogy for diversity.

SOCIOCULTURAL COMPETENCE

Strand One, Sociocultural Competence, focuses on helping candidates to better understand the students and families with whom they will work and the communities in which they will teach. Based on his research, Sternberg (2006) argued "children from non-mainstream cultures often bring to school the kinds of knowledge and skills that are relevant to their lives and upbringing" (p. 30). Educators who are aware of this prior knowledge, and can tap into it in their instructional approach, can more readily promote the academic success of diverse students.

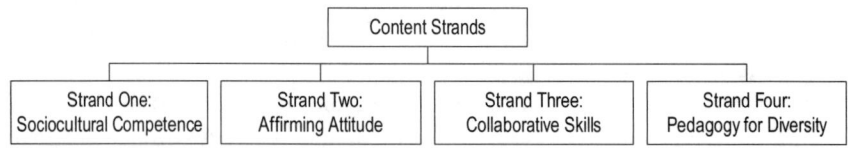

Figure 2.1 Competencies for Success

The need for cultural understanding also was reflected in a focus group study involving 19 teachers from some of Chicago's hardest to staff schools (Fleming, Chou, Random, Nishimura, & Burke, 2004). When asked about the challenges faced by teachers and the knowledge base required for urban teaching, these teachers reported a need for deep understanding of cultural knowledge. According to Fleming et al, participating teachers, "often acknowledged challenges in working with children whose backgrounds were very different from their own . . . teachers suggested the need for course work that breaks down topics related to race and ethnicity into much more specific discussions and experiences to help students better understand the nuances of particular cultures and school communities" (p. 106–107). These nuances included such factors as the impact of poverty on the teaching and learning process, as well as the complexities associated with teaching children who have adult responsibilities.

Based on these and similar research findings related to sociocultural competence, the following competencies for teacher candidates have been developed:

- Understands the influences of culture on learning and behavior, as well as how culture influences teaching
- Is knowledgeable about the local community in which he or she teaches, and is aware of the educational assets of that community (e.g., parks, speakers on specific topics, neighborhood leaders, social service agencies)
- Understands that education broadly defined includes the intellectual, social-emotional, physical, and ethical development of students; and occurs both inside and outside of schools (e.g., neighborhoods, families, and peer groups)
- Recognizes that the context of schooling is complex and reflects the historical, political, social, and economic influences of the community and that teachers must consider these issues in their teaching
- Uses his or her knowledge and experience to advance issues of social justice (e.g., protecting human rights, ensuring effective education for all children) in the broader community and in school-community relationships

AFFIRMING ATTITUDE

Strand Two, Affirming Attitude, focuses on developing in candidates the attitudes necessary to foster high student achievement. It focuses on developing what Corbett, Wilson, and Williams (2005, p. 8) described as a "no choice but success" attitude that has been associated with successful urban teachers. Teacher resilience is an important focus of this strand, as is helping teachers to recognize the many strengths that their urban students bring. It is important for teachers to develop a predisposition toward affirming and working from those strengths.

Likewise, this strand acknowledges the importance of developing students' self-efficacy in the learning process.

A number of research studies support the need for urban teachers to maintain an affirming attitude. For example, a case study of four exemplary urban teachers of African American students revealed that a critical element of their success was their belief in their students' ability to achieve (Howard, 2001a). Participating teachers—nominated by parents, principals, community members, and peers—were interviewed and observed in their classrooms over a four-month period. Findings indicated that:

> Although having a connection to and awareness of the cultural context that students bring from home was important, what seemed to be equally important in the development of these teachers' teaching practices was a belief that their students were capable of being academically successful. Whereas teacher expectations have been associated with student academic performance, students' expectations of their own academic success is often a greater predictor of academic achievement . . . The teachers in this study believed that it was important to convince their students that they possessed the potential to make a difference in their academic development. (Howard, 2001a, p. 198)

The level of trust that teachers have in their students also has been shown to be an important aspect of developing affirming attitudes. In a study involving 452 urban teachers and 2,536 students in 47 schools, Goddard, Tschannen-Moran, and Hoy (2001) found that "trust was a significant positive predictor of differences among schools in student achievement" (p. 3). In the study, participating teachers were surveyed and asked to indicate the extent to which they agreed with statements such as: "Students in this school are reliable," "Teachers in this school trust their students," and "Teachers here believe students are competent learners." The academic achievement of their students was measured by the Metropolitan Achievement Test. Hierarchical linear modeling was used to model teacher trust as a feature varying within and among schools. Results indicated that while the SES level of the school was shown to be related to the level of teacher trust, once school means were adjusted for SES, trust was a significant predictor of differences between schools with respect to achievement. According to the authors, "Trust seems to foster a context that supports student achievement, even in the face of poverty" (Goddard, Tschannen-Moran, and Hoy, 2001, p. 14).

According to Song (2006, p. 496), "Urban teacher education programs need to restructure their curriculum to include experiences designed to strengthen those teacher belief systems that are essential to shaping the way teachers define and understand physical and social realities of today's urban teaching." To this end, the following competencies have been developed:

- Exhibits a strong belief in the capacity of all students to achieve at high levels and communicates this belief to students
- Demonstrates and engages in systematic and continuous inquiry that promotes ongoing teacher reflection, especially in regard to teacher attitudes and beliefs
- Exhibits resilience and a belief that one can achieve what one sets out to do in regard to educational challenges, and promotes similar resilience and belief in his or her students
- Exhibits and encourages respect for students' home community, language, and culture
- Demonstrates a strong commitment to fairness by teaching and reinforcing conflict resolution skills
- Is a reflective, responsive teacher-leader who effectively addresses the inequities of policies, practices, and achievement related to race, class, gender, linguistic differences, and physical or mental exceptionalities

COLLABORATIVE SKILLS

Strand Three, Collaborative Skills, focuses on strategies for building effective relationships with the variety of persons with whom urban teachers must work in order to be effective, including those within schools (e.g., administrators, counselors, other teachers) as well as those external to schools (e.g., parents, social service agencies). Since these collaborative skills must be applied within the organizational complexities that characterize most urban school districts, urban educators must have skills in negotiating bureaucratic structures.

A number of studies have illuminated the importance of collaborative skills in promoting the academic success of urban students. Brown (2002) conducted an ethnographic study of an inclusive urban elementary classroom identified as being exemplary by teachers, administrators, parents, and former students. Based on data collected from observations, interviews, and focus groups, several defining elements of classroom practice were noted. Among these elements, teacher/student/parent interaction was shown to be critical.

Although collaborative skills are important to the success of urban teachers, the practice of collaboration in urban school settings can be complex. Clark and Holmes (2006) studied 12 first-year urban middle and high school teachers. An in-depth interview model was used. Findings indicated that these teachers identified the bureaucratic structure of urban schools and districts as a deterrent to developing collaborative relationships with fellow teachers and administrators. Large school size was noted as a contributing factor, which these new teachers felt led to a lack of staff collegiality and a sense of isolation.

Based on these findings and other research related to collaborative skills, the following competencies for teacher candidates have been developed:

- Demonstrates the ability to plan and problem-solve with parents and other education and social service professionals in order to promote student success
- Engages in collaborative efforts/activities with other teachers that promote mutual respect and high student achievement
- Demonstrates the skills needed to communicate effectively with diverse students, their parents, and the community
- Demonstrates ability to work effectively with diverse families and assure that families feel welcome in the school environment
- Demonstrates knowledge of effective ways to send and receive information to students, parents, and other professionals in order to foster inquiry, collaboration, and engagement in learning environments
- Demonstrates mutual respect, boundary setting, and creative problem-solving skills in collaborative relationships with students, parents, the community, and other professionals
- Recognizes the importance of being a student advocate and change agent, and works effectively with others within and outside of school environments
- Demonstrates understanding of how large school districts function, and understands how change can be accomplished within these complex systems
- Promotes personal and professional resilience in self and colleagues

PEDAGOGY FOR DIVERSITY

Strand Four, Pedagogy for Diversity, focuses on strategies for accelerating achievement for diverse groups of students. Because of the intensity of the academic challenges present in many urban settings, teachers need particularly strong content knowledge, pedagogical skills, and awareness of the instructional nuances that facilitate the learning of diverse populations.

In a study involving 251 sixth grade students, Sternberg (2006) found that those who were taught math by infusing culturally relevant content into instruction performed better on math assessments than did those who were taught through a conventional textbook approach. This finding suggests a need for educators to understand the culture from which their students come in order to maximize their learning.

Turner (2005) conducted an in-depth case study of a highly effective urban teacher of African American elementary students. The purpose of the study was to identify effective practices in orchestrating the literacy success of culturally diverse learners. Twenty classroom observations of approximately two hours each were conducted, along with five teacher interviews of approximately 45 minutes. One of the prominent findings of this study was the facility with which the teacher used practices associated with multicultural education, such as bringing the children's culture into the literacy content, embracing students' learning styles, and promoting interaction among diverse students. Likewise, in a similar study, Brooks (2006) also found that African American students' reading comprehension improved with the use of cultural knowledge congruent with their own experiences. These findings underscore the need for teachers to develop skills in pedagogy that embraces student diversity.

Other studies have focused on classroom contextual variables that support pedagogy for diversity. For example, Howard (2001b) interviewed students of four highly effective urban elementary school teachers and found that three central themes emerged with respect to student perceptions of culturally relevant teaching: "(1) teachers who displayed caring bonds and attitudes toward them; (2) teachers who established community and family-type classroom environments; and (3) teachers who made learning an entertaining and fun process" (Howard, 2001b, p. 131). The author described caring teachers as "warm demanders" (p. 139) who were often stern in their expressions of high expectations for students, but who also provided support and nurturing. A family-type classroom environment was described as one that mirrored some of the communication patterns and interactional styles of the home while promoting a sense of community among students. Making learning fun was described largely as a task of connecting to students' interests and appropriately integrating affect into instruction in order to engage students. Other studies have shown similar trends with respect to student perceptions of culturally responsive instructional and classroom management strategies (Darling, 2005; Weinstein, Tomlinson-Clarke, & Curran, 2004).

Based on this and other research related to pedagogy for diversity, the following competencies for teacher candidates have been developed:

- Plans and implements a variety of developmentally appropriate and culturally responsive instructional strategies
- Demonstrates competence in the use of accommodation strategies and alternative assessments for special needs and ELL students
- Uses classroom management strategies and group motivational techniques that respect cultural differences and establish a classroom climate that promotes positive social interaction, active engagement in learning, and self-motivation

- Demonstrates competence in the use of community resources to meet the needs of diverse students
- Demonstrates competence in alternative assessment strategies that are culturally sensitive
- Demonstrates competence in incorporating students' experiences, cultures, and community resources into instruction
- Demonstrates competence in his or her teaching field, including the ability to present multiple perspectives in the discussion of subject matter

The four strands discussed above, sociocultural competence, affirming attitude, collaborative skills, and pedagogy for diversity, reflect what the research suggests with respect to competencies needed for urban teaching. These strands give guidance to issues related to *what* needs to be included in urban teacher education programs in terms of content. The discussion below will highlight research related to *how* teacher education programs can best go about delivering this content.

Teacher Preparation Program Features

> It is impossible to teach people how to teach powerfully by asking them to imagine what they have never seen or to suggest they "do the opposite" of what they have observed in the classroom. (Darling-Hammond, 2006a, p. 308)

As expressed by Darling-Hammond, teacher education institutions must make significant changes in order to prepare teachers well for urban schools. As teacher educators, we continue to struggle to develop a context for teaching and social justice that will carry urban teachers from preservice through the early years of teaching into ongoing professional development that spans a career. A number of promising practices have emerged from this struggle.

PARTNERSHIPS WITH URBAN SCHOOLS

Evidence has suggested that teacher education institutions partnering with urban school districts is an effective strategy for the preparation of urban teachers (Sleeter, 2001). Often, these partnerships have culminated in the establishment of professional development schools. Darling-Hammond and colleagues at Stanford University examined seven exemplary teacher education programs and identified common features across the programs. These programs were selected because they were noted for producing graduates who are extraordinarily well-prepared for their first classrooms. The common features included:

- A common, clear vision of good teaching that permeates all coursework and clinical experiences, creating a coherent set of learning experiences;
- Well-defined standards of professional practice and performance that are used to guide and evaluate coursework and clinical work;
- A strong core curriculum taught in the context of practice and grounded in knowledge of child and adolescent development and learning, an understanding of social and cultural contexts, curriculum, assessment, and subject matter pedagogy;
- Extended clinical experiences—at least 30 weeks of supervised practicum and student teaching opportunities in each program that are carefully chosen to support the ideas presented in simultaneous, closely interwoven coursework;
- Extensive use of case methods, teacher research, performance assessment, and portfolio evaluation that apply learning to real problems of practice;
- Explicit strategies to help students to confront their own deep-seated beliefs and assumptions about learning and students and to learn about the experiences of people different from themselves; and
- Strong relationships, common knowledge, and shared beliefs among school and university-based faculty jointly engaged in transforming teaching, schooling, and teacher education (Darling-Hammond, 2006b, p. 306).

A teacher education program that attempts to integrate these features above and contribute to goals of social justice while remaining largely a collection of unrelated courses without a common conception of teaching and learning will be a feeble change agent for teacher education. Teacher education institutions must provide integrated opportunities for modeling and participation in high-quality practice that will only come through working with highly accomplished urban teachers and by close collaboration with schools, further developing the quality of urban schools (Darling-Hammond, 2005; Patterson, 2000). Features of high performing teacher education programs can integrate more tightly with the four strands of sociocultural competence, affirming attitude, collaborative skills and pedagogy for diversity in a well-developed school-university partnership or a Professional Development School (PDS).

Partnering with urban districts in the preparation of teachers not only provides opportunities for richer field experiences, but also provides unique opportunities to include urban practitioners as instructional partners in the delivery of coursework. This was a critical element of a successful PDS-embedded urban teacher education program at Indiana University Northwest (Schoon & Sandoval, 2000).

SEPARATE COURSE VS. INFUSION

Much of the content in the four competency strands discussed above revolves around issues of diversity. Many teacher education programs have struggled with how best to address such content. Often it is housed in separate courses (e.g., Multicultural Education, Teaching Diverse Populations, etc.). Among the stated advantages of such an organization is the idea that there is greater assurance that the topic will be covered in some depth—disadvantages include the idea that the information will be isolated to a particular term and not revisited throughout the program of study (Voltz, 2003). A number of studies have been conducted that examined the impact of a single course on student attitudes. For example, Weisman and Garza (2002) used questionnaires to survey 158 prospective teachers before and after taking a required multicultural education course. Results indicated that while gains were made with respect to overall orientation to diversity, students largely remained unable to see the role that schools and society can play in the educational challenges that some students of color face. Other studies also have shown positive, but limited, impact of single-course approaches in the delivery of content related to diverse populations (Sleeter, 2001).

Because of the limited impact of single-course approaches, many teacher education institutions have begun to explore the use of infusion models that distribute competencies related to urban teaching across multiple courses in the program. For example, Indiana University Northwest attempted this approach in their Urban Teacher Education Program (Schoon & Sandoval, 2000). However, the infusion approach was abandoned after a two-year period because "faculty believed that an urban teacher preparation program did need more emphasis on multicultural education" (p. 431). This case study suggested a lack of depth in the coverage of material related to diversity issues under the infusion approach.

Because of the shortcomings associated with both separate course and infusion models, emerging consensus suggests that these approaches be used in combination in order to reduce the liabilities associated with each. Jennings (2002) conducted case studies that examined programs that used both infusion and separate courses. These researchers concluded "multicultural teacher education needs to include but extend beyond particular courses to more expanded venues that provide opportunities for collaboration and critical reflection" (p. 456). These expanded venues included not only infusion throughout other coursework but also related field opportunities in urban settings that allowed for critical inquiry.

Where Do We Go from Here?

As teacher educators, we can no longer afford to ignore the need for well-prepared, successful urban teachers. We must develop bold and innovative strategies to improve what we do in regard to educating teachers and ourselves about teaching effectively in urban schools. First, we must continue serious scholarly inquiry that asks important questions about the competencies needed for successful urban teaching, the types of learning communities necessary to support and nurture those committed to urban schools, and the affiliated questions of social justice. As Ladson-Billings (1999, p. 114) commented, "Despite the changing demographics that make our public schools more culturally and linguistically diverse and the growing body of knowledge on issues of diversity and difference, multicultural teacher education continues to suffer from a thin, poorly developed, fragmented literature that provides an inaccurate picture of the kind of preparation teachers receive to teach in culturally diverse classrooms."

Second, we must analyze efforts to reform teacher education to determine what works. We can only do this by tracking our graduates and their experiences in urban schools. Generally, we shrink from connecting what we do in teacher education with student learning in schools. Yet, without progress in this arena, we will continue to wallow in the unknown and develop program modifications without adequate evidence. Investigation of the multiple factors that influence student and teacher performance holds promise for advancing knowledge and the effectiveness of our programs. To ignore the complete images between teacher actions and student achievement may also open the door for others to pursue that information. Berry (2005) argued that "teaching will not be a profession and teacher education will not earn its rightful status in the university until practitioners link teacher learning to student learning. Teacher educators must take the lead in this regard" (p. 277).

Third, we must consider whether or not modifying existing teacher education programs is sufficient to meet the needs of urban schools. Although specialized programs that prepare students for teaching in urban schools have not always been effective, it is clear that students need extended field experiences in high-quality urban settings that are coherent and integrated with the affiliated teacher education program. More research is needed on these specialized programs. Policymakers need to be informed of the initiatives—including their cost and the costs of replacing teachers. It may also be necessary for these policymakers to take the lead in eliminating duplicate programs within states so that resources can be re-allocated to those that focus successfully on low-performing schools.

Finally, we must use the knowledge gained to create a platform to get others involved in forging quality teacher education that addresses needs of our least served students. If that can be accomplished, we move closer to realizing the goals of social justice and educational equity; for nowhere is the need for renaissance greater than in urban schools.

References

Berry, B. (2005). The future of teacher education. *Journal of Teacher Education, 56*(3), 272–278.
Brooks, W. (2006). Reading representations of themselves: Urban youth use culture and African American textual features to develop literary understandings. *Reading research quarterly, 41*, 372–392.
Brown, E. L. (2002). Mrs. Boyd's fifth-grade inclusive classroom: A study of multicultural teaching strategies. *Urban Education, 37*, 126–141.
Children's Defense Fund. (2001). *Fair start: 2000.* Washington, DC: Author. Available at www.childrensdefense.org/fairstart-povstat2.htm.
Clark, S. R., & Holmes, G. (2006). Demystifying urban teaching: New lessons from the field. In J. Kincheloe & K. Hayes (Eds.), *Metropedagogy: Power, justice and the urban classroom.* Rotterdam: Sense Publishers.
Corbett, D., Wilson, B., & Williams, B. (2005). No choice but success. *Educational Leadership, 62*(6), 8–13.
Darling, D. (2005). Improving minority student achievement by making cultural connections. *Middle School Journal, 36*(5), 46–50.
Darling-Hammond, L. (2006a). Constructing 21st century teacher education. *Journal of Teacher Education, 57*(3).
Darling-Hammond, L. (2006b). *Powerful teacher education: Lessons from exemplary programs.* San Francisco: Jossey-Bass.
Darling-Hammond, L. (Ed.) (2005). *Professional development schools: Schools for developing a profession* (2nd ed.). New York: Teachers College Press.
Fleming, J., Chou, V., Ransom, S., Nishimura, M., & Burke, K. (2004). Putting literacy in context: What practicing teachers say about the realities of teaching in urban schools. In D. Lapp, C. Block, E. Cooper, J. Flood, N. Roser, & J. Tinajero (Eds.), *Teaching all the children: Strategies for developing literacy in an urban setting* (pp. 103–121). New York: Guilford Press.
Goddard, R. D., Tschannen-Moran, M., & Hoy, W. K. (2001). A multilevel examination of the distribution and effects of teacher trust in students and parents in urban elementary schools. *The Elementary School Journal, 102*, 3–17.
Grace, M. (2001, April 24). Teachers ducking certificates: Fear being assigned to bad schools. *New York Daily News.* Retrieved from http://pqasb.pqarchiver.com/nydailynews/index.html?ts=1038787382.
Howard, G. (2007). As diversity grows, so must we. *Educational Leadership, 64,* 23–29.

Howard, T. C. (2001a). Powerful pedagogy for African American students: A case of four teachers. *Urban Education, 36*, 179–203.

Howard, T. C. (2001b). Telling their side of the story: African-American students' perceptions of culturally relevant teaching. *The Urban Review, 33*, 131–149.

Jacob, B. (2007, May) Why is it so hard to recruit and retain teachers in urban districts? *Excellence in the classroom, 17,* 1. Retrieved May 17, 2007, from www.futureofchild ren.org/information_2827/information_show.htm?docid = 469847.

Jennings, L. B. (2002). Examining the role of critical inquiry for transformative practices: Two joint case studies of multicultural teacher education. *Teachers College Record, 104,* 456–481.

Kozol, J. (2005). *The shame of the nation: The restoration of apartheid schooling in America.* New York: Three Rivers Press.

Ladson-Billings, G. (1999). Preparing teachers for diversity. In L. Darling-Hammond & G. Sykes (Eds.), *Teaching as the learning profession* (pp. 86–123). San Francisco: Jossey-Bass.

Lankford, H., Loeb, S., & Wyckoff, J. (2002). Teacher sorting and the plight of urban schools: A descriptive analysis. *Educational Evaluation and Policy Analysis, 24*(1), 37–62.

Monroe, C. R. (2005). Understanding the discipline gap through a cultural lens: Implications for the education of African American students. *Intercultural Education 16*(4), 317–330.

Murnane, R., & Steele, J. (May, 2007). What is the problem? The challenge of providing effective teachers for all children. *Excellence in the classroom, 17,* 1. Retrieved May 17, 2007, from www.futureofchildren.org/information2826/information_show.htm?doc_id = 46895.

National Center for Education Statistics. (2005). *The nation's report card.* Washington, DC: Author.

National Commission on Teaching and America's Future. (2003). *No dream denied: A pledge to America's children.* Retrieved February 3, 2003, from www.actat.org/dream/dream.html.

Obidah, J., & Howard, T. (2005). Preparing teachers for Monday morning in the urban classroom: Reflecting on our pedagogies and practices as effective teacher educators. *Journal of Teacher Educators, 56,* 248–255.

Patterson, J. H. (2000, November). *Impact of professional development schools on teacher education.* Paper presented at the annual meeting of the Mid-South Educational Research Association, Bowling Green, KY.

Rothstein, R. (2004). *Class and schools: Using social, economic, and educational reform to close the black-white achievement gap.* (1st. ed.). Washington, DC: Economic Policy Institute.

Sachs, S. (2004). Evaluation of teacher attributes as predictors of success in urban schools. *Journal of Teacher Education, 55,* 177–187.

Schoon, K. J., & Sandoval, P. A. (2000). Attracting, preparing, and keeping great urban teachers: The Urban Teacher Education Program, Option II. *Urban Education, 35,* 418–441.

Sleeter, C. E. (2001). Preparing teachers for culturally diverse schools: Research and the overwhelming presence of whiteness. *Journal of Teacher Education, 52,* 94–106.

Song, K. H. (2006). Urban teachers' beliefs on teaching, learning, and students: A pilot study in the United States of America. *Education and Urban Society, 38*, 481–499.

Sternberg, R. J. (2006). Recognizing neglected strengths. *Educational Leadership, 64*(1), 8–15.

Turner, J. D. (2005). Orchestrating success for African American readers: The case of an effective third-grade teacher. *Reading Research and Instruction, 44*(4), 27–48.

Voltz, D. L. (2003). Collaborative infusion: An emerging approach to teacher preparation for inclusive education. *Action in Teacher Education, 25*, 5–13.

Weinstein, C. S., Tomlinson-Clarke, S., & Curran, M. (2004). Toward a conception of culturally responsive classroom management. *Journal of Teacher Education, 55*, 25–38.

Weisman, M., & Garza, S. A. (2002). Preservice teacher attitudes toward diversity: Can one course make a difference? *Equity and Excellence in Education, 35*, 28–34.

Young, B. A. (2002). *Public school student, staff and graduates counts by state: School year 2000–01 (NCES 2002-348)*. Washington, DC: National Center for Education Statistics.

Summary and Implications

Cheryl J. Craig

Louise F. Deretchin

As foreshadowed, Ross and Chan's chapter dug deeply into Schwab's scholarship, highlighting themes that inform current issues in teacher education. Moving seamlessly across time and place, Ross and Chan engaged in a point-counterpoint discussion by identifying contemporary teacher education practices that would promote a Schwab-like vision of renaissance in teaching and teacher education.

Through adopting research parameters that did not approach preservice and in-service teaching in a disjointed fashion, Ross and Chan set readers on a course for a re-imagination of the field. They furthermore drew forward for discussion four pressing problems in teacher education: heightened attention to issues regarding teacher quality and teacher preparation, sophisticated new research designs and instruments to study the complexity of teacher preparation, growing emphasis on research and evidence as the basis for decision-making, and working within and against the teacher education system to expand the ways we think about teacher education's purposes in society.

They then analyzed those problems from both contemporary and Schwab-informed perspectives. For example, the failure to attend equally to the commonplaces of teacher, learner, milieu, and subject matter in teacher education programs and in the research designs chosen to study the impact of teacher education is highly problematic to Ross and Chan. This is because such approaches neither address the particularity nor the complexity that Schwab understood as being foundational to a rigorous understanding of practice and practical settings. To further complicate matters, preservice teachers are additionally not cultivated or positioned in the educational enterprise to be curriculum makers—producers of knowledge and researchers of their own practices. All of this contributes to the teaching and teacher education conundrum in which we find ourselves, a conundrum that has been underway for more than five decades as Ross and Chan insightfully pointed out.

Informed by Schwab, Ross and Chan also pulled on research that questioned value-added approaches to studying the effects of teacher education, which factor out human particularity and deny contextual complexity, among other matters. At the same time, the authors' close reading of Schwab caused them to include research practices that were excluded in *Studying Teacher Education* (Cochran-Smith & Zeichner, 2005) due to the boundaries set for the literature searches contained in that volume. To Ross and Chan—as for Schwab before them—both fluid and stable forms of inquiry are vital for growth in the field of education. Not supporting and funding both types of investigations is a mistake in judgment, one that leaves the U.S., as Schwab noted, dependent on international scholars for theoretical and practical advance, particularly where scientific discovery is concerned. Furthermore, focusing exclusively on stable inquiry allows "rhetoric of conclusions" to increase in unbounded ways. This may have led a frustrated Schwab (1958) to additionally write of "the corruption of education by psychology" due to the borrowing of quantification, classification, typification, and the like from that field and the failure to generate research approaches and tools specifically meant for the enterprise of education.

We now turn our attention to Chapter 2, the Voltz, Collins, Patterson, and Sims chapter, which addressed a specific aspect of renaissance: a renaissance in urban teacher education. This imagined rebirth is particularly timely because, as the authors asserted, "nowhere is the need greater." Summarizing studies conducted by others, Voltz et al. presented a vivid picture of the realities within which urban schooling takes place. The authors additionally informed us that preservice education students most often do not represent the racial, cultural, linguistic, and economic backgrounds of the children they teach. Even more troubling, they experience difficulties in communicating appropriately with underserved public school students who tend to be diverse and urban. At the same time, Voltz et al. cited Darling-Hammond (2006) who maintained that "it is impossible to teach people to teach powerfully by asking them to imagine what they have never seen or to suggest that they 'do the opposite' of what they have observed in the classroom" (p. 308).

To attend to these perplexing problems, Voltz et al. offered four strands that summarize the competencies that prospective urban teachers need to develop: sociocultural competence, affirming attitudes, collaborative skills, and pedagogy for diversity. They then worked carefully through these individual strands, providing a set of competencies for each strand as they went along, in addition to a set of sources that provide the rationale for the inclusion of the competencies.

Voltz et al. appropriately concluded their chapter by focusing on promising practices they uncovered. One such practice was establishing partnerships with urban schools; another had to do with how courses dealing with diversity are presented. Readers were informed of the advantages and disadvantages of treating issues of equity and diversity as a separate course and as content distributed throughout a number of courses offered within teacher education programs. Additionally, they were apprised of the possibility of blending both approaches. To end, Voltz et al. returned to the perennial question: "Where do we go from here?" In response to this query, the team of authors reinforced the need for specially prepared teacher candidates for urban schools, the need to connect what is happening in the schools with what is happening in teacher education, and the need to deliberate and modify programs and practices and reflect such changes in educational policy. They concluded by stating that preparation to teach the underserved youth in America's urban centers necessarily involves both practicing and beginning teachers. With assistance from teacher educators, those within the profession and those new to the field will be more able to direct sorely needed attention to social justice and educational equity issues in urban settings. Such attention, coupled with mindful action, would help spur a renaissance in teacher education.

References

Cochran-Smith, M., & Zeichner, K. (Eds.) (2005). *Studying teacher education: The report of the AERA panel on research and teacher education.* Mahwah, NJ: Lawrence Erlbaum.

Darling-Hammond, L. (2006). Constructing 21st century teacher education. *Journal of Teacher Education, 57*(3), 300–314.

Schwab, J. J. (1958). On the corruption of education by psychology. *School Review, 66,* 169–184.

Division 2
SHIFTING PERSPECTIVES AND PRACTICES

Overview and Framework

Cheryl J. Craig

Louise F. Deretchin

In Division 2, Shifting Perspectives and Practices, six chapters appear. In Chapter 3, "Daring to Care: Adding Caring to Our Vision of Teacher Education," Robin McBee and Patrick Westcott introduce some of the harsh realities of today's schools. They suggest that caring is absolutely vital to academic growth and positive social engagement and that teacher education programs must intentionally cultivate an ethic of care.

In Chapter 4, Shelley McIntosh, Iren Chen, Bea Villareal, and Marion Godine, a diverse team of teacher educator collaborators, discuss the "Spiritual Voices of Preservice Teachers" as an avoided topic in teacher education programs. Through the use of concrete examples, they show how their students, who typically represent minority populations, infuse their experiential writing with different aspects of spirituality.

Miriam Ben-Peretz and Gabriella Landler-Pardo also center on an overlooked aspect of teacher education in "Teachers' Thoughts about Rewards and Joys of Teaching: A Neglected Component in Teacher Education Programs," the title of Chapter 5. Taking the position that much of teacher education is cast in the language of dilemmas and issues, Ben-Peretz and Landler-Pardo argue that examples of the joys and rewards of teaching should be made known to aspiring teachers to heighten their attraction to, and satisfaction with, their chosen profession.

In Chapter 6, "Educating for Inquiry through a Reflective Portfolio Process: What are the Imperatives for Teachers or Students to Think Well in Contexts?" Nona Lyons discusses the elements of an inquiry process that scaffold the reflective thinking of faculty and students. Using examples ranging from public school to higher education settings, Lyons inquires into what it means to deliberate a topic and to think well in context through the use of reflective portfolios.

Next in the Division 2 lineup is Chapter 7, "The Wisdom of Fifth-Graders: A Voice in the Renaissance," which is authored by Barbara Morgan-Fleming, Myra Kendrik-Mercer, Susan Myers, and Connie Wilson Anderson. These educators who teach along the K–16 continuum intentionally engage elementary students and probe their thinking concerning their understanding of good teachers and the nature of ideal content in teacher education programs—from children's points of view.

Chapter 8, the final chapter in Division 2, is "Star Tech: The Net Generation!" contributed by Ron Berk, an educator and educational humorist. Berk compels us to consider the degree to which children and teacher education candidates have changed from previous generations. Dubbing these individuals part of "the net generation," he reminds readers that mirroring the high tech environment in which they routinely interact must necessarily be part of any renaissance in teacher education.

CHAPTER 3

Daring to Care
ADDING CARING TO OUR VISION OF TEACHER EDUCATION

Robin Haskell McBee
Rowan University

Patrick M. Westcott
Rowan University

> Robin Haskell McBee, Ph.D., is an associate professor in the Teacher Education Department at Rowan University. Her areas of interest include caring in schools, curriculum integration, multicultural education, and elementary social studies education.
>
> Patrick M. Westcott, Ed.D., is an assistant professor in the Teacher Education Department at Rowan University. His areas of interest include caring in schools, assessment, and best instructional practice.

ABSTRACT

> Today's schools face multiple stressors. Academic and testing pressures, coupled with school violence, lead to dramatic measures that distort curricula and teaching practices. The need to integrate an ethic of caring is of critical importance. This chapter discusses how an ethos of caring can stimulate academic growth and positive social engagement in our schools, how teachers build such an ethos, and how a vision of teacher education programs can intentionally include an ethic of caring in courses and workshops.

Make no mistake. Today's schools confront high stakes: the dual pressures to perform and protect. On one hand we have the looming specter of producing higher test scores to meet "adequate yearly progress" under the deficit-focused eyes of accountability (Cochran-Smith, 2005). On the other hand, lock-down drills force us to practice evasive maneuvers while considering the hate, anger, and frustration that torment and impel students to violent attacks (Poland, 2003). Both conditions cause stress for students and teachers; both can lead to dramatic measures to address them; both reflect the need to integrate greater care into what we do in our schools.

In this chapter, we discuss these conditions, the literature on caring in schools, our own inquiry into how educators conceptualize caring, and our vision for integrating the study of caring approaches and practices into teacher education programs. For us, this vision reshapes teacher education programs, imagining the classroom as a place of caring. Here, educators focus on a thoughtful infusion of materials and activities that build an ethic of care. We believe that the challenging nature of today's classroom environment—one that focuses heavily on preparation for standardized testing and pressing concerns for student safety—make caring a necessity.

The Fallout from the Pressures to Perform

Fear of failure, withdrawal of funds, and job loss drive otherwise well-informed educators to alter the curriculum and their instruction toward a test preparation focus that often eliminates inquiry and replaces critical thinking with fast paced marches through facts and repetitive memorization (Cochran-Smith, 2003). At best, such a focus assures short-term recall of disparate facts at the expense of long-term understanding and retention and the ability to transfer what has been learned to new situations (Weaver, 2004). The over-emphasis on test scores precludes using meaningful, multi-measure assessments to accurately gauge complex student learning and productive teaching that leads to such learning (Cochran-Smith, 2003).

Children who are unable to understand and keep pace with a rapid fact-packed curriculum, are often left behind (Cochran-Smith, 2005; Darling-Hammond, 2004)—a curious perversion of the federal government's purported purpose to leave no child behind. Those failed children are further marginalized as they are relegated to more dull and repetitive supplemental instruction. Eventually, they simply give up on themselves, as their teachers have already been forced to do. Now disenfranchised from the excitement of learning, students cry out to be noticed—"to be constructively 'seen' and heard," (Chaltain, 2006, p. 48)—their invisibility, a reminder of their failed struggles to succeed.

Against this backdrop emerges a concurrent rise in violent antisocial behavior and dropout rates (Fuentes, 2003). Moreover, in yet another left behind twist on No Child Left Behind, the Harvard Civil Rights Project notes the "perverse incentives in many states to push low-performing students out the back door" (Orfield, Losen, & Wald, 2004, p. 3) in order to bypass test-driven penalties.

This is a snapshot of our educational scene today, a troubling picture of teaching and learning. There is neither instructional time nor a culture to support an ethic of care about what we teach, who we teach, or how we teach. In turn, students feel frustrated, bored, unheard (Chaltain, 2006), and alienated from school learning. This situation begs for a new approach that emphasizes the importance of care in schools.

Establishing and maintaining an ethic of care in our classrooms does not mean shedding high expectations or high academic standards. According to resilience researcher, Benson, "we are putting so much emphasis on testing and academic achievement, we risk losing sight of something that is very obvious: Achievement is as much about student development as it is about rigor and curriculum" (as quoted in Walser, 2006). We are reminded by Johnson (2006) that "learning is embedded in relationship. Relationships affect students not only in how they think and act, but also in what kinds of intellectual risks and ethical stands they take" (p. 16).

An ethic of care ensures that we constantly adjust and modify our curriculum to keep it content rich, meaningful, and highly engaging to and challenging for the learners. However, caring also means that we make sure that we are doing this for *all* learners—advanced and struggling, that all learners are appropriately challenged and able to meet the challenges, that we provide the support that is needed to make that happen, and that we are aiming for deep understanding and long-term retention and transferability of knowledge (Cochran-Smith, 2005; Darling-Hammond, 2004).

Caring also necessitates attending to the social and emotional needs of all human beings and recognizing the need to meet these needs in order to establish a learning environment where *all* learners feel comfortable, safe, and inspired to explore, discover, practice, transfer, apply, and share what they are studying (Johnson, 2006). This takes time, intentionality, and an orientation toward deep, meaningful, connected conceptual learning instead of broad coverage, superficial factual memorization, and test driven curriculum planning and instruction (Eisner, 2005; Kohn, 2005).

The Importance of Caring in Schools

Caring in the educational context is an elusive concept that is difficult to define through empirical studies (Goldstein & Lake, 2000). Discussions on caring are largely theoretical, as in the case of the moral imperative for caring in schools. However, caring is also a theme that regularly emerges in the multicultural literature and resilience studies.

The moral imperative to develop an ethic of care and caring communities in schools asserts that caring is the right thing to do and that caring and being cared for is more critical to our well being than any nugget of academic knowledge (Bondy & Davis, 2000; Deiro, 2003; Goldstein & Lake, 2000; Strahan & Layell, 2006). Noddings (2002) advocates intentionally creating a climate of trust and care in schools. We should be dedicated to producing "caring, competent, loving, and lovable people," and this commitment should guide our curriculum design and "everything we do in schools" (p. 33–36). As a leading proponent of caring, Noddings has focused the discussion away from a vague idea of being nice and toward a relational give and take between care givers and receivers. Such relationships are thoughtful and reciprocal in nature, with the care giver considering the needs of those being cared for, and the recipients of that care returning the care in varied forms of responsive engagement (Deiro, 2003; Goldstein & Lake, 2000; Noddings, 1984, 2002).

One critical feature of a caring ethic in schools is teacher knowledge of students' needs and interests. Bondy and Davis (2000) detail novice reading tutors' success after getting to know their urban tutees' interests. Strahan and Layell's findings (2006) indicate that successful urban middle school students "attribute their accomplishments" in part "to the caring relationships they had with teachers" (p. 148) and that teachers' "attempts to get to know their students better enabled them to create" learner-centered environments and "more engaging lessons" (p. 150).

Multicultural educators often note the essential role of caring in a culturally responsive setting. Such settings have strong reciprocal relationships, characterized by teachers truly knowing their learners and engaging in meaningful and respectful dialogue with them (Gay, 2000; Nieto, 2003; Pang, Rivera, & Mora, 1999). Valuing diverse groups and social orientations tends to affirm the academic and social potential of all students. Pang, Rivera, and Mora (1999) call for "caring-centered multicultural education" to "incorporate both a strong ethic of care and the importance of culture as a blended foundation for a strong educational orientation" (p. 3). Nieto (2003) emphasizes the centrality and power of a sense of community and belonging: "For students whose culture and language backgrounds differ from the mainstream, care is especially relevant because when students feel their teachers care about them, they also feel they belong" (p. 42).

High expectations for all students are equally important in a caring multicultural setting. Instructional effectiveness depends on teachers who care enough to demand and expect the best from all of their students (Gay, 2000; Nieto,

2003; Pang, Rivera, & Mora, 1999). Such teachers have a "solid faith in the capability of students to learn" and an "unshakable belief that . . . all students are capable of reaching tremendous heights" (Nieto, 2003, p. 42).

The literature on resilience is rife with data on the role of a caring and supportive adult in students' lives. Such adults may be related to the children, who may be facing many risk factors for delinquency or school failure, or they may be a part of their larger social world, including schools. As is reflected in the other literature, when such adults communicate high expectations, get to know the children, show an interest in their lives, and listen to them, there is a high correlation with increased resiliency and success in schools (Edwards, 2001; Reed, McMillan, & McBee, 1995; Taylor-Dunlop & Norton, 1997; Walser, 2006).

Related to this idea is the notion of engaging such children in schools, in clubs, and in meaningful, caring, democratic communities. When students are engaged (Reed, et al., 1995), listened to and heard (Chaltain, 2006), and have an opportunity to contribute to decisions about what is studied and behavior expectations (Battistitch, 2001; Edwards, 2001), they feel more connected to school, work harder, engage in less misbehavior and delinquency, and perform better academically (Battistich, 2001; Edwards, 2001; Reed et al., 1995; Walser, 2006).

The above literature presents evidence that supports including caring in our school and teacher education curricula; however, defining and delimiting the focus of what is to be taught is challenging. In the next section we consider findings from our own study of teachers' conceptualizations of caring and caring practices. We believe these findings can be helpful in framing a vision for infusing an ethic of caring into teacher education programs.

How Aspiring and Practicing Teachers Conceptualize Caring

In order to better understand the permutations of caring in schools, McBee examined voluntary open-ended survey responses from 144 teachers, teacher candidates, and teacher education faculty members to uncover how they conceptualized caring and carried out those conceptualizations in school settings (McBee, in press; McBee, Bereheiko, & Edmond, 2006, August). A brief background on the study and its outcomes will be followed by a discussion of the use of knowledge gained from the outcomes to contribute to a renaissance in education by including teacher education.

BACKGROUND

Informants were gathered through a mid-Atlantic, university-based, teacher education program serving a range of urban, suburban, and rural communities. Four hundred twenty surveys were mailed or distributed through courses to elementary education teacher education candidates, practicing elementary teachers, and teacher education faculty. Of those, 124 surveys were voluntarily returned by candidates, 13 by teachers, and 7 by teacher education faculty.

The candidate surveys asked what caring means to them in the educational context, what caring behaviors they had observed in college and elementary teachers, and how they had exhibited caring themselves. The teacher and college faculty surveys similarly requested a definition of caring in the educational context. Their surveys further inquired about ways they show their students that they care for them and approaches they use to teach caring to their students.

OUTCOMES

Respondents indicated how they defined caring in school settings. They provided examples of extending care or observing others extend care and described how they taught caring in their classrooms.

Offering Help

Offering help was the most frequently mentioned characteristic of a caring teacher and was central to the caring conceptualizations of both practicing teachers (elementary and college) and aspiring teachers. According to respondents, caring teachers are "concerned with difficulties a student is having and [go] beyond what is required to do everything in [their] power to help that student succeed." One candidate described her own efforts in the following way: "I tutor at an elementary school. A few times I'll see students struggling with an assignment. One girl was actually crying. I went over to her and walked her through the material so she was finally able to do it herself."

A second candidate detailed caring observed in another teacher's behavior: "A teacher had a struggling reader. The parent was concerned and wanted to help but was unsure how. The teacher researched all her sources to find various reading materials the student could practice at home. As a result of their collaboration the student went from a Level C to a Level L (reading A to Z) in four months and is now reading on grade level."

Recognizing the need, responding to it, and providing extra time, input, and resources are typically described manifestations of helpfulness in caring teachers.

Candidates and Compassion

Respondents felt that showing compassion toward students' needs, concerns, and life experiences was a critical component of teacher care. They inquired about students' weekends or their health after an illness, reached out to conflicted students to calm and reassure them, attended family funerals, adjusted expectations to accommodate students' life pressures, and called students at home or in the hospital. The following three comments were typical.

- I ask all of my students who were out sick if they're feeling better when they return.
- I make sure I take the time to talk to [one of my students] about his problems.
- One day she called a sick child at home on his birthday, and the entire class sang "happy birthday" over the phone.

An interesting additional finding was that those who received help or compassionate treatment often provided similar treatment to others. When one receives help, there is a greater tendency to reach out to others and offer help as well.

Showing an Interest in and Getting to Know Students

Comments in this area focused on showing an interest in the students and their lives, as well as their work, accomplishments, and goals. Teachers frequently noted the importance of paying attention to the whole learner and noted learning about their students through chats, check-ins, and questionnaires. "Caring, for many, means knowing learners and treating them as whole people." It is "showing an interest in each student as an individual and taking the time to support the growth and progress of each one." One teacher summed it up this way:

> Caring encompasses the entire person—not just being concerned with students' direct learning, but with their personal lives as well. What happens to the child outside of school affects everything they do in the classroom. It is important to find out about a child's family background, ethnicity, cultural neighborhood, experiences, etc.

Listening to Learners

Listening to students' concerns and views was also important to teachers when describing their conceptualizations of caring. Respondents indicated that they listen to students "when they need to talk," "without judging," through sharing personal anecdotes, and through "their input." One teacher encouraged others to "pay attention to students' behavior—you can catch some learning problems early and help." Another urged that really listening to what students have to say helps build self-esteem. A third described her work this way: "I listen when they speak without interrupting. I answer their questions honestly and promptly. I share their accomplishments and joys and cheer them on! I share their sorrows and failures, too."

Teaching Caring

Teacher respondents reported that they taught about caring through a wide variety of approaches in elementary and college classrooms. At the adult level, there was a greater focus on theme-related readings and discussions, but faculty members often also modeled building caring communities through classroom meeting techniques (Charney, 1992). Elementary teachers also used discussions and class meetings along with children's literature about caring, role playing, and developing rules and norms that focused on caring behaviors. The growth in popularity of character education and anti-bullying programs were also reflected in respondents' comments. Kobak (1997) notes that teachers' caring curricula use three kinds of input: class dialogue, creativity "tools," such as literature and role playing cards, and action projects with the aim of changing attitudes and promoting action.

Including Caring in Teacher Education

Our vision for a renaissance in teacher education programs includes adding appropriate content and instructional practice demonstrations that incorporate the six key characteristics that caring teachers enact in their learning communities. These characteristics are: (1) helpfulness, (2) sincere interest in students, (3) compassion, (4) concern about the individual, (5) generosity with teacher time, and (6) attentive, responsive listening. Following is a discussion of how each characteristic connects with the larger body of literature on caring as well as examples of applications in schools, teacher preparation, and professional development programs.

HELPFULNESS

In a study of two middle schools, students identified helping behaviors as synonymous with caring. Teacher helping behaviors were "helping with schoolwork, explaining work, and checking for understanding" (Bosworth, 1995, p. 686). Strategies for teaching helpfulness are varied but each stems from a teacher's willingness to make time for the individual student. This willingness can take numerous forms. Establishing a regularly scheduled time for meeting with students before and after school each week, for example, is essential. It is important that this time together is not labeled as punitive detention or time for the completion of forgotten or incomplete homework or schoolwork. Instead, this is a time for helping students understand concepts that they misunderstood or did not grasp during class time. In addition to discussing helpfulness, college faculty in teacher education need to model a similar level of helpfulness. This can be accomplished through scheduling extra office hours and through on-line supplemental discussions of challenging concepts for example.

Helping behaviors must also be part of the classroom context. Students should take on roles for "helping" each other in the classroom (Putnam & Burke, 2005) as well as undertake classroom responsibilities such as watering the classroom plants, distributing classroom materials, constructing class bulletin boards, and helping to rearrange desk formations. As Peterson (1992) writes in *Life in a Crowded Place: Making a Learning Community,* "Jobs help students contribute to the quality of life in the learning community as well as negotiate meaning, take on responsibility, and contribute in significant ways to advancing a cooperative way of life" (p. 63).

Students who exhibit helping behaviors in the classroom or school should be honored for their behaviors. Offering certificates for helping behaviors is one strategy. Students can serve as "buddies," who are assigned a partner at the beginning of the school year or the college semester and support each other with schoolwork or when returning to class after an absence. This role can be extended to classroom helpers who aid new students in their navigation of the classroom and the school environment.

Quality children's literature is a resource with constructive exemplars for a caring curriculum that teachers can use for discussing helping behaviors with children and teacher educators. Such varied texts as *The Giving Book: Open the Door to a Lifetime of Giving* by Ellen Sabin (2004), *Number the Stars* by Lois Lowry (1989), *Amelia Bedelia Helps Out* by Peggy Parish (1979), and *Little Red Lighthouse and the Great Gray Bridge* by Hildegarde H. Swift (1970) provide clear examples of caring behaviors. These and many other strategies can be discussed in teacher education programs, and many can actually be modeled as well.

SINCERE INTEREST IN STUDENTS

Showing a sincere interest in students requires that teachers take time to "know" the unique person. Barnett and Morse (1994) point out that students are attracted to teachers who offer personal attention. Demonstrating interest and teaching students to take a sincere interest in one another can be promoted through something as simple as daily morning meeting check-ins, which build "the principle of group," develop the "ethic of an attentive and responsive group," provide time for "sharing events and experiences," and serve as transitions, "connecting lives at home to lives in school" (Charney, 1992, p. 30–31). Regular meetings can similarly be used in teacher preparation courses to model and lend practice to the method.

On a more intimate, individual level, one-on-one weekly meetings with each student can be accomplished through curriculum (e.g., a writing conference); end-of-the-week mini-conferences about the week's events; and weekly lunches with small groups of students where students can share aspects of their lives. Beyond regularly scheduled meetings, teacher educators can incorporate an adaptation of this idea through periodic written reflections and on-line chats.

Finally, acknowledging birthdays and celebrating personal accomplishments provide a natural vehicle for encouraging peer interest and support. These celebrations only require a short break in the course of the classroom day or course period.

COMPASSION

Compassion for life's big as well as little problems is an important part of caring. Noddings (1995b) urges teachers to be prepared to "respond to the needs of students who are suffering from the death of friends, conflicts between groups of students, pressure to use drugs or to engage in sex, and other troubles so rampant in the lives of today's children" (p. 365).

An approach to building an understanding of students' and the community's needs is to invite diverse people into the classroom community to discuss how they navigate the world economically, socially, or physically in the case of impairment. Note can be made of good deeds by others or situations that call for caring acts as told through personal accounts, newspaper articles, and literature. Based on stories, students at any level can be encouraged to propose appropriate acts of caring. Classroom charity work and service projects such as the adopt a group suggested by The Teaching Tolerance Project (1997) promote compassion through the interactions students commit to on a regular basis with groups' members at places such as nursing homes, homeless shelters, etc.

Decades of scientific research have demonstrated that carefully structured cooperative learning strategies are effective means of promoting group work, support, and care. This approach provides a "positive social atmosphere where students learn to like and respect one another and where taunting and bullying are sharply reduced" (Aronson, 2000, p. 17). Professors and staff developers who model cooperative learning techniques in their teacher and professional development sessions provide tangible experience with the effectiveness of the approach.

CONCERN ABOUT THE INDIVIDUAL STUDENT

Bosworth (1995) notes the importance of teachers "who saw students as individuals in their classrooms" (p. 686). Such teachers acknowledged diverse learning styles and rates of learning, observed and inquired about changes in behavior, and continuously sought to recognize students as individuals. In their study of two classroom teachers, McCadden, Noblit, and Rogers (1995) point out that concerned teachers talk with their students.

> Talk cannot be overemphasized, since it was through talk that children revealed their lives and teachers supported and nurtured them. Talk was reciprocal, requiring each to listen and hear as well as to speak . . . [and] became the currency of caring . . . (p. 680)

It is important that class discussions "be ongoing, consistent, relevant and structured into curriculum as a 'period'" (Kobak, 1997, p. 97) or part of the weekly course meeting. In the discussions, empathy for one another is stressed. Conversations focus on how the other person feels or how you would feel under a similar circumstance.

GENEROSITY WITH TEACHER TIME

The caring educator is also willing to expend time with students. "For a professional educator to change students' lives profoundly requires generosity of time and a spirit of commitment . . . Students are directly affected by the generosity bestowed to them by professional educators in numerous ways" (Anderson, 2000, p. 139). Teachers need to provide time before, after, and during school—at lunch, recess, teacher breaks, study hall—to meet with students to discuss academic and social concerns. Such time can be pivotal to students' development, as Allen (2006) reflects when she muses that the boys' weekly lunchtime writing group she has studied is about more than just writing: "These boys yearned to be heard, and they were begging for a sense of belonging" (p. 69–70).

We must also make time in our class work to discuss how to be caring individuals and to respond constructively to emerging situations related to students' or adults' hurtful words or actions. Noddings urges us to create time for students to practice ethical and caring behaviors: "We must help students understand how groups and individuals create rivals and enemies and help them learn how to 'be on both sides'" (Noddings, 1995a, p. 365).

ATTENTIVE, RESPONSIVE LISTENING

Teachers need to learn the skill for, and take the time for listening without comment, moving away from the typical evaluative response or judgment. Practicing respectful, non-evaluative listening can do this. Aaronsohn (2003) worked with teachers to first remove correcting language and then to replace it with "evaluative praise with descriptive encouragement" (p. 93) such as, *I don't understand what you mean; can you say it another way; that reminds me of . . .* ; and *I never thought about it in that way*. Strategies such as the "jigsaw," whereby individual students within a group take responsibility for reading, understanding, and sharing portions of a reading with their group to collectively deepen understanding of the reading and collectively determine further learning, promotes attentive, responsive listening. Aaronsohn (2003) notes that this type of work requires students to "move beyond their own experiences" with the reading toward a more complete understanding of the authors' positions. "It requires them to come to consensus about what is important—and about meaning" (p. 93). Just as in a jigsaw puzzle, each piece or student's part is essential for the completion and full understanding of the text; each student becomes indispensable, and each must learn to listen to the others.

In her study of four fourth-grade classes engaging in mathematical conversations, researcher Atkins (1999) notes the importance of allotting time for students to make meaning, and for teacher and students to honor student talk with careful listening. With mathematical conversations, we can "allow participants to learn about the mathematical constructions of others" while giving them "opportunities to reflect on their own mathematical understandings" (p. 289). Such conversations that honor student talk and collaborative meaning making enhance student listening skills and are relevant even at the adult level. Conversations reflecting on the meaning of subject areas need to be modeled in a host of subject studies within workshops and coursework for both practicing and novice teachers.

Finally, attentive, responsive listening on the part of teachers and students requires a physical environment conducive to interacting. A classroom layout that positions learners so that they can face one another such as the horseshoe, hollow square, or circular layout, encourages richer conversation and careful, interactive listening while also increasing the likelihood that the teacher will become a member rather than a director of the learning community (Atkins, 1999). Again, such classroom configurations can be discussed and modeled in college courses as well as in professional development sessions.

Summary

Knowing our learners is a recurrent theme in this chapter. The theme distinguishes the literature on the ethic of care, multicultural education, and resilience. It is clearly embedded in the six characteristics of caring educational environments we have discussed. Caring teachers recognize the powerful impact they can have on their students' progress by taking time to find out about learners, getting to know what is important to them, listening carefully to them—their individual stories and viewpoints—and taking instructional and personal actions that incorporate that knowledge in support of the learner. Teacher educators need to pay closer attention to the theme of demonstrated caring uncovered by this research and incorporate it into the design of their courses and programs.

Further, we should be more explicit in what we teach about an ethic of care. Many of us may practice aspects of an ethic, but are we intentional about this practice and overt in our discussion of it as a viable and critical curricular component for preparing teachers and for success for all children? We should strive to intentionally and explicitly model a respectful reciprocity in our relationships with our learners so that they might experience the benefits of caring relationships and transfer that experience to their own teaching.

We need to build into our course syllabi and workshop agendas explicit discussions about strategies and the teacher's role in promoting a caring ethic in schools. As teacher educators, we need to develop and conduct role playing scenarios, initiate discussion starters, and collect and use readings and case studies which focus on critical components of the caring ethic. We need to build libraries for thoughtful discourse on the topic with our students. As we become more purposeful and explicit in our inclusion of caring as a part of our own curriculum and instruction, we are likely to promote a greater familiarity and comfort with these ideas on the part of our teachers.

Recommended Annotated Bibliography

The following are examples of quality children's literature that focus on caring:

Bunting, E. (1994). *Smoky Night*. Orlando, FL: Harcourt Brace and Company.
  When a child and his mother must evacuate to a shelter in the middle of the night during the Los Angeles riots, a previously cool relationship with a neighbor warms up as they share relief at being reunited with their rescued pet cats.
dePaola, T. (1979). *Oliver Button is a sissy*. Ft. Worth, TX: Voyager Books.
  Despite the teasing, Oliver stays true to himself with the help of a caring teacher.
Gackenbach, D. (1984). *Harry and the terrible whatzit*. New York: Clarion Books.
  A child conquers his fear in order to save his mother.
Havill, J. (1986). *Jamaica's Find*. New York: Houghton Mifflin Company.
  Jamaica overcomes her reluctance to return a toy found in the park and learns about the satisfaction of returning belongings to their owners.
Lowry, L. (1989). *Number the stars*. New York: Bantam Doubleday Dell Books for Young Readers.
  Ann Marie Johansen shows remarkable courage in helping her Jewish friend during the Nazi occupation of Denmark.
McIntyre, C. (2005). *Flowers for grandpa Dan*. St. Louis, MO: Thumbprint Press.
  Danny learns that, although Alzheimer's disease is steadily altering Grandpa Dan through escalating dementia, there is one significant thing that never changes.
Mills, C. (2005). *Makeovers by Marcia*. New York: Farrar, Straus and Giroux.
  Marcia Faitak is finally asked to the October school dance only to receive word that one of her friends at the local nursing home has suffered a heart attack.
Parish, P. (1979). *Amelia Bedelia helps out*. New York: Avon Books, Inc.
  Amelia Bedelia and her little niece Effie Lou help Miss Emma take care of her house and garden with humorous results.
Sabin, E. (2004). *The giving book: Open the door to a lifetime of giving*. New York: Watering Can.
  Sabin has created an interactive book that aids children in the creation of a "scrapbook" of their journey into empathy and philanthropy.
Spelman, C. M. (2002). *When I care about others*. Morton Grove, IL: Albert Whitman & Company.
  A little bear describes recognizable situations, such as being sick or feeling sad and describes how he was helped or how he offered kindness to someone else.
Swift, H. H., & Ward, L. (1970). *The little red lighthouse and the great grey bridge*. New York: Harcourt, Inc.
  The little lighthouse on the Hudson River recoups its dignity when it discovers that it is useful and has an important task to accomplish.
Viorst, J. (1974). *Rosie and Michael*. New York: Antheneum.
  When his parakeet died, Michael called Rosie, and when her dog ran away, Rosie called Michael.

References

Aaronsohn, E. (2003). *The exceptional teacher: Transforming traditional teaching through thoughtful practice.* San Francisco, CA: Jossey-Bass.

Allen, J. (2006). My literacy lunches with boys. *Educational Leadership, 64,* 67–68.

Anderson, D. R. (2000). Character education: Who is responsible? *Journal of Instructional Psychology, 27,* 139.

Aronson, E. (2000). Nobody left to hate. *The Humanist, 60,* 17.

Atkins, S. L. (1999). Listening to students. *Teaching Children Mathematics, 5,* 289+. Retrieved November 2, 2006, from www.questia.com.

Barnett, M., & Morse, P. (1994). A survey of college students' reactions to their k–12 teachers and schools. *Education, 115,* 133+. Retrieved October 24, 2006, from www.questia.com.

Battistich, V. (2001, April). Effects of an elementary school intervention on students' "connectedness" to school and social adjustment during middle school. In J. Brown (Chair), *Resilience education: Theoretical, interactive and empirical applications.* Symposium conducted at the Annual Meeting of the American Educational Research Association, Seattle, Washington. Retrieved July 6, 2006, from the Wilson Web, Education Full Text database.

Bondy, E., & Davis, S. (2000). The caring of strangers: Insights from a field experience in a culturally unfamiliar community. *Action in Teacher Education, 22*(2), 54–66.

Bosworth, K. (1995). Caring for others and being cared for: Students talk caring in school. *Phi Delta Kappan, 76,* 686+. Retrieved October 20, 2006, from www.questia.com.

Chaltain, S. (2006, October 25). To make schools safe, make all children visible. *Education Week, 26*(9), 48.

Charney, R. S. (1992). *Teaching children to care: Management in the responsive classroom.* Greenfield, MA: Northeast Foundation for Children.

Cochran-Smith, M. (2005). No child left behind: 3 years and counting. *Journal of Teacher Education, 56,* 99+. Retrieved October 24, 2006, from www.questia.com.

Cochran-Smith, M. (2003). Teaching quality matters. *Journal of Teacher Education, 54,* 95+. Retrieved October 24, 2006, from www.questia.com.

Darling-Hammond, L. (2004). From "separate but equal" to "no child left behind": The collision of new standards and old inequalities. In D. Meier & G. Wood (Eds.), *Many children left behind: How the no child left behind act is damaging our children and our schools* (pp. 3–32). Boston, MA: Beacon.

Deiro, J. (2003). Do your students know you care? *Educational Leadership, 60*(6), 60–62.

Edwards, C. H. (2001). Moral classroom communities for student resiliency. *The Education Digest, 67*(2), 15–20. Condensed from *Contemporary Education, 71*(4), 38–41. Retrieved July 6, 2006, from the Wilson Web, Education Full Text database.

Eisner, E. (2005). Back to whole. *Educational Leadership, 63,* 14–18.

Fuentes, A. (2003). Discipline and punish: Zero tolerance policies have created a "lockdown environment" in schools. *The Nation, 277,* 17.

Gay, G. (2000). *Culturally responsive teaching, Theory, research, and practice*. New York: Teachers College Press.

Goldstein, L. S., & Lake, V. E. (2000). 'Love, love, and more love for children": Exploring preservice teachers' understandings of caring. *Teacher and Teacher Education, 16,* 861–872. Retrieved July 6, 2006, from the Wilson Web, Education Full Text database.

Johnson, D. K. (2006). *Education for a caring society, Classroom relationships and moral action*. New York: Teachers College Press.

Kobak, D. (1997). Raising the caring quality (cq) in education: A moral imperative. *Childhood Education, 74,* 97+. Retrieved November 1, 2006, from www.questia.com.

Kohn, A. (2005). Unconditional teaching. *Educational Leadership, 63,* 20–24.

McBee, R. H. (in press). What it means to care: How educators conceptualize and actualize caring. *Action in Teacher Education.*

McBee, R. H., Bereheiko, E., & Edmond, T. (2006, August). *Caring classrooms: The role of caring in university and elementary classrooms*. Presentation at summer meeting of Association of Teacher Educators, Philadelphia, Pennsylvania.

McCadden, B., Noblit, G., & Rogers, D. (1995). In the meantime: The possibilities of caring. *Phi Delta Kappan, 76,* 680+. Retrieved November 2, 2006, from www.questia.com.

Nieto, S. (2003). *What keeps teachers going?* New York: Teachers College Press.

Noddings, N. (2002). *Educating moral people: A caring alternative to character education*. New York: Teachers College Press.

Noddings, N. (1995a). A morally defensible mission for schools in the 21st century. *Phi Delta Kappan, 76,* 365+. Retrieved November 2, 2006, from www.questia.com.

Noddings, N. (1995b). Teaching themes of care. *Phi Delta Kappan, 76,* p. 675+. Retrieved November 2, 2006, from www.questia.com.

Noddings, N. (1984). *Caring: A feminine approach to ethics and moral education*. Berkeley: University of California Press.

Orfield, G., Losen, D., & Wald, J. (2004). *Losing our future: How minority youth are being left behind by the graduation rate crisis*. Cambridge, MA: Harvard University, The Civil Rights Project.

Pang, V. O., Rivera, J., & Mora, J. K. (1999). The Ethic of caring: Clarifying the foundation of multicultural education. *The Educational Forum, 64*(1), 25–32. Retrieved July 6, 2006, from the Wilson Web, Education Full Text database.

Peterson, R. (1992). *Life in a crowded place: Making a learning community*. Portsmouth, NH: Heinemann.

Poland, S. (2003). Congressional testimony: School violence from the perspective of a national crisis response consultant. In M. S. E. Fishbaugh, T. R. Berkely, & G. Schroth (Eds.), *Ensuring safe school environments: Exploring issues, seeking solutions* (pp. 3–12). Mahwah, NJ: Lawrence Erlbaum Associates.

Putnam, J., & Burke, J. B. (2005). *Organizing and managing classroom learning communities*. San Francisco, CA: McGraw-Hill.

Reed, D. F., McMillan, J. H., & McBee, R. H. (1995). Defying the odds: Middle schoolers in high risk circumstances who succeed. *Middle School Journal, 27*(1), 3–10.

Strahan, D. B., & Layell, K. (2006). Connecting caring and action through responsive teaching, How one team accomplished success in a struggling middle school. *The Clearing House, 79,* 147–153. Retrieved July 6, 2006, from the Wilson Web, Education Full Text database.

Taylor-Dunlop, K., & Norton, M. M. (1997). Out of the mouths of babes: Voices of at-risk adolescents. *The Clearing House, 70,* 274–278. Retrieved July 6, 2006, from the Wilson Web, Education Full Text database.

Teaching Tolerance Project. (1997). *Starting small: Teaching tolerance in preschool and the early grades.* Montgomery, AL: Southern Poverty Law Center.

Walser, N. (2006, September/October). "R" is for resilience. *Harvard Education Letter, 22*(5), 1–3.

Weaver, P. E. (2004). The culture of teaching and mentoring for compliance. *Childhood Education, 80,* 258+. Retrieved October 3, 2006, from www.questia.com.

CHAPTER 4

Spiritual Voices of Preservice Teachers

Shelley McIntosh
University of Houston–Downtown

Linlin Irene Chen
University of Houston–Downtown

Beatrice Villarreal
University of Houston–Downtown

Marion Godine
University of Houston–Downtown

> Shelley McIntosh, Ed.D., teaches in the Department of Urban Education, University of Houston–Downtown. Her research interests are holistic education of minority students, transforming school cultures, and social studies.
>
> Irene Chen, Ed.D., teaches in the Department of Urban Education, University of Houston–Downtown. Her research interests are multicultural education, educational technology, and assessment and evaluation.
>
> Beatrice Villarreal, Ph.D., teaches in the Department of Urban Education, University of Houston–Downtown. Her research interests are oral development and multiple intelligences in early childhood.
>
> Marion Godine, Ed.D., teaches in the Department of Urban Education, University of Houston–Downtown. Her research interests are effective instruction in urban schools, critical thinking through mathematics, and improving school cultures for minority children.

ABSTRACT

This qualitative study examines the spiritual characteristics of preservice teachers. Poetry and prose of twenty-five preservice teachers written on the topic of *Where I'm From*, were analyzed for the spiritual characteristics of (1) justice, (2) compassion, (3) personal fulfillment, and (4) community. Findings indicated that preservice teachers spiritually reflected when given the opportunity to reflectively write and they uncovered their personal and moral values and beliefs. Teacher education programs must seriously consider the preservice teachers' multiple expressions of spirituality to address this significant need. This, in fact, spurs a teacher education renaissance acknowledging the "whole" teacher and what he or she has to offer.

Introduction

How do teacher education programs acknowledge and meet the needs of preservice teachers today as well as tomorrow? The challenge lies with the willingness of these programs to embrace the whole preservice teacher: academically, socially and spiritually. Acknowledgment of this wholeness could bring about a renaissance in teacher education that not only embraces the spirituality of preservice teachers but works aggressively to implement it in the curriculum.

Some researchers have called for the importance of differentiating the notion of spirituality from issues of religion, spirit, soul, and faith because these terms are sometimes used interchangeably. *Religion* is viewed as a shared system of beliefs, principles, and doctrines related to a belief in and worship of a supernatural power (Love, 2001). *Spirit* is referred to as a quality of being fully human that ignites our potential to transcend the conditions of our experience (Myers & Myers, 1999). *Soul* is described as a deep and vital energy that gives meaning and direction to our lives (Wink & Wink, 2003).

Parks (2000) views *spirituality* to be a search for meaning, wholeness, purpose, and transcendence. In addition, Ouellette (2002) voiced that spirituality cannot just be understood and studied cognitively because it is experienced differently by different people. Closely associated to spirituality is the concept of *faith*, which according to researchers such as Love (2001), is a process of meaning making, a process of making sense out of the activities of life and seeking order and relation among the disparate elements of living. Researchers' views of spirituality are influenced by various schools of thought. Love (2001) was influenced by both the psychological and cognitive/structural traditions of student development theory. Parks (2000) represents the group of theorists whose perspectives are based on their training in theology. However, Ouellette (2000) describes the concept of spirituality as a new and evolving area of study in social work education. James Comer (2004), author of *Leave No Child Behind: Preparing Today's Youth for Tomorrow's World*, argues that spirituality is not necessarily linked to specific religious practices but has to do with respect for life and the rights and opportunities of other people and appreciation of our environment. We are born with the potential for good and bad, but the way we decide to live is what children will model.

Lately, there has been more attention paid to the relationship between spirituality and education. Mayes (2001), Vogel (2000), and Lake (2000) explored the connection of spirituality from the perspective of holistic education. Fox (1995) in *The Reinvention of Work*, and Palmer (1990) in *The Active Life* honored the restoration of spirituality. "A spirituality of work," Fox notes, "is about bringing life and livelihood back together again" (p. 2).

The discovery of work is shaped by group creativity and personal fulfillment; compassion is the driving force in preparation for meaningful work because it is life affirming and community building. As a result, the new era proposed by researchers taking the holistic approach is characterized by a search for meaningful existence, a mystical feeling that approaches joy at work.

Until recently, there had been some discussion about how spirituality relates to teacher education. While proposing the holistic approach of combining spirituality, work, and education, Fox (1995) also advocated for the spiritual dimension in teaching. He explains:

> Compassion will be manifested in persons volunteering to teach literacy to adults, in persons teaching about our bodies, our diets, and our health care. Compassion can be brought to an analysis of the economic relations between rich and poor, and it can offer solutions for bridging the economic gaps between us. (p. 175)

In a similar way, Purpel (1989) encourages us to view teachers as prophets, individuals who enable children and youth to develop skills and knowledge in the search for justice, community, and joy. "Educators who accept the concept of their profession as having a prophetic function," he declares, "must then affirm a set of sacred and moral principles—a mythos, a set of metaphysical or religious assumptions—or commit themselves to that which has ultimate meaning to them" (p. 105).

As early as 1975, Mattingly's study of teachers in the 19th century pointed out that the American teacher's sense of calling typically "possessed quasi-spiritual properties." In the first half of the nineteenth century, many American teachers saw themselves in a "ministerial" light (Mattingly, 1975). Even though the influence of America's industrial capitalism in the last part of the nineteenth century caused the public schools to serve corporate interests, the view of teachers as moral agents has not disappeared completely. Joseph and Burnaford (1994) found literature on teacher reflectivity that presents teachers as ministers, priests, counselors, mothers, fathers, artists, Zen masters, visionaries, saviors, and even saints.

Mayes (2001) calls for the attention that few subjects are so inadequately explored in teacher education as future teachers' spiritual beliefs and practices. He gives three reasons to address this fairly widespread neglect of spiritual commitments in teacher education programs in the United States. First, it is inauthentic to avoid such issues in the education for teachers. Second, many future teachers are largely motivated by spiritual reasons to become teachers. And third, we need to do a better job of educating our future teachers about what they and their students can legally discuss in the classroom regarding personal spiritual commitments.

The authors of this chapter are urban education professors who are representative of diverse ethnic groups—African American, Hispanic, and Taiwanese, to be specific. Since all are engaged in preparing educators for students of diverse backgrounds, we are interested in the "whole" teacher. This study is one step toward the needed empirical research on spirituality and the passion for teaching as it addresses the question: What are the spiritual characteristics of preservice teachers in their passion to teach?

Methodology

Miller (2000) defines soul, ego, and spirit. First, *soul* connects our ego and spirit. *Ego* is the socialized sense of self; the sense of separateness. *Spirit* is the divine essence within; the part of us that is beyond space and time. *Soul* connects *ego* and *spirit*; more of a sense of depth than of ascendance, as we tend to look down into our souls. As teachers, we must dare to look inside of ourselves and discover that visions and passions are emanations of an innate, creative, and divine inner force.

Passion is described as any powerful or compelling emotion or feeling and teaching as the act of imparting knowledge. In preparing preservice teachers for urban schools, it is critical that they are successful in effective instructional methods; however, it is equally important that they uncover beliefs, values, and reasons they chose teaching. Therefore, opportunities must be provided for them to examine their inner worlds, because this part of their being is taken into a classroom of students.

Preservice teachers attending the University of Houston–Downtown's teacher preparation program in urban education take social studies methods as a requirement. In this class, they write poetry or prose entitled *Where I'm From*, a method described in *Rethinking Our Classrooms: Teaching for Equity and Justice* (Bigelow, Harvey, Karp, & Miller, 2001). This offers preservice teachers a chance to pause and reflect on how they perceive their existence and gives them permission to bring their voices into the classroom.

Four "spiritual characteristics" discussed in the literature review are (a) *justice*, which encompasses a sense of righteousness, (b) *compassion*, which involves acceptance of others, (c) *personal fulfillment*, which involves healing and wholeness, and (d) *community*, which rests on affirmation of self and includes identification with racial and ethnic history. The intent of this study was to examine spiritual characteristic(s) as expressed in the writings of preservice teachers.

Approximately twenty-five poems were examined for spiritual characteristics, some of which appear in this chapter. In addition, the authors wrote selections and these were examined for spiritual characteristics as well. All pieces were written by females. The findings of these examinations are presented in the following passages, often identified by ethnic or racial group for easier detection of patterns specific to particular groups.

Spiritual Characteristics in Poetry and Prose

JUSTICE

Justice is having a sense of fairness and that which is deemed good must meet the needs of human beings. A poem written by a white teacher candidate describes that she was once from the ghetto where babies were born and uncared for. She then moved into the suburb where she says, "They do not look at the homeless. They forget about the babies that are born to people from my past." She concludes with the following statements:

> I have picked up myself, and have compromised between the two lives. I do not want to go back to where I am from, but I do not want to stay here.
> Sometimes I wonder what has happened to those babies?
> What happens to kids that are born, born to those who do not care for them?
> I want to find out. I want to teach them. I want them to know that people do care.

Another preservice teacher education student expresses justice in relationship to education. Her mother was not allowed to attend college but made sure her daughters did.

> I am from a traditional family of four where the father went to work and the mother stayed home.
> I am from a home where dinner was on the table at 6:00 and you got up early every Sunday morning to go to church.
> I am from a mother who was not allowed to go to college, who made sure her two daughters never doubted they would.
> I am from a place where you were told, "The world is not fair" and "We believe you can do it."

Meanwhile, a Hispanic preservice teacher perceives America as a place of justice because of its opportunities and democracy.

> I'm from a beautiful place called America where opportunity awaits me.
> I'm from a country that allows me to be myself, to stand up for what I believe in, and mostly that allows me to dream.
> I'm from a place that does not discriminate against my gender; one that allows women to do the same as men, a place where being a woman is a great thing.

At the same time, injustice experienced in life through low wages, discrimination, and poverty are a poignant reminder that justice is often absent, as another Hispanic preservice teacher wrote:

> Where I'm from, school began in October and ended in April.
> At school, we were slapped or put in the corner for speaking our native tongue. We weren't given much of an opportunity just because we were poor, migrant workers.

A sense of injustice is also reflected in the selection written by another student author from Taiwan. She describes life in her village in this way:

> My earliest memories started with living in a teachers' family as the youngest daughter. The village kids around me could barely meet basic needs such as warm meals, and thin jackets in the cold winter time.
> My parents, the village teachers, would give the kids school supplies so that they could do school work. When my family walked down the street in the village, we were greeted by parents and kids as if we were celebrities.

COMPASSION

Closely related to justice is the idea of compassion, a sympathetic feeling of caring for others. This quality was expressed by several preservice teachers. The example included here is written by a preservice education candidate who was born in Vietnam but grew up in Houston, Texas. Her father was not present until she was seven years old because he was in a communist prison. Without her father, her family was forced to live in poverty. She also had to remain in first grade because no one helped her learn to read or write English. She writes:

> Who am I? I have a husband in the Marine Corps.
> Who am I? As a future teacher, I will teach second grade.
> Who am I? I love kids and have a passion to help them.
> Who am I? I can speak Vietnamese and English.
> Who am I? I am a loving person with compassion and dignity.
> Who am I? I like to spend time with nature. I like to swim in lakes and watch caterpillars.
> Who am I? I respect people who respect me.
> Who am I? I am grateful. I appreciate everyone who helped me become who I am today.

Compassion is also reflected in the assignment of another Hispanic teacher.

> I am from a family of educators with one purpose in mind, to teach.
> I am from a future of educators that pursue to reach each and every one of her students.
> I am from a future of educators that truly believes that children are the future of America.
> I am from a future of educators that dream of the perfect classroom and realize that every classroom is perfect.

In accepting others, a quality critical to compassion, there is tolerance and respect for differences. Undergirding those aspects is a belief that another person is valued because he/she is innately born with value. One preservice teacher, who is white, shares that she overcame society's taboo of developing an intimate relationship with someone of another race.

> I'm from an old-fashioned family that raised me to believe that an out-of-race relationship was never to exist.
> But much to their surprise I did not listen, and now Poria and I have made a new bi-racial family list.
> I'm from eight years with a man, who helped me invent the meaning of true love.
> A man who has stayed by my side through thick and through thin, a man who has exceeded my family's expectations time and time again.

Justice, compassion, acceptance of others are interlocking and overlapping spiritual qualities. These are shown in actions toward others but also can include a quest for personal fulfillment, the quality and exemplars of which follow.

PERSONAL FULFILLMENT

Personal fulfillment is a healing journey to wholeness, a state of being in healthy or sound conditions. In poetry that reflected personal fulfillment, preservice teachers expressed a sense of wholeness through their interdependency upon those who loved, supported, and encouraged them. These included parents, spouses, and grandparents.

In her poem, a white preservice teacher, for example, expresses how interdependency plays an important part in her life.

> I come from a place where dinner was always home cooked and sadness was erased with a "cuppa" tea.
> I come from a place where my mom is my best friend and my dad is finally no longer a stranger.
> I come from a place where my older brother still makes me cry and though I've heard them all my life, his words still sting.
> I come from a place that has proven money doesn't buy happiness and material items aren't substitutes for love and companionship.
> I come from a place that I am blessed to be from, a life rich with culture and family I am proud of.

Healing and wholeness were also expressed in everyday struggles to become the best one can be as reflected by this Hispanic preservice teacher.

> I am from being a single mom and struggling everyday to being a good mother.
> I am from partying all night to reading *Green Eggs and Ham*, weekly visits to Chuck E Cheese, and being the only person who can comfort my daughter when she is sick.
> I am from a family who, no matter what, will always be there for me and in their weird ways love me unconditionally.
> I am from believing that through all my hardships it has made me a stronger person.

Recollecting the tragedies of her life, a white preservice teacher reveals how she overcame everyday struggles by encountering and experiencing people in the present.

> I was born on an island south of here, born of fire and born of ice.
> The fire killed a mother—I raged.

> The orphanage was cold—I cried.
> But this is not where I am from.
> These are the old ghosts that have left the haunt.
> They still sometimes drop in to visit.
> Mother, fathers, siblings; a man I called husband,
> babies who toddled and grew,
> things and places passed through on the way
> are not where I am from.
> Within the eyes of each person I meet,
> Within my heart, within my soul,
> I am from here.

Personal fulfillment, through individual spiritual quests, finds ultimate expression through a sense of community. The poems that follow reflect that quality.

COMMUNITY

Identification with racial history connects a person of the present with the past through spirit. In essence, that individual is influenced by the historical experiences of the racial group to which he or she belongs. As Sobonfu Somé says as he describes his identification, "Dagara people are known for their spiritual practices and their visionary ability. We live at the threshold between the ancestor world—the world of spirit—and the human world. The element of fire is about dreaming, passion, keeping our connection to the ancestors, and keeping our visions alive" (Somé, 1999, p. 22).

An African American preservice teacher expresses that she is from a life of tears, a man who left her, friends who turned their backs on her, and schools where teachers were abusive. However, she ends with an affirmation of self in connection to her race.

> Where I'm from I have two sisters who I love.
> Physically, they were bright and I was brown.
> Where I'm from that made me different—an outcast in the crowd.
> People didn't understand—they thought I came from another man.
> Where I'm from I endured a lot of scars and bruises not physical.
> You can't see them. They are a part of me.
> Where I'm from is the past and something I'll always see because
> Where I'm from makes me the strong black sista you see.

Another African American describes her homestead in Northeast Houston and the hot water cornbread, mustard greens, and fried chicken her "momma" cooks. The following lines express her feelings of identification with racial history.

> I am from ancestors who were given a chance to freedom
> But were so anxious that they couldn't defeat them (slave masters).

Additionally, a Hispanic shares an awareness of her history to which she links her identity.

> Where I'm from, Spaniard met Aztec,
> Colonist met Mexican, and Texan met American.
> I come from a union of John and Yolanda, Alvina and Semprisio, Elvira, and Jose.
> I come from no education to some education, to college education.
> I come from a family overflowing with faith and love.
> I come from a long line of strong women dedicated to family.
> I come from now knowing where I'm going to being where I am . . .

Another Hispanic preservice teacher begins her writing by drawing a contrast between a middle-class life and her impoverished life. She writes:

> White picket fence, beautiful two story house, tailored gardens, two-car garage, a pet poodle named Fiffy, and what mattered the most was education; that is not where I'm from. It was more like a dirt yard, a one-room home, outhouses, and old beat-up truck and as for education, what was that? Now, that's more like where I'm from.
> Where I'm from meant overcrowded labor camps, long lines for the government cheese, waiting for the farmer to choose us to work their crop, being taken advantage by choosing the cheapest labor and school didn't matter.

The next Hispanic preservice teachers tell of experiences in migrating to the United States, support of family, and the perception of a better life.

> I am from a family that migrated to the United States with a dream in mind, freedom from poverty.
> I am from a family that believes that the only way to reach your goals is by working hard and never giving up.
> I am from a family that believes that the only way to reach paradise is through education . . .

A white preservice teacher also expresses a sense of community experienced through ethnic identity and a sense of extended family.

> Where I am from, I come from a long line of Italian heritage that defines my customs. I come from a large tight-knit family where my cousins are more like brothers and sisters than distant relatives.

> Where I am from, I am from a very devoted family who has made me who I am. My life has been truly blessed to be a part of such an amazing group of people and I am grateful to have them in my life.

In the final example, one of the African American authors reflects community through a sense of identification in the experiences of African Americans in this country.

> I am from the black migration looking for hope in the north.
> I am from the eastside of Detroit of days filled with music, barbeque and watchful neighbors.
> I'm from build a nation on earth for my race to be free, to live, to work, to play, to stay happy eternally.

According to Love (2001), faith is a process of meaning making, which is the journey of making sense out of the activities of life and to seek order and relation among the disparate elements of living. Possessing spiritual qualities of justice, compassion, personal fulfillment, and community help make sense out of the activities of life. As the student authors affirmed in their poems, these qualities are integral parts of the lives of preservice teachers.

Discussion

As indicated, there has been widespread neglect of the spiritual commitments of students in teacher education programs and, for the most part, such issues are highly avoided and neglected even though many students are largely motivated by spiritual reasons to become teachers (Serow, Eaker, & Ciechalski, 1992). What are the implications then for inclusion of spirituality in such programs? If teacher education programs recognize, value, and embrace students' spiritually as being an essential foundation for personal pursuit of teaching in the classroom, there is a fundamental acceptance of the individual's spiritual commitments which include an ethic of compassion, service, and reflectivity.

Spiritual commitments focus upon the notion of the sacred, or the symbolic frameworks that are set apart from everyday life, and give a sense of transcendent, holistic meaning (Parks, 2000). These aspects of spirituality are socially and personally foundational to preservice teachers but are highly neglected and avoided in teacher preparation programs. The spiritual impulse is not only primary but also essential in the formation and maintenance of society.

Many teachers persist in seeing their roles as primarily the emotional and moral nurturance of children (Goodlad, 1990; Noddings, 1993, 1994; Stokes, 1997). Serow, Eakere, and Ciechalski (1992) studied teacher education students at five public universities in the United States and found that over 90 percent of the respondents had chosen to become teachers because of a desire to serve and nurture others. In a similar study, Pajak and Blaire (1989) in a study of 200 teachers concluded that:

> Teachers identified their own spiritual beliefs as having a beneficial effect on their professional lives. Most spoke generally of religious values or a belief in God without naming any religion in particular. Many specified Christianity, but Zen, Yoga, and a belief in the inherent dignity of man were also mentioned as sources of stability, meaning, and direction. (p. 299–300)

We must ask ourselves why we need to explore, discuss, and recognize the inherent value of including our preservice teachers' spiritual beliefs and practices in their education programs. Inclusion of spiritual commitments in teacher education programs such as the one at the University of Houston–Downtown is essential due to the fact that preservice teachers are highly motivated by spiritual reasons to become teachers, as reflected in their poetry and other writings. College education programs must find ways to honor and embrace preservice teachers' spiritual motivations and commitments to become teachers who express personal desire and interest as foundational in the service of others.

Conclusion

As our preservice teachers reflected through writing, they expressed personal and moral values and beliefs as well as their emotions regarding the meaning of their lives. They strongly expressed the relationship between spiritual commitment and their desire to improve educational opportunities for children they will teach in the future.

In writing "Where I'm From," our preservice teachers expressed, of their own free will, their spiritual principles. University professors have a great deal of latitude regarding reflective practices where students and teachers can explore spiritual connections that impact teaching, and thus afford a renaissance in teacher education. As Hansen (1996) confirms, "Teachers would be well served if they sought to be cognizant of not just the curricula and instructional methods but also of their very outlooks on life itself . . . those outlooks infuse the teacher's every day work with more meaning than first meets the eye."

References

Bigelow, B., Harvey, B., Karp, S., & Miller, L. (2001). *Rethinking our classrooms: Teaching for equity and justice.* Williston, VT: Rethinking School, Ltd.

Comer, J. (2004). *Leave no child behind: Preparing today's youth for tomorrow's world.* New Haven, CT: Yale University Press.

Fox, M. (1995). *The reinvention of work: A new vision of livelihood for our time.* New York: Harper-Collins.

Goodlad, J. (1990). *The moral dimensions of teaching.* San Francisco: Jossey-Bass Incorporated.

Hansen, D. (1996). Teaching and the moral life of classrooms. *Journal for a Just and Caring Education, 2,* 59–74.

Joseph, P. B., & Burnaford, G. E. (1994). *Images of Schoolteachers in twentieth-century America.* New York: St. Martin's Press.

Lake, R. (2000). Spirituality, work, and education: The holistic approach. *Journal of Vocational Education Research, 25*(2), 199–219.

Love, P. (2001, Fall). Spirituality and student development: Theoretical connections. *New Directions for Student Services, 95,* 7–16.

Mattingly, P. (1975). *The classless profession: American schoolmen in the nineteenth century.* New York: New York University Press.

Miller, J. (2000). *Education and the Soul: Toward a Spiritual Curriculum.* New York: University of New York Press.

Mayes, C. (2001, Spring). Cultivating spiritual reflectivity in teachers. *Teacher Education Quarterly, 28*(2), 5–22.

Myers, B. K., & Myers, M. E. (1999, Fall). Engaging children's spirit and spirituality through literature. *Childhood Education, 76,* 28–32.

Noddings, N. (1993). *Educating for intelligent belief or unbelief.* New York: Teachers College Press.

Noddings, N. (1994). Conversations as moral education. *Journal of Moral Education, 23*(2), 107–110.

Ouellette, B. (2000). Marrying the head and the soul: Teaching spirituality in an academic environment. *Teaching Perspectives, 2.*

Pajak, E., & Blasé, J. (1989). The impact of teachers' personal lives on professional role enactment: A qualitative analysis. *American Educational Research Journal, 26*(2), 283–310.

Palmer, P. (1990). *The active life: A spirituality of work, creativity, and caring.* San Francisco: Jossey-Bass.

Parks, S. (2000). *Big questions, Worthy dreams: Mentoring young adults in their search for meaning, purpose, and faith.* San Francisco: Jossey-Bass.

Purpel, D. E. (1989). *The moral and spiritual crisis in education: A curriculum for justice and compassion in education.* Granby, MA: Bergin & Gravey.

Serow, R., Eaker, D., & Ciechalski, J. (1992). Calling, service, and legitimacy: Professional orientations and career commitment among prospective teachers. *Journal of Research and Development in Education 25*(3), 136–141.

Sklar, K. (1973). *Catherine Beecher: A study in American domesticity.* New Haven, CT: Yale University Press.

Some, M. (1999). *Ritual power, healing, and community.* New York: Penguin Putnam, Inc.

Stokes, D. (1997). *Called to teach: Exploring the worldview of called prospective teachers during their pre-service teacher education experience.* An unpublished dissertation. Salt Lake City, UT: University of Utah.

Tillich, P. (1956/1983). *The religious situation*. London, England: Thames and Hudson.
Vogel, L. (2000). Reckoning with the spiritual lives of adult educators. *New Directions for Adult and Continuing Education, 85*, 17–27.
Wink, J., & Wink, D. (2003). *Teaching passionately: What's love got to do with it?* Boston: Allyn & Bacon.

CHAPTER 5

Teachers' Thoughts about Rewards and Joys of Teaching

A NEGLECTED COMPONENT IN TEACHER EDUCATION PROGRAMS

Miriam Ben-Peretz
University of Haifa

Gabriella Landler-Pardo
University of Haifa

>Miriam Ben-Peretz, Ph.D., is Professor Emeritus of Education at the University of Haifa. She is former dean of the School of Education at the University of Haifa, and past President of Tel-Hai Academic College. The major fields of research and teaching of Professor Ben-Peretz include curriculum studies, issues of teacher education, the culture of teachers and teaching, and policy making in education. She has been a visiting professor and lecturer at American, Canadian, and European universities. She authored numerous articles and chapters in books, as well as several books. In 1997, Professor Ben-Peretz was awarded the Lifetime Achievement Award, in recognition of outstanding contribution to curriculum studies over an extended period of time, Division B, Curriculum Studies, of the American Educational Research Association. In 2006 she was awarded the Israel Prize for Research in Education.
>
>Gabriella Landler-Pardo, M.A., is a doctoral student at the University of Haifa in the Faculty of Education where she is a teacher's assistant. She is presently an Arabic Language teacher with twenty years of experience. She has facilitated teacher workshops concerning subject matter, teaching methods, and classroom management. She also served as principal of a Jewish day school in San Diego, California. Her areas of interest are moral education, teacher education, and curriculum development.

ABSTRACT

Teachers tend to relate to the psychological-emotional rewards of teaching as a central component of their work. Yet programs of teacher education, introducing student teachers to the problems, dilemmas and difficulties of teaching, neglect this important, motivating aspect of the profession. This chapter presents teacher narratives concerning the rewards of teaching. Several explanations for focusing on psychological-emotional rewards are discussed. The chapter ends with some suggestions for introducing issues of professional rewards into teacher education programs.

"Variety is the mother of enjoyment"
—B. Disraeli, in *Vivian Grey* (1926, p. 196),
London: University Press Edinburgh

Teacher education programs tend to focus on present day problems, challenges, and complexities of teaching. Such a view of the profession might even deter people from entering it and might create a rather gloomy perception and anticipation of the world of schooling. Our paper seeks to balance this perspective. What keeps teachers coming back to the classroom year after year besides a monthly paycheck? Jackson (1968) raises this question and interviewed teachers in order to uncover "the personal satisfactions that come from being a teacher" (p. 117). Several sources for what Jackson called "the joys of teaching" (p. 134) were identified in his study. Students' success in tests and the achievement of prescribed educational objectives are part of teachers' rewards. Teacher rewards entail many more aspects of the practice of teaching. Jackson organizes these aspects of joy and satisfaction according to their emotional intensity. These are the feeling of serving a good cause and being useful, the perception of student progress and the sense of accomplishment that comes with it, and the excitement and thrill created by unexpected classroom events and outcomes. In the words of one of the teachers interviewed by Jackson: "I just wish that everyone could feel the excitement that there is in teaching—the eagerness to get into the classroom" (p. 135). Another teacher speaking about her work said: "I just don't think there is any other job that provides you with the depth of feeling" (p. 138).

Lortie (1975) has written about the rewards of teaching and differentiated between extrinsic rewards, for instance salaries; ancillary rewards, namely, characteristics of teaching, such as long vacations; and psychic, psychological and emotional, rewards. According to Lortie psychic rewards are those that touch the inner self of teachers—their feelings, attitudes, and dispositions. It is difficult to measure such rewards quantitatively, but they play an important role in the lives of teachers.

Teachers tend to connect their major rewards with classroom events, mainly with reaching classroom objectives and anticipated outcomes. According to Lortie, most teachers in the survey emphasized, "that satisfaction accompanied desirable results with students; respondents experienced gratification when they felt they had influenced students" (Lortie, p. 104).

Joys and Emotional Rewards in the Context of the Teaching Profession

Lortie (1975) also stated that, "cultural and structural aspects of the occupation influence teachers to emphasize psychic rewards in their work" (p. 101). According to Lortie:

> The culture of teachers and the structure of rewards do not emphasize the acquisition of extrinsic rewards. The traditions of teaching make people who seek money, prestige, or power somewhat suspect; the characteristic style in public education is to mute personal ambition. The service ideal has extolled the virtue of giving more than one receives; the model teacher has been "dedicated." (p. 102)

In line with this image of teaching, it is to be expected that teachers will voice their enjoyment of work in terms of psychological rewards such as the success level of their students, and not in terms of financial advantages. Joys and rewards of teaching are not only part of teachers' experiences; they are, as well, part of the structure of education and the nature of subject matter domains.

In *Eros and Education,* Schwab (1954) relates an important aspect of education that seems particularly relevant, namely, the establishment of a community of learners, embracing both students and teachers, establishing personal relationships, which connect affect and cognitive operations. This view of teaching situations, emphasizing interpersonal relationships in a community of learners, may lead teachers to assign prime importance to emotional rewards.

The joys of teaching are related, as well, to the nature of subject matter domains. In a paper called "Rediscovering the Joys of Poetry," Keil (2005) describes how a gifted teacher can make school subject matter come alive for students, for instance, by creating classrooms that celebrate poetry. This is one example of how subject matter becomes a source of joy.

Mathematicians, biologists, historians, and experts in other disciplines often tell us about the beauty of their domains and the joy associated with their research. Many teachers who love the discipline they teach are able to create delightful and emotionally satisfying experiences for their students, enabling them to encounter the joys of learning. In these circumstances teachers are apt to focus on affective rewards.

A gap between the extrinsic rewards teachers receive and their own beliefs about the value of their work, may lead to a feeling of "cognitive dissonance." According to Festinger (1962) cognitive dissonance is an inconsistency between what a person believes and what he does. In our case the inconsistency may be between teachers' actions and beliefs. This issue will be further treated in our discussion.

In spite of numerous teacher testimonies concerning the rewards, satisfactions, and joys of teaching, these tend to be a neglected component of programs of teacher education.

In the following parts of this chapter we introduce some narratives of teachers that can be found in the literature concerning the joys of teaching. We will further elaborate empirical evidence provided by teachers in Israel; we then analyze several curricula of teacher education programs, showing their tendency to focus on the problems, dilemmas, and difficulties of teaching. Interviews with teacher educators concerning their views on this issue are next discussed. The last part of our chapter offers some possible ways of introducing elements of joys and rewards into teacher education programs.

Teacher Narratives and the Joy of Teaching

"I always enjoyed teaching . . . at any level, I've taught every grade from third on up and whenever anyone asks me that question I always have the same answer, I like what I'm doing" (Millies, 1992, p. 31). Many teachers proclaim that they find enjoyment and satisfaction in their profession. The book by Shubert and Ayers, *Teacher Lore* (1992), presents multiple examples of this position. Sometimes it is expressed through affirming one's love of the subject matter one teaches:

> Imagination is letting your love be translated into your classroom. Because imagination really comes from love through loving something, through loving what you do, through loving your subject matter, through loving your students, or loving your profession. So many of us are so afraid to be passionate about what we teach or how we feel about it. (Jagla, 1992, p. 65)

There are teachers who speak explicitly about the excitement of teaching:

> The excitement comes from two places: the subject and the children. You have to think what you're teaching is valuable for the children

> to know. When you teach it and they learn it, to me, how can that help but be exciting? That excitement . . . makes me want to be imaginative because you want to get that high and do it again. (Jagla, 1992, p. 65)

With love of subject matter and the excitement of teaching one finds mentioning of "love of learning" that makes teaching fruitful and enjoyable:

> Most teachers that I have ever met who are good teachers do enjoy learning themselves. You could be a professional student. It's a difference between somebody being stagnant as opposed to alive and alert. (Jagla, 1992, p. 176)

Imagination and intuition are considered to be requisites for this kind of teaching (Jagla, 1992). Noddings and Shore (1984) confirm the importance of love of subject matter and the importance of intuition in teachers' work. Teachers' intuition is important for communicating their passion of a subject to students:

> In order for this communication to happen, several things must be present: a fascination with the particular subject, an intuitive sense of some (but not necessarily all) of its relationships and concepts, a desire to give this knowledge to others, and the ability to communicate effectively and engagingly. Intuition needs to be cultivated and trusted as the teacher decides how, when, and in what amount information about the subject should be communicated. But we must keep in mind that not only factual information but love of the subject area can be communicated and for the latter we have no simple procedures, no foolproof strategies. The most specific statement we can make is that a caring teacher who is genuinely excited about a subject or approach will convey this excitement to some of the students . . . (Noddings and Shore, 1984, p. 168)

In a study of retired teachers' memories (Ben-Peretz, 1995), it was found that though there were fewer memories of positive experiences than of job difficulties, the participating teachers tended to have fundamentally positive views of their professional careers. Connelly in his foreword to this book writes that teachers:

> look back with warmth, humor, and a sense of accomplishment at a lifetime of teaching. They remember the end of teaching cycles as being satisfactory moments; they remember long hours, hard work, and the satisfaction they brought; they remember individual students; they remember difficult non-homogeneous classes and the success of a curriculum struggling to serve diverse students; they remember improved student achievement perhaps, it seems, more than

achievement itself; and they feel, as one teacher said, "we made a difference." (Connelly, 1995, p. xiii–xiv)

Israeli Narratives

We next introduce empirical evidence from Israeli teachers. It is our intention to show that teachers' focus on psychological and emotional rewards extends beyond geographical and cultural boundaries.

METHOD

In order to find answers to the main question of our study, "What do teachers think about the rewards and pleasures of teaching?" 20 practicing primary and secondary Israeli teachers were interviewed. All teachers, 17 female and 3 male, were personally approached and provided with a brief overview of the study. They all agreed to participate in it.

The teachers were not chosen randomly. We knew most of the participants from professional interaction with them, either as colleagues, or from in-service workshops. The teachers represented a wide range of years of teaching experience, age group of children being taught, and a diversity of urban schools in several cities in Israel (Jerusalem, Haifa, Tel Aviv, and Ramat Hasharon). Their teaching experience ranged from 1 to 35 years. Ten teachers taught in elementary school and ten in secondary school. Their students came from a range of social and economical backgrounds. The teachers were asked to respond to the following questions:

1. What gives you pleasure, satisfaction, and joy in your teaching?
2. Do you feel rewarded being a teacher? When and how?

We asked most of the teachers (15 out of 20) these questions personally and the rest of them (5) by telephone interview. We posed all the questions at once leaving teachers the choice to answer them in their own order.

As the participant began responding, we wrote down their words. Once they finished we read their answer aloud so they could confirm their responses. Each interview lasted about 15 to 20 minutes.

Most of the respondents began their answer with hesitation, but as they progressed they became confident and enthusiastic. We got the impression that they were eager to talk about their sources of joy and pleasure in teaching and educational work, and were glad to share it with us. All 20 teachers mentioned several sources for joy, pleasure, and rewards in teaching.

It is important to note that we did not ask the teachers about the challenges or the difficulties they face in their teaching. Our focus was on the joys, rewards, and satisfaction they experience in their practice.

FINDINGS FROM THE ISRAELI STUDY

Analyzing the teachers' responses (all names were changed), we identified several sources for "the joys and rewards of teaching." These sources can be organized into four categories as follows: (a) teachers' love of learning and personal growth; (b) the process of instruction: love of subject matter, love of teaching; (c) students, the target population: impact on students, interpersonal relationship with students; and (d) evaluation by others.

In the following section we discuss each of these sources and introduce some examples from the teachers' responses.

TEACHERS' LOVE OF LEARNING AND PERSONAL GROWTH

For several teachers, "love of learning" is a major source for rewards and joy while teaching. This aspect connects them with the personal inner-self and the desire for self-improvement. According to the teachers, it entails an ongoing process of self-evaluation followed by growth: 'I enjoy the fact that in order to teach the kids, I need to be engaged in an ongoing process of studying and learning myself. I especially love this part" (Michelle, a literature teacher in an elementary school with 14 years of teaching experience). This assertion is an example of teachers' yearning for personal growth through ongoing learning accompanied by a sense of joy.

THE PROCESS OF INSTRUCTION

Love of Subject Matter

Several teachers expressed enjoyment and satisfaction with teaching through affirming their love of the subject matter taught. ". . . I love the subject of my teaching [English]. I like the language and enjoy very much teaching it" (Hava is an English teacher [ESL] in an elementary school and has 10 years of experience), or as Noa, a Bible and homeroom teacher in 9th and 10th grades, with 4 years of teaching experience stated, "I love the subject matter I teach, Bible, and I enjoy teaching it."

Love of Teaching

The love of teaching source contains several aspects which give teachers feelings of reward and satisfaction: developing instructional material, instilling the love for learning, being able to reach all students and meet their needs, and developing learning materials to fit students' needs.

There are teachers who speak explicitly about the excitement of teaching: "I really like the teaching. It is the best part of my job, the instruction in the classroom," offered Danielle, a literature and a homeroom teacher in an elementary school who has 14 years teaching experience. Tom, a math teacher in a secondary school, with five years seniority, also explained his love of teaching in this way: "I love their thinking, the way they handle a problem, the way they approach it, I enjoy teaching them how to think mathematically—what is a mathematical thought. That gives me great pleasure."

Some teachers stated that they most enjoy developing instructional materials and matching them to students' needs. Orna, a language arts teacher in a secondary school who taught in the 7th–9th grades with 16 years of teaching experience, considered this part a real adventure:

> I like it when I have a topic and I need to develop it into a teaching unit. After you get to know your students, their levels, abilities and learning styles, then it's a challenge to plan your teaching. It's real fun for me. When I prepare my lessons and teaching materials, I see my students in my mind and I match the materials especially to them. It is an adventure for me.

Orna's narrative especially serves as an example of the joy experienced by teachers in their role of creative curriculum adapters. Many teachers interpret curriculum materials and expand their use in different ways. (Ben Peretz, 1990)

Ella, a geography teacher in a secondary school (7th–9th grades), who had 34 years of teaching experience, liked the challenge of surprising her students with new materials,"I like looking for new and challenging materials I can share with my students. It revives me. I like the challenge of developing new materials for them and looking for a method to teach it." This is a case of teachers not only adapting existing materials but creating their own innovative ones. Both teachers justify Disraeli's statement that "Variety is the mother of enjoyment." New ideas and activities clearly are important sources of satisfaction.

STUDENTS, THE TARGET POPULATION

Impact on Students

Students' accomplishments and advancement caused by teachers' care and efforts are a source of teacher satisfaction as well. The impact teachers have on their students is accompanied by feelings of reward. This impact has various forms of expression. Motivating students to reach higher levels of learning and achievement is one of them. "Mostly I enjoy watching a student who didn't like math and was even resentful toward it and after teaching him or her, the student likes it, participates in class discussions and understands the material. For me, this is the real satisfaction and reward," remarked Inbal, a novice math teacher in an elementary school. Sara, a literature teacher in a secondary school, 8th–9th grades, with 30 years of teaching experience, added, "If I, with some assistance of 'one on one' tutoring, a hug, and some words of encouragement, helped a student read or if I triggered an interest where there was none, I feel satisfaction and joy."

Another aspect of impact is students' achievements. Once students experience success and demonstrate the joy which comes along with it, teachers experience comparable feelings of satisfaction and contentment. "I really like being part of their learning process. I enjoy guiding the students; broadening their knowledge and helping them improve their achievement," offered Amos, a social studies teacher in a secondary school with 8 years of teaching experience. As for Tammy, a special education teacher in an elementary school with 12 years of teaching experience, providing students with opportunities to succeed is the reason to feel rewarded: "Since I mainly work with students who have learning difficulties, I find it very important to allow these kids to experience and feel a true success. I take much pleasure watching them discover something new and feel good about themselves."

Together these teacher statements and others are reminiscent of Lortie's (1975) insight that teachers experience satisfaction and gratification when they feel they have influenced students.

Watching students in moments of discovery and understanding was mentioned by all teachers as a source of feeling joy and reward. Several metaphors were reiterated throughout their accounts to illustrate this point. "Seeing the light in the students' eyes or faces" was the most common one. Sharon, for example, a primary grades teacher, 1st and 2nd, in an elementary school who has 15 years of experience, offered: "As a primary grades homeroom teacher I get pleasure from watching the students in the moments of discovery, when they realize they understand and they know. The light in their faces is always rewarding for me." "Making a difference" in a student's life or, in other words, being a significant and influential figure for the student and thus causing him or her to change is a major component of teachers' feeling of reward and pleasure. Whether the change is in conduct, attitude, learning habits, knowledge, or social behavior does not matter; the fact that it happened and that the teacher evoked it is the reason for satisfaction. "I feel joy knowing that my teaching broadens the students' horizons," said Hanna, a math and homeroom teacher in an elementary school, with 4 years of experience. "I love the learning process because it makes a difference in the kids' lives. After learning something they are not the same person they have been before, they have changed," was what Nili, a 3rd grade language arts teacher in an elementary school with 35 years of experience, shared with us.

Interpersonal Relationship with Students

In addition to instruction itself, teachers are engaged in a variety of interactions with the students. They develop interpersonal relationships with students, which at times become a meaningful source of joy for them. "For me the most exciting and challenging component of teaching is the interaction with the students. I feel very close to my students in spite of the age difference. Being part of their adolescence years, guiding and directing them is a true joy for me," offered Mona, a physical education and homeroom teacher in a secondary school with 21 years of teaching experience. Meanwhile, Tom, a math teacher in secondary school with 5 years seniority, perceives his relationship with students as an "ongoing" dialogue: "I love the daily interaction with them, I like watching them, seeing them, talking with them, they make me laugh. There is a bond, a friendship between us and a lot of respect." Teachers' testimonies about the importance and joys of their social relationships with their students are illustrative of the kind of community that was envisioned by Schwab in *Eros and Education* (1954).

EVALUATION BY OTHERS

Positive feedback from students, parents, and colleagues validates teachers' practice. It illuminates its values and importance. Receiving positive forms of evaluative comment grants the teachers a feeling of worth. "Kids who appreciate good teachers—this is so rewarding. I also feel satisfaction and reward when I am appreciated by my students. It's a natural high. It's the kids who make me happy," said Dana, an English teacher in secondary school, with 15 years seniority. Students' displays of affection and love toward their teachers is often perceived by them as an expression of appreciation. Positive feedback can come also from a third party, such as parents and colleagues, and is generally interpreted by the teachers as a sign of reassurance of their work's value and an endorsement of it. Nona, a Bible and homeroom teacher with 4 years of teaching experience, noted: "The parents in our school are very much involved in the learning process of their kids. So it feels really good when I am being complimented by them, when I get positive feedback from the parents and from my students. It has a huge impact, it supports me and it encourages me to continue." Tom, a math teacher in secondary school (grades 10–12), depicted it as a source of enjoyment: "Receiving positive feedback and compliments from parents, students, and colleagues is very rewarding. That's fun," was what he had to say. This source of professional satisfaction is far removed from the usual extrinsic rewards that are conceived to be of major importance for teachers. Careful analysis of teachers' statements led us to the following overarching observations:

1. In teachers' responses we often find an integration of several sources of satisfaction. None of the teachers interviewed reported only one source for the joys of teaching.
2. Students' knowledge growth and their level of comprehension and acquisition of new materials being taught were aspects which were mentioned by all teachers, regardless of their age, their teaching experience, grade level, or the subject matter they were teaching. One reason for this can be that the students' knowledge can be measured and hence it serves as an indication of the quality of instruction—a source of satisfaction.
3. Teachers from both schools, primary and secondary, share most of the same sources for the joys and rewards of teaching. However, there are some differences. One of them is in the domain of interpersonal relationships with students. While secondary school teachers talk about developing a mature relationship with their students based on mutual respect which could develop into friendship, primary school teachers perceive their interactions with students as those of adults with children.
4. A perception of impact on students that we find in secondary school teachers only is that they talk about "making a difference" in their students' lives and playing a significant part in their students' worlds.

It is important to note that these observations relate only to our study, which included only 20 teachers.

In summary, teachers like to speak about the joys and rewards of teaching. The sources for these rewards are intrinsic and might function as motivating factors for teachers to continue their work.

Teacher Education Programs

Teacher education programs in universities and colleges aim at providing their students, the future teachers, with a solid professional foundation. These programs try to prepare their candidates for the complexity of present-day teaching.

In analyzing several teacher education programs offered in universities and colleges in the USA (6) and in Israel (4), we found that in addition to obtaining a strong theoretical framework that incorporates knowledge of subject matter, philosophy, sociology, pedagogy, method courses, and practicum, students of these programs are also introduced to today's urban education milieu with its diversity and dynamic change. For example, at Mills College in the U.S. (Oakland, California) and the University of Haifa in Israel, there is a strong emphasis on diversity and equity. Courses such as "Building Structures for Equity, Excellence, and Access," dealing with the question of "how can we teach each child well in a racist society," or "Working with Families and Community" are offered at Mills College. At the University of Haifa we found awareness of the challenges of the rapidly changing conditions of modern societies. Topics such as "Values and Morality in Teaching and Education," the "Multi-cultural Curriculum," or "Acclimation Problems" that are being taught in Haifa are evidence of this phenomenon.

Other examples of courses dealing with the difficulties and challenges within teaching are "Teaching Linguistic and Cultural Minority Students" (Berkeley, California), "Principles of Teaching Exceptional Individuals" (UCLA, California), "Elements of Diversity: English Language Learners" (Harvard, Massachusetts), "Teaching Heterogeneous Classes, Adolescence—a Challenge for the Teacher" (Hebrew University, Israel), or "Management and Discipline in Heterogeneous Classes" (Hebrew University).

We noted that teacher education programs are dynamic curricula constantly being reformed and revitalized. A recent research report on the "Teacher Education Curriculum in Relation to Changes in Israeli Society" (Shagrir, 2007) found a connection between social changes that occurred in Israel and the contents of curricula of teacher education institutions. This study, which examined the curricula of elementary teacher education in three different colleges, found that "some of the social changes [were] reflected in the curricula of the colleges, and even relate to specific events. . . . Topics were related to educational reform, the education laws, and the demographic properties of Israeli society. The manner in which these topics are dealt with recurs in the various courses that are studied in the educational sciences in the three colleges. The influence of these components can be explained by the fact that they affect everyday life in the school, as well as the ongoing work of teachers" (Shagrir, 2007, p. ix).

It can be assumed that the teacher candidates in these programs will encounter experiences of success in their practical work, which might eventually grant them feelings of joy and satisfaction. Yet, the overall image of teaching created by courses in these teacher education programs seems to present an image of tensions, problems, and difficulties. We believe that a course that centers on the joys and rewards of teaching might provide some needed balance. Such a course would enable teachers to identify and clarify the pleasures in their teaching and use these as a source of professional growth.

Interviews with Teacher Educators

Concerning this topic, two leading teacher educators in Israel were interviewed. One is the former chair of a large department of teacher education at a research university. The other is head of academic planning in a large, well-respected teacher education college. Both were asked whether there are learning experiences focusing on teacher rewards and the joy of teaching in their respective institutions. Also, we inquired whether they thought this could be an important component of teacher education, and, if so, how could one go about it? Both responded that these issues are not explicitly treated in their programs. The university chair of teacher education emphasized the feelings of fear and anxiety prevailing among student teachers in relation to teaching experiences. She claimed that student teachers usually lack experiences of positive rewards in their practicum and are therefore unable to focus on the joys of teaching to overcome their sense of anxiety and failure.

The director of academic planning in a teacher education college offered that in her college students are a-priori oriented toward a teaching career and tend to accept the conditions of the profession. An important aspect of the college program is the gradual introduction into teaching situations, starting with a one-to-one experience and assisted by ongoing mentoring. The intention is to focus on small "successes," thus building a culture of rewards. Teacher educators at her college meet regularly to share such experiences. She also believes that more explicit attention should be given to the general issues of teachers' careers and reward system.

According to these two teacher educator leaders, ways to introduce issues of rewards would include analysis of films portraying teacher success and emotional rewards as well as student involvement in the study of rewards of teaching, and a seminar focusing on these components of teaching.

Discussion

We have established that teachers do tend to speak about the joys and rewards of teaching. By this they don't mean extrinsic or ancillary rewards, but what Lortie (1975) calls "psychic rewards," namely, psychological and emotional rewards. Several reasons for this preference of teachers will be offered now.

An important aspect of these kinds of rewards is that, unlike salaries and work conditions, they are, at least partially, under the control of the teachers themselves. Classroom practices of teachers might vary according to their professional knowledge, and their ability to match teaching to their students' needs. Improved pedagogic decisions and the growth of pedagogic content knowledge of teaching (Shulman, 1986) has the potential to increase their work-related satisfaction. There might yet be another explanation for the tendency of teachers to emphasize psychological and emotional rewards, namely, the inherent cognitive dissonance of their work situation. Teachers sense the gap between the manifold duties they fulfill, the time and energy they give to their work and the low status of their profession. Lortie (1975) found that in comparison with other professions teachers have fewer rewards, less formal recognition, and usually lower salaries. Teachers might resent this situation. One of the teachers in Lortie's study proclaimed, "I think the thing that aggravates [teachers] most is in that no one else takes their job, considers their job, as seriously as do teachers. I think teachers consider their job most seriously and expend themselves to no end in it and I think it bothers them because people are not aware how they feel, how important this particular job is and I think it annoys them no end" (Lortie, p. 180).

The cognitive dissonance ensuing from the gap between the extrinsic rewards they receive, and their beliefs about the value of their work, might lead teachers to intensify their statements of joy and emotional rewards. Their emphasis on these rewards might be read as an expression of the need to minimize the cognitive dissonance they experience (Festinger, 1962). According to Festinger, when there exists dissonance, inconsistency, between what a person believes and what he does, people are motivated, "to reduce the dissonance and achieve consonance" (p. 3). One way of reducing dissonance is changing one's actions or one's feelings. Festinger has shown that when rewards for an action are relatively weak changes of opinions are frequent (p. 94–95). Teachers cannot change their teaching situation, or the external reward system, so they tend to enhance their beliefs about other aspects of teaching.

Empirical studies could be conducted concerning teachers' tendency to relate to the joys of teaching in countries where the status of teachers is high, combined with significant extrinsic rewards. It would be interesting to study whether teachers' leaving the profession soon after their graduation from teacher education might be connected to the dissonance between their experience in school and their beliefs, and a lack of a critical mass of emotional rewards.

The Important Role of the Joys and Rewards of Teaching in Teacher Education

Whatever the sources of teachers' relation to rewards, rewards are an important feature of their professional lives and should have an appropriate place in their teacher education.

We see a strong connection between joys and rewards of teaching and the lifelong learning expected of teachers (Day, 1999). As stated above, the sources of psychological rewards, such as students' successes, positive feedback of the environment, and a sense of accomplishment, can be enhanced by teachers' own classroom actions and their growing professional competence. The growth of their professional knowledge depends on the lifelong learning of teachers in a variety of ways.

Neglecting emotional rewards in teacher education is part of a wider phenomenon. According to Day (1999), "Many writers on reflection tend to ignore or downplay the importance of attending to emotional development" (p. 33). Day quotes Hargreaves (1998), who found that emotions are acknowledged ". . . only insofar as they help administrators and reformers 'manage' and offset teachers' resistance to change, or help them set the climate or mood in which the 'really important' business of cognitive learning or strategic planning can take place" (p. 33).

Joys and rewards of teaching belong to the emotional domain and should not be ignored. We have seen that in spite of the importance of teachers' rewards this issue is mostly neglected in teacher education programs.

What Can Be Done to Change the Situation?

The following are several suggestions for including the joys and rewards of teaching in the curriculum of teacher education programs.

It seems to us that programs of teacher education should devise special learning opportunities for dealing with these important issues. These opportunities could entail lectures, analysis of films, videos, television programs, and classroom observations. Student teachers could be asked to interview teachers concerning rewards and joys of teaching. Personal narratives of teachers could be part of the relevant literature. One of the particularly powerful learning experiences is sharing insights with colleagues in a "community of learners" (Schwab, 1954; Shulman, 1993). Narratives of practice (Connelly & Clandinin, 1985, 1986) are vehicles for sharing and building knowledge. In Connelly and Clandinin's (1985) words, "personal practical knowledge is experienced, embodied and reconstructed out of the narratives of a user's life" (p. 183). In telling stories of how one has solved difficult problems, practitioners show themselves as being competent—and are being competent—through the preservation and circulation of knowledge. The narrative form of community memory is perceived as fulfilling another important function, namely, the construction of the professional identity of members of the community (Orr, 1992). The sharing of narratives of rewards is conceived by us as contributing to teachers' sense of belonging to a professional community of teachers who view their work as satisfying. Jalongo and Isenberg with Gerbracht (1995) claim that stories can contribute to teachers' renewed enthusiasm for learning and teaching.

A central site for dealing with joys and rewards is the practicum. Cooperating teachers and mentors can raise these issues and make the students aware of different kinds of rewards. Method courses could focus on subject matter aspects that are conducive to experiences of joy in learning, such as the pleasure of solving math problems, or seeing the beauty in biological phenomena. Teacher educators could plan special occasions for sharing their own narratives of rewards with each other as well as with their students. A word of caution is necessary. This is not an attempt to create a "Pollyanna" view of teaching. Teaching is highly complex, uncertain, and fraught with problems. What is proposed is to introduce a balance between focusing mainly on problems, difficulties, and dilemmas, and the inherent rewards of teaching.

Concluding Comments

In this chapter we have focused on a neglected component in teacher education programs, namely, the psychological and emotional rewards of teaching. We have presented empirical evidence concerning teachers' own perceptions of these rewards. Analysis of several programs of teacher education, as well as interviews with teacher educators, have shown that though rewards play a major role in the professional lives of teachers, they are not dealt with explicitly in teacher education.

Education in the professions has always grappled with the tension between theory and practice. Shulman (2004) claims that "one of the sources of those tensions is the conflict between standards and conceptions of practice affirmed in the academy and those typically manifested in the field" (p. 533). Shulman offers the following as a possible solution to this enduring conflict:

> When we seek a pedagogy that can reside between the universal principles of theory and the narratives of lived practice, we invent approaches—such as the varieties of case review. We render individual experiential learning into 'community property' when we transform those lessons from personal experiences into a literature of shared narrative. Such connections between theoretical principles and practical narratives, between universal and the accidental, forge professional knowledge. (p. 536)

It is our claim that these cases and narratives should focus not only on the problems of classroom life, but should celebrate and illuminate, as well, the joys and emotional rewards of teaching. This, for us, would contribute to a renaissance in teacher education.

References

Ben-Peretz, M. (1990). *The teacher-curriculum encounter: Freeing teachers from the tyranny of texts*, in the series: *Curriculum issues and inquiries*. Albany: SUNY Press.

Ben-Peretz, M. (1995). *Learning from experience: Memory and the teacher's account of teaching*. Albany: SUNY Press.

Connelly, F. M. (1995). Foreword. In M. Ben-Peretz, *Learning from experience: Memory and the teacher's account of teaching* (pp. xiii–xiv). Albany: SUNY Press.

Connelly, F. M., & Clandinin, D. J. (1985). Personal practical knowledge and the modes of knowing: Relevance for teaching and learning. In E. Eisner (Ed.), *Learning and teaching ways of knowing* (pp. 174–198). Eighty-fourth Yearbook of the National Society for the Study of Education, Part 2. Chicago: University of Chicago Press.

Connelly, F. M., & Clandinin, D. J. (1986). On narrative method, personal philosophy, and narrative unities in the story of teaching. *Journal of Research in Science Teaching*, *23*(4), 293–310.

Day, C. (1999). *Developing Teachers: The Challenges of lifelong learning*. London and Philadelphia: Falmer Press.

Disraeli, B. (1926). *Vivian Grey*. London: University Press Edinburgh.

Festinger, L. (1962). *A theory of cognitive dissonance*. London: Tavistock Publications and Stanford University Press.

Hargreaves, A. (1998). The Emotional Practice of Teaching. *Teaching and Teacher Education*, *14*(8), 835–854.

Jackson, P. W. (1968). *Life in classrooms*. New York: Holt, Rinehart and Winston.

Jagla, V. M. (1992). Teachers' everyday imagination and intuition. In W. H. Shubert and W. C. Ayers (Eds.), *Teacher Lore: Learning from our own experience* (pp. 61–79). New York: Longman Publishing Group.

Jalongo, M. R., & Isenberg, J. P., with Gerbracht, G. (Eds.) (1995). *Teachers' stories: From personal narrative to professional insight*. San Francisco: Jossey-Bass Publishers.

Keil, K. (2005). Rediscovering the joy of poetry. *English Journal, 95*(1), 97–102.

Lortie, D. C. (1975). *Schoolteacher: A sociological study*. Chicago: The University of Chicago Press.

Millies, P. S. G. (1992). The relationship between a teacher's life and teaching. In W. H. Shubert & W. C. Ayers (Eds.), *Teacher Lore: Learning from our own experience* (pp. 25–42). New York: Longman Publishing Group.

Noddings, N., & Shore, P. J. (1984). *Awakening the inner eye: Intuition in education*. New York: Teachers' College Press.

Orr, J. E. (1992). Sharing knowledge, celebrating identity: Community memory in a service culture. In D. Middleton & D. Edwards (Eds.), *Collective remembering* (pp. 169–189). London: Sage Publications.

Schwab, J. J. (1954). Eros and education. *Journal of General Education, 8,* 54–71.

Shagrir, L. (2007). *Teacher education curricula in relation to changes in Israeli society*. Ramat Aviv, Israel: Dor Ledor & MOFET Institute.

Shubert, W. H., & Ayers, W. C. (1992). *Teacher Lore: Learning from our own experience*. New York: Longman Publishing Group.

Shulman, L. S. (1986). Those who understand: knowledge growth in teaching. *Educational Researcher, 15* (2), 4–14.

Shulman, L. S. (1993). Teaching as community property: Putting an end to pedagogical solitude. *Change Magazine,* 6–7.

Shulman, L. S. (2004). *The Wisdom of Practice: Essays on teaching, learning, and learning to teach*. San Francisco: Jossey-Bass.

Shulman, L. S. (2004). Theory, practice and the education of professionals. In L. S. Shulman (Ed.), *The Wisdom of Practice: Essays on Teaching, Learning, and Learning to Teach* (pp. 523–544). San Francisco: Jossey-Bass.

WEB ADDRESSES FOR TEACHER EDUCATION PROGRAMS

Beit Berl College: www.beitberl.ac.il/education/default.asp
Harvard University: www.gse.harvard.edu/academics/masters/tep/index.html
Hebrew University: http://education.huji.ac.il/prog_ba.asp?cat
Levinsky College of Education: www.levinsky.ac.il/levinsky/doa_iis.dll/serve/level/hebrew/1.11.html
Mills College: www.mills.edu/academics/full_course_list.php
New York University: http://steinhardt.nyu.edu/teachlearn
UCLA: www.centerx.gseis.ucla.edu/tep/
University of Haifa: www.edu.haifa.ac.il/main/index.php?Itemid=230&option=com_data&task=show_contentpage&page_id=23&site_id=49
University of Pennsylvania: www.gse.upenn.edu/degrees_programs/eld_tlc.php
Yale University: www.yale.edu/tprep/tprep/index.html

CHAPTER 6

Educating for Inquiry through a Reflective Portfolio Process
WHAT ARE THE IMPERATIVES FOR TEACHERS OR STUDENTS TO THINK WELL IN CONTEXTS?

Nona Lyons
University College Cork

> Nona Lyons, Ed.D., has a background in developmental psychology from the Harvard Graduate School of Education and is a Visiting Research Scholar at University College Cork where, for the last six years, she has been coaching faculty and students in creating reflective teaching portfolios. Her current research is examining and documenting the results of these efforts and what portfolio-makers claim they are learning from the process, especially their awareness of themselves and their students as knowers, of what they know and how they know it. She is the editor of *With Portfolio in Hand: Validating the New Teacher Professionalism* (1998) and co-editor of *Narrative Inquiry in Practice* (2002).

ABSTRACT

> This chapter examines and explores elements of an inquiry process that served as a scaffold for faculty and students at University College Cork, Ireland, for engaging in a reflective portfolio process to document their own investigations into their teaching and learning practices. It celebrates and advocates the serious and systematic exploration of the contexts of teaching and learning while at the same time warning of the need for documenting how to teach the processes of inquiry, of thinking well in contexts; and it invites and encourages such inquiries for education's future.

Recently when scientist James Watson, the discoverer of DNA, and Nobel Prize holder Paul Nurse, the President of Rockefeller University, joined Charlie Rose as guests for one of his Science Series Programs, they were asked to predict the likely scientific discoveries of the next few years given the possibilities offered by the genome project. Arguing that the achievements of the genome project which identified all known genes clearly laid the grounding for future scientific work and discoveries, Watson averred how the greatest challenge today is for science to uncover the role *contexts* play in how genes operate and interact, and how they influence human development and disease.

"Contexts are so variable," Watson exclaimed, throwing up his hands. "They are so complex. But now that we can hold genes constant, we can begin to take up the impact of contexts." Paul Nurse elaborated, saying, "We know, for example, that there is not just a single cancer but rather there are all kinds of cancers, with sets of genes. There are many different types of lung cancers and breast cancers. The mapping of genes makes it possible to now turn to the messy complexities of the variable of the contexts of cancer, including the human body. The challenge is to sort out the significance and the impact of different contexts." He summed up, "We have the names of the characters of the play, now we have to write the narrative, setting the script in context and opening the story" (Rose, January 9, 2007).

No one knows and appreciates the challenge of contexts more than educators of all persuasions. No one has been more criticized or excoriated than educational researchers for not sorting out the role of contexts in determining what works best in educational practices (Cochran-Smith & Zeichner, 2005; Lagemann, 2000; Feuer, Towne, & Shavelson, 2002). It is precisely because education research could not predict, for example, which educational innovations were most likely to raise reading and other test scores that the No Child Left Behind law of 2001 set new standards for education research. Any new research project would be funded only if it were deemed scientific; that is, carried out with experimental designs and randomized trials that could contribute to prediction.

But what is it that can be held constant when contending with educational contexts? No such project similar to the genome project has been designed and carried out for education practices in settings. Even when educational goals can be agreed upon and a curriculum program chosen with full consent of a faculty, there is no telling how contexts of different schools, communities, parents, students, or teachers will make a difference. Any K–12 teacher, or college teacher as well, has experienced having had an excellent lesson or even a course one semester only to discover it as a baffling failure the next.

Not surprisingly, little confidence is accorded to what is learned from such experiences, if they lacked predictability. How are differences in education contexts manifested? What difference do they make? How can education contexts be studied, mapped? Could it be that like the future of scientific discoveries, contexts are to be education's future as well, the source of significant discoveries?

It is easily apparent that no one has better access to educational contexts than teachers themselves. Questions arise: What would happen if teachers were to study their own and their students' contexts of learning? What would they uncover? How? How valuable would that knowledge be? What resources would faculty need to carry out this kind of inquiry? To date, much important research has already begun on this task, especially self-study in teacher education (Loughran, Hamilton, LaBoskey, & Russell, 2004). But much remains to be done (Kuhn, 2005; Schön, 1995).

Introduction to Practitioner Inquiry

This chapter takes up this issue of practitioners studying their own education settings. It tells the story of one set of teachers who have been examining their teaching practices and it reports on faculty research being carried out today in Ireland at University College Cork (UCC). The project began in 2001 when a new UCC president initiated an award for excellence in teaching at UCC. Faculty would apply for the award by documenting their teaching efforts and their inquiries into what worked and why. The method chosen was a reflective portfolio process. Faculty were to conduct inquiries into their teaching and the learning of their students and simultaneously engage in a thoughtful, reflective interrogation and documentation of the process and their own learning.

Inquiry is a challenging undertaking for students and their teachers, often the subject of serious misconceptions (Kuhn, 2005). It is a process that needs to be scaffolded for all its practitioners. Common usage defines inquiry as an investigation; that is, to probe, explore, research, question, query, interrogate, etc. (Oxford, 2001, p. 427). But these definitions fail to hint at the skills involved. Here, following psychologist Deanna Kuhn (2005, p. 4), inquiry is defined preliminarily as *thinking well* in undertaking the investigation of a problem arising in a real life setting. Reflective inquiry of a portfolio process highlights the inquiry task as a meta-cognitive one; that is, of thinking about one's own processes of thinking and knowing needed to document the investigative process as well as the meaning and understandings one achieves through it, as this chapter will make clear. This chapter reports on the result of efforts by faculty members of various disciplines from one institution—University College Cork—to document their teaching for the first round of the teaching awards program and then, later, for other program developments. The chapter addresses three issues: (a) practitioners' perspectives on their inquiry experience, the subjects investigated in their inquiries, the skills they actually used, and what they learned from the reflective process; (b) the course designer's (and author's) perspective on the elements necessary for scaffolding the inquiry and portfolio processes; and (c) perspectives gained from research on significant results of faculty inquiries through a reflective portfolio process, especially the claims of new ways of knowing and a new conscious awareness about teaching and students' ways of learning and knowing.

The chapter begins by outlining the UCC project, indicating how the project came about, where it is today, and the wider set of concerns that first and still inspire it; it then discusses the skills of reflective inquiry and their challenges, along with how they were introduced in the program; and, finally, it looks at results, that is, research data and observations from faculty on what they feel they have learned from their inquiries into their own teaching and the learning of their students, including vignettes of practitioners engaged in inquiry.

Here I turn to the larger setting for these concerns; that is, the state of how students today are faring as inquirers in their own right.

Context

A striking discovery in the recent critiques of higher education in the U.S. and Europe is how the critiques today of higher education echo those leveled at elementary and secondary education. For example, there is the charge that although most undergraduate students make gains during their college years, they accomplish far less than they should. Derek Bok, interim president of Harvard University, writing in *Our Underachieving Colleges* (2006), finds college students lack critical thinking skills and the ability to make sound judgments beyond a naive epistemology; that is, an understanding of what knowing and knowledge are and how we know:

> Many seniors graduate without being able to write well enough to satisfy their employers. Many cannot reason clearly or perform competently in analyzing complex, nontechnical problems, even though faculties rank critical thinking as the primary goal of a college education. (Bok, 2006, p. 8)

Equally surprising is the fact that most colleges neglect to collect data on what exactly their students learn and know how to do at graduation, in contrast to the number of courses students have taken. Although some professors are aware of the problems of student learning and do try new methods of teaching, their concerns are not always shared by faculty as a whole.

Highly pertinent to these concerns are the observations of Mary Huber and Pat Hutchings of the Carnegie Foundation for the Advancement of Teaching who, since the 1990s, have been working to advance a scholarship of teaching at the university level. They argue for the need for what they call *a teaching commons,* a place of exchange for faculty to share their teaching experiences. Huber and Hutchings (2006) find that:

> ... teaching is a private activity for most faculty taking place behind doors that are both metaphorically and physically closed to colleagues. Not surprisingly, teachers have developed few habits or conventions for exploring what they do in the classroom and how it affects their students, or for sharing what they know with colleagues who might build upon it. In contrast to most professions, teaching at all levels, as Lee Shulman argued in a 1987 essay, is *"devoid of a history of practice."* (p. 26)

Complicating this situation is the challenge of uncovering what it takes to engage in inquiry and how to teach its skills. Developmental psychologist Deanna Kuhn (2005), in her groundbreaking book, *Education for Thinking,* documents the sobering difficulty for both children and adults of doing inquiry, from identifying a question, to constructing an investigation, to distinguishing evidence from assertion, and to connecting research with findings, not just with what was done. Kuhn argues that students must have not only the skills but the opportunity to engage in increasingly complex forms of inquiry and grow in epistemological understanding of the nature of knowledge. At present, she argues, "we lack sufficient understanding of what it means to be an 'independent learner and thinker' . . . to make this a readily implementable goal in classrooms today" (Kuhn, 2005, p. 4).

Thus, three problems emerge for teachers of inquiry at all levels: (1) the failure of students to do well, especially in developing thinking and inquiry skills; (2) the challenge to knowing how to teach students inquiry and its skills; and (3) the lack of exchange between college or K–12 teachers of these pedagogical strategies.

The UCC Project

This chapter addresses these issues as it takes up the case of University College Cork and how faculty there responded to the opportunity to engage in inquiries into teaching and student learning and share that knowledge with their colleagues, creating a history of practice of their own, in their own contexts. Here three building blocks for engagement and inquiry are described. They were first tried out six years ago in spring of 2001 at University College Cork when I was asked to introduce staff to a reflective portfolio process by Vice-President Aine Hyland. A portfolio was to be the method of documentation that faculty would prepare in order to participate in the newly announced competition at UCC for an award for Excellence in Teaching (Lyons, 1998; Lyons, Hyland, & Ryan, 2002). The three procedures include:

1. The introduction of a *conceptual framework;* in this case, the idea of a Scholarship of Teaching and Learning, to provide the intellectual rationale for the program, in other words, to cast teaching and inquiries into teaching into a framework of a scholarly activity;
2. The initiation of a *series of portfolio seminars* to serve as a scaffold for faculty to meet regularly to exchange teaching practices and their inquiries into student learning; and
3. The development of a *meta-cognitive reflective review through a portfolio development process* to encourage and engage faculty in documenting and making public inquiries/investigations into teaching and student learning and to identify what is learned from this process of reflective inquiry.

The chapter first describes the three procedures and some of their challenges. It then discusses results of these exchanges and inquiries.

Three Elements of Reflective Inquiry and Their Challenges

1. A CONCEPTUAL FRAMEWORK: A SCHOLARSHIP OF TEACHING AND LEARNING

A conceptual framework defines the values of a program and its intellectual tasks and challenges. Here the idea of a scholarship of teaching as first championed by Ernest Boyer, the president of the Carnegie Foundation for the Advancement of Teaching, provided that conceptual framework.

When in 1990 Ernest Boyer published his prescient book, *Scholarship Considered,* he launched a challenge to the closed doors of teachers in academia and to the wall between teaching and research. Although Boyer rightly saw that it was time to bury the old teaching versus research controversy and create new forms of scholarship at universities, he asked, "Is it possible to define the work of faculty in ways that reflect more realistically the full range of academic and civic mandates? . . . to give the familiar and honorable term 'scholarship' a broader, more capacious meaning, one that brings legitimacy to the full scope of academic work":

> Surely, scholarship means engaging in original research. But the work of the scholar also means stepping back from one's investiga-

> tion, looking for connections, building bridges between theory and practice, and communicating one's knowledge effectively to students. Specifically, we conclude that the work of the professoriate might be thought of as having four separate, yet overlapping functions. These are: the scholarship of *discovery;* the scholarship of *integration;* the scholarship of *application;* and, the scholarship of *teaching.* (Boyer, 1990, p. 16)

For Boyer, the work of the professor becomes consequential through teaching, only as it is understood by others. Yet, today, teaching is often viewed as a routine function, tacked on, something almost anyone can do. When defined as *scholarship,* however, teaching both educates and entices future scholars. Indeed, as Aristotle said, "Teaching is the highest form of understanding" (Boyer, 1990, p. 23).

In the years since Boyer's injunction, academics have taken up his challenge, nowhere more profitably than in exploring the idea of a scholarship of teaching. A rich history of scholarly work has been published by the American Association of Higher Education and the Carnegie Foundation for the Advancement of Teaching as well as by individuals across Europe, America, and the world (Becker & Andrews, 2004; Hutchings, 1998; Skillbeck, 2001). From my work with faculty at UCC, I share Huber and Hutchings's belief about "the power that comes with viewing teaching as challenging intellectual work. The scholarship of teaching and learning invites faculty from all disciplines and fields to identify and explore interesting questions in their own teaching and especially, in their students' learning and to share what they discover with colleagues who can build on their insights" (Huber & Hutchings, 2006, p. 24; Shulman, 1993).

I believe this is the power that enticed faculty at UCC in the spring of 2001 to respond positively to the invitation to attend a series of seminars on the portfolio creation process and to share their own inquiries into puzzles of teaching and learning. The portfolio seminars were in support of the newly announced competition for awards for Excellence in Teaching at UCC, and that was a drawing card. At the very first seminar, four people, when asked, volunteered to come the following week prepared to share one of their experiences of teaching, something they felt might become a potential entry for a portfolio of their own. Impressively, at that seminar two members from the medical faculty reported on a teaching experience of theirs that failed. When those present learned that these teachers had already tried out their unit and been roundly told by their students that it was a failure, faculty caught their breath. Why had the teachers used the unit again, another year? What were the teachers clinging to, or trying to convey? Why was that so important? Seldom had the people present engaged in such conversations. As one member said, not in all his thirteen years at UCC had he ever participated in a discussion about teaching, to say nothing of discussing failure.

2. WEEKLY PORTFOLIO SEMINARS FACILITATE EXCHANGE

Participants were so eager to have a forum for exchange that the seminars were continued the next fall. It also helped that the competition for the Awards for Excellence in Teaching at UCC were to be completed and teaching portfolios were to be submitted in March 2002. But the power of the seminars came from faculty members themselves. As they acknowledged, what slowly dawned on them was that someone in economics, or law, or food services engineering could have a teaching approach or a story they would find compelling, even challenging to their own practice. For instance, the way a biochemist told how he had, through his own research, revised a course on proteins that had taken him over some ten years to develop. He held his audience's rapt attention as he described the mysteries of protein-unfolding problems that might be clues to the cure of several diseases, such as BSE, or Alzheimer's. Here the intellectual power of the subject caught and held his audience.

Similarly, faculty members responded to the doctor who developed a program for training medical personnel in resuscitating newborn infants and used a research model to document his work in creating a teaching portfolio entry. He held everyone's attention as his audience realized the teaching problem he faced. Because the procedures medical personnel were trained in were only rarely required, usually in emergencies, there was always a need for re-training over time.

This diversity of issues of teaching and student learning had never been so easily available for interrogation in such an open forum. It also helped that the sessions were held in the high domed Council Room, the ancient place of university governance meetings. The noon discussions about teaching went on over a light lunch made available to participants. Sessions were open to all. The first round of the competition for teaching excellence yielded five awards. But twenty-three teachers submitted portfolios, and some 300 faculty participated in the seminars from 2001 to 2004 (Lyons, Hyland, & Ryan, 2002). Boyer had reminded us all that:

> Good teaching means that faculty, as scholars, are also learners. . . . While well-prepared lectures surely have a place, teaching, at its best, means not only transmitting knowledge, but transforming and extending it as well. Through reading, through classroom discussion and surely through comments and questions posed by students, pro-

fessors themselves will be pushed in creative new directions. (Boyer, 1990, p. 26)

The teaching commons created by these portfolio seminars nurtured the exchanges of UCC faculty and their unique ways of approaching the scholarship of teaching and the investigations of their own teaching they conducted.

3. THE REFLECTIVE PORTFOLIO INQUIRY PROCESS

Of all of the procedures for inquiry and exchange developed at UCC none is more challenging than creating a reflective portfolio. It is an explicit metacognitive task; it demands a reflective review of what any teaching act was attempting to do and what it achieved, asking what have students learned and what do they now know how to do: How do we know, by what evidence? The portfolio, long a familiar creation of artists, writers, photographers, and even financial planners, was transformed into something new when adopted for teaching and its inquiries. Now, not only would it be a mode of documenting teaching practices, it would become a means of inquiry, of investigation into teaching itself, presenting a question driving the research, evidence, the data of student learning, findings and their interpretation. As such, it gained prominence in teacher education circles. Then, in the pursuit of a scholarship of teaching, it became a method of choice at the American Association of Higher Education to document the inquiries teacher practitioners were making in pursuit of teaching as a scholarly activity. The teaching portfolio became popular in colleges and universities allowing faculty to document all aspects of their teaching tasks. These investigations then created new innovations of the portfolio itself.

For example, when teacher William Cerbin, a psychologist at the University of Wisconsin at La Crosse, began working on a teaching portfolio as part of a scholarship of teaching project, he found himself taking a new focus not on his teaching as a whole but on a single course and, in the process, invented the course portfolio:

> Being a social scientist, I began to think of each course . . . as a kind of laboratory—not a truly controlled experiment, of course, but as a setting in which you start out with goals for student learning, then you adopt teaching practices that you think will accomplish these, and along the way you can watch and see if your practices are helping to accomplish your goals, collecting evidence about effects and impact. In this sense, each course is a kind of discrete entity. . . . So the course portfolio was a natural way to go . . . I'm not sure I saw this immediately, but one thing I now see is that the course portfolio is

really like a scholarly manuscript . . . a draft, of ongoing inquiry (1996, 53). (Hutchings, 1998, p. 33)

It was this design of a course as comprised itself of a design (that is, a plan, what is usually called a syllabus), an enactment in teaching (that is, what students were asked to do), and having *results* in student learning (that is, what students learned) that became an important conceptual framework for putting together a course or a teaching portfolio. The course portfolio highlighted, too, data of the results, what exactly students got out of the course, what they now learned and knew how to do.

Foundational Inquiry Issues

DEFINING REFLECTIVE INQUIRY

The critical element of developing a portfolio is the reflective element, one that has recently come under fire and created controversy. Recent research on reflective inquiry undertaken as part of a portfolio process has identified two significant problems: there is little agreement about what reflective inquiry is; and, without an agreed definition, there is little *comparable research* that can document or verify the purported, but highly regarded, benefits of reflective inquiry (Rodgers, 2002; Zeichner, 1999). Lacking description, the tasks of an inquiry process remain hidden from view and understanding that might guide new inquirers. As a developer of the new portfolio seminars course I share how I define reflection, that is:

> Reflection is an intentional act engaging a person alone, but especially in collaboration with others—students, teachers, practitioners, other researchers or colleagues—in *systematic inquiry* [our emphasis], interrogating a situation of teaching or learning, usually one presenting some puzzle, to construct an understanding of some aspect of it. Such an act looks both backwards and to the future. It is in service of understanding and meaning that will shape action. It involves gathering and documenting evidence of the inquiry. It likely involves narrative for it is the story of meaning and it can raise ethical issues for the people involved. (Lyons, 2002a, p. 99)

This definition incorporates the idea of an intentional investigation of some real-life puzzle or problem which has as its goal meaning and understanding gained through serious investigation, the assessment of evidence, and collaborative reflection. Kuhn (2005), a developmental psychologist, bringing insights from developmental psychology and her own innovative empirical research with children and adolescents as well as her review of adult development in inquiry, suggests the complexity of inquiry for students of all ages:

> Students must have not only the skills and the opportunity to engage in increasingly complex forms of inquiry . . . it is equally essential that they develop a firm belief that engaging in inquiry is worthwhile. Such a belief can be grounded only in their own experience. But inquiry experiences have the advantage of revealing their value and power as they are engaged. No further argument for their worth is necessary. Nonetheless, understanding of the nature and value of inquiry itself develops, as do the skills that inquiry requires . . . patterns in the development of this epistemological understanding of the nature of knowing have been identified by developmental psychologists, and their findings stand to inform the stated intentions of educators to include understanding of inquiry as a curriculum standard. (Kuhn, 2005, p. 59)

STUDENTS' PERSPECTIVES TOWARD KNOWING

With other researchers, Kuhn (2005) argues that a perspective toward knowing is the foundational beginning of inquiry; that is, an awareness of oneself as a knower and of the process of knowing. Unfortunately, this is a seldom acknowledged starting place. Yet, as William Perry (1970) first demonstrated in his groundbreaking work, *Forms of Intellectual and Ethical Development in the College Years*, most students are likely to begin their educational careers with a naive, dualistic perspective on knowledge, knowing, truth, and so on. In other words, they expect that knowledge is known and that someone—usually an authority figure—knows the one right answer. Perry found that as students develop, they come to realize that there are or can be multiple perspectives on what is known. The danger of this perspective of multiplicity is that any opinion may then be termed as good as any other and all knowledge and truth can be relegated to "just an opinion." But growth beyond is possible and there comes the realization that some positions have a better grounding in evidence. Then can come the revolutionary leap to the realization that all knowledge is relative (considered in relation to something else, values, degrees, or frames not absolutes) and constructed; but, unfortunately, not all adults or students reach this point. Perry outlined these perspectives as five epistemological positions (see Kuhn, 2005; see Hofer & Pintrich, 2002, for similarities in models of epistemological development).

But the journey to developing richer and more complex perspectives on knowing and knowledge—that is, to developing an epistemological perspective—takes rich nurturing, according to Kuhn (2005). Inquiry is in the service of changing understandings. Learning involves changing understandings. Yet epistemological assumptions can have serious implications for how a learner will approach the task of learning, and of seeing new perspectives on a subject. Teachers encounter these assumptions all the time—for example, the university student who told her lecturer, a medical doctor, that she did not want to participate in a small group discussion with other students because she said "it would be a waste of time. I only want to hear from the lecturer who knows." Or the high school philosophy teacher who hesitated to give his students his opinion in a debate about a case of euthanasia: "Do I give my opinion . . . running the risk that twenty-two kids will change their vote because this is what the teacher thinks?" This teacher also found that his students thought the only way to convince someone was to keep saying their opinion louder and louder, "rather than searching for some evidence" (Lyons, 1990, pp. 166–167). One junior high school student, addressing his small group, directed students to their group investigative task: "You choose what to look at and I'll say what we found," seeing no connection between the two tasks (Kuhn, 2005, p. 100).

DEVELOPING SKILL IN REFLECTIVE INQUIRY

One path out of these dilemmas is knowing how to connect, read, and evaluate evidence, an ability critical to developing understanding of the inquiry process. But to develop this ability, students must first be able to sustain observation; connect both observation and evidence to the central question of their investigation; and then write up what they have discovered, not just what they have done. In fact, data and conclusions are sometimes not linked, and students rarely connect what they discovered to their own knowledge (Kuhn, 2005, p. 54). Some researchers in this area have argued for the necessity to move toward more highly structured sequences of activities in support of the inquiry process, identifying and breaking down each step of the process, such as those listed here.

Dewey insists that reflective thinking is not "just mulling things over"—a common, popular definition. Nor is simply introspection of one's thoughts or feelings. Rather for Dewey it is the "kind of thinking that consists in turning a subject over in the mind and giving it serious and consecutive consideration" (Dewey, 1933/1998, pp. 3–16). In addition, Dewey distinguishes reflective inquiry from stream of consciousness, uncontrolled coursing of ideas through our heads; from mental pictures of something not present; and, from belief, simply an assertion about some matter or fact, principle or law. For Dewey, reflective thinking has a purpose, "it must lead somewhere . . . implies belief in evidence" (Dewey, p. 9).

Reflective thinking usually has its origins in some kind of puzzle or doubt. "In distinction from other operations to which we apply the name of thought, it involves: (1) a state of doubt, hesitation, perplexity, mental difficulty in which thinking originates; and (2) an act of searching, hunting, inquiring, to find material that will resolve the doubt, settle and dispose of the perplexity" (Dewey, 1933/1998, p. 12). To be genuinely thoughtful, Dewey averred, "we must be willing to sustain and protract that state of doubt which is the stimulus to thorough inquiry, so as not to accept an idea or make positive assertion of a belief until justifying reasons have been found" (Dewey, 1933/1998, p. 16).

This is the challenge and the work of reflective inquiry. And it is what psychologist Deanna Kuhn has well documented that is so difficult to learn and to teach. The reflective portfolio process has the advantage of making the process explicit, in its demand for evidence of results of teaching and identification of the implications of the research. Reflective inquiry is a systematic, thoughtful investigation in service of discovering evidence to resolve the doubt, dissolve the perplexity, and the puzzles of teaching and learning.

Given both the participants' lack of familiarity with reflective inquiry, and the lack of understanding of the inquiry process more generally, the inquiry process needs to be taught, mentored, modeled, and supported in collaboration with others. Therefore, in this portfolio course, the process is scaffolded in several ways. We:

- review the definitions of reflective inquiry by John Dewey, Donald Schön, and ourselves, all of which emphasize the serious, systematic work of inquiry that is built on the requirement of evidence and deliberation
- introduce and mentor students through the process of creating portfolio entries with their evidence, the building blocks of the portfolio
- monitor students' reflective writing
- invite them to share in presenting and critiquing their portfolio entries over the course of the program, and, at its conclusion, articulating what they had found and learned from the process

But what are its results? Here we look at results UCC faculty indicate from their inquiries.

Outcomes: Results of Faculty Inquiries into Teaching and Student Learning

To explore the results of the reflective inquiries of UCC faculty I present data from two studies. The first is data from interviews with some twenty UCC faculty members who participated in the first round of the competition for an award for excellence in teaching. The second study comes from work currently happening with faculty members who have now completed three years of study and portfolio documentation of investigations into their teaching and student learning. In the last three years they have been pursuing inquiries of their own through a reflective portfolio process in new course formats that have evolved at UCC. These formats are important formal institutional programs for study introduced and developed under the leadership of Aine Hyland and others. They include the introduction of a Certificate in Teaching and Learning in 2004, a Diploma program in 2005, and a Masters in Teaching and Learning program in 2006–2007. All of these programs emphasize the study of theory and practices of teaching and learning with a particular emphasis on Howard Gardner's (1983) theory of multiple intelligences, teaching for understanding, and assessing student learning to uncover what they know.

The three UCC teachers presented in brief vignettes below have been engaged in portfolio making and in the study of teaching and learning in the three new programs. Results of the first study of UCC faculty provide a base point: They revealed some of the power of reflective inquiry. That study took place in 2002–2003 in interviews with twenty of the twenty-three faculty members applying by portfolio for the first award competition of 2002. In an analysis of that study's interview data, especially in response to the questions, "Looking back over the portfolio process, what stands out for you?" and "What would you say you learned from the process?" findings revealed that nineteen out of twenty UCC staff members cited that reflective engagement through the portfolio process created a new "consciousness" of their own teaching practice (Lyons, 2002b; see also Lyons, Hyland, & Ryan, 2002). For most faculty, seventeen out of twenty, this conscious awareness triggered a set of four related actions: (1) the new consciousness led them to articulate a greater explicitness about their teaching goals and practices, both for themselves and their students; (2) they began to ask, "What exactly do students learn and know from my teaching and how do I know?"; (3) they identified changes they would consider in their practice; and (4) they then said they actually changed their practice. I argue that these elements point to a new meta-cognitive awareness of what these teachers know and how they know it. Other researchers support this claim of a new consciousness. Perry (1970) refers to the achievements of understanding that all knowledge is contextual and relative as the "radical reperception of all knowledge" (1970, p. 109). Jack Mezirow (1991) terms it a "perspective transformation" (p. 109). Reflection is the central dynamic of intentional learning, involving the reinterpretation of the meaning of experience.

But when faculty members take an additional step and continue in their own learning about teaching and learning, what kinds of results and understandings do they acknowledge?

Three Vignettes—When Teachers Inquire into Their Own Contexts of Learning

The three UCC staff members presented here provide a brief glimpse into how faculty responded to deeper engagement in teaching and learning, what they were inquiring in continuing to engage in a reflective portfolio process, and what they say they have learned. Of special interest is how they encourage their own inquiry process and that of their students, if they do. Data are from interviews conducted in 2006 with participants in the new Masters in Teaching and Learning program. In this study, participants are asked: What were you trying to achieve and understand by continuing to engage in the portfolio process of the new programs? What would you say you have learned? What stood out for you in the process?

Results varied in terms of peoples' disciplines, their prior knowledge, and current professional goals. But two findings from this clearly small sample are important to verify: *how faculty link inquiries into teaching to their research, suggesting a new integration of research and teaching in this work; how faculty are further developing a meta-cognitive awareness of the links they are making in their own understanding of ways of knowing through the inquiry process; and, how they now try to scaffold that inquiry process for others, either their own students or other faculty members.* These findings clearly need further testing. We look here at three faculty members and their three perspectives on the relation between teaching and research and ways of knowing.

1. THE FINANCE TEACHER INITIATES A STUDY: HOW DO YOU FOSTER REFLECTIVE INQUIRY IN STUDENTS?

This faculty member, a teacher of finance for some ten years, described how she became a self-chosen mentor to a group of some twenty students in a Bachelor of Science in Finance program. She had designed a new third year practicum, a Placement Program, that gave advanced students a six-month work experience in a local financial organization. She had created the program with a deliberate inquiry goal to initiate an investigation into how to foster reflection in the UCC finance students. The teacher had in fact created the program as an inquiry into her own question: Could students be encouraged to engage in reflection on their own? She reveals:

> My initial reflection on the program was that it was good but not as good as it could be. . . . My overarching learning objective for the course module was that students would practice active reflection on both prior theoretical knowledge and on the experiential learning they would achieve in the work environment. . . . Reflective learning fosters in students a capacity for critical thinking and facilitates continuous learning. The corollary of this is that there can be no real development, deep learning, if experience is not accompanied by a process of inquiry into that experience. . . . I encourage and facilitate learners in the process of conducting a dialogue with themselves, through the medium of compiling a weekly learning log. . . . By asking "how do the things I am doing connect?" learners themselves become active participants in learning.

Toward that goal, the teacher asked students to keep learning logs during the six-month practicum, to communicate with her at least once a week, emailing learning log entries, that is, their questions and comments about their placement, and connections they found.

The origin of the program for the teacher was a deep-seated respect for students and a desire to integrate students more fully into her teaching, "How could I bring students more into the mainstream of learning. . . . I wanted to gain more insight into that. And I saw the opportunity to look at that" (Lyons, 2006). Here this teacher illuminates how a new teaching program is put into operation as a research investigation.

When asked what she had learned from this project, she responded: "I was reassured of the benefits of reflection. I believe that students have a latent capacity to reflect if we can engage them in the process. I mentored them by interacting with emails each week. I could see what puzzled them, how they resolved it. I believe over time they, not all, about half, got to learn how to do it" (Lyons, 2006). She is left with a new puzzle: why did the other half of the students not grasp reflection? But she has already raised the important question and advanced some answers to, "How can students see themselves as inquirers, as knowers conscious of how they know?"

2. THE DOCTOR AS A RESEARCH EDUCATOR: MAKING META-COGNITIVE INQUIRY ROUTINE IN MEDICAL TEACHING

The medical doctor had created a teaching portfolio and won an award for Excellence in Teaching in 2002. But he continued his studies in the new UCC Teaching and Learning program, achieving a Certificate and then a Diploma and creating portfolio entries for these programs. Currently he is enrolled in the

Masters program. Although there are many roles a doctor must fill, he acknowledges how as a doctor he must also be an educator. He describes how for him teaching and research must be intimately linked and how he strives to achieve that linkage. In one instance he acknowledges the need to create and pursue a pilot program as a way to provide evidence to justify a new medical procedure for a new education program. Toward that goal, he commits himself to research that is connected to his teaching. Introduced to a program inspired by Howard Gardner's work, the doctor has adopted a teaching technique that trains medical personnel working with premature infants to create *still videos* when they enter the environment of the infant. For example, "I get my students to ask and record what they see as they enter an infant's environment: What is going on here? Who is in the picture? How would the parent put the situation? What story is the parent creating? The nurse? The doctor? What is going on outside the room? The goal is to help those involved to see that there is more than one story in a medical emergency, to empower them with ways of knowing how to uncover more than one perspective" (Lyons, 2006).

Presently this doctor is exploring the effects of this process and also considering introducing the idea of a Standardized Patient, that is, an actor who can portray the symptoms of someone sick so that medical personnel can practice how they would respond. He believes this model can also be used to teach communication skills, so that a new level of competency in communication can be taught and measured. But the doctor is trying to figure out: Can it be introduced to doctors in training? Could it also be used as well to educate medical and related personnel in communication and consultation skills? How would it be measured? Could it train people from different medical cultures, gain an international perspective? But as he says, "I like to do things in terms of measuring, and teaching. I always have enjoyed teaching. I am much more interested in teaching." Thus he plans to pilot an inquiry for the Standardized Patient project. He is also clear about why, that is, not only to try out a new pedagogy but to research its potential results. He sums up his approach to teaching through inquiry research and the skills it yields: "And I like to do research, to bring in research, to use it to empower people. There is more than one way. Every time you teach you must get feedback. You can then say, 'Let's look at this. What is going on here?'" (Lyons, 2006). Teaching and research inquiries are joined not only at the planning stage for a new program but at every stage buttressed by evidence from feedback to be carefully reviewed.

3. THE LANGUAGE TEACHER: DISCOVERING WHAT INQUIRY AND RESEARCH MEAN TO UNDERSTANDING

The language teacher similarly is working toward a Masters in Teaching and Learning, having already completed the other portfolio programs. His dominant sense of what he is learning is how to question what he is doing in his teaching every day. "In slow and simple ways this program makes me question what I do all the time. I have been teaching for over ten years and yesterday I asked myself why I was doing something. I looked at the students and some did not seem hooked in. So I wonder, 'Are these students' power pointed out?'" So he begins the idea of testing his hunch. In addition, he says, "I understand much more what my responsibility is, and how to check it out. I see my responsibility to students has matured as has my partnership with students." Thus inquiry has become a daily habit that can alert him to his own responsibilities to students.

But what is the most dramatic learning for this teacher is a new understanding of the nature of knowledge and knowing of the research inquiry process itself.

> From our inquiries in the program I find that for the first time I understand what research is about! Even when I did a Ph.D., I did it like it was another essay, the thing to do, to do it and get out on the road. But I was never really satisfied with it. Last year when we talked about the Masters and what it entailed, about boundaries in a field, and others in the Teaching and Learning program began to talk about their research work, I could see the research process for the first time, what is meant by research. And I could relate to the people around me, to what they were interested in. I could see exactly where I was and what my research topic was, I could see where it fit into language and where it fit into my teaching and my students' learning. The portfolio process as inquiry into something worthwhile. (Lyons, 2006)

The Future: Testable Hypotheses and Imperatives for Inquiry Learning

While it is still early to suggest the full impact of this Scholarship of Teaching project, there are several telltale statistics: some seventy faculty members signed up for the Certificate program three years ago and some forty-five of those are now completing the Masters. But several hypotheses do emerge from these brief investigations and suggest a future research agenda for understanding the contexts of education for inquiry. These hypotheses are:

- The portfolio inquiry process fosters a new integration between teaching and research. Research is embedded in the teaching process as new techniques are tried out, tested, and assessed.
- As a perspective on inquiry develops it leads to increased investigations and creative experimentation in teaching.

- The inquiry process enhances a teacher's sense of responsibility to students and may induce heightened ethical concerns or awareness of ethical dimensions of teaching.
- Engaging in inquiries into teaching and learning can foster new ways of seeing and knowing one's own discipline, new perspectives toward knowledge and knowing and how you know, that is a meta-cognitive awareness.

A rich set of questions remains to be explored in the future. A set of imperatives for advancing inquiry teaching and learning can now be suggested:

1. Identify and scaffold all stages of the inquiry process, for all students;
2. Encourage inquiry projects in real contexts and in collaborations;
3. Document and make public the inquiry skills needed and used; and
4. Share findings and plan to use and build on the results of inquiry projects.

The sample of faculty inquiries reported here, though modest, offers some sense of the building blocks useful for inquiries into the study of education contexts, the possible future for education research. But it remains to bring all of these small studies together, to coalesce the potential of this work. Dare we ask: What if education had a genome-scope project to keep track of and map investigations into the contexts of learning?

References

Becker, W. C., & Andrews, M. L. (2004). *The scholarship of teaching and learning in higher education.* Bloomington: Indiana University Press.

Bok, D. (2006). *Our underachieving colleges.* Princeton: Princeton University Press.

Boyer, E. (1990). *Scholarship reconsidered: Priorities of the professoriate.* Princeton: The Carnegie Foundation for the Advancement of Teaching.

Cochran-Smith, M., & Zeichner, K. (2005). *Studying teacher education: The report of the AERA panel on research and teacher education.* Washington, DC: American Educational Research Association.

Dewey, J. (1933/1998). *How we think: A restatement of the relation of reflective thinking to the educative process.* New York: Houghton Mifflin Co.

Feuer, M. J., Towne, L., & Shavelson, R. (2002). Science, culture and education research. *Educational Researcher, 32*(80), 21–24.

Gardner, H. (1983). *Frames of mind: Theory of multiple intelligences.* London: Fontana.

Hofer, B., & Pintrich, P. (Eds.) (2002). *Personal epistemology: The psychology of beliefs about knowldge and knowing.* Mahwah, NJ: Erlbaum Associates.

Huber, M., & Hutchings, P. (2006). Building the teaching commons. *Change, 38*(3), 24–31.

Hutchings, P. (1998). *The course portfolio.* Washington, DC: American Association for Higher Education.

Kuhn, D. (2005). *Education for thinking*. Cambridge, MA: Harvard University Press.
Lagemann, E. (2000). *An elusive science: The troubling history of education research*. Chicago: University of Chicago Press.
Loughran, J., Hamilton, M. L., LaBoskey, V. K., & Russell, T. (Eds.) (2004). *International handbook of self-study of teaching and teacher education*. Boston: Kluwer Academic Publishers.
Lyons, N. (1998). *With portfolio in hand*. New York: Teachers College Press.
Lyons, N. (2002a). Personal self in a public story. In N. Lyons & V. LaBoskey (Eds.), *Narrative Inquiry in Practice*. New York: Teachers College Press.
Lyons, N. (2002b). Results: What faculty said they learn and value. In N. Lyons, A. Hyland, & N. Ryan (Eds.), *Advancing the scholarship of teaching and learning through a reflective portfolio process*. Cork, Ireland: University College Cork.
Lyons, N. (2006). *The portfolio research project*. Unpublished research interviews. University College Cork, Cork, Ireland.
Lyons, N., Hyland, A., & Ryan, N. (Eds.) (2002). *Advancing the scholarship of teaching and learning through a reflective portfolio process*. Cork, Ireland: University College Cork.
Mezirow, J. (1991). *Transformative dimensions of adult learning*. San Francisco: Jossey-Bass.
Oxford American Desk Dictionary and Thesaurus. (2001). New York: Berkley Books.
Perry, W. (1970). *Forms of intellectual and ethical development in college years*. New York: Holt, Rinehart and Winston, Inc.
Rodgers, C. (2002). Defining reflection: Another look at John Dewey and reflective thinking. *Teacher College Record, 104*(4), 842–866.
Rose, C. (2007). *Science Series* TV program.
Schön, D. (1995). The new scholarship needs a new epistemology. *Change, 27*(6), 28–34.
Shulman, L. (1993). Teaching as community property: Putting an end to pedagogical solitude. *Change, 25*(6), 6–7.
Skillbeck, M. (2001). *The university challenged: A review of international trends and issues with particular reference to Ireland*. Dublin: HEA.
Zeichner, K. (1999). The new scholarship of teacher education. *Educational Researcher, 28*(9), 4–15.

CHAPTER 7

The Wisdom of Fifth Graders
A VOICE IN THE RENAISSANCE

Barbara Morgan-Fleming
Texas Tech University

Mya Kendrick-Mercer
Wheatley Elementary School

Susan Myers
Texas Tech University

Connie Wilson Anderson
Texas Tech University

Barbara Morgan-Fleming, Ph.D., is an associate professor of Curriculum and Instruction at Texas Tech University. She has taught in elementary schools and adult education programs, and currently teaches preservice teachers in collaboration with professional development schools. Her research interests include classroom performance of curriculum and informal aspects of teachers' knowledge.

Mya Kendrick-Mercer, M.A., has taught in elementary schools for six years and has recently completed her Masters in Educational Administration. She is interested in doing research with elementary school students in order to improve the practice of preservice and veteran educators.

Susan Myers, Ed.D., is an assistant professor at Texas Tech University in the Secondary Education Program of the Curriculum Studies Department. Her interest in school/university partnerships evolved from her eighteen years of public school experience at the elementary and secondary levels, both as a classroom teacher and a guidance counselor. Dr. Myers' research and professional interests include mentoring and induction of new teachers, characteristics of effective mentoring, and collaborative partnerships with professional development schools.

Connie Wilson Anderson, Ed.D., is an assistant professor at Texas Tech University in the College of Education's Secondary Education Program.

She has over thirty-four years' experience in educational institutions in Oklahoma, Nebraska, and Texas. Her experience at the public school and university levels includes extensive involvement teaching and working with diverse ethnic and cultural student populations in rural and urban public schools identified as "at-risk" and association with field-based teacher education programs. Dr. Anderson's research interests include the mentoring and induction of new teachers and the professional concerns of first-year teachers.

ABSTRACT

This chapter discusses a study that asked fifth grade students to describe a good teacher and offer insight into how teacher education programs can help people become good teachers. The students were predominantly African American, and underserved. The outcomes of the study support the contention that student voice is an important, although neglected, resource for a renaissance in teacher education. Their insights are presented and discussed with reference to the literature, the experience of the authors, and the theme of this edited volume. Sensitivity to what students have to say, in the authors' view, contributes to a renaissance in teacher education.

We agree with the editors of the Yearbook about the importance of seeking different perspectives from the multiple constituents of teacher education. As we begin this process, we must consider who are the authors of, and participants in, this renaissance. For growth to occur, differing voices and constituents must be brought into contact with one another. If change is to occur, hegemony must be avoided. Said (1982) speaks of the importance of including multiple perspectives in academic institutions and discourse:

> A principle of silent exclusion operates within and at the boundaries of discourse; this has now become so internalized that fields, disciplines, and their discourse have taken on the status of immutable durability. Licensed members of the field, which has all the trappings of a social institution are identifiable as belonging to a guild, and for them words like "expert" and "objective" have an important resonance. To acquire a position of authority within the field is, however, to be involved internally in the formation of a canon, which usually turns out to be a blocking device for methodological and disciplinary self-questioning. (p. 16)

It is the purpose of this chapter to include one voice that is often missing from educational discussions: that of K–12 students. Although they are the recipient, audience, and target of educational practice and reform, all too often the most important people involved in education are left out of conversations about instructional change. Today's students are bright, well-informed, and have knowledge to contribute. We ask students to share their perspectives about what works and what doesn't work in K–12 schools, experiment with different ways of interviewing, and write articles about how to encourage student involvement and create participatory environments for learning, but seldom actually sustain student voices in the scholarship of teaching, learning, and teacher education. As educators, we know that students have valuable ideas about what would make their learning more meaningful and engaging, but how often do we seek out their perspectives about improving our practice as teacher educators? Student participation is a necessary component if we are to make the move from "in the head" to "between heads" analysis described by Denny Taylor (1993):

> "in-the-head" analysis of human behavior is beyond our present capability. Instead I suggested a "between heads" view of human learning . . . we consistently underestimate the enormous potential of children to participate in the construction of their own learning environments. (p. 2–3)

Preparing new teachers for the diverse classrooms they will encounter has become one of the greatest priorities for teacher preparation programs. Numerous studies have examined in-depth the concerns, professional development, and career stages of preservice and beginning teachers (Steffy, Wolfe, Pasch, & Enz, 2000). As a result, programs are being designed and implemented not only in an attempt to address teacher preparation, but as an impetus for educational renewal and reform (Fullan, 2001; Zeichner, Melnick, & Gomez, 1996).

The collaborative inquiry described in this chapter is based on the premise that creating an environment where researchers, practitioners, and students work together to examine their practice increases the opportunity for shared power and voice. Additionally, it allows for all involved to become co-constructors of the lived experience of the research, creating the dissonance that is required for regeneration and invention, and making possible what Turner (1986) calls the growth of reflexivity:

> If social drama regularly implies conflict of principles, norms, and persons, it equally implies the growth of reflexivity; for if all principles and norms were consistent and if all persons obeyed them, then culture and society would be unselfconscious and innocent, untroubled by the shadow of a doubt. But few indeed are the human groups whose relationships are perpetually in equilibrium, and are free from agonistic strivings. (p. 103)

By utilizing and including the student voices of the K–6 students in this study, we attempt to bring a new perspective to teacher education as we seek to inform and improve practice (Wasser & Bresler, 1996).

The four authors of this chapter have found great benefit from including children in their research. Morgan-Fleming began her research as a fifth grade teacher (see Morgan, 1993; Morgan-Fleming, 1994; Morgan-Fleming & Doyle, 1997). Anderson, Myers, and Morgan-Fleming teach preservice and in-service teachers, and have longstanding relationships with public schools in the area. Kendrick-Mercer has taught at the elementary school discussed in this chapter for six years, and has recently completed certification in educational administration.

Methodology

The contributions to this chapter come from fifth grade students in a small elementary school in West Texas. The student body is primarily African-American, and a majority of the students qualify for free or reduced lunch. The school is rated as "recognized," the second highest rating in the Texas system. Mercer is the fifth graders' math teacher and has taught at the school for six years. Morgan-Fleming has taught field-based methods classes at the school for seven years and has developed a relationship over time with the students, helping with field trips, judging science fairs, and participating in other activities with the children. Over the years, Morgan-Fleming has thanked students for their help with the university students who were placed in their classrooms, and has asked the students to provide insights to the university students and the research community (see Morgan-Fleming, Marbley, & White, 2005). The students were given a handout with the following questions and asked to complete it:

What does a good teacher look like?
What's in her/his head?
What's in his/her heart?
How can teacher educators help people become good teachers?

Kendrik-Mercer and Morgan-Fleming discussed the importance of the students' participation in the project, and asked them to help those of us who work in the preparation of teachers to improve our programs. The first part of the exercise was relatively simple. Students quickly drew a picture of a good teacher—many drawings were of specific teachers with whom they had studied (see Figure 7.1).

As the students were writing, Morgan-Fleming noticed that two students

Raykeisha	Tobi	Anthony
Kody	Ashtyn	Alexa

Figure 7.1 Student Drawings of a Good Teacher

THE WISDOM OF FIFTH GRADERS 123

Angelica	Chadsidi
Rachel	Marcos

Figure 7.1 *Continued*

had interpreted two of the questions ("What's in his/her head?" and "What's in her/his heart?") literally, answering "brain" for the former, and "blood" for the latter. We explained that we were speaking metaphorically about the knowledge and attitude that a good teacher would have. Below are presented the students' answers to each of the four questions.

What's in her/his head?

- Math, reading, algebra, social studies, science. (Marcos)
- In her/his head they should think how should they make students learn but have fun. (Rachael)
- Knowledge. What they need to know to be a teacher. (Chadsidi)
- Not to be prejudiced to other people. To be kind to others. To be patient with others if they are doing it too long. (Anjelica)
- How will I make this day as educated as possible? (Alexa)
- "Education is a key." Smart role model. (Ashtyn)
- Teach children to love one another. Always have a smile. (Kody)
- She wants me to do what I can, wants me to achieve all that I can, and wants me to be a leader not a follower. She is behind me 100%. (Anthony)
- I'm going to show my students what they got to learn to go on. (Tobi)
- Brain, knowledge, what they need to know to be a good teacher. (Raykeisha)

What's in his/her heart?

- Blood, ability to listen to kids. (Marcos)
- In the teachers heart they should love all the students. (Rachael)
- They do not need to be prejudiced. They need to tell students they are doing well. (Chadsidi)
- Not to be mad at others when they are mad at somebody else. To be responsible to work with others. To have faith in others. (Anjelica)
- I love to teach these hard workers. (Alexa)
- Attitude. (Ashtyn)
- Have fun and be willing to help others out and teach them to their full potential. (Kody)
- To never ever give up. Do not want to yell all the time at one person. Let the students have a little fun every blue moon? (Anthony)
- Teacher educators can help teachers by giving them more education and passion. To teach a teacher to be patient you have to be patient with them. (Tobi)
- A good person, an excellent teacher, a trustworthy person. (Raykeisha)

On the back of the handout students were asked, "How should teacher educators help people become good teachers?" This question was harder for the students, so Morgan-Fleming explained that it was her job as a teacher educator to help college students become good teachers. Kendrick-Mercer and Morgan-Fleming asked the students what colleges needed to teach in order to reach this goal. Here are the students' answers.

How can teacher educators help people become good teachers?

- Show how to keep their cool and not get mad. Take time to listen. Respect their boss and show respect. (Marcos)
- The teacher educators should let the student teacher learn before they start teaching, and to make them patient, you have to be a role model so they can be like you. (Rachael)
- Teacher educators can help others by tuffing them up and teaching them the math, science, reading and social studies. We can also send them to other schools to see how to do that certain kind of thing. To teach a teacher to be patient, you got to be patient yourself. (Chadsidi)
- Teach others not to judge people by the way they look or act by asking teachers that are nonprejudiced how not to be prejudiced. When you are mad before you come to work you should not take it out on others like your students. Not to tell others you do not want to work with them because they will feel bad. (Anjelica)
- Learn more to teach more, and to be a strong and caring teacher so you can do and know more about the child and NOT be prejudiced. Smile and make them feel better. Help them with their anger against others. If you are talking to the child, ask if they dream of anything and if they are having problems. (Alexa)
- I think they should experience college success, fun, knowledge, happy, victory, patience, responsible, smile, kindness, athletic, against prejudice, algebra, mathematics, understanding science, passion, calm attitude, available, dependable. (Ashtyn)
- To become a leader you have to be a follower. Lead them to education and success, because it is the key to victory. Teachers have to know how to spell. Kids need to know knowledge. Teachers cannot be prejudiced to one either. Maybe have some experience with the life they are going through. Try to have some friends and teach them with respect and with love not hatred. Show and tell about your life and how it got better. Have history of all the people we know. (Kody)
- Stay on them. Teach them not to be mean. Show them not to be prejudiced. Tell them it's okay to have fun. Teach them to do the right thing. Tell them why it is good to work with one another. Give them some homework. Teach

them not to pick on one student because others are. To help, teach them how to be nice. (Anthony)
- By teaching them not to be prejudiced, to be kind to students and treat others like you want to be treated. (Tobi)
- You teach them. You tell them to stand up for myself. You do what you have to do. You have to model what they need to do to slow your rode [sic] with the students [i.e., take it easy on us, calm down]. (Raykeisha)

What We Learned from Students

While there are numerous accounts reported in the literature about the concerns of preservice teachers as they begin teaching, there are far fewer accounts from a K–12 student perspective. In an effort to bring a renaissance to teacher preparation, student voices provide additional support and insight into how we as teachers can work collaboratively for equity. Some of the lessons learned from the interactions with the fifth graders in this study added a different lens through which to view ourselves and our practice. In light of becoming more reflective about our teaching and engaging ourselves by listening closely to all of the voices of those we encounter, we discovered an interest in descriptive inquiry as well. The lessons presented here reflect a few of the salient themes that emerged during this inquiry.

Because the students were central to this investigation, we lead with some of the lessons learned from their participation as it pertains to their impressions about preservice teachers. Our intent is to draw from the collaborative nature of the interactions and connect them in ways that improve our professional conversations with students, preservice teachers, and teacher educators.

Students expect their teachers to provide an educationally challenging place where they feel safe to share their dreams, problems, and differences. Additionally, students appear to want their teachers to control their emotions (especially anger), model patience and passion, and overcome prejudice.

A majority of the students wrote of the importance of teachers overcoming prejudice. It is important for teachers to understand how children perceive their treatment of them, as the perception that students bring to the classroom is strongly linked to student performance. While *Brown v. Board of Education of Topeka*, a landmark decision of the United States Supreme Court, declared the establishment of separate public schools for black and white students inherently unequal, equality of educational opportunity is still an issue that is being debated in American education. Marcus, Gross, and Seefeldt (1991) asked fifth-grade Black and White students of similar achievement levels about their perception of how their teachers treat them and found continued discrimination against Black students in favor of White students as one explanation for achievement differences. Good (1981) also found that equality of educational opportunity is related to teacher practices as perceived by students. Each student's reality is based on his/her perception of the school and its practices and although there is just one school, each student's experience in that school is different. If students perceive unequal treatment, then that is the reality and one possible source of lower achievement.

While the number of culturally diverse students in public schools is steadily increasing, the teachers preparing to teach them are predominantly White and middle-class. These teachers recruited to teach culturally diverse students find that they feel unprepared to handle the challenges associated with the instructional needs of culturally diverse students. The need for teachers to have an understanding of the cultural differences they will encounter when teaching culturally diverse students is reported in current research on culturally responsive teaching. Brown (2004) describes culturally responsive teaching as:

> Purposively responding to the needs of the many culturally and ethnically diverse learners in classrooms. It involves implementing specifically student-orientated instructional processes as well as choosing and delivering ethnically and culturally relevant curricula. (p. 268)

The students they encounter today are quite different than those they may remember as students. This transition into classrooms that are decidedly more diverse makes it even more imperative that teachers feel equipped to address challenges of differences other than their subject area. Teachers must consider voices of their students as a source of advice from the classroom that could not be more important to help them better understand why their students think and behave as they do.

Cushman (2003) reports that in the 2001 MetLife Survey of the American Teacher national survey, 65 percent of students agreed with the statement, "My teachers don't understand me," and 33 percent of the teachers reported inadequate preparation to reach students with backgrounds different from their own. She also suggests teachers foster a habit of paying close attention to what students say, whether they speak through words or actions. Some ways that Cushman suggests for incorporating student voice include knowing students well, teaching to the individual student, and not expecting the work of one student from another. She acknowledges that having adolescent students advise their own teachers often strikes educators and other adults as audacious, but still insists we provide a structure to expand understanding and improve practice by finding out what students have to say. Cushman asked, "how can young people still in their teens be expected to summon the necessary know-how and perspective to help the adults charged with their very development and learning" (Cushman, 2003, p. 184)? Her answer—it is as simple as coming up with questions you really care about and gathering a group of students willing to express their thoughts. Write everything down and analyze the information collected!

A renaissance in teacher education will require reflection and action at the individual and institutional levels. We must look at the hidden curriculum (Jackson, 1968) in our institutions, and ask ourselves how we can help ourselves and our students work to overcome prejudice in our schools and society. Anjelica and Chadsidi suggest involving preservice teachers in public schools as one potential method for overcoming prejudice, a practice that we have found helpful. University students doing field experience at Anjelica and Chadsidi's school often express surprise at how wonderful the school is. The majority of the university students are white, and many entertain stereotypes about schools on the black side of town. When they enter the school, see the excellent, caring teaching and the high achievement and creativity of the students, their pre-judgments are made visible and vulnerable to change.

Teacher preparation programs have been implementing numerous changes in how we prepare highly qualified new teachers to meet the needs of increasingly culturally and linguistically diverse student populations (Abbate-Vaughn, 2006; Feiman-Nemser, 2001; Chan, 2006). Furthermore, teacher educators are encouraging veteran teachers to assist in preparing new teachers for diverse classrooms. The involvement of teachers and teacher educators in collaborative inquiry and thoughtful discussion is evidenced by the increase of professional development schools and field-based teaching opportunities. Veteran teachers have the experience, longevity, and intimate knowledge of the students—they are the perfect conduit to mediate these reflective opportunities (Marston, Courtney, & Brunetti, 2006).

The examples of collaborative inquiry provided in this chapter highlight how students can become an important and valued voice in the preparation of new teachers. Descriptive inquiry can also allow us to more closely examine our beliefs and practice about students, teaching, and learning. While the current trend in education appears to be focusing on management skills and instructional programs teachers can employ to improve learning, perhaps we need to take a somewhat different tack to include a more reflective stance as we prepare new teachers. Descriptive inquiry allows and encourages each of us to take a moment to critically observe and accept what is occurring in the here and now. The ability to mentally shift gears and focus on the moment in a non-judgmental way reflects what the students quoted earlier described as, "How will I make this day as educated as possible?" Changing the focus from "What can I do to fix this child?" to one of simply observing what is occurring at a particular given moment provides opportunities to listen intently to what our students may be trying to say.

Conclusion

As we move toward a renaissance in teacher education, we must work in community, listening to one another, challenging assumptions and institutional "givens." If it is to succeed, this community cannot include only teacher educators. We must also seek out views of preservice and veteran teachers, as well as K–12 students and their parents. Establishing the relationships necessary for these conversations to take place is the first step in achieving the renaissance.

Perhaps we should all begin by asking ourselves to "draw a good teacher," "what's in her/his head," "what's in his/her heart," and how can we make it so.

References

Abbate-Vaughn, J. (2006). "Not writing it out but writing it off": Preparing multicultural teachers for urban classrooms. *Multicultural Education 8*(3), Summer, 41–48.

Brown, E. L. (2004). The relationship of self-concepts to changes in cultural diversity awareness: Implications for urban teacher educators. Urban Review, 26(2), 119–145.

Brown Foundation for Educational Equity, Excellence and Research. (2004, April 11). *Brown v. Board of Education.* Retrieved May 2, 2007, from http://brownvboard.org/summary/index.php.

Chan, E. (2006). Teacher experiences of culture in the curriculum. *Journal of Curriculum Studies, 38*(2), 161–176.

Cushman, K. (2003). *Fires in the bathroom: Advice for teachers from high school teachers.* New York: The New Press.

Feiman-Nemser, S. (2001). From preparation to practice: Designing a continuum to strengthen and sustain teaching. *Teachers College Record, 103*(6), 1013–1055.

Fullan, M. G. (2001). *The new meaning of educational change (3rd ed.).* New York: Teachers College Press.

Good, Thomas L. (1981, February). Teacher expectations and student perceptions: A decade of research. *Educational Leadership, 38*(5), 415–422.

Jackson, P. W. (1968). Life in classrooms. New York: Holt, Rinehart & Winston.

Marcus, G., Gross, S., & Seefeldt, C. (1991). Black and White Students' Perceptions of Teacher Treatment. *Journal of Educational Research, 84*(6), 363–367.

Marston, S., Courtney, V., & Brunetti, G. (2006). The voices of experienced elementary teachers: Their insight into the profession, *Teacher Education Quarterly, 33*(2), 111–131.

MetLife, Inc. (2001). *The MetLife survey of the American teacher 2001: Key elements of quality schools.* New York City: MetLife, Inc. Retrieved from www.metlife.com/WPSAssets/26575530001018400549V1F2001ats.pdf.

Morgan, B. A. (1993). Practical rationality: A self-investigation. *Journal of Curriculum Studies, 25*(2), 115–124.

Morgan-Fleming, B. (1994). *The enactment of a curriculum event.* Unpublished doctoral dissertation. University of Arizona.

Morgan-Fleming, B., & Doyle, W. (1997, August). Children's interpretations of curriculum events. *Teaching and Teacher Education, 13*(5), 499–511.

Morgan-Fleming, B., Marbley, A., & White, J. (2005). Letters from my grandstudents: Recommendations for future teachers. In J. Brophy & S. Pinnegar (Eds.), *Learning from research on teaching: Perspective, methodology, and representation*. New York: Elsevier.

Said, E. (1982, September). The politics of interpretation. *Critical Inquiry, 9*(1), 1–26.

Steffy, B. E., Wolfe, M. P., Pasch, S. H., & Enz, B. J. (Eds.). (2000). *Life cycle of the career teacher*. Thousand Oaks, CA.: Corwin Press.

Taylor, Denny. (1993). *From the child's point of view*. Portsmouth, NH: Heinemann

Turner, Victor. (1986). Images and reflections: Ritual, drama, carnival, film, and spectacle in cultural performance. *The anthropology of performance*. New York: PAJ Publications.

Wasser, J. D., & Bresler, L. (1996). Working in the interpretive zone: Conceptualizing collaboration in qualitative research teams. *Educational Researcher, 25*(5), 5–15.

Zeichner, K., Melnick, S., & Gomez, M. L. (1996). *Currents of reform in preservice teacher education*. New York: Teachers College Press.

CHAPTER 8

Star Tech: The Net Generation!

Ronald A. Berk
Johns Hopkins University

> Ronald A. Berk, Ph.D., is professor emeritus of biostatistics and measurement at Johns Hopkins University. He served as assistant dean for teaching and has received several teaching awards. He is a fellow in the Oxford Society of Scholars. Dr. Berk has published nine books and more than 125 journal articles and book chapters on teaching methods, evaluation of teaching, and humor.

ABSTRACT

> Today's students are super-savvy with technology, experiential, participatory, visual, kinesthetic learners who crave interaction with other students. Their world revolves around music, movies, music videos, PC and video games, and TV programs. It is a remixed, digital, mobile, always-on media environment. This chapter examines the characteristics of these *Net Geners* and how elementary and secondary teacher education programs need to respond to adapt to their needs. How can teachers compete with their level of overstimulation? They can't, but they can tap into it. Teachers can activate the students' prior knowledge of the cultural elements in their world to generate motivation, interest, and attention to learn new material from our world. Teachers need to leverage the music to which the *Net Geners* are listening, the videos and TV programs they're watching, and the games they're playing as teaching tools. These tools can be executed in a cooperative, social, learner-centered environment in which every student can succeed.

Disclaimer: No, this chapter is not about William Shatner or Leonard Nimoy. They are busy on *Boston Legal*, commercials, and whatever. The operative word is "Tech," not "Trek." Technology has changed this generation of students and will change those in utero even more. (*Author Alert:* Before we continue, you need to know that I'm not a teacher educator and don't know whether I could even pick one out of a line-up if he or she were right in front of me. However, I am an educator and I did take teacher preparation courses to teach at the secondary level and actually taught elementary and junior high school for several years in Washington, D.C. That being said, let's get back to the disclaimer.) "How different is this current generation of K–12 students, who have grown up with the Internet and the burgeoning technology?" Try visualizing a typical tween or teenager text messaging her buddy, while listening to her favorite pop singer on her iPod, watching *Real World* on TV, and Googling the local movie theater to order tickets online *all at the same time.* Answer to the question: Really different from all previous generations. "How much has teacher education changed over the past decade to address these differences?" Not enough to keep pace with student changes. A renaissance in teacher preparation is needed. Teacher education has to reinvent itself. Teachers must change along with their students. Hang on to your laser pointer and smart phone. You are in for an exciting, but fun, ride. See you at the end of the chapter.

What We Know about Teaching and Students

The current foundation of what happens in K–12 classrooms throughout the U.S. rests on the preparation of in-service teacher candidates receive and what they know about how students learn. Let's briefly examine those elements before considering what might be changed to redirect teacher preparation in the future.

TEACHER EDUCATION CURRICULA

The curricula of teacher education programs for K–12 consist of three components:

1. Content or "what" is taught in the classroom,
2. Pedagogy or "how" the content is delivered, and
3. Practice or "live student teaching" in real school settings.

The "what" is defined by district and state level standards that describe the knowledge, skills, and abilities (KSAs) for every grade level and subject or course. I could not even begin to cover the "what" in this chapter because I do not have a clue what KSA means. The practice, as far as I am concerned, is the application of the "what" and the "how" in actual classrooms.

By a process of elimination, I have chosen to cover the "how"; otherwise, this chapter would be filled with blank pages. Over the past decade, two major trends or shifts in teaching methods emerged: (1) *learner-centered teaching*, such as active, collaborative, and cooperative learning techniques, with more than a thousand journal articles and 119 studies on its effectiveness (Cornelius-White, 2007), and (2) burgeoning *instructional technology*, which may be online, offline, inline, or outtaline. Based on this method's foundation, the remainder of this section examines students' characteristics and how they affect the teaching process.

STUDENT CHARACTERISTICS

Teaching methods must be built on what we know about our students. They:

- *possess 8.5 intelligences* and each student has a unique intelligence profile (Gardner, 1983, 1993, 1999, 2005; Gardner & Hatch, 1989; Marks-Tarlow, 1995; White, 1998; Williams, Blythe, White, Li, Sternberg, & Gardner, 1996);
- *have 3–7 different learning styles* (Conner & Hodgins, 2000; Felder & Soloman, 2000; Kolb, 2005; Rose, 1985; Schroeder, 1993);
- *learn by inductive discovery*, participating, by doing rather than being told what to do, experiential, hands-on, engaged, constantly connected with first-person learning, games, simulations, and role playing (Oblinger & Oblinger, 2006b; Tapscott, 1998);
- *are intuitive visual communicators*, visually literate, comfortable in an image-rich rather than text-only environment, able to weave together images, text, and sound easily, move between the real and the virtual instantaneously (Frand, 2000; Manuel, 2002);
- *crave social face-to-face interaction* and gravitate toward activities that promote and reinforce conversation, collaboration, and teamwork (Howe & Strauss, 2000; Manuel, 2002; Ramaley & Zia, 2006; Windham, 2005); can move seamlessly between physical and virtual interactions;
- *are emotionally open* to express their feelings, meet new people, and experience different cultures; open to diversity, differences, and sharing personal information with others, whether online or in class (Lenhart, Rainie, & Lewis, 2001; Oblinger & Oblinger, 2006b);
- *respond quickly and expect rapid responses in return*, multitask, moving quickly from one activity or medium to another, such as using instant messaging (IM), the cell or smart phone, and e-mail all at once, while surfing the Web and watching TV (Prensky, 2001; Roberts, 2006); and
- *shift attention rapidly from one task to another*, extremely short attention span,

thrive on immediate gratification, accustomed to the twitch-speed, multitasking, random access, graphics-first, active, connected, fun, fantasy, quick pay-off world of video games, MTV, and Internet (Foreman, 2003; Prensky, 2001).

MULTIPLE INTELLIGENCES AND LEARNING STYLES

The content teachers usually teach is in a verbal or quantitative form. Most often teachers teach reading or English verbally and math quantitatively. That is natural and, perhaps, the easiest for the teacher. However, learning that content is not as easy. Every student has strengths and weaknesses and, for example, if Jerome does not have a strength in quantitative ability, he will struggle in his math courses.

Fortunately, Jerome has other abilities or intelligences according to the latest research in cognitive psychology, up to 8.5 in all. In addition to the aforementioned verbal and quantitative intelligences, there are visual/spatial, bodily/kinesthetic, musical/rhythmic, interpersonal and intrapersonal (equivalent to Goleman's [1998] emotional intelligences), naturalistic, and environmental. (*Note:* Gardner [2005] assigns environmental intelligence a .5 based on current evidence.) Jerome's strengths may lie in visual/spatial and musical/rhythmic. Just imagine: If all teachers could teach by drawing on these intelligences AND quantitative ability, how much more effective could they be? In fact, if they could teach so that four to six intelligences are tapped simultaneously, probably every student could learn the material on most topics without struggling. Such strategies build on students' strengths rather than their weaknesses. Those strengths are translated into their learning styles (Kolb, 2005). Designing teaching methods that systematically consider students' multiple intelligences and their different learning styles is essential for effective teaching of all students (Berk, 2001).

IMPACT OF TECHNOLOGY

The remaining six characteristics listed previously relate to the Millennials (Howe & Strauss, 2000), this *Net Generation* of students who have grown up with the Internet and the related technology (Oblinger & Oblinger, 2006b), born between 1981 and 1994, and post-Millennials, 1995 to present. They have been described as "digital natives" (Prensky, 2001) whereas those of us born before 1981 are "digital immigrants," because we have had to learn the technology on the fly. Among children ages 8–18, 96% have gone online; 74% have access at home, and 61% use the Internet every day (Oblinger & Oblinger, 2006a). Instant messaging (IM) is nearly as common a form of communication and socializing (70%) as e-mail (81%) among teenagers. Almost 13 million use IM.

These experiential, technology savvy *Net Geners* with the attention span of goat cheese (Berk, 2002) want interactivity in the classroom with their peers, the teacher, tools, and concepts. Team experiences provide these students with the active, participatory, visual, collaborative, fast moving, quick thinking, rapid responding, emotionally freeing, spontaneous, combustible vehicle they so badly desire. The learning environment must be active, collaborative, social, and learner-centered for these students to thrive and be successful. Anything less will be considered boring.

Tweaking the Direction of Teacher Preparation for the Future

The foundation described in the preceding section still is not adequate to address the needs of all students in an ever-changing culture. Teachers will need to incorporate the students' culture if they are to be effective. That means knowing the ingredients in a student's world and incorporating those ingredients in the methods teachers are already using, plus creating new and over-the-top strategies to reach all students. An image of our students in 2009 and what can be expected in the future are described next. Recommendations for how all that we know about teaching and learning can be integrated into teacher preparation programs so teachers will be effective in tackling future challenges are also proffered. Four salient issues are examined: (1) ingredients in a student's world, (2) active, social, learner-centered environment, (3) activating prior knowledge, and (4) unique, over-the-top learning experiences.

INGREDIENTS IN A STUDENT'S WORLD

"School is boring. Everything is boring." Ring a bell? I hear this from almost every kid, regardless of age, K–16+. What teacher or parent has not heard those complaints? UCLA's Higher Education Research Institute conducts a national survey of 250,000 college freshman at nearly 500 colleges and universities every year. One of their findings is that more than 40% of the students report that "they are frequently bored in class." That percentage keeps climbing. Despite the fact that we know more about student characteristics, how to teach, how students learn, and technological applications to learning than at anytime previously, nearly half the class of students is probably unmotivated and disinterested in learning now more than they ever have been. Where is the disconnection?

STUDENTS' USES OF TECHNOLOGY

It is a function of what these students deem important. This *Net Generation* has grown up with *Sesame Street*, MTV, PCs, video games, iPods, MP3 players, PDAs, cell/smart phones, and TV/DVD remotes as appendages to their bodies. More than 2 million children ages 6–17 have their own Web site. These are key ingredients in their world. Their use of the technology focuses on music, music videos, movies, PC and video games, and TV programs. They live in a complicated remixed, mashed-up, digital, mobile, always-on media environment (Jenkins, 2006). Their world involves instant communication and produces media overstimulation, where from 6.5–11 hours per day are consumed with multitasking using multimedia. As the lyrics to the Peabo Bryson and Regina Belle hit song from *Aladdin* tell us, we are entering "A whole new world/A new fantastic point of view . . ."

The students' world is not better than or inferior to the teachers'; it is just different. When the students cross the threshold of the classroom door, they enter culture shock. They're numb with understimulation. How can you possibly compete with their world? You cannot. Therein lies the disconnection and it will worsen as their stimulation accelerates with the cultural manifestations of the technology in the future. That is the problem. Now, how do we fix it?

Recommendations

The characteristics of the *Net Geners* should be clearly communicated in foundation courses so future teachers are thoroughly informed from the get-go of the types of students they will be teaching. The impact of these characteristics should be communicated throughout the curriculum as a distinctive strand. The "what" and "how" of teaching at the different levels need to be systematically linked to those characteristics to be able to tailor teaching methods and content to the students at each level. The methods course links are described in the next three sections.

ACTIVE, SOCIAL, AND LEARNER-CENTERED ENVIRONMENT

Effective teaching must consider all of the students' characteristics in order to build novel learning experiences in the classroom; otherwise, students will find ways to access the required information from home, a library, or a retail mall. That means going far beyond the traditional modes of lecture and textbook-based instruction to innovative and creative techniques that draw on their multi-mediated world, multiple intelligences, multiple learning styles, and technological skills as well as what we know about effective teaching practices, such as "learner-centered" teaching (i.e., active and cooperative learning), blended learning, and online teaching. These *Net Geners* want interactivity with their teachers, peers, and technology that permit them to discover their own solutions. They are experiential learners, part of what Jenkins (2006) calls a *participatory culture*; they are not spectators.

Effective Teaching

The most appropriate mantra for "effective teaching" is: *Teaching is all about the students, not about the teachers!* If the students' world and characteristics are ignored and teachers simply use their content expertise and learner-centered teaching methods taught in teacher education methods courses, they will probably be ineffective with many students now and in the future. Teachers have to get into their students' brains and think like them, not like teachers. They need to mentally perform neurosurgery on their right hemisphere and cerebral cortex to find out what makes them tick and view how they teach from their students' perspective, through their eye-sockets (Berk, 2003, 2005).

Recommendations

Methods courses must integrate the elements in the students' world into learner-centered teaching strategies. Collaborative learning techniques may range from the most highly structured cooperative learning exercises (Johnson, Johnson, & Smith, 1991; Kagan, 1992; Millis & Cottell, 1998) at one end of a continuum to the less-structured spontaneity of improvisation at the other. Courses should emphasize how to design new "team" approaches to learning. That's what *Net Geners* want.

 The application of theatrical techniques to teaching would be an asset in the live classroom (Berk, 2002, 2003; Millbower, 2003; Patterson, McKenna-Cook, & Swick, 2006; Timpson, Burgoyne, Jones, & Jones, 1997). Just as theatre can be scripted and also unscripted (improvisation), so can these team activities be scripted cooperative learning exercises and unscripted collaborative learning (improvisation) exercises. For example, one *theatre model* could involve five students role-playing the following:

 Director. Guides everyone to focus on a content topic, concept, or process to develop a skit/parody with/without script

Designer. Creates scenery, costumes, props, lighting, sound, music, videos, and games

Technician. Determines equipment, tools, and resources to execute skit/parody

Writer. Prepares script, if required, and sequence of steps to execute skit/parody

Actor(s). Performs skit/parody

This production team will flesh out the visual image they want to create using the following teaching tools: music, videos, sound effects, games, props, costumes, lighting, sets, and movement. When the final product is performed to illustrate a concept, principle, or process, it will be an unforgettable experience for the team, performers, and entire class. Not only does this collaborative learning activity match the aforementioned characteristics and cultural world of these students, but it draws on their multiple intelligences (i.e., verbal, quantitative, visual/spatial, bodily/kinesthetic, musical/rhythmic, interpersonal, and intrapersonal) and learning styles, plus it fosters deep learning.

Another variation on the theme of collaborative learning is *improvisation* with groups of four or five students. The spontaneity of improvisation can build trust, respect, and team spirit as well as listening, verbal and nonverbal communication, ad-libbing, role-playing, risk-taking, and storytelling skills (Barkley, Cross, & Major, 2005; Moshavi, 2001). A content-generic, easy-to-execute activity, such as "one word at a time/one sentence at a time," "freeze tag," "speech tag," or "gibberish" (Gesell, 1997; Koppett, 2001; Spolin, 1986, 1999) may be more palatable to *Net Geners* at first than the more structured, formal cooperative learning methods. Improvisation involves the co-creation of ideas rather than a teacher-directed or scripted group activity. It can serve as the warm-up or segue to cooperative learning exercises. The methods courses should include all of these strategies in a future teacher's repertoire.

ACTIVATING PRIOR KNOWLEDGE

Teachers need to leverage the music to which the students are listening, the videos and TV programs they're watching, and the games they're playing as instructional tools. These activities are driven by *their* interests and passions as well as by *their* gifts and abilities. Teachers can capitalize on those activities to increase learning. From a cognitive psychology perspective, teachers can activate the students' prior knowledge of these cultural elements in *their world* to generate motivation, interest, and attention to learn new information in the *teachers' world* (Berk, 2001). Only by entering the students' world will teachers be able to connect with them, draw on their interests and what they already know, and extend their knowledge base. That is how teachers can connect with their students.

Recommendations

Technology courses in the teacher preparation program should emphasize the pedagogical value of music, videos, and games in teaching. They can be powerful teaching tools (Berk, 2001, 2002). Teachers should be taught PowerPoint skills beyond the basics of just text material on slides. The classes must cover custom animation, transitions, extracting and converting music to wav format and videos to mpeg, avi, and wmv formats for PCs (Macs don't require the same conversions), video streaming, and other techniques to arm teachers with the latest skills.

Pertinent legal issues related to copyright infringement in the use of these various forms of media should also be covered. The U.S. copyright law supports this broad approach to mediated teaching. All of the preceding media as well as print materials can be used by teachers in their classrooms. Title 17 of the U.S. Code in Chapter 1§107 defines the "fair use" provision: "The fair use of copyrighted work . . . for purposes such as . . . teaching, scholarship, or research, is not an infringement of copyright." Teachers should be aware of the requirement that an acknowledgment be given of the copyright holder as the source of the material (e.g., print, music, video clips, and cartoons).

UNIQUE, OVER-THE-TOP LEARNING EXPERIENCES

When students are present in the classroom, teachers need to stretch their imaginations to design learning activities to justify their physical presence in that venue. The time should be used for meaningful, valuable, and unique, yet non-replicable experiences the students could not obtain anywhere else. The students need to be engaged, interacting with peers, and connected to the learning activity. Teachers need to produce learning experiences that students would perceive as worthy of being in class, experiences that will be unforgettable (Berk, 2001, 2005). Over-the-top exercises are appropriate if that is what it takes to get the job done. What can be executed in the live classroom environment that cannot be transmitted online or in any other context? That is the standard or criterion all teachers should strive to attain.

Recommendations

Before entering the classroom for student teaching, maybe the future teachers could take a capstone course in their teacher education programs that would provide an inventory of all the possible teaching and testing strategies one could possibly use. Sorting out the appropriate venues where they may be best implemented would furnish a useful perspective for their application in the classroom. What activities could be completed online, at home, in the library, in the mall, and in class? Consider which activities would waste in-class time and could be assigned elsewhere. What collaborative, theatrical, mediated, participatory exercises could be executed in real class time that would take advantage of the live interaction of students with other students and the teacher? The classroom is the stage for that live performance that can never be repeated. If that is the "how" teachers and students see in their futures, then everyone will be excited to come to class and, maybe, even learn the "what."

A Metaphor for Teaching

How do you conclude a humor-laden chapter like this one? The content has been presented and the recommendations for redirecting teacher education have been proffered. But something is missing. Why go to all the trouble of preparing the various activities for the students, day after day? Teaching is unlike any other profession. There is something special or unique about it. Teaching is more of a calling than a chosen job. It draws on our gifts and intelligences and applies them in creative ways in the classroom. Why do we do it?

I have taught for 37 years. Maybe you have taught even longer. As noted in the opening disclaimer, I taught elementary school and junior high for several years before completing a 30-year stint at Johns Hopkins University. I thought some type of "timeless" metaphor that represents my passion for teaching and its significance as a profession would be appropriate. Hopefully, those of you who share that passion now or in the past will agree.

PUTTING IT ON THE LINE

My search for a metaphor for teaching brought to mind a Broadway musical that opened 33 years ago and then again two years ago: *A Chorus Line* (original in April 1975; revival in October 2006). That show was all about *putting it on the line*, literally and figuratively. A white tape line was placed on the floor across the width of the stage, downstage (near the front), on which the dancers auditioning for the show (within a show) were told to stand. The musical is all about dancers (the gypsies who go from show to show) and the sacrifices they make mentally, physically, and emotionally when they walk onto that stage and put themselves on the line in every performance. They bare their body and soul before a live audience every day, sometimes twice a day; every part of their being is tested. There is nowhere to hide.

Putting it on the line could be a metaphor for other careers and even life in general. The show's creator, director, and choreographer, the late Michael Bennett, did not realize the symbolism in this line until it was drawn on the stage before one of the out-of-town pre-Broadway try-outs. The significance and meaningfulness of that line became apparent as members of the theatre audience communicated how the line related to their occupations and lives.

Consider for a moment how soldiers in Iraq and Afghanistan, police officers, and firefighters put their lives on the line every day. Many other professionals put their skills on the line in a variety of ways through the manner in which they execute their jobs. Examples include physicians, lawyers, athletes, bank robbers, and Jack Bauer on *24*.

The line has personal significance to most anyone who saw *A Chorus Line*. He or she could relate to that line and what it meant through the songs in the show:

- the commitment ("The Music and the Mirror"),
- the sacrifices ("What I Did for Love"),
- the preparation ("I Can Do That"; "At the Ballet"; "Nothing"),
- the performance ("One"), and
- the satisfaction.

APPLICATION TO TEACHING

Do teachers *put it on the line*? They must or the preceding paragraphs are totally pointless. The parallels between Broadway dancing and teaching in the classroom are striking:

- Have you made the *commitment* to be the best teacher you can be?
- Have you made significant *sacrifices* in the process?
- What teacher *preparation* did you complete to become the teacher you are today? Do you continue learning new techniques to add to your repertoire? Do you pass down your knowledge and experiences through your *preparation* for every class?
- Are you *performing* every day in real time? Do you feel you are constantly being tested or challenged by your students? Do you bare your mind, heart, and soul before your students? It's almost impossible not to, given the time you're together. Do you lose your mind?

- Are you *satisfied* at the end of your class or day? Do you experience a "teaching high"?

Certainly, the best teachers experience all of the satisfactions listed above, and more. They probably finish their performance exhausted, but also extremely satisfied with what they accomplished. What a feeling when you know you have given it everything you have. That is *putting it on the line* for your students. *Ultimately, it is the students' futures that are on the line.*

Challenge to Teacher Education

Teacher education programs represent the "working rehearsals" for the live performance of a career in teaching. Those rehearsals must be thorough and demanding in addressing the content and the pedagogy. The latter, in particular, will need to shift direction with this new generation of students and those to come in the future. Basic foundations and methods courses in elementary and secondary level teacher preparation programs need to address all of the characteristics of these students by incorporating the following in the curricula: music, videos, TV programs, and games; improvisation and cooperative learning methods; theatrical techniques; and the latest technology. These strategies will draw on the students' multiple intelligences, learning styles, uses of multiple media, and their abilities to multitask.

The challenge will be to make these changes to facilitate the teacher-student connection and effective teaching before student teaching begins. Student teaching is the "dress rehearsal" and "previews." All of these preparation experiences in the programs lead to opening day. Of course, in between graduation and opening day, it is assumed that the state teacher licensure/certification exam has been passed.

"Opening day" in the classroom is just like a Broadway opening. The students will immediately size up the first class as a smash hit or a flop. The reviews will come in quickly. The quality of the teacher preparation and student teaching rehearsals will ultimately determine the nature of the opening as well as the success and run of the production for the rest of the year. The challenge is clear. May the efforts invested to update and refocus teacher education programs in the areas described in this chapter result eventually in lots of long-running hits in classrooms nationwide that would contribute to—and help constitute—a renaissance in teacher education that resonates with the Net Generation.

References

Barkley, E. F., Cross, K. P., & Major, C. H. (2005). *Collaborative learning techniques: A handbook for college faculty.* San Francisco: Jossey-Bass.

Berk, R. A. (2001). Using music with demonstrations to trigger laughter and facilitate learning in multiple intelligences. *Journal on Excellence in College Teaching, 12*(1), 97–107.

Berk, R. A. (2002). *Humor as an instructional defibrillator: Evidence-based techniques in teaching and assessment.* Sterling, VA: Stylus Publishing.

Berk, R. A. (2003). *Professors are from Mars, Students are from Snickers.* Sterling, VA: Stylus Publishing.

Berk, R. A. (2005). Laughterpiece theatre: Humor as a systematic teaching tool. *Teaching Excellence, 17*(2). (Available from www.ronberk.com.)

Conner, M., & Hodgins, W. (2000). Learning styles. Retrieved November 9, 2006, from www.learnactivity.com/learningstyles.html.

Cornelius-White, J. (2007). Learner-centered teacher-student relationships are effective: A meta-analysis. *Review of Educational Research, 77,* 113–143.

Felder, R. M., & Soloman, B. A. (2000). Learning styles and strategies. Retrieved July 14, 2006, from www.ncsu.edu/felder-public/ilsdir/styles.html.

Foreman, J. (2003, July/August). Next generation: Technology versus the lecture. Retrieved April 10, 2007, from www.educause.edu/ir/library/pdf/erm0340.pdf.

Frand, J. (2000). The information-age mindset: Changes in students and implications for higher education. *EDUCAUSE Review, 35*(5), 15–24.

Gardner, H. (1983). *Frames of mind: The theory of multiple intelligences.* New York: Basic Books.

Gardner, H. (1993). *Multiple intelligences: The theory in practice.* New York: Basic Books.

Gardner, H. (1999). *Intelligence reframed: Multiple intelligences for the 21st century.* New York: Basic Books.

Gardner, H. (2005, May). *Multiple lenses on the mind.* Paper presented at the ExpoGestion Conference, Bogota, Columbia.

Gardner, H., & Hatch, T. (1989). Multiple intelligences go to school: Educational implications of the theory of multiple intelligences. *Educational Researcher, 18*(8), 4–9.

Gesell, I. (1997). *Playing along 37 group learning activities.* Duluth, MN: Whole Person Associates.

Goleman, D. (1998). *Working with emotional intelligence.* New York: Bantam Books.

Howe, N., & Strauss, W. (2000). *Millennials rising: The next great generation.* New York: Vintage Books.

Jenkins, H. (2006). *Convergence culture: Where old and new media collide.* New York: New York University Press.

Johnson, D. W., Johnson, R. T., & Smith, K. A. (1991). *Cooperative learning: Increasing college faculty instructional productivity* (ASHE-ERIC Higher Education Report No. 4). Washington, DC: The George Washington University School of Education and Human Development.

Kagan, S. (1992). *Cooperative learning*. San Juan Capistrano, CA: Resources for Teachers, Inc.

Kolb, D. A. (2005). *The Kolb Learning Style Inventory—version 3.1: Self-scoring and interpretation booklet*. Boston: Hay Resources Direct.

Koppett, K. (2001). *Training to imagine: Practical improvisational theatre techniques to enhance creativity, teamwork, leadership, and learning*. Sterling, VA: Stylus Publishing.

Lenhart, A., Rainie, L, & Lewis, O. (2001). *Teenage life online: The rise of instant-message generation and the Internet's impact on friendships and family relationships*. Washington, DC: Pew Internet and American Life Project. (Also available from www.pewinternet.org/pdfs/PIP_Teens_Report.pdf.)

Manuel, K. (2002). *Teaching information literacy to generation Y*. New York: Haworth Press.

Marks-Tarlow, T. (1995). *Creativity inside out: Learning through multiple intelligences*. Reading, MA: Addison-Wesley.

Millbower, L. (2003). *Show biz training*. New York: American Management Association (AMACOM).

Millis, B. J., & Cottell, P. G., Jr. (1998). *Cooperative learning for higher education faculty*. Phoenix, AZ: Oryx Press.

Moshavi, D. (2001). Yes and . . . : Introducing improvisational theatre techniques to the management classroom. *Journal of Management Education, 25*(4), 437–449.

Oblinger, D. C., & Oblinger, J. L. (2006a). Is it age or IT: First steps toward understanding the net generation. In D. C. Oblinger & J. L. Oblinger (Eds.), *Educating the net generation*. EDUCAUSE. Retrieved November 14, 2006, from www.educause.edu.

Oblinger, D. C., & Oblinger, J. L. (Eds.) (2006b). *Educating the net generation*. EDUCAUSE. Retrieved November 14, 2006, from www.educause.edu.

Patterson, J., McKenna-Cook, D., & Swick, M. (2006). *Theatre in the secondary school classroom: Methods and strategies for the beginning teacher*. Portsmouth, NH: Heinemann Drama.

Prensky, M. (2001). Digital natives, digital immigrants, part II: Do they really think differently? *On the Horizon, 9*(6), 15-24. (Also available from www.marcprensky.com/writing/.)

Ramaley, J., & Zia, L. (2006). The real versus the possible: Closing the gaps in engagement and learning. In D. C. Oblinger & J. L. Oblinger (Eds.), *Educating the net generation*. EDUCAUSE. Retrieved November 14, 2006, from www.educause.edu.

Roberts, G. R. (2006). Technology and learning experiences of the net generation. In D. C. Oblinger & J. L. Oblinger (Eds.), *Educating the net generation*. EDUCAUSE. Retrieved November 14, 2006, from www.educause.edu.

Rose, C. (1985). *Accelerated learning*. New York: Dell.

Schroeder, C. C. (1993). New students—New learning styles. *Change 25*(4), 21–26.

Spolin, V. (1986). *Theatre games for the classroom: A teacher's handbook*. Evanston, IL: Northwestern University Press.

Spolin, V. (1999). *Improvisation for the theatre* (3rd ed.). Evanston, IL: Northwestern University Press.

Tapscott, D. (1998). *Growing up digital: The rise of the net generation*. New York: McGraw-Hill.

Timpson, W. M., Burgoyne, S., Jones, C. S., & Jones, W. (1997). *Teaching and performing*. Madison, WI: Magna Publications.

White, J. (1998). *Do Howard Gardner's multiple intelligences add up?* London: Institute of Education, University of London.

Williams, W. M., Blythe, T., White, N., Li, J., Sternberg, R. J., & Gardner, H. (1996). *Practical intelligence for school.* New York: HarperCollins College Publishers.

Windham, C. (2005). Father Google and Mother IM: Confessions of a net gen learner. *EDUCAUSE Review, 40*(5), 45–59.

Summary and Implications

Cheryl J. Craig

Louise F. Deretchin

In Division 2, McBee and Wescott alerted readers to the demands and stresses placed on teachers and the degree to which these pressures detract from positive human interactions and relationships based on an ethic of caring. They particularly centered on "the fallout from the pressures to perform" on both teachers and students. Needless to say, the snapshot the authors presented was bleak and provided ample reason for the need of renaissance.

McBee and Wescott next introduced the philosophical roots of caring and then their study of how aspiring and practicing teachers conceptualize caring in the context of schools. Through the use of open-ended survey questions, the authors elicited what caring means to flesh-and-blood educators in real-life situations. According to McBee and Wescott, caring, as perceived by their research participants, fell into such categories as offering help, candidates and compassion, showing an interest in and getting to know students, listening to learners, and teaching caring. Then McBee and Wescott revisited the literature, unearthing other dimensions of caring teachers. This served to further embellish the categories and provided grist for their inclusion of an annotated bibliography of relevant children's literature, among a number of other teaching strategies that promote caring teaching practices.

McBee and Wescott ended their chapter with an appeal to readers and those who they teach. The authors acknowledged that prospective teachers, practicing teachers, and teacher educators frequently exhibit the characteristics of caring in the course of their work. What McBee and Wescott urged, however, was for readers to be deliberate and intentional about practicing an ethic of care in their relationships and interactions and creating an ethos of care in their classroom and school contexts. They especially emphasized that role-modeling is important, particularly on the part of teacher educators. For the authors, mindful attention to caring and the qualities of caring would do much to spur a renaissance in teaching and teacher education.

Somewhat like McBee and Wescott, McIntosh, Chen, Villareal, and Godine also argued for a quality that restores a sense of wholeness to teaching. For these authors, however, the quality was spirituality. To McIntosh et al., spiritual characteristics can be defined as justice which encompasses a sense of righteousness, compassion which involves acceptance of others, personal fulfillment which involves healing and wholeness, and community which rests on affirmation of self and includes identification with racial and ethnic history.

Using these characteristics as a framework for analysis, McIntosh et al. introduced a *Where I'm From* poetry writing activity in which the preservice teachers at their institution probed their origins and their identities and shared their passions for teaching. In the process, all sorts of connections and disconnections between the teacher candidates and their future urban students surfaced. Additionally, barriers to growth and progress became known.

In conclusion, McIntosh et al. maintained that the inclusion of the spiritual in teaching and teacher education is entirely dependent on teacher educators who realize that "spiritual connections . . . impact teaching" and hence, take important actions that contribute to this dimension of a renaissance in teaching. Furthermore, like McBee and Wescott, McIntosh et al. viewed the teacher educator as being absolutely integral to spearheading this much needed change.

Ben-Peretz and Landler-Pardo additionally addressed a neglected component in teacher education programs. However, their topic was not a dilemma or a problem, which is the dominant way of approaching teacher education, as current reviews of the literature suggest. On the contrary, the authors argued that the problematic nature of teaching is given far too much emphasis in teacher education programs and the joys, rewards, and pleasures of the profession are given short shrift.

Ben-Peretz and Landler-Pardo made their case by interviewing experienced teachers and surveying course offerings of several prominent national and international teacher education programs. While teacher education programs are constantly under revision, the authors found that none appeared to have taken into account the psychic satisfactions—the eros (Schwab, 1954)—that experienced teachers repeatedly identify as part of what sustains them in their chosen profession.

But the author team did not leave the discussion hanging here. They shared the omission they uncovered with administrators of teacher education programs, inquiring how such an oversight might be ameliorated. In response, a number of viable approaches were offered. To Ben-Peretz and Landler-Pardo, these approaches, together with the overall attention afforded the joys and rewards of teaching, would do much to showcase the fruits of teaching. In turn, this appreciation would create movement in a positive direction toward renaissance in the field.

Nona Lyons's chapter came next. It centered on education for inquiry through reflective portfolio-making and discussed the complexities of context that the human genome researchers bafflingly encountered. Lyons's opening vignette caused readers to imagine the complexities present in experiments even when variables are controlled. Lyons then introduced the details of the University of College Cork (UCC) project around which her chapter took shape.

Lyons's discussion focused on three major issues: practitioners' perspectives of their engagement in an inquiry context, the author's view concerning scaffolding for inquiry, and perspectives gained as a consequence of the reflective portfolio process and the new understandings afforded by it. Lyons then guided readers through her work by strategically placing inquiry questions in her discussion. Readers subsequently learned of three building blocks in the UCC project that promoted engagement and inquiry: the introduction of a conceptual framework, a series of portfolio seminars, and a meta-cognitive reflective review through reflective portfolio development.

Through Lyons's meticulous attention to detail, readers came to know the intellectual heft and rigor that formed the nexus of the UCC project. Additionally, reflective portfolio development was presented as a vehicle for professors to think hard about the context of their teaching in ways that spilled over to—and affected—student engagement and learning.

All in all, the implications of Lyons's study were many. The raised consciousness of learning meant that professors better understood themselves as learners, became more creative in their teaching, and became increasingly awakened to the ethical nature of their work. Such practices and perspectives significantly add to our understanding of a renaissance in teacher education.

On the heels of Lyons's chapter dealing with faculty development, readers were introduced to the Morgan-Fleming, Kendrik-Mercer, Myers, and Anderson chapter, which wisely included the voices of children who were predominantly African American in imagining a renaissance in teaching education. Desirous of avoiding exclusions and hegemonies that favor adults or children of other races, the author team created an environment where researchers, teachers, and students worked together to share voice and power.

The shared activity began with a handout that invited students to draw their versions of good teachers, to describe what was in his/her head and heart, and to offer advice concerning how teacher educators could help people become good teachers. The students then provided many thoughtful responses to the aforementioned queries. What was in the good teacher's head, for example, included subject matter knowledge, teaching strategies, ways to motivate students, and ideas about how to be a good role model. But what was also there was the desire to make the day as educative as possible and to not show prejudice. In addition, in the teacher's heart, there was a love for all children, a positive attitude, and a sense of never giving up. But, additionally, there was an absence of prejudice, a desire to be a good person, a feeling of trustworthiness, and the ability to handle stress without taking it out on the wrong people.

Finally, when the question concerning how teacher educators could help people become teachers was broached, the students had much advice to offer. Once again, statements about avoiding premature judgment and acting in prejudiced manners appeared. Then, too, lessons about being strong, patient, caring, happy, fun, and "tuff" were emphasized. The idea of sharing your life and how you overcame obstacles with others was additionally stressed. So, too, was the notion of actively developing a personal knowledge of the students with whom you work. In the end result, Morgan-Fleming et al. recommended that adults and children work in community and listen closely to the voices of individuals while at the same time challenging assumptions and institutional givens. For the team of authors, relationship, conversation, and culturally responsive pedagogy were absolutely necessary for achieving the renaissance to which they—and the K–12 and preservice teacher education students with whom they work—are moving toward.

Following the Morgan-Fleming et al. chapter was the Berk chapter. If the Morgan-Fleming et al. chapter reminded us of the wisdom of children, the Berk chapter reminded us that serious matters can be approached in humorous ways. Working from the assumption that humans have 8.5 intelligences, Berk took the position that we are using only a small number of these intelligences at too high a frequency and that it is possible to teach so that four to six intelligences can be tapped simultaneously. He also asserted that technology needs to be used in the ways that students encounter it in the context of their lives. To Berk, teacher education especially lags behind in this area.

Consequently, Berk recommended that teaching and teacher education programs be "tweaked" through drawing "ingredients from students' worlds." For example, teachers and teacher educators must take the locus of attention away from themselves and place it on their students. One way to do this would be to embrace a theatre model in which each of five students have specific roles to play and are dependent on one another for the success of their shared enterprise. Another way would be to focus on improvisation, which includes game-playing, role-playing, risk-taking, and storytelling. Still other approaches would be to integrate music and increase the pedagogical value of music, videos, and games in teaching.

Berk then went on to unpack the "putting it on the line" metaphor. For him, the metaphor connects with the Broadway musical, *A Chorus Line*, as well as the notion of serving on the frontline in Iraq or Afghanistan. But the metaphor also has applicability to education. Berk concluded his lively chapter with a number of deadly serious questions, all of which pertained to teachers laying their teaching commitment "on the line."

Combined, the six chapters in Division 2 introduced readers to a wide range of practices and perspectives that would greatly enhance teacher education as we currently know it. These included infusing teacher education with an ethic and ethos of caring, mindfully addressing the spiritual dimensions of teaching, promoting the joys and rewards of teaching over the career span, scaffolding the reflective portfolio process to enable teacher educators and prospective teachers to think well in contexts, listening to the voices of children, and becoming attuned to the technological milieu within which the current generation of teacher educators and students learn. Aggregated, this set of chapters illuminated specific dimensions of a renaissance in education as envisioned by particular authors and co-authors.

Reference

Schwab, J. J. (1954). Eros and education. *Journal of General Education*, 8, 54–71.

Division 3
ALTERING CONTENT

Overview and Framework

Cheryl J. Craig

Louise F. Deretchin

In Division 3, Altering Content, our attention turns to what Schwab referred to as subject matter in his curriculum commonplaces. However, this set of chapters extends well beyond content area considerations to include theoretical and legal adjustments to teacher education curriculum.

Chapter 9, "The Reimagination of a Graduate Reading Program: Roles and Responsibilities, Themes, Reflections, and Implications" written by Kathleen Malu, Salika Lawrence, and Geraldine Mongillo, provides a detailed description of the process these co-authors went through to reimagine a graduate reading program. What provoked the authors to shift their practices and the kinds of changes they made are included in the discussion as well as the recommendations they offer other teacher education programs.

In Chapter 10, "Preservice Teachers' Beliefs about Curriculum Theory: Is It Meaningful and/or Useful?," Elida Giraldo examines the absence of curriculum theory in early childhood education classes. She argues for revisiting the role of curriculum studies in preservice education and the richer kinds of discourses that curriculum insights can offer teachers and teaching.

Chapter 11, "Professionalism vs. Reality: Student Awareness of Legal Rights and Responsibilities," is written by former principal and teacher association director Rita Pokol Poimbeauf. In it, she presents situations she encountered in the public schools in which teachers, due to their lack of knowledge of their rights and responsibilities, found themselves in legally charged circumstances. In her opinion, teachers and prospective teachers must be aware of the problematic situations in which they find themselves. To Poimbeauf, teacher education most certainly has a role to play here.

Meanwhile, Chapter 12, "Student Teachers' Diversity Rights: The Case Law," is authored by legal experts, Zorka Karanxha and Perry Zirkel. These professors argue that student teachers are largely unprotected when problems emerge in their student teaching situations. The small body of available case literature indicates that outcomes typically favor defendant institutions. For Karanxha and Zirkel, a renaissance in teacher education would necessarily include the instruction of preservice teachers in preventative law.

These four chapters, one rooted in subject matter, one advocating for curriculum theory, and two addressing law as a necessary component of teacher education, comprise the ways that the authors in Division 3 imagined altering the content of teacher education programs.

CHAPTER 9

The Reimagination of a Graduate Reading Program
ROLES AND RESPONSIBILITIES, THEMES, REFLECTIONS, AND IMPLICATIONS

Kathleen F. Malu
William Paterson University

Salika A. Lawrence
William Paterson University

Geraldine Mongillo
William Paterson University

Kathleen F. Malu, Ph.D., teaches in the Graduate Reading Program. Her research interests include middle level and multicultural education, qualitative research, and teacher education. Her recent publications include "Ways of Reading *Harry Potter*: Multiple Stories for Multiple Reader Identities," contained in E. Heilman (Ed.), *Harry Potter's World: Multidisciplinary Critical Perspectives* (New York: Routledge/Falmer) and "Framing an Urban School-University Partnership: A Critical Analysis," found in M. Caskey (Ed.), *Making a Difference: Action Research in Middle Level Education—A Volume in the Handbook of Research in Middle Level Education* (Greenwich, CT: Information Age Publishing).

Salika A. Lawrence, Ph.D., teaches courses in the Graduate Reading Program and undergraduate courses in the preservice secondary education program. Her research interests include adolescent literacy, secondary instruction, and teacher education. Her most recent publication is "Teaching adult learners: Effective techniques," which is published in the *Language, Literacy and Learning Newsletter*, 3(1), 3–4.

Geraldine Mongillo, Ph.D., is the director of and teaches courses in the Graduate Reading Program. Her research interests include teacher preparation, adolescent literacy, and professional development of reading teachers. Her most recent publication is "Improving Expository Writing of Preservice Teachers in an Online Environment (with H. Wilder), in *Contemporary issues in technology & teacher education* (2007).

ABSTRACT

This chapter examines the process that three professors in higher education engaged in to reimagine their graduate reading program. This reimagination began when the authors asked: What knowledge, experiences, and dispositions do reading professionals need to ensure children's success? To answer this question the authors engaged in a yearlong process of discussion, reflection, and curriculum mapping. This process resulted in the production, interpretation, and application of knowledge that they used to reimagine the reading program. This chapter presents the knowledge and findings from this process. Beginning with a program overview and the roles and responsibilities that candidates are expected to assume as reading specialists, the authors highlight the theory and research that support the program. The three principle themes of knowledge, experiences, and dispositions are used to present the activities that are scaffolded through the program. The article concludes with reflections on the process of reimagination and the implications for future teacher preparation programs.

For children to become successful, critical participants in our democratic society, we know they will need to be fluent, thoughtful readers and writers. But what knowledge, experiences, and dispositions do reading professionals need to ensure children's success? This was the question we asked ourselves during a yearlong process in which we reimagined our graduate reading program by engaging in discussion, reflection, and curriculum mapping.

The chapter begins with a rationale for engaging in this reimagination of our program. Next, we present an overview of our program and the roles and responsibilities that our candidates need to assume as reading professionals. This is followed by highlights of our program and the theory and research lenses that inspire our professional work. We next identify the three principle themes in our program and the activities we use to scaffold these themes throughout the program. We conclude with our reflections on this process of reimagination and the renaissance we envision for teacher preparation programs as we move forward.

Graduate Reading Program: Roles and Responsibilities of Reading Professionals

The authors are three full-time faculty members who teach seven of the nine required courses in the graduate reading program. Mindful of Schwab's (1969/ 1978) call for a renaissance in the curriculum, we decided to meet on a regular basis throughout the year to try to reimagine our teaching and the courses we offer in our reading program. It was important for us to engage in this activity because we taught the same courses for several years and did not want to perpetuate what Schwab would consider a "moribund" approach. We wanted our curriculum to be dynamic, creative, and fluid.

The graduate reading program at William Paterson University is open to candidates who hold a state teaching license and have two years of teaching experience. Our program complies with the International Reading Association (IRA) standards for the preparation of reading professionals (IRA, 2004a) and the reading certification requirements set forth by the State of New Jersey.

Our 33 credit program typically takes candidates three years to complete and is designed to become increasingly more challenging as candidates progress through the program. On average we have 25 graduates per year and approximately 100 candidates enrolled in our courses. We, the authors, joined the university faculty at different points in our professional careers. We have a combined total of 30 years of P–12 classroom experience and 15 years of experience teaching in this reading program. Graduates of our program typically obtain positions as reading specialists or reading/literacy coaches. These professionals are expected to assume roles and responsibilities in three broad areas: instruction, assessment, and leadership (IRA, 2000; IRA, 2004b).

In the area of instruction, reading professionals must be excellent, experienced classroom teachers who can work successfully with children in and outside of classroom settings. These professionals are expected to work collaboratively with teachers to improve and enhance literacy teaching in the classroom. Reading professionals must be able to model what they consider best teaching practices and observe, thoughtfully critique, and offer suggestions to teachers. In the area of assessment, reading professionals need to have in-depth knowledge of reading processes, reading acquisition and development, assessment tools, and reading programs and curricula. Reading professionals additionally must be able to diagnose student literacy learning needs and remediate them by designing effective instruction for such students. These professionals are also expected to identify and evaluate schoolwide and districtwide literacy programs.

Leadership may be the most important role that reading professionals must assume. They need to lead teachers and school administrators in professional development workshops, inform school communities of literacy policy and research, and assume leadership roles in all curricula decisions. They need to be skilled in making and maintaining home-school connections and serving as resources for all of these constituencies.

These "real world" roles and expectations for reading professionals guided our inquiry into and reimagination of the curriculum. With these areas in mind, we examined and reshaped our program to better prepare our candidates for the demands they will encounter as literacy specialists.

Lenses Used to Examine the Graduate Reading Program

In our roles as graduate reading faculty, we integrate the lenses of theory and research to frame our teaching, reflection, and reimagination of the graduate reading program. A sampling of the theory and research we draw on follows.

First, Vygotsky's (1934/1987) theory of social interaction is critical to us. Discussions are important components in all our classes and in our own professional growth. It was through our reading program discussions that we identified areas for planning and reflection. Second, Freire and Macedo (1987) maintained that literacy learning needs to engage readers with immediate problems that they encounter in their worlds. We use their scholarly contributions to help our teachers problematize reading experiences and make them meaningful and immediately relevant for their learners. Third, Rosenblatt (1994) theorized that reading may be a transactional process in which readers bring their unique experiences and interpretations of text to their readings. This theory also underpins a majority of our work with texts throughout the program.

Although there is a nationwide call to increase the number of reading professionals (IRA, 2000; IRA, 2004b; United States Department of Education, 2002), reports on the preparation of teachers to teach reading typically address the quality of preservice teacher preparation. Walsh, Glaser, and Wilcox (2006) report that few reading programs adequately prepare preservice teachers to work successfully with children in K–12 settings. Most elementary education programs do not teach the science of reading instruction or provide opportunities for teacher candidates to learn how to teach using a balanced literacy approach (Walsh, Glaser, & Wilcox, 2006). Studies that report on the use of action research in teacher preparation examine the preparation of preservice teachers (Collier & Meyers, 2002) as well. To our way of thinking, these reports that seek better teacher preparation programs support a renaissance in teacher education to better prepare candidates for current and future P–12 settings.

One of the most significant areas in teacher preparation that needs scrutiny is the preparation of candidates to work with students from diverse backgrounds to meet their diverse needs. It is clear from our experiences, the settings in which our candidates work, and a wide variety of studies and discussions (e.g., Battle Vold & Pattnaik, 2002; Robinson, 2002) that the typical American classroom is and will continue to include a rainbow of multicultural children. We believe it is imperative that the candidates in our program learn to work successfully with children from diverse social and cultural backgrounds (Banks, 2003).

Due to the increasing demands for technology and information literacy skills in our society, another area to examine is the opportunities candidates have to develop technology skills. Leu and Kinzer (2000) note the need for all teachers to become technologically fluent and critical consumers of Internet information. Given the deictic nature of literacy and technology, they note that teachers may not be able to learn all aspects of technology. What may be more important is that teachers understand how they learn and become expert learners so they can learn whatever technology may be relevant and useful for classroom instruction at the time.

It is through the lenses of these theories and research that we are inspired in our practices as teacher educators. We use these lenses as we work to prepare our candidates to meet the needs of their students and other constituents including school administrators, teachers, and parents.

Program Themes

Using the workplace roles and responsibilities that our graduates are expected to assume and our college National Council for the Accreditation of Teacher Education (NCATE) theme of *"preparing inquiring educators,"* we reimagined our program. In this reconceptualization, we identified the themes of knowledge, inquiry, and dispositions. We sequenced the courses, identified content, and scaffolded activities to become progressively more challenging. We included multicultural education and technology in all of these themes and across all courses. For example, one course, Socio-Psycholinguistics and Reading, focuses almost exclusively on multicultural experiences of P–12 students and how these experiences may impact their literacy development. Two courses offered online give candidates intense technology experiences.

Reading professionals need a broad knowledge base within the area of reading. They need to demonstrate this knowledge and use it to inquire, investigate, and problem solve. One of the knowledge activities that threads through the program is the synthesis of research (see Table 9.1).

In two first-year courses, Theoretical Foundations of Literacy and Socio-

Table 9.1 Knowledge Activity

Knowledge Activity	Year 1	Year 2	Year 3
Read and synthesize research	Synthesize one theory (5- to 7-page paper) Synthesize 3 research studies	Report on a commercial reading program Research and critique a school-wide reading program	Synthesize 5–7 literacy theories and 1–15 research studies for master's thesis, Chapters 1 and 2 (included in the literature review are studies conducted in multicultural settings)

Psycholinguistics and Reading, candidates prepare a synthesis of one theory and three research studies of their choice on a literacy topic. In the second-year course, Administration and Supervision of Reading Programs, candidates work in groups to investigate and learn about commercial reading programs and individually select a schoolwide literacy program to research and critique. In the third-year courses, Practicum in Reading and Research in Reading, candidates complete a master's thesis—a qualitative research study of a professional problem in the area of teaching and literacy that concerns them in their classroom. Typically, they must synthesize 5–7 literacy theories and 10–15 research articles as part of their literature review for their proposed study. By giving candidates choices in these activities, they develop critical literacy skills which engage them in reflection and encourage them to explore relevant issues they encounter in their own professional lives.

Another theme that is evident throughout the graduate program is teacher inquiry. We define the theme of inquiry as a process of investigating a teaching and learning problem (see Table 9.2), identifying a solution, and reflecting on the experience. This is evident in the coursework mentioned above and in other courses throughout the program. In a few courses, inquiry and technology merge to help candidates develop their critical and information literacy skills. For instance, in two first-year courses conducted online in an asynchronous environment (Children's Literacy in the 21st Century and Adult and Adolescent Literacy in the 21st Century), candidates prepare presentations that rise to the challenge of Leu and Kinzer (2000). Candidates must solve the problem of preparing a class critical issues presentation without meeting face-to-face. Exam-

Table 9.2 Inquiry Activity

Inquiry Activity	Year 1	Year 2	Year 3
Investigate problem, solve and reflect	Critical issues: Online presentations with reflective essay using research-based strategies	Child literacy study to diagnose and remediate reading problems	Select several research participants; Research question and problematize, gather data, analyze, reveal findings, and reflect on research

ples of critical issues presentation topics include "The Digital Divide," "Gender and Ethnic Bias," "Intergenerational Literacy and Technology," "Politics and Literacy," "Censorship," "Standard English, IM-ing and Youth Culture." During their presentation week, candidates lead the discussions online and are responsible for prompting and provoking controversy, critical thinking, and discussion. Candidates must present a reflective essay at the end of the week's presentation.

As shown in Table 9.2, candidates conduct a yearlong child study in the courses Diagnosis of Reading Problems and Remediation of Reading Problems in which they must diagnose and remediate a child's reading problem. Then, in year three is the master's thesis in which candidates identify a research question, problematize it, gather data, and analyze them. For this study candidates must use several research participants. In their final chapter candidates reflect on their findings and their classroom work, suggest changes to improve their work with children, and recommend directions for future research. These research studies result in a five chapter thesis.

The third program theme is dispositions (see Table 9.3). Using the standards

Table 9.3 Dispositions

Dispositions	Year 1	Year 2	Year 3
IRA standard: follows through on suggestions/ recommendations for further study	Critical issues: Presentations in online courses	Child study in reading diagnosis and remediation courses	Master's thesis research report

from the IRA (2004a), we developed dispositions for our program and identified specific courses in which we expect to observe them. The disposition that states, "Candidates in our program follow through on suggestions/recommendations for further study," can be observed in all courses. Specifically when candidates prepare their critical issues presentations in the two online courses, the university faculty review the presentations and make suggestions for changes to the information contained in their presentations and additions that will improve these presentations. If candidates follow through on these suggestions then they have met this disposition in these courses.

This sequence of activities—faculty review with feedback, suggestions on a candidate product, and the expectation that candidates follow through on these suggestions—is evident in the second-year courses with the child study. In this course the university faculty supervises the candidate's work of diagnosing and remediating the child's literacy needs and offers suggestions and feedback that candidates are expected to use to improve their work with the child. In the third-year courses with the master's thesis, there are considerable opportunities for candidates to receive feedback and suggestions from the faculty mentor and their classmates. Multiple drafts of research chapters are systematically viewed, reviewed, and re-viewed numerous times with many opportunities for candidates to reconsider, reframe, and reshape their studies to reimagine their practice, drawing on current research-based knowledge.

Reflections

After our reading program passed the IRA folio review and our college was awarded NCATE re-accreditation, we decided that we wanted to better understand the experiences our candidates had as they proceeded through our program. We began to discuss our program by following the sequence of courses from the perspective of candidates experiencing our program. These discussions led us to consider reimagining the program. There was one moment, in particular, that we attribute to our desire to change it. It was, specifically, after one program meeting when we struggled with the notion of requiring candidates to join a professional organization, based on IRA Standard 5.2 (IRA, 2004a). Through our discussion we learned that two of us required our candidates to join the IRA in two different courses. Based upon that realization we became curious about what we each required in our courses. Consequently we sought to reform our program so our candidates obtained experiences that were more cohesive and built upon prior knowledge gained through earlier courses in the program. Another goal was to increase the communication among faculty members about program goals, curriculum reimagination, and the needs of our candidates.

We decided to meet systematically, which we did, holding formal monthly graduate reading program meetings. We also found ourselves holding informal office and hallway "chats" whenever we could. As we listened to each of us discuss the courses we taught, we asked each other questions about our teaching styles, assignments and activities, rubrics and expectations, and our use of dispositions. Based upon these discussions we began to revamp our program and recognized that we needed to hold ourselves to the same standards we required of our candidates, specifically IRA Standard 5.3: Work with colleagues to observe, evaluate, and provide feedback on each other's practice (IRA, 2004a).

When we reflect back on this process, we find there were three patterns in our discussions. Our discussions focused on the areas of repetitions, omissions, and academic challenges within and across the courses in our program. We created a simple, blank curriculum map (see Table 9.4) and systematically shared the content we addressed in our courses, the articles, texts, and theory we assigned candidates to read, the technology used, the areas of multicultural focus, the assignments and activities, and the workplace roles and responsibilities we believed our courses addressed. Once we gathered all of this information and we all understood what we each taught and how, we brainstormed to identify repetitions in our program. One example was our duplication of the professional membership requirement. Another was our assignment to synthesize three to five research studies in two different courses. Once identified, these repetitions were easily eliminated.

Similarly we used the curriculum map to identify overlapping learning experiences or omissions in our curricula. For example, we identified content, experiences, and dispositions that were omitted in our curricula. An example of overlap we found was in the yearlong child study and the research course. In the child study course, candidates were required to work with one child. In the

Table 9.4 Sample of Blank Curriculum Map

Course Number	Content Covered	Theory/ Readings	Technology Used	Multi-cultural Focus	Assignment/ Activities	Workplace Role or Responsibility; IRA Standard
CIRL 623						
CIRL 624						

yearlong research courses we realized that some candidates designed and conducted a study with only one research participant. Candidates did not have experiences studying and managing a progressively larger number of children. We decided to scaffold the number of children with whom the candidates worked, progressing from one student in the second-year courses to several (5–10) in the third-year research sequence of courses.

Another area for which we identified omissions in the curricula was theory. We found that some of us had candidates read about various literacy theories but few of us required them to read the primary source writings of specific theorists. We realized we were supplying our students with "rhetoric of conclusions," not "narratives of inquiry" consistent with our college's preparing inquiring teachers NCATE theme (Schwab, 1962, p. 24). Hence, our discussions led us to identify appropriate original sources to match our courses and the future needs of our candidates.

Unlike the ease with which we were able to identify and make the curricular changes noted above, the pattern of academic challenges has been more difficult to elucidate because the roles and responsibilities of reading professionals continue to evolve. We wonder whether some activities are beyond the scope of a graduate program—reading the original, translated work of Vygotsky (1987). We also wonder if some activities we facilitate in our courses are not rigorous enough. For example, in the Administration and Supervision course before our reimagination, candidates were asked to prepare a professional development workshop, present it to five faculty members at their school, and hand in five completed evaluations as proof of having completed the assignment. We wondered whether this was challenging enough. Candidates could present their professional development workshop to a handpicked, sympathetic group of colleagues. We realized that in the online courses candidates were already preparing professional development workshops, albeit to their classmates, through the critical issues presentations, so we decided to modify the workshop activity in the Administration and Supervision course. To make this activity more relevant to the workplace expectations of reading professionals and increase the academic challenge for this course, we redesigned this activity so that the candidates in this class plan, administer, and conduct a one day literacy conference at the university. We expect this conference to eventually grow to include presentations of research conducted by the candidates from the master's thesis courses, other interested candidates in the program, program graduates, neighboring school faculty, and university faculty.

A second academic challenge we face is the need to have our candidates work with students who do not attend the candidate schools. Throughout our program we always had candidates work with the children in their classrooms. This meant that candidates never developed skills to work with students from different socio-economic, cultural, linguistic, religious, and ethnic backgrounds. This has been our biggest challenge: Finding ways to have our candidates work in different settings with populations of students who are different from their typical classroom students. We hope to resolve this issue by partnering with neighboring after school literacy programs sponsored by the local YMCAs and Boys and Girls Clubs located in the surrounding urban communities.

By identifying repetitions, omissions, and academic challenges within and across the courses in our program, we reconceptualized our graduate reading program to ensure that we maximized the time, effort, and learning of our candidates.

Implications for Teacher Preparation Programs

Despite the fact that we engaged in this deliberative work less than a year after our graduate reading program successfully passed our IRA portfolio review and our college NCATE reaccreditation was awarded, the various activities and reports we prepared for these reviews surprisingly did not engage us in a critical reimagination of our program. However, the NCATE process led us, as individuals and concerned faculty, to engage in this reimagination work.

The reform of our graduate reading program contributes an important component to the literature on the renaissance and reimagination of curriculum and teaching. On the one hand, there is little discussion of explicit curriculum review as reflected in Schwab's call. On the other, faculty may assume they review and revise curriculum when they have no evidence to support their claim. The rationale, strategies, activities, and suggestions for making such curriculum work explicit can be used at any level of education and in any content area.

Through our professionally intriguing discussions, we collaboratively completed a curriculum map which led us to discover the weaknesses in our program and to address them. We drew upon theory and research to inspire us and give us a common language and perspective on our work. We used the Specialty Professional Association Standards for Reading Professionals (IRA, 2004a) regarding the roles and responsibilities of reading professionals to redesign a course of study that prepares reading professionals to work effectively and successfully in the field of literacy development.

Based on our cumulative experiences we identify two important implications for teacher preparation programs. Faculty in teacher education programs should systematically engage in collegial discussions that explicitly examine courses within and across programs to identify repetitions, omissions, and academic challenges that candidates experience. All faculty members who teach in a program should be engaged in and committed to these discussions. In our reading program, we have a total of four faculty members who teach in the program. Thus, we were able to schedule meetings so that we could all meet to engage in these discussions. Our deliberations were typically lively, thought-provoking, inspiring, and intriguing. We agreed that we "got on well" together and this, we believe, was reflected in our work.

Through our discussions about our program, we learned that reflective, collegial conversations, on-going program review, and critical examination are essential. It may not be enough to examine a program prior to an NCATE review. Rather, teacher educators may need to model the reflective processes we expect of our candidates by engaging in on-going, collaborative conversations in our own teacher education communities. These conversations may provide opportunities for identifying success, help teacher educators maintain connections to practitioners, and be instrumental in creating programs that can effectively prepare professionals who are empowered to become dynamic school-based community leaders who can work with all children to become critical, active participants in our democratic society and assume vital responsibilities in the workplaces of tomorrow.

Acknowledgments

The authors are grateful for comments received from the ATE Yearbook blind reviewers and the review panel members. The authors acknowledge the leadership and vision of Dorothy Feola who set us on the path to reimagination of the reading program.

References

Banks, J. A. (Ed.). (2003). *Handbook of research on multicultural education, Second Edition*. New York: John Wiley & Sons.

Battle Vold, E., & Pattnaik, J. (2002). Educators working in culturally diverse schools: Linking Colleges of Education and partnership schools. In J. R. Dangel & E. M. Guyton (Eds.), *Research on preparing teachers who can meet the needs of all students: Teacher education yearbook XVI* (pp. 121–128). Duque, IA: Kendall/Hunt Publishing.

Collier, S., & Meyers, B. (2002). Developing preservice teacher-researchers to meet the needs of individual children. In J. R. Dangel & E. M. Guyton (Eds.), *Research on preparing teachers who can meet the needs of all students: Teacher education yearbook XVI* (pp. 45–66). Duque, IA: Kendall/Hunt Publishing.

Freire, P., & Macedo, D. (1987). *Literacy: Reading the word and the world.* New York: Bergin & Garvey.

International Reading Association. (2000). *Teaching all children to read: Roles of the reading specialist, a position statement of the International Reading Association.* Newark, DE: Author.

International Reading Association. (2004a). *Standards for reading professionals, revised 2003.* Newark, DE: Author.

International Reading Association. (2004b). *The role and qualifications of the reading coach in the United States.* Newark, DE: Author.

Leu, D., & Kinzer, C. (2000). The convergence of literacy instruction with networked technologies for information and communication. *Reading Research Quarterly, 35*(1). 108–127.

Robinson, C. (2002). Forward. In J. R. Dangel & E. M. Guyton (Eds.), *Research on preparing teachers who can meet the needs of all students: Teacher education yearbook XVI* (pp. vii–ix). Duque, IA: Kendall/Hunt Publishing.

Rosenblatt, L. (1994). *The reading, the text, the poem: The transactional theory of the literary work.* Carbondale, IL: Southern Illinois University Press.

Schwab, J. J. (1962). *The teaching of science.* Cambridge, MA: Harvard University Press.

Schwab, J. J. (1969/1978). The practical: A language for curriculum. In I. Westbury & N. J. Wilkof (Eds.) *Science, curriculum, and liberal education: Selected essays* (pp. 287–321). University of Chicago Press.

United States Department of Education. (2002). *No Child Left Behind Act: Public Law 107–110.* Retrieved November 2, 2006, from www.ed.gov/policy/elsec/leg/esea02/107-110.pdf.

Vygotsky, L. S. (1987). Thinking and speech. In R. W. Rieber & A. S. Carton (Eds.), *The works of L. S. Vygotsky* (Vol. 1, pp. 39–288). New York: Plenum Press. (Original work published 1934.)

Walsh, K., Glaser, D., & Wilcox, D. (2006). *What education schools aren't teaching about reading and what elementary teachers aren't learning.* Washington, DC: National Council on Teacher Quality.

Chapter 10

Preservice Teachers' Beliefs about Curriculum Theory
IS IT MEANINGFUL AND/OR USEFUL?

Elida Giraldo
University of Antioquia (Colombia) and Southern Illinois University, Carbondale

> Elida Giraldo, M.S., teaches at the College of Education at the University of Antioquia, Colombia. She is also a Curriculum and Instruction doctoral candidate at Southern Illinois University. Her scholarly interests include curriculum theory, gender issues, early childhood education, and qualitative research.

ABSTRACT

> In early childhood education, curriculum theory does not always have an important place. Typically, preservice teachers are exposed to a technical vision of curriculum that does not allow them to understand the educational practices in which they participate. This chapter emerges from a qualitative case study that takes place in a preschool setting. It is an initial exploration of early childhood preservice teachers' beliefs about curriculum theory and its usefulness in their practice. Findings such as the lack of connection between curriculum theory and practice, the prevalent technical approach to curriculum, and the absence of a comprehensive curriculum theory in the preservice teachers' narratives show that we need to rethink the role of curriculum theory in education as well as the kinds of curriculum discourses that are presented to prospective teachers through the theory offered/enacted in classrooms.

In teaching, theories, skills, and qualities should blend together. Yet, despite the importance of theory, many people seem to believe that the teacher is primarily a technician and that the appropriate preparation for such activity consists of acquiring various technical and procedural skills (Beyer, 1992; Pinar, 2004). In the teacher education literature, little attention has been given to the relevance that curriculum theory has in the preparation of preservice teachers. When theory is addressed, it is often talked about as separate from educational practice and the day-to-day activities of teaching.

Curriculum theory is an interdisciplinary field committed to the study of educational experience (Pinar, 2004). The role of this theory is to provide educators with a broad understanding of the fundamental assumptions, priorities, and values of the practices in which they participate. For that purpose, ideally there should be a dialectical relationship between the practical and theoretic that allows educators to have a more inclusive view of the world (Hooks, 2000; Simon, 1992; Reid, 2001) and engage in more thoughtful and theoretically enriched practice (Beyer, 1992; Darder, 1991; Pinar, 1999).

As the foundation for educational practice is set during teacher education, it is important to examine the place that curriculum theory has in the preparation of teachers and how this is connected to their practice. In this case study, I explore the significance that curriculum theory has for early childhood preservice teachers and the connection that they see between curriculum theory and practice. I present their experiences with curriculum theory as well as the implications that they have for teacher preparation. I argue that not only to imagine but also to create new possibilities in teacher education, we need to do a better job of teaching curriculum theory and connecting it to personal and professional preservice teachers' experiences.

Literature Review

CURRICULUM THEORY

Theory usually refers to "a 'scheme of ideas' that attempts to both describe and explain a particular set of events or practices" (Simon, 1992, p. 80). It offers possible explanations and/or understandings of a particular reality (Koetting & Combs, 2002); it is a way of doing and thinking about that way of doing. It is a set of beliefs that guide both thought and enactment. In this sense, theory has "an integral connection to questions of practice" (Simon, 1992, p. 92), but this connection is not unilateral. Rather, there is a bilateral connection between the two. Theory and practice inform and enrich one another. We need to transcend the false dichotomy that divides theory from practice (Pring, 2000) and/or that subjugates practice to simply an application of theory (Deng, 2004).

Although theory is usually connected to the realm of abstract thinking, we need to link it to the concrete experiences and practices of everyday life (Darder, 1991). "Everything we do in life is rooted in theory" (Hooks, 2000, p. 19). Whether we are aware or not of the rationale for our perspectives, assumptions, and actions, there is an underlying system shaping and directing our thought and practice. Hence, our teaching always reflects what we believe, do, and are.

Curriculum theory involves an exploration of educational experience, "especially (but not only) as that experience is encoded in the school curriculum, itself a highly symbolic as well as institutional structuration of (potentially) educational experience" (Pinar, 2004, p. 20). It is intended to help us to understand and explain the educational significance of the relationships among the curriculum, the individual, society, and history, using multiple lenses and perspectives as well as providing spaces for comprehensive and interdisciplinary analysis. It moves "in multiplicities and lines of flight, not in dualisms or either/ors" (Reynolds & Webber, 2004, p. 2).

A comprehensive curriculum theory should describe and explain curriculum from biographical, cultural, political, and historical perspectives as well as in terms of gender, class, race/ethnicity, sexuality, and geography. In so doing, it needs a multidisciplinary framework that includes attention to different theoretical backgrounds such as phenomenology, postmodernism, poststructuralism, psychoanalysis, gender and sexuality studies, critical theory, and aesthetics.

In contrast to this comprehensive vision of curriculum, we talk about it as if it were simply a set of activities and resources that we use to transmit information to students. Alternatively, Doll (2002) argues that we need to *"reconceptualize the nature of curriculum,* to see it not in terms of plans preset or ideologies advocated, but as an image hovering over the process of education, giving direction and meaning to that process" (p. 23–24, emphasis in original). This means shifting away from the view of curriculum as simply a noun (the courses, plans, methods of instruction and evaluation) and instead thinking of it as a system of relationships, as a "process or method of 'negotiating passages' between ourselves and the text, between ourselves and the students, and among all three" (p. 45).

If we begin with this more comprehensive conception of curriculum, it follows that the preparation of teachers requires transcending mere technicality and understanding curriculum as interdisciplinary. When presented as simply a set of guidelines, the vision of curriculum is distorted and limited as it does not encourage teachers to reflect upon their practice and to confront different views. We see consequences of this limited view of curriculum in Olson's (2000) two year study of six preservice teachers. She writes that "When teachers believe they know what needs to be done and how to do it . . . [t]hey do not feel the need to discuss the possibility of different visions" (p. 181); they do not feel the need to engage in intellectually challenging situations or theoretical reflections.

CURRICULUM THEORY IN (EARLY CHILDHOOD) TEACHER EDUCATION

Teacher preparation programs "constitute a powerful set of professional and institutional values that shape teachers' ways of thinking [and performing] in particular ways" (Beyer, 1992, p. 250). The narratives and discourses to which prospective teachers are exposed in their programs usually become the narratives and discourses that guide their teaching. Yet these discourses do not always promote intellectual engagement and reflection. The dominant culture of teacher education has contributed to creating an image of teachers as technicians as opposed to more reflective, interdisciplinary practitioners (Beyer, 1992; Pinar, 2004).

Theory, and curriculum theory in particular, is often undervalued in teacher education. Although most educators would acknowledge the idea that theory alone is insufficient for developing a good practice (Cassidy & Lawrence, 2000) and/or find competing and conflicting curriculum stories between what they learn in the university classrooms and practice in the school (Olson, 2000), I argue that curriculum theory remains a critical requisite in the preparation of teachers.

We need to cultivate teachers who critically embrace the dialectical curriculum theory/practice relationship (Grundy, 1987). Though early childhood educators have been deeply concerned about curricula, there has been little discussion of critical curriculum issues in early childhood curriculum programs (Schoonmaker & Ryan, 1996). Also, there has not been a comprehensive approach to early childhood curriculum that allows early childhood teachers to transcend a limited perspective of curriculum (Pinar, 2004): "For many practicing teachers, 'curriculum' is understood as what the district office requires them to teach, what the state education department publishes in scope and sequence guides. For many prospective teachers, curriculum denotes a course syllabus" (p. 185).

What teachers "believe about curriculum affects what they believe needs to be taught in schools. How they know reality suggests how they should teach" (Koetting & Combs, 2002, p. 138) and what they know about curriculum will guide their relationships with themselves, the students, and different texts. A more comprehensive, contextualized, and interdisciplinary approach to curriculum will help early childhood teachers to have a better understanding of their educational practices and a more meaningful theory-practice connection.

Despite the importance that curriculum theory has in the preparation of early childhood teachers, there is a lack of empirical research in the field that addresses the value of this theory. While recent research on the effectiveness of teacher education programs addresses the issue of "theory into practice orientation" as one of the critical factors that makes an education program successful (Darling-Hammond, 2006; Volante, 2006), few studies address the importance of curriculum theory in teacher preparation. Nor do they question what theory is worthy to teach and learn, from what perspective(s), and for what purposes.

Overall, the significance of curriculum theory in the formation of early childhood teachers has not been addressed adequately by the literature. Current research on the effectiveness of early childhood education programs highlights the importance of other elements in the preparation of teachers such as self-reflection and awareness (Baum & King, 2006; Landerholm, Gehrie, & Hao, 2004; Ward & McCotter, 2004) and the integration of information technology into early childhood teacher education (Kelley, Wetzel, Padgett, Williams, & Odom, 2004; Landerholm et al., 2004; Rowley, Dysard, & Arnold, 2005). Attention to the value of curriculum theory is conspicuously missing.

Although studies which address the preparation of early childhood teachers have been done, research that explores preservice teachers' beliefs about curriculum theory and its relevance to their practice is needed. We know little about what early childhood preservice teachers think about curriculum theory, how they conceptualize/define curriculum, and what connection they see between curriculum theory (what they are taught and have learned) and practice (being a preservice teacher/inservice teacher and performing as such). In this study, I begin to address this gap in literature with an exploratory case study of how a group of preservice teachers think about and enact the relationship they see between theory and practice.

Methodology

To study the relationship between curriculum theory and practice, I developed a case study of a group of six early childhood preservice teachers who were doing their eight-week student-teaching in a laboratory preschool. There were two groups of preservice teachers: one of four students who did their practice the first eight weeks of the school semester and the other of two students who practiced during the second eight weeks. These six preservice teachers were in the last semester of an undergraduate early childhood program at a large Midwestern public university. Their age ranged from 22 to 47 years. Their work experience also varied: Two of them had had no previous work experience and the rest had between 2 and 10 years of experience working in early childhood centers.

To have a broad and in-depth view of this particular group, I gathered data during a 16-week period. I conducted two 35- to 60-minute semi-structured interviews with each preservice teacher and conducted three hour observations of each student in the classroom. I also attended the 60-minute weekly planning meeting that both groups had, during the 16 weeks. I reviewed written schedules, planning sheets, and evaluation forms and had informal conversations with their Master Teacher and two cooperating teachers: preschool teachers who were also graduate assistants pursuing their masters in early childhood. Having different sources of information and using different tools to collect it allowed me to have a comprehensive view of this particular group (Patton, 2002).

Data Analysis

I used *constant comparison* (Glaser & Strauss, 1967) to analyze the data during the whole period of the study. I compared information within a single source (interview, observation, document, conversation, field-notes) and then, compared the information among the different sources and participants. After the final comparison of the data, I developed themes in three major areas: learning from the classes and the teachers, being in the schools, and moving between two different educational scenarios.

LEARNING FROM THE CLASSES AND THE TEACHERS

The preservice teachers had different perspectives about the content of their curriculum classes and what they learned and did in these classes. When asked about their curriculum classes, these students talked about "methods" and "lessons" classes. One of the students said that those classes "cover[ed] science and math methods . . . and reading and literature for children." Another said: "I'm taking . . . a class on math and science lessons and also one on language arts and social studies." According to these preservice teachers, the classes were focused on how to teach and how to write lesson plans; students were expected to learn how to do both accurately.

Other students referred to the same classes stating explicitly that they were curriculum classes. These students, for example, said that "One of the classes was social studies and language arts curriculum and the other one was science curriculum and math curriculum," that "all the education courses had to do with curriculum," and that "all classes are like tied with curriculum," even as one of them reflected that "there isn't probably one class in which we actually talk about curriculum."

Whether these preservice teachers spoke about curriculum classes or methods/lessons classes, it seemed that the classes were geared toward the procedural part of the instruction. Theoretical discussion and reflection were not present in these preservice teachers' narratives. When asked about what they did in their curriculum classes, one of the preservice teachers said that "[Y]ou have to write about the lesson plans for those classes, turn them into the instructor here, and get them graded. And then, you have to go out and implement them." "In the classes," stated another student, "You have to write a lesson plan and explain everything in it, what standard's been met, how it's been met, what objectives you have in this lesson."

What these students learned in their curriculum courses varied. Although the majority of the teachers seemed to have learned to write lesson plans and align them with the standards, some of them said that "from those classes [math and science curriculum and language arts and social studies curriculum], I don't think I gain too much at all about curriculum . . . No, I don't really think I had a class that really focused on curriculum at all." This comment was supported by a different student who asked "And what's the curriculum theory?" Reflections on curriculum and/or curriculum theory did not appear to be part of what the students were exposed to and/or expected to learn in the curriculum classes.

Not only did some of these students express they had learned about curriculum (lessons and methods) while students in the early childhood program, but also while students at elementary or secondary school: "when growing up you always see the teacher with the teacher's edition book, so I thought it [curriculum] was pretty much what I saw." Likewise, two different students remarked: "I remember my teacher using the textbooks and doing everything out of the textbooks; I thought it was the curriculum" and "using textbooks and fact sheets . . . still is pretty much the same. . . . I think it is easier."

These preservice teachers' comments highlight how important it is that we explore the experiences that education students bring with them into their programs as well as their assumptions about the meaning of curriculum. In these cases, the students thought that the curriculum was simply about guidelines and textbooks because that was what they saw enacted by their teachers. Their teachers were the role models for these preservice teachers' conceptualization of curriculum.

BEING IN THE SCHOOLS

The preservice teachers' experiences in the particular educational settings in which they position and see themselves as "teachers" allow them to theorize about curriculum in different ways. They also speak differently about curriculum when they speak as "teachers" more than as "students." From the classes they took, it seems that these preservice teachers did not learn as much about curriculum as they did being in the educational setting. When they were asked about what was curriculum for them, they answered contextualizing curriculum both in the higher educational institution and in their practice/experience as teachers. It appears to be that their teaching experience offers them a different framework for them to talk about and/or define curriculum.

Curriculum means different but related things to all these preservice teachers. Curriculum "is more setting goals and then meeting those goals"; it "is the tool that the teacher uses to teach the children . . . is like the plans and the goals that you want the children to learn." Likewise, it "is the guidelines you need to follow as a teacher" and "the skills that are . . . developmentally appropriate and that are taught to the children in my classroom." One of the preservice teacher's comments summarizes the general perception of curriculum held by all the preservice teachers:

> To me it is the planning, the guidelines and directions that you follow. . . . It kind of keeps me aligned as a teacher. You know, by having a curriculum, those guidelines to follow, I'm more organized. . . . I'm meeting the standards and the needs of each area of development because I consider that curriculum covers each area of development.

Likewise, when they spoke as teachers, they thought it was important to *know the curriculum* and *know about the curriculum* for different reasons. It is important to *know about the curriculum* because "whatever you're teaching is part of the curriculum . . . everything's involved then." And, it is also important to *know the curriculum* "to know what resources you can use; that's when curriculum comes in, what resources you can use [and] where can you go to get the resources." Another preservice teacher stated that it is important to "understand the guidelines . . . of the center or of the district you're teaching in, and that's a thing that you have to consider . . . though I may have something in mind, I need to follow and know their curriculum."

When these preservice teachers conceptualize curriculum, they use their teaching experiences and contexts to do it. However, the ways in which they state their definitions of curriculum and frame the importance of knowing about curriculum still refer to the "how to"—the procedural approach to the instruction. These preservice teachers do not refer to curriculum as a way to understand educational experiences and/or to reflect upon their practice.

MOVING BETWEEN TWO DIFFERENT EDUCATIONAL SCENARIOS

The interaction in and between two different educational settings (university and school) allows these preservice teachers to think about the usefulness (or lack of) of what they learn about curriculum. Being teachers while also being students offer opportunities to preservice teachers to find the connections between what they learn in the classes that they take and what they practice at schools. One of the preservice teachers clearly illustrated the usefulness of what she learned and the interaction that she saw between the classes she took and the classes she (student-) teaches:

> The way we have to do our lesson plans now is the way we are taught in the classroom. They're exactly the same and all the stuff on portfolios and how to do portfolios and how to write a lesson . . . basically, learning how to do a science activity or how to make a math activity, you know, all those are things that I learned in my [curriculum] classes. . . . What you learn in your classroom, when you're actually in the classroom doing the work, is what you're really gonna do when you get to your student teaching.

There was another preservice teacher who remarked that "everything you learn is useful. . . . I apply what I learn." However, he goes on to say, "You have to adapt to each setting" because "each school curriculum is different. . . . Every school has a curriculum, and if you have an idea, you have to make it fit." The idea he alludes to in the second part of his statement is present among all these preservice teachers: "When you go to a school you have to adapt to that school"; You find "that there's difference depending on where you are." These comments illustrate that—to some extent—the methods and techniques of what they learn could be applied when teaching, but that technicality does not provide them with ways and means to understand contextualized educational practices, to understand curriculum from different perspectives.

At the same time, preservice teachers also expressed a tension between what they learned and did in their university classes and what they learned and did in schools. For them, theory and practice were disconnected from one another: "You learn how to plan, but then being there it changes" and "In class . . . I did a lot of lesson plans based on the standards, but I mean, when I was in the public school I followed their curriculum, so I became familiar with their curriculum and they do it differently." Another preservice teacher affirmed:

> We learn about curriculum theories and what it should be, you know, we could still learn about important stuff like that. But in schools is where you have your own ideas of what you're going to

end up using, like if you like standardized textbooks and you like teaching out of those textbooks, then you'll probably have a job where you can teach out of the textbooks. And if you don't like textbooks, then you gotta find a job in preschool or maybe in a school that's more open. I think you can come up with your own ideas of what curriculum should be and if you fit into the school where that curriculum is [pause] then, I don't know. [laughing]

Another preservice teacher stated that there was no need to learn about curriculum. When asked about its usefulness, she responded: "Useful? I'm not sure. And it's something sad. Like I said, I went to this school and I learned things that worked for me . . ." A different student's observation is similar: "You don't need to know about curriculum; you'll learn it from the school. . . . You learn about curriculum in the school that you're teaching at." If these preservice teachers were exposed to a comprehensive and interdisciplinary curriculum theory that transcended simply standards, textbooks, and lesson plans, they would be better able to understand the complex realities that they are enmeshed in. If a non-technical perspective on curriculum were presented to these early childhood preservice teachers, they would probably be able to see connections between theory and practice and find theory useful in their experience.

These preservice teachers' statements reflecting a limited vision of curriculum were consistent with the last page of the *Daily Schedule Information* of the laboratory school where these preservice teachers were doing their practice. This document clearly states what is expected from the preservice teachers in this specific setting:

> Student teachers are expected to have all lesson plans in the room. . . . All materials should be gathered and left in the appropriate location. Student teachers must leave instructions for staff. . . . Student teachers are responsible for keeping accurate counts of children and staff at all times. Student teachers are to bring in 5 new books each week. . . . Lesson Plans for Head Teaching Days consist of . . .

This information describing what (not) to do and how to do it illustrate how preservice teachers are introduced to a particular form of being a teacher, into certain curriculum narratives and performances. It states not only what the preservice teachers should do—to leave, to have, to gather, to bring, to be responsible, and to include—but also what they need to focus on: lesson plans, materials, instructions, number of children, and books. If preservice teachers know what they need to do and be and where to concentrate their efforts, if they know what is expected, they will hardly engage in situations different from the expected ones. If they are not encouraged and/or expected to engage in theory and/or look for different alternatives, they will hardly feel the need to do it.

When the "how to" is more important than the "why," preservice teachers do not have space for critical academic engagement.

In a similar fashion as the *Daily Schedule Information*, the *Student Teacher Evaluation* also provides a limited view of curriculum. This evaluation "is based on the five NAEYC Professional Standards that relate to expectations for teachers of young children" and calls for assessing "student's work" on each of the following items: *Promoting Child Development and Learning; Building Family and Community Relationships; Observing, Documenting, and Assessing to Support Young Children and Families; Teaching and Learning; and Becoming a Professional.* The words curriculum and theory are hard to find in this form.

When *Becoming a Professional*, an early childhood preservice teacher needs to know about and perform "Classroom Management, Supervision Skills, Self Reflection, Cooperation, Dependability, Initiative, Poise, and Appearance." Comprehending and applying (basic) theoretical curriculum foundations and/ or making connections between curriculum theory and practice are not noted as part of *Becoming a(n) (Early Childhood) Professional*. Although preservice teachers were reminded that as teachers "We need to have an explanation of why we're doing what we're doing" by their Master Teacher in some of the planning meetings, being able to articulate their rationale for practice was not expected in their evaluations.

Discussion

The purpose of this study was to explore early childhood preservice teachers' beliefs about curriculum theory and the importance it had in their student-teaching experience. In the course of this study, I uncovered important aspects about curriculum theory taught in university classes, how early childhood preservice teachers conceptualize curriculum, how they understand the relationship between curriculum theory and practice, and how preservice teachers are evaluated.

According to these six early childhood preservice teachers, the content of early childhood curriculum classes is mostly about methods and lessons; and, to some extent, curriculum models. In these classes, early childhood preservice teachers learn how to write lesson plans, align them with the early childhood learning standards, and select developmentally appropriate activities. Yet at the same time, they also learn to conceptualize curriculum from the largely implicit theory that is both presented as well as enacted in those classes (Beyer, 1992). These early childhood preservice teachers conceptualize curriculum as primarily goals, planning, tools, guidelines, directions, developmentally appropriate activities, and/or standards (Pinar, 2004).

Ultimately, they conceptualize curriculum as a noun—goals, tools, guidelines—and not as an adjective or as a verb: as actions and performances. They see curriculum as a set of guidelines that an institution has but not a set of activities, beliefs, and performances that an institution enacts. It is mostly related to issues of methodology and content but not connected to ways of understanding educational practices as contextualized, historical, and social (Doll, 2002; Pinar, 2004). Although preservice teachers' participation in different educational settings, whether as teachers or students, plays an important role in their conceptualization of curriculum, it is also clear that the content of their curriculum classes has a direct relation with the way they think about curriculum and, therefore, how they conceive curriculum theory.

Regarding the importance of knowing about curriculum theory, these preservice teachers clearly state that it is important to know about curriculum because this entails learning to make lesson plans, to know what the guidelines are, and to know what resources they can use. Other than these things, it does not seem important to them to know about the assumptions, values, and beliefs that undergird curriculum and/or to learn about curriculum theory in their classes. For them, curriculum theory is not "useful" because everything they need to know about curriculum they can learn from their teaching in a particular setting; practice will teach them about it. Curriculum theory, is then, irrelevant for teaching (Cassidy & Lawrence, 2000) because is it not applicable in a direct/explicit way in their professional experience (Darder, 1991; Simon, 1992).

Early childhood preservice teachers' evaluation is also an important part of this picture. Although my study was not intended to explore evaluation issues, it seems that what is expected to be known and done by the preservice teachers determines the students' outcomes and, therefore, what they learn. If it is not expected that they theorize about curriculum, know about it, connect it to their practice and use it to understand their experience, they will not do it. Preservice teachers will learn and do what it is said that they have to, but nothing more. I wonder what would be the case if it was expected/required that early childhood teachers use curriculum theory to inform and understand their practice as well as use their practice to understand and inform theory. Would curriculum theory be more meaningful and useful to the students and would the theory-practice dichotomy be overcome?

Implications

Like any other discipline, education requires the cultivation of critical thinking, independence of mind, and intellectuality (Pinar, 2004). Education should not merely involve technical and/or vocational preparation. Teacher preparation requires understanding the importance of theory and promoting spaces for mutual engagement in intellectual curiosity. Also, it requires overcoming the dichotomy that often exists between theory and practice and creating the contexts for students to establish a dialectical relationship between their personal and professional experiences and theory, as well as encouraging them to enrich theory with their narratives.

Teacher educators have an important role in compelling preservice teachers to appreciate their professional practice as an ongoing theoretical preoccupation. They need to offer a variety of curriculum scripts that allow students to engage in theoretical discussion as well as to critically evaluate existing education and curriculum theories and policies. They also need to acknowledge the multiple ways in which curriculum is constructed and enacted and the importance that they have being not only theory providers but also theory performers. More question-asking, exploration of different ways of knowing, and less programming and prescription are indispensable in the education of any teacher.

We also need to ask more critical questions about the kind of curriculum theory we teach, its quality, and its purpose. We also need to explore the outcomes we should expect for early childhood preservice teachers. Not only do teacher educators and supervisors need to revisit what kind of early childhood teachers they want to prepare and for what purposes, but also they need to better bridge the gap between university classrooms and schools. Involving cooperating teachers and schools in this process is critical. Ultimately, early childhood education programs need to reconsider the role of curriculum theory as well as the place it has been assigned.

Conclusions

Curriculum theory is not about reading curriculum texts or following textbooks; it is about truly understanding and contextualizing our educational, social, and personal experiences, their past, present, and future and what has been said about them as well as what we would say about them afterwards. Although education programs and teaching experiences are not the only components of preservice teachers' exposure to curriculum theory, they are critical in offering possibilities for constructing personal curriculum theories/narratives.

This study is an initial step in addressing the role and importance of curriculum theory in teacher education. Findings such as the lack of connection between curriculum theory and practice, the prevalent technical approach to curriculum in the classes, and the absence of a comprehensive curriculum theory in the preservice teachers' narratives show that we need to rethink the role of curriculum theory in education as well as the kinds of curriculum discourses that are presented to prospective teachers through the theory offered/enacted in the classrooms.

More research on these issues is needed. We need more studies which explore the kind of curriculum discourses available to preservice teachers in their education programs; possible ways to address curriculum theory to make it meaningful to the students/teachers; and the role of the school teachers, teaching experience, school classrooms, cooperating teachers, supervisors, standards, and personal history in framing preservice teachers' curriculum theorizing and performances. Not only will these studies help to improve the quality of teacher education but also to expand the horizons of curriculum theory. Teacher educators should provide opportunities for preservice teachers to use theory to understand their practice and vice versa. If we want to envision a renaissance in teacher education, we should revisit the place that we have assigned to theory in the preparation of teachers as well as its significance in understanding their (and our) everyday experiences.

References

Baum, A. C., & King, M. A. (2006). Creating a climate of self-awareness in early childhood teacher preparation programs. *Early Childhood Education Journal, 33*(4), 217–222.

Beyer, L. E. (1992). The personal and the social in education. In E. W. Ross, J. W. Cornett, & G. McCutcheon (Eds.), *Teacher personal theorizing: Connecting curriculum practice, theory, and research* (pp. 239–255). New York: SUNY Press.

Cassidy, D. J., & Lawrence, J. M. (2000). Teachers' beliefs: The "whys" behind the "how tos" in child care classrooms. *Journal of Research in Childhood Education, 14*(2), 193–204.

Darder, A. (1991). *Culture and power in the classroom: A critical foundation for bicultural education.* New York: Bergin & Garvey.

Darling-Hammond, L. (2006). Constructing 21st-century teacher education. *Journal of Teacher Education, 57*(3), 300–314.

Deng, Z. (2004). The role of theory in teacher preparation: An analysis of the concept of theory application. *Asia-Pacific Journal of Teacher Education, 32*(2), 143–157.

Doll, Jr., W. E. (2002). Ghosts and the curriculum. In W. E. Doll, Jr. & N. Gough (Eds.), *Curriculum visions* (pp. 23–70). New York: Peter Lang.

Glaser, B. G., & Strauss, A. L. (1967). *The discovery of grounded theory: Strategies for qualitative research.* Chicago: Aldine.

Grundy, S. (1987). *Curriculum: Product or praxis?* Philadelphia: The Falmer Press.

Gutek, G. L. (1988). *Philosophical and ideological perspectives on education.* Boston: Allyn and Bacon.

Hooks, B. (2000). *Feminism is for everybody: Passionate politics.* Cambridge, MA: South End Press.

Kelley, M., Wetzel, K., Padgett, H., Williams, M., & Odom, M. (2004). Early childhood teacher preparation and technology integration: The Arizona State University West experience. *Information Technology in Childhood Education Annual, 2004*(1), 245–260.

Koetting, J. R., & Combs, M. (2002). The importance of theory and theoretical discourse. *Curriculum and Teaching Dialogue, 4*(2), 137–145.

Landerholm, E., Gehrie, C., & Hao, Y. (2004). Educating early childhood teachers for the global world. *Early Child Development and Care, 174*(7–8), 593–606.

Olson, M. (2000). Curriculum as a multistoried process. *Canadian Journal of Education, 25*(3), 169–187.

Patton, M. Q. (2002). *Qualitative research & evaluation methods* (3rd Ed.). Thousand Oaks, CA: Sage.

Pinar, W. F. (1999). Not burdens: Breakthroughs. *Curriculum Inquiry, 29*(3), 365–367.

Pinar, W. F. (2004). *What is curriculum theory?* Mahwah, NJ: LEA.

Pring, R. (2000). *Philosophy of educational research.* New York: Continuum.

Reid, W. A. (2001). Rethinking Schwab: Curriculum theorizing as a visionary activity. *Journal of Curriculum and Supervision, 17*(1), 29–41.

Reynolds, W. M., & Webber, J. A. (Eds.) (2004). *Expanding curriculum theory: Dis/positions and lines of flight.* Mahwah, NJ: LEA.

Ross, E. W. (1992). Teacher personal theorizing and reflective practice in teacher education. In E. W. Ross, J. W. Cornett, & G. McCutcheon (Eds.), *Teacher personal theorizing: Connecting curriculum practice, theory, and research* (pp. 179–190). New York: SUNY Press.

Rowley, J., Dysard, G., & Arnold, J. (2005). Developing a new technology infusion program for preparing tomorrow's teachers. *Journal of Technology and Teacher Education, 13*(1), 105–123.

Schoonmaker, F., & Ryan, S. (1996). Does theory lead practice? Teachers' constructs about teaching: Top-down perspectives. *Advances in Early Education and Child Care, 8,* 117–151.

Simon, R. I. (1992). *Teaching against the grain: Texts for a pedagogy of possibility.* New York: Bergin & Garvey.

Volante, L. (2006). Essential elements in teacher education: Preservice student perspectives. *Alberta Journal of Educational Research, 52*(2), 167–180.

Ward, J. R., & McCotter, S. S. (2004). Reflection as a visible outcome for preservice teachers. *Teaching and Teacher Education, 20*(3), 243–257.

CHAPTER 11

Professionalism vs. Reality
STUDENT AWARENESS OF LEGAL RIGHTS
AND RESPONSIBILITIES

Rita Pokol Poimbeauf
University of Houston

> Rita P. Poimbeauf, Ed.D., was a school administrator for twenty-seven years and an executive director of a professional teachers' organization for eight years. Presently, she is teaching aspiring principals and preservice teachers at the University of Houston. Her current interest is in the preparation of preservice teachers for the realities they will encounter in schools.

ABSTRACT

Through the use of interviews and presentation of case studies, this chapter discusses my contention as an administrator in multiple leadership roles that preservice teachers need more than what a majority of colleges of education are providing in terms of their understandings of their rights and responsibilities as educators. Teaching methodologies, pedagogy, and content area curriculum appear to be taught remarkably well. Yet, some colleges neglect to fortify teachers with the knowledge that they need to protect themselves in classroom and school situations. Teachers need to brace themselves with information on the laws, policies, and procedures of the district, state, and federal agencies that they are bound to observe. They need to understand how to handle difficult situations, the what ifs, and they need to know where to turn for assistance when there are problems. These are teacher survival skills. Future curriculum for preservice teachers should include such courses so that not only will a teacher be qualified to teach mathematics or reading but also will be prepared to deal with the realities of today's classroom. This position paper is a recollection of incidents and events that sparked my quest for urgent change in teacher education. I, by no means, started out as a researcher on this topic. My life evolved in the public school arena and with it shaped my thoughts on teacher education and eventually the questions researched in this chapter.

Introduction

In reflecting on a *Renaissance in Teacher Education*, my mind was filled with images of the countless new teachers and the more experienced, yet uninformed, teachers whose lives have crossed mine over the thirty-five years of my career. Having been a school administrator in a large urban school district for twenty-seven years and later an executive director of a professional teachers' organization for eight years, I feel compelled to call for a change in a system that is causing concern and upheaval in our young teacher population. In a nutshell, they are simply not in the position to deal with the realities of today's classroom and the teaching profession.

As a principal, I witnessed, year after year, the new, energy-filled teachers leaving their sheltered college settings to enter the teaching profession. Some of these teachers were young whereas others were more experienced in the ways of the world. All were equally determined to have a positive effect on their students. Yet, each one was a bit too naïve and unable to imagine the real classroom and students who were not motivated to the extent that others expected them to be.

All of my new teachers were too optimistic in that they overwhelmingly believed that they could single-handedly make the difference in each student's life. They believed that all they had to do was be a good teacher. Granted, this is what has been instilled in preservice teachers in the colleges of education and this is what administrators look for in newly anointed teachers. Without exception, they come out of our colleges filled with enthusiasm and the ambitious desire to become top-notch educators. The idealism that is instilled in new teachers is commendable, but maybe, not practical for teacher survival as I contend in this chapter.

Anyone involved in the schools knows this is sheer madness since the evolution of a first-rate educator takes years of hard work, mistakes involving trial and error, and countless classes of overly active youngsters who are just waiting to make their mark at the expense of the teacher. The idealism that we instill in teachers should be tempered with the practical knowledge of how schools operate and what are the boundaries of teachers in regards to their relationships with students and the school community.

In addition, common sense plays a key role in the success of a teacher. Common sense is not taught like mathematics. The best that we can offer preservice teachers is a chance to work with scenarios close to the real school settings and to provide preservice teachers with opportunities to work in the schools. Moreover, do teachers know where to find the support they need both in and out of their school contexts? They need to know how to seek legal support when in trouble and how to react when they find themselves in a disconcerting situation.

The present mentor system cannot function in this capacity since the mentors many times are not that experienced and lack this basic information themselves. Principals, and I was one of them, are hardly able to find quality mentors willing to spend extra time with new teachers. Yet, preservice teachers need a more realistic view of their profession along with information on how to survive the realities encountered in classrooms and schools.

Observations and Conversations

Through the years, I have witnessed the enthusiasm of the newly hired teachers wane. Some of these inexperienced teachers do not last the year. Others plug along for a couple of years, then determine that they are not in the right profession and leave with bitter memories. The school life was not what they thought it would or should be. The most heart-wrenching cases of teachers leaving the profession happen when the truly dedicated teachers are drummed out of the profession because they have made an unforgivable mistake that could not be tolerated or overlooked by the school district's upper administration. Preservice teachers and new teachers rarely understand how all encompassing the life of the educator actually is.

The teacher is going to be 'on the job' twenty-four hours a day. Time in school is when the teacher's behavior is especially scrutinized but there will be a 'halo effect' that carries over to out-of-school activities. This 'halo effect' will be dictated by two distinct (though connected) concerns. First, the teacher will be expected to be a person whose character engenders the trust of parents and/or school authorities. Second, the teacher will be expected (to a variable degree) to exemplify a certain morality that fits him or her in the judgment of 'society' to instruct the young (Piddocke, Magsino, & Manley-Casimir, 1997, p. 219–220).

In talking to teachers who are terminated for grievous offenses, one thing stands out. They frequently report, "I didn't know that *this* could not be done." The *this* can be substituted with a hundred different interpretations such as: 1) Teachers should not drink alcoholic beverages in front of students even when they are off hours and away from school; 2) Teachers should not humiliate or tease students of any age in the classroom; 3) Teachers cannot require students to do physical activity (push-ups) as a form of corporal punishment in districts that prohibit corporal punishment; and 4) Teachers are required to follow the verbal or written directives of their administrators. The offenses of a majority of teachers in trouble are errors of judgment. It appears that many beginning teachers lack a clear understanding of their professional status and do not possess the common sense to relate or react to unfavorable situations in a manner that would protect their careers. As a result, they are caught up in a major misunderstanding that escalates to termination. (Please note that I am not advocating all teachers deserve a second chance. There are educators—child molesters, drug offenders, and those involved in illegal activities—who do deserve immediate termination.) Moreover, new teachers are hit the hardest with terminations that could have been prevented if only the teachers had the proper knowledge on how to handle the situations that they found overwhelming. It may come as a surprise that new teacher terminations do not require good cause. New teachers, many times, are stunned with this information whereby they sum up their state of affairs with a quick "That's not fair." Their administration needs no reason to recommend a new teacher's dismissal; the administration can just make the recommendation. After all, because new teachers are probationary, their status allows for dismissal at any time during the year determined by the administration.

Teachers caught in this statute depart their school districts totally devastated. It usually is a matter of the new teacher not having the common sense and appropriate knowledge necessary to survive. New teachers do not enter schools armed with information that includes federal, state, and local school laws and procedures. Nor do they enter teaching equipped with the sense of how to protect themselves from the happenings in schools that could hurt them professionally and ruin a career teacher. These could include goings-on such as a child breaking his arm, or a minor approaching the teacher in a confidential manner about an illegal activity, or an irate parent threatening the teacher.

In a discussion with preservice teachers with whom I work, I asked what they needed from classes that would have been helpful in their student teaching. Their response surprised me in that they uniformly agreed more discipline management classes were needed. As we talked about this need, I further inquired about their understanding of school policies and state guidelines that they needed to observe. I questioned them on their ability to respond to different "what-if" situations as described in the incidents presented later in this chapter and by selections excerpted from *Cases for Teacher Development* (Goldblatt & Smith, 2005), a project of the Ontario College of Teachers.

Almost immediately, the group reversed their opinion and realized that they lacked specific knowledge that was needed to make wise decisions on a daily basis. They also concluded that they were unaware of many of the policies and that they could have easily disregarded them in the course of their day. It became obvious that the particular student teachers were well versed in teaching the content, understood the pedagogy and learning theories, and could recite all the growth development concepts pertinent to their assignment. However, this group was not fortified with the practical skills to make good choices and quick responses that are necessary on a daily basis. In *Cases for Teacher Development* (Goldblatt & Smith, 2005), Margaret Olson, Assistant Professor in the School of Education at Saint Xavier University in Nova Scotia, quotes Bullough and Baughman in her commentary on a case study: "Within education, 'teaching is complicated by the nature of education related problems that are especially messy, overlap, and come in clusters rather than rows' (Bullough & Baughman, 1997, p. 131). This complexity mostly leads to ethical dilemmas rather than solutions" (p. 206–207).

Realizing this, the student teachers quickly changed their first suggestion of discipline management classes to survival classes for the teacher. Discipline was still important, but their lack of practical knowledge could cause them to fail as a teacher. Remember school things are, as Bullough and Baughman pointedly state and Olson (2005) duly noted, messy and overlapping in nature. What struck me during the course of this conversation was that this group was too naïve to even understand their vulnerability in messy school and classroom situations.

To further substantiate my claim that colleges must teach preservice teachers the skills to survive, I interviewed two individuals closely associated with teachers in peril. The first was F. Carter Crain (October, 2006), an employment attorney in Houston, Texas, who represents teachers experiencing legal difficulties. Attorney Crain had unique ideas on teacher training. He stated that students should know the state Teacher Code of Ethics. He suggested:

> It [Code of Ethics] is both a shield and a sword. If you know what you are supposed to do and do what you are supposed to do—that protects you to some extent. If you are supervised by someone who is violating it, it can be a shield to protect you from some unfair situation.

He continued that the code should form a basis for the actions of a teacher and as well a basis for their ethical foundations. Crain reported that the most common disciplinary issues he encounters are those of physical force. He advised, "Be aware that when you touch children, you open yourself up for charges of abuse and improper physical force." A teacher may think they are playing with a student or just having fun and their actions can be misinterpreted. Crain's example reinforces the fact that teachers need to know the laws and guidelines that they are bound to observe. He reflected that this sort of preservice training would certainly reduce future misunderstandings and protect teachers before they find themselves in situations that require legal assistance. In addition, Crain suggested helpful hints for preservice teachers and practicing teachers:

- Be aware that there are corrupted administrators and that teachers need to protect themselves from them
- Be true to your own values
- Be aware that "students have a full range of capacity for all kinds of bizarre inappropriate behavior" and know what is going on in your classroom
- Keep a journal and be factual, but leave judgment, feelings, and evaluations out of it

It makes good sense in the preparation of teachers that a course offering what Attorney Crain is suggesting be available to preservice teachers. In that way, colleges of education can provide preservice teachers with a better grasp on the realities of schools.

My second interview was with Gayle Fallon (October, 2006), the president of the Houston Federation of Teachers who processes several hundred cases of troubled teachers each year. When asked what advice could be offered to new teachers, Fallon quickly replied:

> The first thing that I would tell (a new teacher) before you walk into class join something (organization) and pick up the phone and call them the first time you have an uneasy feeling. Don't wait till you're in trouble. The other thing I would tell them is that when you look at the class of students, remember there is a line between you and them. The days of taking them home, hugging them, picking them up if they are little are over. You are going to have to be professional, but there is a degree of social distance that will keep you out of trouble.

Offering advice to universities, Fallon commented:

> One or two realistic courses would help because everything they [teachers] get is theory. . . . They need to know law. They also need some type of course where they are exposed to what really happens in a school, where they talk to people who really can explain behaviors, the pitfalls, the areas where they can get into trouble and how to seek help. Because the other thing we found is that they don't have a clue how to seek help. They need to get out of their vocabulary the phrase, "It's not fair." Because the school district is just like life. It is not going to be fair . . .

Fallon continued,

> Some type of training in how political their system is [is needed for preservice teachers]. They don't understand the role of politics on

the state level. They need to know they cannot be friends with their students. There is a social distance. . . . The other thing we found is that they are not prepared to the extent they need to be for teaching in a school of a different culture or ethnicity and they have no clue as to communication there. They don't understand the mores. It's a recipe for disaster.

Crain's and Fallon's suggestions are similar in that none of their suggestions fit readily into a methodology or content class. Both advocates indicated a need for the practical knowledge that requires a different kind of university course. Universities have to prepare preservice teachers in a way that makes them capable of handling the various real life situations (what ifs) that play out in schools. A survival skills course would assist preservice teachers and contribute to a renaissance of teacher education through aiding teacher retention.

What Ifs

To clarify what I am stressing as far as being prepared for the unknown, an overview will be presented of several possible "what if" scenarios. These situations were presented to preservice teachers while they were fulfilling their student teaching or soon would be doing their student teaching. Their common response was "I don't know," which was quickly followed by "What should I do?" Inasmuch as these cases can be endless, I have chosen six for your reflection. All six caused some consternation to the preservice teachers involved. They revolve around the following situations:

- What if a student reports something confidentially to you that is happening in the home and is illegal?
- What if you accidentally use a bad word in front of your class?
- What if your principal demands that you pay for lost and stolen textbooks at the end of the year?
- What if you have a parent that demands a full report by telephone every evening of her child's day?
- What if you are threatened by a student?
- What if you are called to the principal's office to be told you are being reassigned duties pending an investigation into your actions with a specific student?

As you can quickly determine, each "what if" situation requires quick action on the part of the teacher. Each also requires that the teacher give the appropriate response. In some instances, a teacher, by responding inappropriately to a what if, could escalate the situation and subsequently place herself in jeopardy. These situations easily become arenas for a legal battle. The teacher must make smart decisions daily in schools and handle reasonably the reality of such dilemmas. Sometimes, a teacher protecting herself/himself may take a course of action that is not the most professional path.

An example of this would be the teacher threatened by a recently released student from a juvenile detention center. The particular teacher was coaxed by administration to work with the student who has seriously threatened school personnel in general and more specifically this teacher. The teacher was encouraged to put aside her doubts and to develop a relationship that would help the student overcome his hostility to the school environment.

The novice teacher, however, must think of the seriousness of this threat, even when administration tends to ignore it. The teacher may fear for his/her family as well. The teacher could request to be transferred to another building or, by exercising his/her right, demand that the student be removed from the campus. In this case, what is best for the teacher is not always what is best for the student. There are no happily-ever-after solutions here. It is questionable that our preservice teachers are prepared to cope with these types of situations even though they are realistically a part of school life.

Case Studies

The following authentic teacher cases, which were drawn from my years as the executive director of a professional teachers' organization that provided legal aid to teachers in trouble, will now be presented as a means of demonstrating teachers' lack of practical knowledge and the professionally and personally dangerous situations arising as a consequence. These cases are offered to strengthen the position that the curriculum for preservice teachers needs to be altered to include the perils of teaching in today's schools. Each case resonates with costly mistakes that need not have happened if the teachers were equipped with the appropriate knowledge and information necessary to manage such an episode in their school lives. Although we believe experience teaches, for the teachers involved, it came too late in their career path to save them from their school systems' rulings, many of which are upheld in a court of law.

PULLED UP BY THE EARS

A male teacher was beginning his fifteenth year of teaching in intermediate grades in an urban school district. His wife and other members of his family were teachers in the same school system. His campus enjoyed a good student body and active parents. Discipline problems were minimal on this campus. Up until this incident, the teacher was not involved in any major incidents with students and had been given consistently exceptional performance ratings on his assessments. He was considered an innovative teacher who helped other teachers whenever called upon. No previous reprimands or disciplinary actions had been taken against him.

One day, he wanted to make an impression on his class that homework was important and had to be completed. The class was not doing assignments as required. The teacher devised a plan to startle the class when he did his "homework is important" lecture. His plan to make an impression involved one of his male students with whom he had good rapport. He kept this youngster after school and taught him a trick. He explained how he would use this trick on him the next day to fool the class. The student was more than willing to go along with the teacher's plan.

When the time came the next day and the teacher began his lecture on homework, he was especially animated and loud. He told the class that he was about to demonstrate what would happen to anyone not bringing homework to class. The teacher said he would pick them up by their ears at which time he grabbed the student that he had previously collaborated with and picked him up at least two feet off the floor by holding on to his ears. His class gasped. The students got the message that the teacher was serious about homework. The demonstration student acted like he was hurt (he was not!). The class did not know this.

The class went home and all discussed how the teacher physically handled the demonstration student. The other students' parents called the demonstration student's mom who did not know anything about her child being hurt by the teacher. The boy's mother immediately went to the principal to complain about her son's rough treatment. When the boy was questioned, he did say that he was picked up by his ears in front of the class. (Remember this was a trick and the student was not hurt.)

One thing led to another and it was determined that the trick employed by the teacher did not hurt the boy in any way. However, the teacher was removed from his class and reassigned to a district office for "teacher time out" with pay because he did admit to having physical contact with the boy. The principal notified the school district authorities in spite of his investigation that cleared the teacher because rumors were flying around the school that the principal could not control. The district office conducted a second investigation and found that it was a trick and the boy was just fine. The young student said it was a trick and the teacher maintained that it was a joke. This incident should have been over. But it was not.

The school district terminated this teacher for violation of their corporal punishment policy. The attorneys for the school district determined that the teacher was threatening physical harm in his demonstration to the class and that the teacher improperly touched one of his students. The attorney for the teacher subsequently filed for a hearing on the state level to appeal the termination. All who heard about the case were astonished that the district pursued this aggressive course of action against a good teacher with no prior record.

At the hearing, the state's hearing officer heard the case presented by the district as well as the teacher's claim of a joke. This hearing lasted two weeks with students, parents, former principals, and expert witnesses called in to testify either for or against a rather bewildered teacher. How did the hearing officer rule? His decision was the final and permanent ruling in a teacher termination case. There is no higher authority to execute an appeal. Was the termination left standing?

After a few weeks of deliberation, the hearing officer ruled in favor of the teacher. The district had to restore the teacher to the classroom. The district, however, requested that this teacher be transferred to another campus because the district felt by now the teacher was turning into a hero. The hearing officer granted the district's request and the teacher was moved to another campus. Although the grade level was similar to his original campus, the school was not comparable to the original campus. There were severe discipline problems, gangs, vandalism, and violence prevalent on this campus.

The teacher completed the last two months of the school year and resigned from the district. He could not accept the fact that the district did not value him as an employee. Although he originally agreed to be transferred, he did not expect the transfer he received. He felt the transfer was punitive and a direct result of his fighting the district for the sake of his job. He was a good teacher who was caught in an unfortunate chain of events. Since the incident, he has not returned to the classroom and is working in another field. Yes, this teacher made mistakes in his class. Listed briefly, they included:

- Threatening students with physical force
- Allowing the students to be dismissed without letting them in on the joke
- Making physical contact with a student
- Failing to inform the parents of what was planned with their child
- Failing to obtain parents' permission to use their child in this class demonstration

HIS UNDERWEAR SAYS IT ALL

A fifth year, middle school science teacher who was married with two small children enjoyed a reputation of being friendly and fair with his students. On the day in question, he had his school computer in the classroom turned on as students entered the room. This class period followed the teacher's planning period. The teacher entered the room with the class and stated that he was not on the computer during the planning period. He said later that he always kept his computer on and that on this day he was not using it. He repeatedly denied that he had any idea of the contents being exhibited on the computer. The students discovered pornography on his computer. The teacher quickly turned off the computer and resumed class. As the day progressed, the story spread throughout the school. A student went home and told his mother about the pornography on the teacher's computer. The child's mother informed the principal. The principal immediately informed the district's Professional Standards team. The teacher was reassigned while Professional Standards conducted an investigation. Most definitely, it was against school policy to display or use district computers for pornography.

The school district confiscated the computer with the intention of checking to see whether or not the computer was used to view pornography. The district wanted proof that pornography viewing during planning time was a common practice of the science teacher. Although such a computer search would be costly to the district, the district was determined to conduct this search.

The teacher was asked by his attorney if there were other incidents that could come into play in this investigation. The teacher reported that he played the guitar for his students on Fridays in class and that he cleaned his guitar with a rag. The rag was his old underwear, which turned out to be a joke among the students. When students first discovered this, they laughed so he would occasionally change his underwear rag for a laugh. He also reported that he and his students viewed rock band websites on the computer after their class work was completed. The attorney knew his defense depended on the outcome of the computer search because the information he obtained from the teacher was even more damaging.

This teacher then shared important information about a school intruder. It seemed that a tall man in a black raincoat was seen several times in the halls on different days. The intruder was chased from the building and there was a written record of this. The teacher believed this man used his computer during the time he was absent from his room prior to class starting. The classroom was never locked because in this particular school, keys were not available to all the rooms. The attorney began to center his case on the unidentified intruder. But the attorney was never given a chance to defend his case.

Almost immediately the district superintendent called the teacher at home and said that he would meet him after hours if the teacher would sign a resignation. He also told the teacher that he must meet him alone without representation. This superintendent knew nothing about the conference with the attorney where the teacher divulged information on his classroom routines and the intruder. The school district had not yet done the computer search or started their investigation; therefore, nothing would show on this teacher's record except his resignation. The science teacher met with the superintendent and signed the resignation effective immediately.

Whether or not the teacher was guilty of viewing pornography on a school computer was never proven. The teacher maintained his innocence. Yet, this teacher lacked good judgment in his work with students. His friendliness and playfulness with the students would have come out and would have played negatively against his case in court. His apparent ease with the underwear joke would have been viewed with disapproval. The intruder defense would probably be enough to establish some doubt as to who was using the computer. Yet, this teacher, when offered the chance, resigned. His explanation was that he had to consider support for his wife and children. He moved to another town in the state and was hired without problems as the head of a science department.

Yes, this teacher made mistakes in his class. Listed briefly, they included:

- Using an underwear rag in front of middle school students
- Becoming too much of a friend with the students by viewing rock bands and playing guitar on Fridays
- Failing to report the computer incident to the office or administration immediately

A SLAP IN THE FACE

A twenty-five year veteran teacher was accused of slapping a girl in front of her class. This white teacher taught first grade in an all-black neighborhood that was politically active and deeply involved in school and local church activities. The teacher was very small in stature and for the most part had a good reputation in the community. The teacher commented that her size probably served to her advantage in this school in that she was never viewed as a threat to the students.

The teacher was presenting material in front of the class and waving her hands around as part of her presentation. One of her students walked up beside her out of the sight of the teacher. As the teacher continued her explanation, she accidentally "hit" the student under the chin. This caused the student's teeth to clamp shut with a loud noise. The student was not injured. Some of the class heard the girl's mouth shut and made the usual clamor about it. The teacher immediately checked that the girl was okay, apologized, and kept teaching. However, the girl went home and reported that she was slapped.

The girl's mother appeared the next day at the new principal's door with her minister and several community activists calling for the teacher's termination. The teacher was called to the office to explain before the group what happened. By way of clarification, the teacher admitted she hit the girl, but that it was an accident. The teacher said that she checked with the girl to make sure she was okay and apologized to her immediately. The teacher continued to report that she thought nothing more about the incident and kept teaching.

The new principal of the school allowed the meeting to take place between the teacher and the group without the teacher's prior knowledge. The parent and her supporters were not satisfied with the teacher's explanation. The principal had to act, so in front of the group, he reassigned the teacher and said the school would conduct an investigation. The teacher remained reassigned for months. It may have been the district's way of not making a judgment and of hoping that the incident would resolve itself.

But, as time went on, the community became outraged. They wanted this teacher fired. It did not matter that she had taught in the school for a number of years and was a highly sought after teacher. The principal finally requested her termination as a result of pressure from the neighborhood. At the next school board meeting, the teacher was terminated. An attorney for this teacher appealed the board's decision and requested a state hearing. Her students were called as witnesses and they all agreed that the girl was hit. The teacher's former principal of fourteen years appeared in her defense.

Can you determine what happened at the state hearing? The teacher stuck to her story. The outcome of this case did not look good for the teacher. In a surprise move, the hearing officer called on the young girl to demonstrate on him how the teacher "hit" her. The girl obliged.

The hearing officer closed the case right on the spot. He delivered a lecture to the teacher that this could have been avoided if the teacher chose her words more carefully and had not inflamed the group with the word "hit." Likewise, he lectured the school district for putting such a decision on him when clearly it was the district's responsibility to defend this teacher to the community. The girl apparently had demonstrated this act to both the principal and the school district's attorneys.

The teacher's attorney requested that the district move the teacher to another campus because he feared the teacher would continue to experience difficulty on her current campus. All parties agreed, and the request was approved. The teacher was transferred to an intermediate/middle alternative campus. The details of the site were not discussed in the attorney meeting. Remember this teacher was of a very small stature and all the alternative students towered over her. The teacher resigned from the district two weeks after her reassignment. She was, in her words, "disgusted, disheartened and ashamed." Yes, this teacher made mistakes in her class. Listed briefly, they included:

- Using a provocative verb—"hit" to describe her actions instead of "My hand came up on her chin."
- Failing to inform the principal of all classroom incidents
- Failing to call the mother before the child returned home
- Talking to the principal and mother's group without representation. (Teachers have a right to seek counsel and have representation.)

In all fairness, the newly appointed principal, although not on trial, made numerous mistakes in his investigation and procedures as well.

THE BOOBY TRAP

A middle school female student began telling her friends that she was afraid of the gym teacher. She told them how the female gym teacher caught her in the locker room after class and began to touch her in ways that made her uncomfortable. You can imagine how word spread throughout the school. When the principal heard this rumor, he summoned the gym teacher to conference with her about this allegation. The gym teacher responded that she knew nothing about it. But this initial conference frightened the gym teacher and she reacted beyond what would have been a normal response to this type of accusation. The teacher lived an alternative lifestyle and had kept this information private from school personnel. Her students also were not aware of their teacher's lifestyle.

The teacher was reassigned pending an investigation by the principal who at once began looking into the matter without a formal complaint from a student or her parents. No charges were filed against the gym teacher; the student and her parents did not complain to administration. The teacher, however, was totally devastated by the rumor that had spread throughout the building.

Before seeking counsel with her professional organization, she consulted one of the best lawyers in town. He agreed to take her case for a $5,000.00 immediate deposit. She paid him the money. A few days later, she called her professional organization because another payment to the lawyer would be due when he represented her in a meeting with her principal. The teacher hoped her liability insurance from the organization would cover it.

The principal proceeded to question several girls in the gym class. As her case was investigated, the teacher was questioned again in the presence of her attorney. The teacher continued to claim that she knew nothing about this incident. The female student who made the initial allegation was finally questioned about her locker room story. As the principal talked to her, the student burst out laughing and said she made up the story to see what would happen. The student was a bit shocked that the principal even knew about it. In her mind, it was just a tall tale to gain the attention of her friends and was all a big joke. She could not understand why everyone was making such a big deal about it. What outcome do you think this case produced?

The teacher was subsequently returned to her teaching position. As far as the principal was concerned, the incident was a false alarm and forgotten. The teacher, however, lost her money. She wanted her liability insurance to cover her attorney fees, but she did not get prior approval to hire an attorney. The female student who started this rumor went back to her classes as if nothing happened, although she was sternly rebuked. The case ended with the teacher's career remaining unscathed. Yet, the teacher lost a substantial amount of money due to her panic.

Yes, this teacher made mistakes in her reaction to this false allegation. Listed briefly, they included:

- Hiring an attorney before calling on her professional organization for counsel and approval to hire an attorney
- Becoming panic stricken from the onset of the incident, before a charge was filed
- Contacting and paying an attorney before all the facts were sorted out in the case and a formal charge was made against her

In review, each teacher in the four cases presented made unfortunate mistakes that resulted in damaged careers and financial loss. Each teacher was not headed for district termination when they made their mistakes. All were innocent of the charges brought against them. However, each teacher under duress responded in a way that exhibited a lack of knowledge in how to address such a pressured position.

REVIEW OF CASE STUDIES

In the first case, the teacher used poor judgment and did not understand the district's policy on corporal punishment. In the second case, the teacher never waited to hear his rights and bolted. He, too, used poor judgment in working with his students. In the third case, the teacher did not properly know how to protect herself from false accusations and also did not know her rights when she was brought face-to-face with a community group. Finally, the teacher in the fourth case had no idea what procedures were in effect that would or could be used against her. She acted without knowing the policies and procedures of her school district and her professional organization.

Conclusions

Preservice teachers as well as practicing teachers have not been prepared for what awaits them today in real-life situations. Colleges of education must take this into account and change program offerings in order to prepare their soon-to-be teachers in all aspects of their prospective careers. The biggest challenge for incorporating know-how into the curriculum would be in making their experiences as real as possible through case studies, "what-if" situations, and contact with practicing teachers.

This can be accomplished by either of two approaches. The first approach would be to integrate teacher survival skills in the present courses. The responsibility for making young teachers aware of the laws, policies, and procedures, (federal, state, and local), would rest with the present instructors charged with dispensing teacher preparation through theory, methods, and content courses. The second approach is to develop and initiate new courses on teacher survival into the curriculum for both preservice and veteran teachers taught by practicing school people. In this way, teachers would be better equipped to handle the "what ifs" of the school day.

Although there are universities training preservice teachers with the skills that are needed for success in classrooms and schools, I do, nevertheless, see a need to revamp teacher education. It is imperative to include survival curriculum of the nature I have proposed. Some universities have incorporated this type of knowledge into their programs and are frontrunners in this dimension of a renaissance in teacher education. Until such practices become more common, as educators of educators, we must crusade for changes in our teacher education programs to ensure that competent and professionally savvy teachers will be readied for the challenges of today's classrooms and schools.

References

Bullough, R. V., Jr., & Baughman, K. (1997). *First year teacher eight years later: An inquiry into teacher development.* New York: Teachers College Press.

Crain, F. C. (2006, October 26). Audio-taped Interview, 8 pages.

Fallon, G. (2006, October 30). Audio-taped Interview, 8 pages.

Goldblatt, P. F., & Smith, D. (Eds.) (2005). *Cases for teacher development: Preparing for the classroom.* Thousand Oaks, CA: Sage Publications, Inc.

Olson, M. (2005). Case Commentary by Margaret Olson. In P. F. Goldblatt & D. Smith (Eds.), *Cases for teacher development: Preparing for the classroom* (pp. 206–208). Thousand Oaks, CA: Sage Publications, Inc.

Piddocke, S., Magsino, R., & Manley-Casimir, M. (1997). *Teachers in trouble: An exploration of the normative character of teaching.* Toronto: University of Toronto Press Inc.

CHAPTER 12

Student Teachers' Diversity Rights
THE CASE LAW

Zorka Karanxha
University of South Florida

Perry A. Zirkel
Lehigh University

> Zorka Karanxha, Ed.D., is an assistant professor of educational leadership at the University of South Florida. She has been a public school teacher at both middle and high school levels. Her research interests include charter schools, parent involvement, teacher and principal preparation, and education law.
>
> Perry Zirkel, Ph.D., J.D., and LL.M., is university professor of education and law at Lehigh University, where he formerly was Dean of the College of Education and more recently held the Iacocca Chair in Education for a five-year term. He has written more than 1,100 publications on various aspects of school law.

ABSTRACT

This chapter provides a concise and up-to-date synthesis of the published case law where a student teacher was the plaintiff, the defendant was an institution of higher education or cooperating local school district, and the issues in dispute were related to diversity. The number of such court decisions was surprisingly small, and the outcomes generally favored the defendant institutions. The court cases fall under three categories: 1) student teachers' diverse views on religion, 2) student teachers' diverse forms of free speech, and 3) student teachers with special needs. Constitutional claims were the predominant avenue of litigation against school districts and those institutions of higher education that were public, whereas breach of contract was the primary claim against private higher education institutions. Helping to fill a gap in the professional literature for both students and educational institutions, this chapter serves as a step forward for institutional policies and practices of preventive law and provides case study material based on published precedents for teacher preparation programs. Additionally, it provides an opportunity for renaissance in the field of education.

In recent years, the preparation of teachers has become a central subject of attention. Educational reform efforts, including the No Child Left Behind Act, have recognized the importance of preparing highly qualified teachers. Thus far, such attention has focused on content mastery and teaching methods. Yet, despite the increasing impact of education legislation, regulations, and litigation generally and the particular vulnerability of teacher education candidates during the culminating, student-teaching phase of their preparation, legal knowledge has been largely neglected (Schimmel, in press; Zirkel, 2006) in preservice programs. The need includes issues specific to not only teachers in general but also—amounting to a glaring gap in the professional literature—student teachers in particular. This, in our view, maps a possible renaissance in the field of education.

In this chapter, we first provide a quick overview of the published research, showing the need for both legal literacy among teachers as well as more systematic information about student-teaching case law. Second, the chapter provides a synthesis of court decisions specific to student teachers' diversity suits. Combined, we illustrate how the inclusion of this special set of knowledge assists prospective teachers, thus contributing to a needed renaissance in teacher education.

Background

Survey studies have confirmed the importance of legal literacy in teacher preparation programs. For example, Traynelis-Yurek and Giacobbe (1992) surveyed teachers in Virginia to determine the relative significance of 20 issues for preservice teacher training programs. They found that "laws and litigation" ranked third overall among the respondents, only surpassed by classroom management and reading preparation. Various other survey studies have found a prevailing perception that preservice teacher education programs lacked sufficient study of education law (Gullat & Tollet, 1997; Paterson & Gibbs, 1999; Pell, 1994).

Yet, as Garner (2000) more recently observed, few teacher preparation programs provide coverage of education law. For example, Patterson and Rossow's (1996) survey of 700 teacher preparation institutions found that only 18 offered an undergraduate course in education law. Moreover, our informal review of a sampling of textbooks used in basic teacher preparation courses revealed that most contained negligible, if any, information on legal issues specific to student teachers.

As a start toward filling the gap in the literature, Johnson and Yates (1981) conducted a survey of the directors of 902 teacher education programs in the country concerning student teaching. Only 1 of the 21 items in their questionnaire asked directors whether either their programs or their student teachers had ever been "involved in a law suit growing out of any aspect of student teaching" (p. 26). Although 46 directors responded "yes," the tabulated "circumstances and outcome" comments did not yield sufficiently specific details.

Only two studies came closer to identifying the published court decisions pertinent to student teachers, but neither one was recent or sufficient. In their separate studies Swalls (1976) and Hall (1991) identified 14 and 26 published court decisions respectively, but the boundaries for relevance were not clear, and the coverage was far from up-to-date.

Method

The boundaries in this chapter for pertinent court decisions were specific to the parties, the subject matter, and publication. The criterion for including a case in terms of the parties was that the plaintiff, or suing party, was a student teacher, and the defendant was an institution of higher education or a school district. The criterion for subject matter was that the case concerned diversity, which for the purposes of this chapter meant an issue of a legally protected group or activity, such as race, disability, religion, or freedom of expression. Finally, "published" in this context refers broadly to the court opinions not only in the official reports, such as the Federal Supplement, but also those available in the two major legal databases, LEXIS and WESTLAW.

Results

The overall search yielded 24 published court decisions that met the first and third criteria but only 7 that also met the second criterion. We divided them into three categories: a) issues of diverse views on religion, b) issues of other diverse forms of free speech, and c) student teachers with disabilities.

STUDENT TEACHERS' DIVERSE VIEWS ON RELIGION

Of the seven pertinent court cases, three fit in this category—two featuring student teachers who expressed atheistic views and, in polar opposition, one initiated by a student teacher who advocated strong Christian views.

In the first decision in this category—*Robinson v. University of Miami* (1958)—a private university "withdrew its acceptance" (p. 443) of a student teaching candidate after the principal of the cooperating school called the university's attention to a letter the student had written on atheism in a local newspaper. The university's committee on student teaching subsequently met with the student, concluding that he was so fanatical in his views in favor of atheism that he would seek to express and impose them on the students he would be assigned to teach. He sued, claiming the university violated its contract of enrollment with the student. The appellate court affirmed the trial court's rejection of his contractual claim, ruling that the university had not acted arbitrarily or with malice and that it had a right to withdraw a student at any time after his acceptance on the implicit grounds of suitability. Additionally, the court reasoned that the university has an "obligation" not to graduate and thereby place "the stamp of its academic approval" on a new teacher "having fanatical ideas" (p. 444) on atheism.

In the second case, a dismissed student teacher prevailed on a constitutional claim, which only applies against a public institution (Moore v. Gaston, 1973). The student teacher had been performing his duties well, but trouble arose one day when he substituted for one of the teachers. He had no problem until a class on the history of religion in the Middle East. During the discussion, he gave "unorthodox" (i.e., atheistic) answers to students' questions about creation, evolution, immortality, and the nature and existence of God. After receiving heated complaints from parents, the superintendent arranged a quick meeting with the student teacher, inquired about the previous day's statements, and dismissed him. The student teacher filed suit in federal court on various constitutional grounds, including First Amendment expression and Fourteenth Amendment due process. The federal trial judge sided with the student teacher on the First Amendment claim of overbreadth, which overlaps with the Fourteenth Amendment safeguard against vagueness, concluding that the balance between the plaintiff's interest in academic freedom and the public school's interest in protecting impressionable minds lies in school officials' providing the educator with adequate notice of the boundaries between permissible and impermissible expression. Here, the court reasoned that "we are concerned not merely with vague standards, but with the total absence of standards" (p. 1041) that would unconstitutionally result in the unfettered discretion of school officials to censor or censure expression. Additionally, the court reasoned that to discharge a teacher without warning because "his answers to scientific and theological questions do not fit the notions of the local parents and teachers" (p. 1043) is a violation of the First Amendment's establishment clause, which prohibits the government from promoting religion. Finally, the court also vindicated the student teacher's Fourteenth Amendment procedural due process claim, finding that he had a reasonable expectation, i.e., property right, to continue his student teaching. Interpreting student teachers as having the same protection as certified teachers regardless of compensation or tenure, the court concluded that the school district had deprived the plaintiff of this property right via a "hearing with twenty minutes notice before a hostile ad hoc committee without eyewitness testimony" and with the questioning focused on a few "unorthodox statements" (p. 1042). The relatively early date and limited jurisdiction for this decision, however, cautions against over-generalizing its applicability in light of more defendant-friendly constitutional precedents.

In contrast, the third court case deals with a very religious student teacher and provides a more representative view of modern constitutional jurisprudence. In *Hennessy v. City of Melrose* (1999), the court rejected this student teacher's constitutional claims. He had started his student teaching and was doing well until three incidents revealed that his strong Christian beliefs superseded his responsibilities as a student teacher. The fourth and final incident occurred when the principal called him to inquire about the previous events. During the meeting, the student teacher called the principal "the devil" (p. 243) and persisted in arguing against the alleged denigration of religion in the school curriculum. Citing the four incidents, the principal informed the college official that she would not allow the student teacher to continue at her school. The college temporarily suspended the student teacher and notified him that he was entitled to an immediate hearing. Upon learning that the principal would not testify at the hearing, the college officials dropped the disciplinary proceedings and rescinded the temporary suspension. The student teacher received a failing grade in his teaching practicum based on four of the basic teaching competencies—communication skills, self-evaluation, equity, and professionalism—that the state required for teaching certification. The student teacher filed suit against both the college and the district, claiming a violation of his First Amendment and Fourteenth Amendment rights. The federal trial court granted the defendants' motion for summary judgment. The student teacher appealed. The First Circuit Court of Appeals affirmed for each of his constitutional claims.

First, the appellate court rejected the student teacher's First Amendment freedom of speech claim. Finding the "apprentice-type" relationship to more closely approximate the employee than the student relationship, the court used the modern three-step test for public employment expression rather than the school-sponsored versus substantial-disruption framework that applies to public school student expression. At the first step, the court determined that the student teacher's expression during the four incidents was at least partially a comprehensive message of public concern, thus warranting a balancing of interests. Doing so, the court concluded that, "the school's strong interest in preserving a collegial atmosphere, harmonious relations among teachers, and respect for the curriculum while in the classroom outweighed the [student teacher's] interest in proselytizing for his chosen cause" (p. 247), thus disposing of his speech claim. Next, the court made short shrift of the student teacher's overlapping First Amendment free exercise of religion claim, concluding that, "to whatever extent religious beliefs dictated the student teacher's actions critical of the curriculum, those beliefs did not excuse him as an apprentice teacher in the public school system from complying with legislatively mandated curriculum and implementing that curriculum" (p. 244). As for procedural due process under the Fourteenth Amendment, the court questioned whether the plaintiff had been deprived of a property or liberty interest and concluded, in any event, that the college's action was academic, rather than disciplinary, and thus did not require a hearing. The court explained that, in light of the state's requirement for certification, the plaintiff's inability to communicate effectively with his colleagues and his unwillingness to work "reasonably" within the prescribed curriculum were as important, "from an academic standpoint, as his ability to prepare a lesson plan" (p. 250). Finally, the court summarily disposed of his substantive due process claim, ruling that—in light of the pertinent precedents that afforded wide latitude to public institutions of higher education—the college's decision-making was "reasonable" within the boundaries of academic decision-making (p. 252).

STUDENT TEACHERS' OTHER DIVERSE FORMS OF FREE SPEECH

A limited triad of court decisions also fit within this overlapping category, where the expression was not connected to religion. The plaintiff in each case was one or more student teachers terminated from student teaching after participating in demonstrations on campus.

In the earliest case in this category, a federal trial court dismissed the constitutional claims of a group of approximately 50 college students, including student teachers, who had participated in a demonstration that resulted in the closing of the defendant state college (Scott v. Alabama, 1969). The college had sent notice, listing the charges, and had subsequently held a hearing for the students. At the hearing, the students' attorney objected to the charges as being unconstitutionally vague, but the hearing committee denied his request to make the charges more definite. The students declined further participation in the hearings, and the college suspended or expelled each of them. They filed suit in federal court, relying not only on Fourteenth Amendment procedural due process but also First Amendment freedom of expression. The court rejected the Fourteenth Amendment claim, concluding that even if one of the charges was vague, the rest were sufficiently specific to satisfy the "rudimentary element of fair play" (p. 166) of constitutional due process. The court also summarily disposed of their First Amendment claim because their disruptive conduct, beyond their expressions of protest, was not protected speech. The judge explained, Freedom of Speech does not mean that just because someone believes "strongly enough that his cause is right, then one may use in advancing that cause any means that seem effective at the moment, whether they are lawful or unlawful and whether or not they are consistent with the interests of others" (p. 168). Instead, people who do so "must expect to be punished when they violate laws and college regulations which are part of a system designed to protect the rights and interests of all" (p. 168).

In *James v. West Virginia Board of Regents* (1971), the defendant public college failed to place the student teacher in a public school of his choice after the college had suspended him from his original student teaching location, which was a local high school. The suspension had arisen in the wake of the bombing of the college's physical education building; the police arrested him along with several other students who had participated in racial demonstrations, charging them with felonious conspiracy to bomb said building, and the resulting media coverage branded him as a militant. Following the dismissal of the charges, the student teacher requested readmission to the college and a student teaching assignment in one of the public schools in the immediate county. Due to the student's militant reputation, the college was unable to arrange a placement of his choice but succeeded in assigning him to a school in another county. Refusing the assignment, he sued the state board of regents, college officials, and the local county school board in federal court, claiming violations of his First Amendment and his Fourteenth Amendment rights.

First, the federal district court in West Virginia summarily rejected James' constitutional claims against the state board and college defendants, concluding that they had fulfilled their "duty of making a good faith effort to place those of its students majoring in education in an accredited school [for student teaching]" despite "much provocation from him" (p. 227). Specific to the First Amendment, the court concluded that his threatening conduct went beyond the protection of the speech and assembly clauses. Second, the court similarly denied his constitutional claims against the school district. Specific to Fourteenth Amendment substantive due process and equal protection, the court concluded that the refusal of the school officials to accept the student teacher was solely predicated on his reputation as a militant on and off campus, which was reasonable and not racial. More specifically, the court found that the public school officials had applied to him "relevant... and proper" (p. 228) selection criterion for student teachers and that he had received the same treatment as white applicants. The Fourth Circuit Court of Appeals subsequently affirmed the district court's decision without further opinion.

Much more recently and similarly, the Ninth Circuit Court of Appeals affirmed the federal trial court's summary rejection of a former student's claim that one of the California state universities violated his First Amendment freedom of expression by not letting him start his student teaching assignment (Holt v. Munitz, 1996). Assuming without deciding that his participation in a press conference in response to a controversial racial incident—specifically, the police beating of Rodney King—was protected expression, the court pointed to undisputed evidence that the reason for his removal was his failure to complete a final examination that was a prerequisite to commence one's assignment to student teaching. Thus, the university proved that it would have disallowed him from participating in student teaching regardless of any protected expression, defeating his claim. However, in using the framework for First Amendment litigation concerning public employees, the court did not address the potential counterargument based on his student status, probably because he proceeded in court *pro se*, i.e., without a lawyer, and thus did not raise such distinctions.

SPECIAL NEEDS STUDENT TEACHERS

In the only court case in this category, a federal appellate court upheld the rejection, based on untimeliness, of a former student teacher's claim of disability discrimination under Section 504 of the Rehabilitation Act and the Americans with Disabilities Act (Everett v. Cobb County, 1998). The plaintiff had multiple sclerosis and bilateral joint dysfunction, which required her reliance on an electrically powered scooter for mobility. She alleged that the supervising teacher had refused to allow her to use the scooter in the classroom and had made various disparaging comments about her disability. After the supervising teacher recommended a grade of Unsatisfactory, and the college faculty decided to give her an Incomplete, she sued both the college and the school district under these interrelated federal civil rights statutes. The fatal problem was that she did not file her suit on time. The court concluded that the applicable limitations period was two years, commencing when she first received notification of the Incomplete. She filed suit exactly two years after receiving the letter confirming the faculty's decision, but that letter was one week after she received the grade. Applying the timeline strictly, the court denied hearing her claim.

Conclusions and Implications

A systematic search uncovered a paucity of published court decisions on student teaching generally and connected to diversity in particular. More specifically, we found only seven court decisions pertaining to the three criteria, i.e., 1) the student teacher was the plaintiff, 2) a higher education institution and/or school district was the defendant, and 3) issues of legally protected group or activity, such as race, disability, religion, or freedom of expression. This number is surprisingly small in the context of our litigious society and in light of the high stakes of professional certification and the vulnerable nature of student teachers. The obvious explanation that universities or school districts settled student teachers' lawsuits before they reached the courts is too simplistic; the same factors that lead to settlement apply to other areas of higher education litigation, yet they continue to yield a robust amount of published case law (Zirkel, 1998b).

The outcomes of these court decisions, i.e., which party ultimately won, are not as surprising and may help explain their limited frequency. Specifically, in six (84%) of the seven cases the ultimate decision, whether at the trial or appellate level, was in favor of the defendant education entities. The pro-institution trend was especially evident for the constitutional claims, which amounted to the main highway for litigation against public institutions of higher education and school districts. The general doctrine of deference to administrative officials, which favors the institutional defendants, is even more powerful for educational matters, often referred to as the doctrine of academic abstention (Kaplin & Lee, 2006). The one decision in favor of plaintiff-student teacher was at least partially an outlier because the plaintiff was substituting for a regular teacher and, thus, was within the employee role rather than in the marginal neither-fish-nor-fowl position of student teacher.

More specifically, in the majority of the cases where the defendant was a college or university, the institution was public, thus providing the avenue of the individual Bill of Rights in the Constitution, which is a dead-end in relation to private colleges or universities. However, this route was unsuccessful in light of 1) the deference and academic abstention doctrines, 2) the flexible and broad lenses in constitutional claims, and 3) the modern trend in student cases generally (Zirkel, 1998a). In the minority of the cases where the defendant was a private institution of higher education, the courts have similarly construed the limited available avenues, primarily breach of contract and torts, with wide latitude for the "ivory tower."

Student teachers face many challenges in their student teaching experiences at both the sponsoring higher education institution and the host school district, with the potential of filing a lawsuit lurking in the background in the mind of both the student teacher and the institutional officials. This chapter helps fill a gap in the professional literature for both audiences. It serves as a step forward for institutional policies and practices of preventive law and for study material in teacher preparation programs, including case studies based on these published precedents.

On the institutional side, public universities and school districts must pay particular attention to the First Amendment freedom of speech rights of student teachers, which accounts for the bulk of litigation to date. However, both the student teachers and those who select and supervise them must recognize that this freedom is not absolute, and it does not prevent public institutions from disciplining those who abuse it. The basic rights of the First Amendment in terms of free exercise of religion and free exercise of other expression are subject to the special interests specific to student teaching, which include those of the children to whom they are assigned and the profession to which they seek entrance. The secondary alternatives of Fourteenth Amendment rather simply mean that public institutions should apply rules and procedures similarly in comparable situations—i.e., equal protection—and provide procedural safeguards, such as notice of specific charges, and substantive grounds in accordance with fair play—i.e., due process. For student teaching programs in private institutions, the primary legal foci are the student handbook and other institutional policies that form the contract that is the primary analog for the Constitution.

Even though there is only one case directly related to students with disabilities thus far, which was decided on technical procedural grounds, both public and private institutions may expect more litigation within the student teaching context, as they are experiencing more generally (Zirkel, 2004; Zirkel & McMenamin, 1999), under Section 504 and the ADA. The key issues concern whether the plaintiff qualifies under these statutes' definition of disability and, if so, whether the defendant institution—whether a college or university or the cooperating school district—has engaged in discrimination, which includes applying the concepts of causation and reasonable accommodation.

Because this chapter only represents one step, additional research on legal issues for student teachers is warranted. We recommend research that includes surveys of legal knowledge and prevailing practice as well as qualitative studies of cases of potential and ongoing litigation, including the perceptions of the participants and the propensity for settlement. Such qualitative research should include an exploration of the reasons for the paucity of published litigation where student teachers are plaintiffs, during a period when published court decisions in both basic and higher education remains at a relatively high level (Zirkel, 1996, 1998b).

Finally, a truly reformed teacher education program should include in its curriculum education law in general as well as preparation of student teachers of the legal issues they face while conducting their field experiences. Student teachers and teacher preparation programs more generally at the preservice and inservice level need more specific and accurate information about the law, particularly in light of the American penchant for litigation and the accompanying misconceptions among teachers and the public (Zirkel, 2006). A true renaissance of teacher education must include adequate preparation of future teachers to deal with legal issues so they do not become deterrents to entering, remaining in, and succeeding in the profession.

References

Everett v. Cobb County Sch. Dist., 138 F.3d 1407 (11th Cir. 1998).
Garner, D. R. (2000). *The knowledge of legal issues needed by teachers and student teachers.* (ERIC Document Reproduction Service No. ED 451 139).
Gullat, D., & Tollet, J. R. (1997). Education law: A requisite course for preservice and inservice teacher education programs. *Journal of Teacher Education, 48,* 129–135.
Hall, G. C. (1991). Legal relationship of student teachers to public institutions of higher education and public schools. (Doctoral dissertation, Indiana University, 1990). *Dissertation Abstracts International,* A51/11, p. 3705.
Hennessy v. City of Melrose, 194 F.3d 237 (1st Cir. 1999).
Holt v. Munitz, 1996 U.S. App. LEXIS 16578 (9th Cir. 1996).
James v. West Virginia Bd. of Regents 322 F. Supp. 217 (S.D. W. Va. 1971), *aff'd mem,* 448 F.3d 785 (4th Cir. 1971).
Johnson, J., & Yates, J. (1981). *A national survey of student teaching programs. Supplemental report 1: Lawsuits growing out of student teaching.* DeKalb: Northern Illinois University. (ERIC Document Reproduction Service No. ED 232 963).
Kaplin, W. A., & Lee, B. A. (2006). *The law of higher education: A comprehensive guide to legal implications of administrative decision making* (3rd ed.). San Francisco: Jossey-Bass.
Moore v. Gaston County Bd. of Educ., 357 F. Supp. 1037 (W.D.N.C. 1973).
Paterson, F., & Gibbs, A. (1999). Graduate education students' attitudes toward preservice education law training. *ELA Notes, 34*(1), 8–9.
Patterson, F., & Rossow, L. (1996). Preventive law by the ounce or by the pound: Education law courses in undergraduate teacher education programs. *National Forum of Applied Educational Research Journal, 9*(2), 38–43.
Pell, S. W. (1994). Preservice teachers' knowledge of education law: Ignorance is no excuse. *Illinois School Law Quarterly, 14*(4), 23–24.
Robinson v. Univ. of Miami, 100 So.2d 442 (Fla. Dist. Ct. App. 1958).
Schimmel, D. (in press). Classroom management, discipline and the law. In C. Everston & C. Weinstein (Eds.), *Handbook of Classroom Management.*
Scott v. Alabama State Bd. of Educ., 300 F. Supp. 163 (M.D. Ala. 1969).
Swalls, F. (1976). *The law on student teaching in the United States.* Danville, IL: Interstate.

Traynelis-Yurek, E., & Giacobbe, G. A. (1992). Teacher preparation areas described as most valued and least valued by practicing teachers. *Teacher Educators Journal, 3*(1), 23–30.

Zirkel, P. A. (1996). The "explosion" in education litigation: An update. *West's Education Law Reporter, 114,* 341–351.

Zirkel, P. A. (1998a). National trends in education litigation: Supreme Court decisions concerning students. *Journal of Law & Education, 27*(2), 235–248.

Zirkel, P. A. (1998b). The volume of higher education litigation. *West's Education Law Reporter, 126*(1), 21–27.

Zirkel, P. A. (2004). *Section 504, the ADA, and the schools.* Horsham, PA: LRP Publications.

Zirkel, P. A. (2006). Paralyzing fear? Avoiding distorted assessment of the effect of law on education. *Journal of Law and Education, 38,* 461–496.

Zirkel, P. A., & McMenamin, M. (1999). *Section 504 and the Americans with Disabilities Act in relation to postsecondary education.* Boston, MA: AHEAD.

Summary and Implications

Cheryl J. Craig

Louise F. Deretchin

In Division 3, Malu, Lawrence, and Mongillo provided readers with an inside view of the reimagination of a graduate reading program. They informed readers that their college successfully completed its national accreditation review but it was their personal recognition of the duplication and gaps in the aftermath of the formal evaluation that prompted the changes they made.

Keeping in mind their college's theme of "preparing inquiring educators," they reviewed their graduate reading program with respect to the themes of knowledge, inquiry, and dispositions. Additionally, they rearranged reading courses and course content, and built sequences of activities so that rigor increased in proportion to the time spent in the program. Another change they instituted was moving from the study of an individual child to an inquiry of a complex situation. Also, the process of revamping the program caused Malu, Lawrence, and Mongillo to want to meet regularly as a team to share not only matters relating to the program, but to their teacher candidates and their teaching practices as well. Indeed, their shared work led to the collaborative writing of the yearbook chapter presented here.

But the revamping of the reading program also caused them to continue to examine their expectations and to want their preservice teachers to work with students with whom they previously have not had experiences. Malu, Lawrence, and Mongillo ended their chapter by encouraging other teacher educators to engage in a deliberative process concerning their subject area offerings. In their opinion, the attention afforded details and sequencing would do much to enhance teaching and teacher education and spur a renaissance in the field.

In chapter 10, Giraldo conducted a small study with preservice teachers in the early childhood area concerning their beliefs about curriculum theory. She embarked on this investigation because she recognized that curriculum theory typically does not have a place in early childhood teacher preparation. Wanting to know what the consequences of that omission might be, Giraldo searched the literature to define curriculum theory in common terms—explanations and/or understandings of a particular reality (e.g., Koetting & Comb, 2002)—and the ramifications of approaching curriculum from a narrow point of view—preservice teachers do not feel the need to engage in intellectually challenging situations or theoretical reflections (e.g., Olson, 2000).

Giraldo then adopted a case study approach to examine how six early childhood preservice teachers made theory-practice connections in their eight-week field placements in a laboratory preschool. Through classroom observations and semi-structured interviews, the author found three themes emerging from the data: learning from classes and the teachers, being in the schools, and moving between two different educational scenarios, all of which have a great deal to do with Schwab's milieu commonplace that Ross and Chan introduced at the beginning of this volume.

Giraldo concluded that, for the early childhood preservice teachers with whom she worked, curriculum was a noun—"goals, tools, guidelines"—and not an adjective or a verb—"actions, performances." In Giraldo's estimation, teacher educators have a vital role to play in addressing this problematic situation. They can open up avenues to inquire more deeply into practice and create spaces where rich, instructive conversations can serve to enrich teaching and learning. To Giraldo, this change in teacher education content would help bring about a renaissance in teaching and teacher education.

The final two chapters in Division 3 were authored by Poimbeauf (11) and Karanxha and Zirkel (12). While distinctively different in outlook and substance, these bookend essays arrived at the same conclusion: that prospective and practicing teachers need to know more about their legal rights and responsibilities so that they can avoid problem-riddled situations, particularly when matters relating to diversity are involved.

Poimbeauf walked readers through five case studies she experienced as a school administrator and as an executive director of a teacher association. In them, a number of "what if" situations occurred before the case study teachers had the opportunity to weigh the magnitude of the situations in which they were involved. As a result, "mistakes" were made that were litigious or potentially litigious. Even when the teachers were not found at fault, personal loss (money, pride, transfer, job change, etc.) was involved.

To round off her chapter, Poimbeauf sought out the views of an employment attorney and a current leader of a teachers' federation. Both agreed that teachers routinely interact in situations where other adults and children may not frame their actions in a positive light. They, like Poimbeauf (and the literature), advised that teachers regularly be apprised of their rights and responsibilities so that "what if" situations can be dealt with in appropriate and timely manners. As readers, we came to know that including content such as the case studies Poimbeauf presented in her chapter would help promote change in teacher education curriculum.

If Poimbeauf would advise that field-based case studies be added to the content of teacher education programs, the final set of authors in this division, Karanxha and Zirkel, would include case law, particularly where student teachers' diversity rights are concerned. To make their point, Karanxha and Zirkel synthesized the published case law where a student teacher was the plaintiff, the defendant was an institution of higher learning or a school district, and the dispute had something to do with diversity. The authors' search of the literature amounted to a small number of court cases dealing with student teachers' diverse views on religion, student teachers' diverse forms of free speech, and student teachers with special needs.

Karanxha and Zirkel summed up their chapter by asserting that there is a need for the institutionalization of policies and practices of preventative law. They also declared that student teachers need to know of potential outcomes, particularly when they find themselves on the opposite side of an issue to an educational institution.

Taken together, the four chapters in Division 3 suggested altering the content of teacher education programs from a subject matter point of view, a curriculum theory perspective, and from considerations arising from both questionable school-based practices and legal precedent. Each provided glimpses of what different renaissances in teacher education could entail.

References

Koettling, J. R., & Combs, M. (2002). The importance of theory and theoretical discourse. *Curriculum and Teaching Dialogue, 4*(2), 137–145.

Olson, M. (2000). Curriculum as a multistoried process. *Canadian Journal of Education, 25*(3), 169–187.

Division 4
PROBLEMATIC CONDITIONS

Overview and Framework

Cheryl J. Craig

Louise F. Deretchin

In Division 4, four chapters addressing problematic conditions appear. These chapters center on the challenges encountered in field-based experiences, students' noncommittal attitudes toward social responsibilities and social structures, ruptures and fissures between teacher education and teaching practice, and the ongoing failure to acknowledge relational complexity in teaching and teacher education.

The division begins with Chapter 13, "Preservice Teachers Leading the Way: Improving Field Experiences by Cultivating Candidates' Voice and Agency." Written by Wendy Burke, Ryan Cowell, Russ Olwell, and David Osta, the chapter discusses how a space was created for undergraduate secondary preservice teachers to examine the state of their field experience with an eye to improving its educative value.

Chapter 14, authored by Thomas Lucey, is titled "Fence Sitting: Preservice Teachers' Agreement with Tenets of Economic Responsibilities and Social Justice." It tells of a survey administered to preservice teachers that indicated that prospective teachers were neither positive nor negative where their attitudes toward economic responsibilities and social justice were concerned.

In Chapter 15, Renée Clift, Raúl Mora, and Patricia Brady take up the topic of "The Categories that Bind: Connecting Teacher Education to Teaching Practice." In the chapter, the authors argue that the current disjointed view of teaching and teacher education means that neither preservice nor in-service education can be revitalized in isolation and that a more inclusive view of practice and structures needs to be embraced.

The final chapter in this division, Chapter 16, is contributed by Margaret Macintyre Latta. In "Encountering Relational Complexity: On 'The Arts of the Practical' in Learning to Teach," Latta uncovers the problems preservice teachers encounter largely due to the denial of relational complexity in the understanding of practice and what it means to be a practitioner.

Thus, in the manners described, the four chapters in Division 4 wrestle with problematic conditions identified by particular authors and co-author teams. These chapters, from the perspective of our contributors, map troubling areas where educational renaissance is most necessary.

CHAPTER 13

Preservice Teachers Leading the Way

IMPROVING FIELD EXPERIENCES BY CULTIVATING CANDIDATES' VOICE AND AGENCY

Wendy Burke
Eastern Michigan University

Ryan Cowell
Eastern Michigan University

Russell Olwell
Eastern Michigan University

David Osta
Eastern Michigan University

>Wendy Burke, Ph.D., is an associate professor in the Department of Teacher Education at Eastern Michigan University. Areas of expertise include teacher education, professional development, teacher communities, and school reform and improvement. She is a co-author of *Teaching as Decision Making: Successful Practices for the Secondary Teacher* (2nd edition) and has other published work examining school-university partnerships, teacher induction, and professional development.
>
>Ryan Cowell, B.A., was born and raised in Iron Mountain, Michigan, a town in Michigan's Upper Peninsula. He received a B.A. in English from Michigan State University and a Post-Baccalaureate certificate in Secondary Spanish and English Education from Eastern Michigan University.
>
>Russell Olwell, Ph.D., is an associate professor of history at Eastern Michigan University. He holds a Ph.D. in the history of science and technology from the Massachusetts Institute of Technology, and earned his teaching credentials at Wellesley College (Massachusetts).

David Osta, M.A., earned his B.A. from the University of Illinois, Urbana-Champaign, and an M.A. in public policy from the University of Michigan. David was the research associate for the 2006–2007 Michigan Department of Education Teacher Preparation Policy Study Group. He has taught elementary and middle school in Washington, D.C., and Chicago.

ABSTRACT

During the 2005–2006 school year, twelve undergraduate secondary preservice teachers initiated an alternative cohort with two university faculty in order to chart a new course for their field experiences with a goal of improving the field experience program for all students in a large teacher preparation program. Firstly, these students compared their expectations for the field experiences with their experiences during the three required phases of field experiences. Secondly, several students conducted a survey of randomly selected preservice teachers in the same program to evaluate students' levels of satisfaction with the program and preparedness. Finally, the cohort of students presented their insights, findings, and recommendations for improving the program to the teacher education faculty. This chapter is the first of a three part longitudinal study that shares preservice teachers' finding their voice, assessing their experiences in light of their expectations for levels of preparedness for the classroom, and making recommendations for improving the program.

Educational researchers have long discussed the need for well-coordinated field experiences as a key component of improving the quality of teacher preparation programs (Darling-Hammond, 2000; Darling-Hammond, 2006; Feiman-Nemser & Buchmann, 1985; McBee, 1998; Metcalf & Kahlich, 1998; Zeichner, 1980; Zeichner & Tabachnick, 1981; Zeichner, Melnick, & Gomez, 1996). Clift and Brady's (2005) detailed summary of 105 empirical studies clearly indicates a lack of attention given to field placements in large teacher education programs, as well as the impact of field experience on preservice teachers' preparedness for teaching, and the need to cultivate preservice teachers' voice and agency in their own professional development. Given what we currently know and do not know about this critical dimension of teacher preparation programs, how should teacher educators purposefully approach addressing what could be characterized as the formidable black box of teacher education and preparation?

Perhaps the biggest variable and least researched factor that impact the quality of preservice field experiences can be found within the assumed role of the individual preservice teacher. As Clift and Brady's (2005) review of literature suggests, little attention has been given to the impact of the individual preservice teacher's ability to navigate the teacher education program in its entirety and how expectations for the program relate to perceived levels of preparedness. Few empirical research studies about field experiences have given preservice teachers voice and agency in influencing the questions asked, the methodology used, and how well the "findings" reflect their cumulative lived experiences as those required to construct meaningful points of coordination between the actual courses, field experiences, and instructors. Further, Clift and Brady's (2005) review suggests that the ways in which teacher educators and educational researchers conceptualize the research on field experiences narrows and limits our ability to learn about what is and what is not effective from the perspective of preservice teachers.

Cultivating Voice and Agency for Preservice Teachers

In his most recent work, Covey (2004) argues that in finding one's voice and inspiring others to find theirs, individuals become much more effective in leading desired change within any organization, personal, or professional relationship. If preservice teachers were to assume a more active role in determining, assessing, and reflecting on their own development as teachers within the context of the university coursework and field experiences, would they be better prepared to be leaders ready for the realities of the classroom? What is the role of preservice teachers in effecting change in a teacher education program? Is there an appropriate role of preservice teachers in addressing the larger issues of teacher quality, public accountability, and teacher professionalism? Finally, how might the voice of the preservice teacher become valued and audible within the public discourse about learning to teach, determining what's valuable within teacher education programs, and articulating appropriate expectations from their university coursework and field experiences in the schools? These questions prompted a group of 12 preservice teachers and several teacher educators to investigate this "coherency of experience" by reflecting on their perceived levels of preparedness in light of what they expect from what should be a well-coordinated program that includes university coursework and field experiences.

This chapter is the first of a three part longitudinal study that shares preservice teachers' finding their voice, assessing their experiences in light of their expectations for levels of preparedness for the classroom, and recommendations for improving the program. The second part of this study will share their experiences as student teachers and revisit their expectations and levels of preparedness in order to supplement their recommendations. Finally, the third part will focus on the students' experiences after they have graduated from the program and possibly as beginning teachers within their first year of teaching. It is our belief that this longitudinal examination of the transformation spanning the novice preservice teacher to practicing teacher continuum will offer needed perspective from those that these programs affect most. These preservice teachers believe that the future teacher's voice, after all, has been absent from the discourse far too long, and is perhaps the catalyst that can move educational research of field experience from discussion to reformation or renaissance, the theme of this volume of the *ATE Yearbook*.

Charting a New Course for Field Experiences?

Field experiences of preservice teachers have now been criticized by the last three generations of educational policy reformers. Beginning with the 1963 Conant Report, the 1986 Holmes Group study, to the Arthur Levine (2005) critique, educational policy analysts and many practicing teachers and school leaders have been united in their plea for improving field experiences in order to better prepare beginning teachers for a successful transition from their teacher preparation programs to the P–12 classroom. Now that teacher education and preparation programs are facing increasing measures of accountability, the consequences for not better supporting beginning teachers' professional development and their ability to bridge their use of educational theory to guide their decision making in everyday classroom practice are increasingly grave and public in that they affect programs' reputations and viability.

In 2000, Darling-Hammond explored the question, "What are the characteristics of exemplary teacher education programs?" The seven programs shared six common features, one of which was a well-crafted and implemented field experience that was tightly coupled with university coursework. Recently, the *Educating School Teachers* (Levine, 2005) report commissioned by the Educating Schools Project identified several exemplary teacher preparation programs. The cornerstone for each of the featured programs was well-coordinated field experiences that provide the contexts for learning how to construct and apply pedagogical theory, knowledge, and practice that are well presented in the university courses. The most critical aspect of the programs was an intentional continuous and reiterative communication loop in which teacher candidates experienced high quality instruction and management in the schools and classrooms and these experiences became salient topics of discussion and assignments within the university courses. These exemplary programs have well-addressed the dysfunctional disconnect that has been historically present between well-intentioned programs and instructors and the ways in which field experiences have been operationalized for preservice teachers.

Most teacher educators are painfully aware that the intention to make these connections explicit is insufficient to insure more tightly coupled learning experiences for preservice teachers. "Research documents numerous situations in which prospective teachers and even teacher educators want to teach in desirable ways but are not able to move from intention to action," according to Levine's *Educating School Teachers* report (p. 16). From a programmatic perspective, there are many instances in which methods courses and fieldwork experiences are described by researchers. The researchers are often the instructors of the courses, and, programs they are researching are described as "tightly coupled" aspects of teaching candidates' pre–student teaching experiences. But would preservice teachers characterize this connection in similar ways?

Some research studies have explored this question as they relate to the use of the professional development school model (Bullough, Hobbs, Kauchak, Crow, & Stokes, 1997; Cobb, 2000; Mantle-Bromley, Gould, McWhorter, & Whaley, 2000). A powerful example of such research that considered the holistic experience for students was Arends and Apple's (1994) examination of preservice teachers' levels of satisfaction and feelings of preparedness to teach after they had participated in an intensive teacher preparation program. This program reflected a professional development school model whereby preservice teachers' field experiences and methods courses were offered within the school context. The overwhelming positive response from the preservice teachers suggests that this program's basic qualities deserved consideration from programs of all sizes. The most salient of these qualities was noted as being the beneficial nature of a holistic approach to teacher education in which university faculty, cooperating teachers, and students work simultaneously within the program. A quote from a participating student explains its benefits most succinctly when he stated, "You have lectures which give the content and theories, but you also have to go into the classroom and see how they work and get to plan them yourself. So it's more beneficial to us as practicing teachers to work with students than to hear about how they should work" (p. 15).

Others have examined the question retroactively, "How would practicing teachers characterize the connections between their coursework and field experiences?" from a program evaluation perspective. One example is Darling-Hammond, Chung, and Frelow's (2002) survey of 2,302 teachers with three or fewer years of experience in order to compare different types of teacher preparation programs on teachers' feelings of preparedness for teaching in their current classrooms. Another example is Haberman's (1999) telephone interviews and administered principal questionnaires to 137 graduates of the University of Wisconsin-Milwaukee teacher preparation program to assess the quality of its program for teachers' level of preparedness. Finally, other studies have examined this question in light of exploring other agendas, such as traditional versus alternative routes to teacher certification, recruitment and retention issues, and supervisors' ratings of beginning teachers' job performance as it relates to teachers' feelings of preparedness.

From our review of the literature, it is apparent that preservice teachers have had little voice or agency when sharing their experiences. Clift and Brady's (2005) review of research on field experiences reveals that there is a need for more research that can conclusively identify the impact of field experiences on teachers' practices and effectiveness, provide more joint inquiries and collaborations between university researchers and classroom teachers, and have the inclusion of voices of cooperating teachers and prospective teachers. Our student-initiated research examines one early field experience program and its alignment with university coursework in order to provide the Department of Teacher Education with student recommendations for current faculty discussions of the redesign of this program.

The Study: Preservice Teachers Investigate Field Experiences in Teacher Education

During the fall of 2006, 26 undergraduate students were enrolled in a secondary curriculum methods course with an associate professor from the Department of Teacher Education at Eastern Michigan University, a very large midwestern comprehensive teacher preparation program. For most of the students, this second of four phases in their professional education sequence involved taking a methods, assessment, and social foundation course while also being placed in a secondary classroom for a minimum of 25 hours during the same semester. This one-credit-hour field experience course did not meet face-to-face but required students to participate in an online web caucus to share their written reflections. Because a primary objective of the secondary curriculum methods course was to engage students in learning about instructional strategies in order to make more informed pedagogical decisions in the classroom, students soon routinely shared their observations and experiences while teaching, tutoring, and being in these classrooms.

By mid-semester, students voluntarily shared their insights and questions about these field experiences and the degree to which the university methods course was preparing them for what they already understood to be the realities and demands for the classroom teacher. According to students, they were becoming both empowered and informed about effective classroom practice as a result of the coherency within this phase of their program. They also became critical consumers about the quality of their teacher education program. At first hesitantly, then later boldly, students shared their frustrations about the web caucus forum for completing their written reflective assignments about their field experiences and noted its lack of a learning community, inquiry process, and accountability for students' learning.

Having heard from peers that the next field experience would be even more frustrating for them, students inquired about what could be done to improve their learning experiences to better prepare them for the classroom. These conversations revealed students' keen insights into the lack of agency, leadership, and voice they currently held within the decision-making and governance of this teacher education program. One student suggested we create an alternative format for the next field experience course to replace the online web caucus that would involve a voluntary cohort of students from our current class to continue our work together during winter 2006. After several more class discussions, a group of 12 students agreed to a hybrid course that involved at least nine face-to-face meetings and online discussions. We agreed to complete the required assignments of the online course and an evaluation of the current field experiences required for every teacher candidate in order to make recommendations to the department for ways to improve the course effectiveness. As a step beyond merely complaining, the students investigated fellow students' opinions of the field experience program by developing and administering a survey for a random sampling of students.

Mode of Inquiry

Our research project is grounded in the qualitative mode of inquiry and relies on a mixed method design for data collection. Together we examined what we have called "the coherency of experience" as students moved through Phase I, II, and III of their teacher preparation program. Students and the faculty member recorded observations, comments, and insights during our winter 2006 meetings. Every student made the effort to attend at least nine of the 15 scheduled meetings. The discussions during these meetings were student-led and, only when necessary, did the instructor guide the conversations with questions such as: What did you learn about students in this moment? What did you learn about teaching from this example? What do you still need to learn in order to address this issue? How did your observation relate to what you now know about learning, teaching, equity, diversity, etc.?

Two of the students, Ryan and David, also conducted a more formal survey of randomly selected preservice students to analyze students' self-reported experiences during each of the three traditional field experience courses. During the final spring meeting, students formally presented their conceptualization of their experiences and recommendations to the Department of Teacher Education for improving aspects of different components to improve overall quality and effectiveness of the course.

A Possible or Probable Coherency of Experience?

The students' culminating presentation to the department provided the evidence of their learning during the semester. Students identified the motivation for participating in this alternative cohort as: 1) a common belief in the importance of the current field experience program objectives; 2) a belief that the program is not meeting its potential; and 3) a desire to improve the field experience for future students. Students next organized their discussion by focusing on each of the phases prior to student teaching through a sequence of questions: Phase I: Do I want to be a teacher and what does it really mean to be a teacher? What is available to me as I search for this answer? Phase II: How do I connect my knowledge and experience to teaching in the classroom and what resources are available to me? Phase III: What is it really like on a daily basis to be a teacher?

From the perspective of the 12 preservice students who volunteered to participate in the alternative section of the course, the presumed goal of this program was for the university to produce highly qualified and effective educators who will eventually make the largest possible positive impact within their profession. It was partially because of this lofty and admirable goal that the following study came into existence.

Each of the 12 students located themselves on a graph that pinpointed the correlation between their expectations and experiences of the field experience program at the end of each phase. This activity was prompted by their interest in assessing the "coherence of experience" as students in the program. By organizing their insights in this way, students were able to articulate the differences among their experiences in terms of their level of leadership and voice in designing their placements, relationships with teachers, and activities in the classroom. Where individual students assumed a more proactive role in these relationships and placements, their field experiences were more closely correlated to the expectations. For instance, when a student sought out additional professional dialogue with classroom teachers, she was then invited into their classrooms and had additional opportunities to work with students, teach lessons, and discuss the teachers' daily decision-making about instructional and classroom issues.

The field experience program at our university is referred to as FETE (Field Experience in Teacher Education). Each FETE section (201, 301, 302, 401, and 402) has its own manual that contains detailed descriptions of required assignments to be completed by the preservice teacher in an assigned cooperating teacher's classroom and then submitted as a reflective journal entry via a section's specific web caucus—a type of online forum. In most cases, there is virtually no peer-to-peer meeting time required of the preservice teachers and minimal interaction at most between the web caucus facilitators and preservice teachers.

A ten question, standard Likert scale survey was administered to 106 students within the teacher education program. The scale of this survey was as follows: 1 = Strongly Agree, 2 = Agree, 3 = Neutral, 4 = Disagree, and 5 = Strongly Disagree. In addition to the 10 Likert scale questions, the survey also contained an optional "Comments" section to which 56 students responded. In an attempt to obtain an equal sampling from all three phases of the FETE program, the survey was administered to students from courses known to contain students from a specific FETE level. The following statements were distributed in a written survey:

1. I feel that the FETE program has successfully met my prior expectations of what pre–student teaching should be.
2. At times, the FETE program seems disconnected from my other College of Education courses.
3. I believe that the web caucus is an effective way to share my FETE experiences.
4. I believe that the program will sufficiently prepare me for student teaching.
5. I always complete my web caucus assignments to the best of my ability.
6. I believe that the FETE program should be changed.
7. I wish I could discuss my FETE experiences face to face with an instructor and my peers.
8. It is my opinion that the current FETE program does not require much effort on the part of the student.
9. The FETE assignments seem to fit naturally within my cooperating teacher's classroom.
10. I am completely satisfied with my FETE experience.

By using a statistical analysis of the survey results in conjunction with the survey comments, common themes emerged that illuminated shortcomings of the current FETE program.

Analysis and Discussion of Preservice Teachers' Survey

The survey questions represent two broad categories for analysis and discussion: preservice teachers' feelings toward the program and preservice teachers' feelings about specific deficiencies of the current FETE program. The first theme to emerge from the results was one that can be classified as students' feelings toward the current FETE program. These feelings can be categorized into three specific categories that are as follows: 1) Expectations for the program; 2) Satisfaction with the program; 3) Preparedness for student teaching.

EXPECTATIONS FOR THE PROGRAM

Item one from the survey asked whether students feel that the FETE program has successfully met their prior expectations of what pre–student teaching should be. The average response of students was 3.01 and shows relative neutrality on the Likert scale. This neutrality, however, should not necessarily be construed as a positive by the teacher education program. The distribution of responses clearly shows the negative sentiment of the student body in regard to the ability of the current FETE program to meet their expectations. In total, 59% of the students located their experiences as either neutral or strongly disagree. This is not to say that all of the responses to this item were negative, but that only 36% of the students agree that the program met their expectations points to the inherent inconsistencies within the program. The data clearly shows that the program's ability to meet students' expectations is possible but not probable.

SATISFACTION WITH THE PROGRAM

Item ten from the survey asked students whether they were completely satisfied with their FETE experience. Similarly to item one, the students' average response of 3.45 on the Likert scale indicates relative neutrality, but it is once again the distribution of responses which most clearly shows the students' sentiments in regard to their satisfaction with the program. While 22% of students feel satisfied with the current program, clearly the vast majority of students feel dissatisfied, with 19% strongly disagreeing with the item and a total of 77% of students who feel either neutral or unsatisfied with their FETE experience. This data points to an alarming inconsistency within the program that makes satisfaction of the students possible but not probable. One student in Phase II of the program remarked:

> I think I feel that FETE is an easier class because it's online and I get to meet with my peers. Doing this, however, gave me a reality check at schools. For me it's more helpful online because of my load, but I'd hope that one day to share my experiences in person.

The students in the advisory group believe this quote passage is representative of many students' sentiments about the program. This quote further highlights the preservice teacher's positive regard for portions of the program, in particular the opportunity to meet with P–12 students within an authentic school setting. However, the statements point to flaws within the system, most significantly, a lack of face-to-face meetingtime with peers and professors. It is these shortcomings of the current program that make successful experiences for the preservice teachers possible but not necessarily probable. "FETE seemed to be a waste of time. I feel that changes need to be made for students to get more out of the program," said another preservice teacher in Phase III. Unfortunately, the 12 students in our hybrid group believe this is an all too common sentiment, and therefore provides an excellent reference point for examining the common themes that emerged from the survey's results.

PREPAREDNESS FOR STUDENT TEACHING

Item four from the survey asked students about their feelings of preparedness for student teaching upon completion of the FETE program, and the students' overwhelmingly negative responses undoubtedly make this category the most disturbing of the three (expectations, satisfaction, and preparedness). While meeting student expectations and creating student satisfaction are not necessarily essential outcomes of the FETE program in the preparation of a prospective teacher, feelings of preparedness for their student teaching experience are fundamental. This data clearly shows a lack of success by the current FETE program in this regard; a field experience program that leaves 70% of its students feeling at best unsure of and at worst unprepared for student teaching is failing students. The specific areas in which the current program seems to be insufficient are visible when the data is examined further.

The second theme to emerge from the statistical results is specific deficiencies of the current FETE program: 1) Problems with the web caucus; 2) A desire for face-to-face interaction with peers and instructors; and 3) FETE assignments which do not integrate smoothly into the cooperating teacher's classroom.

PROBLEMS WITH THE WEB CAUCUS: LOST IN CYBERSPACE

Item three from the survey asked the students about the effectiveness of the web caucus for sharing field experiences. The web caucus could be an invaluable tool for students and faculty to connect and discuss coursework and other academic issues outside of the classroom, especially for commuter students. A caucus system is only valuable, however, if it is used to supplement course material; it is simply inadequate as the sole contact point between students and instructors. This is the problem exposed by students' quotes such as this one from a student in Phase III of the program. The student explains, "The courses should encourage students to be active and work with the students with some accountability. As it is, fiction is more common than the professors in the program might think." Such a comment highlights students' perceptions and experiences with a lack of accountability within a program that relies exclusively on a web caucus. The "fiction" being referred to is the fictitious pre–student teaching experiences that are quite often passed off as completed assignments by students within the current program. The results of the survey testify further to the students' dissatisfaction with the web caucus system as it is currently being implemented within the FETE program. The data shows that 61% of students either feel neutral or dissatisfied with the web caucus as an effective means to share their FETE experiences.

A DESIRE FOR FACE-TO-FACE INTERACTION WITH PEERS AND INSTRUCTORS

Item seven from the survey asked preservice teachers if they wished that they could discuss their FETE experiences face-to-face with an instructor and their peers. In theory, online discussions allow for the free flow of ideas and experiences and could potentially result in rich and engaging learning opportunities for students. In practice, however, this does not appear to be happening. Unfortunately, few students within the current FETE program seem to have the rewarding experiences that the university intended them to have when the program was designed. The following quote from a student in Phase II speaks to this issue, "I understand what FETE is getting at, but I need face-to-face interaction with my peers in order to get a richer experience out of such a class."

This student's comment is succinctly summarizing a sentiment that is heard repeatedly. No one questions the instructors' good intentions in designing the current incarnation of the FETE program, but many preservice teachers question how the program has been implemented. Fifty-six percent of preservice teachers reported that they wanted to discuss their FETE experiences with peers and professors in face-to-face interactions. Nineteen percent did not have strong feelings either way and 25% did not wish to change the online format.

FETE ASSIGNMENTS AND INTEGRATION WITH COOPERATING TEACHER'S CLASSROOM

Item 9 from the survey asked students whether the FETE assignments seemed to fit naturally within their cooperating teacher's classroom. It appears that an inherent lack of flexibility within the design of the current FETE program makes it difficult or impossible to integrate the FETE assignments into the cooperating teacher's classroom in a way that reflects the daily routines of the class. Preservice teachers believe this creates feelings of imposing an artificial teaching and learning experience on the cooperating teacher and more importantly, the middle and high school students in the classroom. "My required lessons in this FETE were disconnected from the students' learning in their normal classroom," said one student. Another said, "None of my assignments have fit in with the cooperating teacher's classroom, and I've found myself apologizing for things being random." The survey data lends more credibility to these students' frustration, by showing the widespread nature of this frustration among preservice teachers. Seventy-three percent of students feel neutral or disagree that the FETE assignments integrate easily into the classroom.

The preceding themes reveal a program rife with inconsistencies which more times than not leave students feeling unsatisfied with their professional development and unprepared for student teaching. In summation, this survey data indicates a lack of positive regard by preservice teachers for many aspects of the current field experience courses that include poorly aligned assignments with student expectations for program outcomes, inadequate preparation for the realities of the classroom, high dissatisfaction with the strictly online web caucus format, and the general lack of accountability for candidates' learning and quality of submitted online work.

Student Recommendations for Changes in Field Experiences

The results of the survey prompted the 12 preservice teachers to reflect on their expectations for their field experiences and led to their articulation of criteria for a well-coordinated field experience. These students believe that field experiences should provide preservice teachers the opportunity to:

- Examine interactions of students' learning with school and community environments.
- Examine the impact of culture on your development and that of others.
- Reflect on teaching and assessment practices.
- Tryout individual and group lessons and assessments.
- Reflectively analyze, interpret, and integrate current classroom practices as they relate to assessment and curriculum classes.
- Apply teaching strategies introduced in reading and methods classes.
- Plan and implement instruction based on student needs.

Throughout the presentation to faculty, students identified the multiple ways in which students were left to their own devices to establish their learning experiences but were not encouraged to have an active role in manipulating, improving, or assessing their impact when these experiences did not meet their expectations. Students repeated the phrase, "Success in field experiences is possible but not probable" to highlight the need for faculty to consider other ways to structure, facilitate, and manage this vital component of their program. Students' recommendations to the faculty for ways to improve the program included more face-to-face interactions between students and between students and faculty, greater coherency and alignment among courses within and across each of the phases in the professional education sequence, and better integration between field activities and the cooperating teachers' classroom activities.

Students further recommended that preservice teachers have a choice between traditional or independent study. The latter could be created with a university professor, allowing students some flexibility to create more classroom-based assignments in collaboration with their cooperating teacher as opposed to university-based coursework. This would provide preservice teachers the freedom to assume a much more active role in shaping their professional development.

FOLLOW-UP

In keeping with our promise to provide a follow-up about these 12 preservice teachers, two authors of this article, Wendy and Russ, will continue to remain in contact with members of the cohort as they enter and complete their student teaching practicums. Using survey instruments and regular email correspondence, our hope is to be able to further follow and link their experiences with cultivating voice and agency during their preservice coursework with their developing roles as student teachers and eventually as beginning teachers in their own classrooms. We believe this information will further inform our efforts to revise and improve our teacher preparation programs while also learning more about how these 12 students transition and negotiate new roles in different classroom contexts.

Contribution to the Field

When given the opportunity, preservice teachers can assume a role that reflects a much higher level of responsibility and leadership within their teacher preparation programs than usually expected. While students can articulate problems in the program, the implementation of real change remains problematic but not impossible. Cost issues, lack of an appropriate number of faculty, and the inertia of teacher education programs all conspire to cripple reform efforts. While faculty are willing to listen to student presentations and ideas and applaud them as an example of democracy in action, the field experience system at the large midwestern comprehensive university resists the changes students (and other faculty) suggest, and remains the weak link in the teacher education process. And yet, there is so much to be learned from these conversations initiated by these preservice teachers that are transferable to other programs in a variety of teacher preparation institutions. The primary lesson we believe should be learned: Preservice teachers who experience a particular program are quite capable of helping us all rethink how we structure and coordinate our courses, field experiences, and their assignments.

When we as teacher educators create forums such as this *ATE Yearbook XVI* to focus on a renaissance in teacher education, we believe such change is made probable through our roles as teacher educators by creating leaders for change to meet the changing demands of P–12 schools. It then becomes in our best interest to invest in providing such opportunities for preservice teachers to gain experiences in cultivating their own agency, leadership, and voice as a central dimension of our teacher preparation programs. It is possible to improve these field experiences for our preservice teachers in order to increase the probability of their becoming highly effective and qualified teachers in their future classrooms.

References

Arends, B. W., & Apple, M. (1994). *Pre-student teaching field-based semester.* Paper presented at the Annual Meeting of the Mid-Western Educational Research Association, Chicago, Illinois.

Bullough, R. V., Jr., Hobbs, S. F., Kauchak, D. P., Crow, N. A., & Stokes, D. (1997). Long-term PDS development in research universities and the clinicalization of teacher education. *Journal of Teacher Education, 48,* 85–95.

Clift, R. T., & Brady, P. (2005). Research on methods courses and field experiences. In M. Cochran-Smith & K. M. Zeichner (Eds.), *Studying teacher education: The report of the AERA panel on research and teacher education.* (pp. 309–424). Washington, DC: American Educational Research Association.

Cobb, J. (2000). The impact of a professional development school in preservice teacher preparation, inservice teachers' professionalism, and children's achievement; Perceptions of inservice teachers. *Action in Teacher Education, 22*(3), 64–76.

Cochran-Smith, M., & Zeichner, K. M. (Eds.) (2005). *Studying teacher education: The report of the AREA panel on research and teacher education.* Washington, DC: American Educational Research Association.

Conant, J. B. (1963). *The Education of American teachers.* New York: McGraw-Hill.

Covey, S. (2004). *The 8th habit: From effectiveness to greatness.* New York: Free Press.

Darling-Hammond, L. (2000). *Studies of excellence in teacher education* (3 volumes). Washington, DC: American Association of Colleges for Teacher Education.

Darling-Hammond, L. (2006). Constructing 21st-century teacher education. *Journal of Teacher Education, 57*(3), 300–314.

Darling-Hammond, L., Chung, R., & Frelow, F. (2002). Variation in teacher preparation: How well do different pathways prepare teacher to teach? *Journal of Teacher Education, 53*(4), 286–302.

Feiman-Nemser, S., & Buchmann, M. (1985). Pitfalls of experience in teacher education. *Teachers College Record, 87,* 49–65.

Haberman, M. (1999). Increasing the number of high-quality African-American teachers in urban schools. *Journal of Instructional Psychology 26*(4), 208–212.

Holmes Group. (1986). *Teachers for tomorrow's schools.* East Lansing, MI: Author.

Levine, A. (2006). *Educating school teachers.* Washington, DC: Educating Schools Project, Inc.

Mantle-Bromley, C., Gould, L. M., McWhorter, B. A., & Whaley, D. C. (2000). The effect of program structure on new teachers' employment and program satisfaction patterns. *Action in Teacher Education, 22,* 1–14.

McBee, R. (1998). Readying teachers for real classrooms. *Educational Leadership, 55*(5), 56–58.

Metcalf, K., & Kahlich, P. (1998). Nontraditional preservice teacher development: The value of clinical experience. *Journal of Research and Development in Education, 31*(2), 68–82.

Zeichner, K. (1980). Myth and realities: Field Based Experiences in preservice teacher education. *Journal of Teacher Education, 31*(6), 45–48, 51–55.

Zeichner, K., & Tabachnick, B. R. (1981). Are the effects of university teacher education washed out by school experiences? *Journal of Teacher Education, 32,* 7–11.

Zeichner, K., Melnick, S., & Gomez, M. L. (1996). *Currents of reform in preservice teacher education.* New York: Teachers College Press.

CHAPTER 14

Fence Sitting

PRESERVICE TEACHERS' AGREEMENT WITH TENETS OF ECONOMIC RESPONSIBILITIES AND SOCIAL JUSTICE

Thomas A. Lucey
Illinois State University

> Thomas Lucey, Ed.D., is an assistant professor of Curriculum and Instruction at Illinois State University, Normal, Illinois. His research interests include financial education, social justice, teacher education, and related technology issues.

ABSTRACT

The attitudes among a sample of preservice teachers toward economic responsibilities and social justice enrolled at a Midwestern institution of higher learning are presented in this chapter. Results were based on the responses from the 75 respondents who completed all items within the interpreted subscales. Large percentages of respondents expressed neutrality about items concerning social responsibilities and social structures. More decisiveness was associated with responses to items involving general impressions of social goals. The author calls for examination of teacher preparation programs and the extent to which they enable students' consideration of these issues.

As the 21st century unfolds, it witnesses a reductionist environment that streamlines interpretations of performance and achievement. In this setting, teacher educators face increasing pressure to develop candidates who conform to the standards of practice. This situation limits the patterns of knowledge and thinking among preservice teachers and the K–12 students in their care. Applying Freire's (1970) theoretical framework, teacher educators prepare candidates to implement legislators' "one-size-fits-all" curriculum and maintain professional order. A renaissance in teacher education necessitates the development of candidates who facilitate students' discussion, promotion, and pursuit of social justice.

Psychological theorists interpret the nature of social justice as procedural (Tyler & Blader, 2003) with dispositions and values inspiring member involvement. Respect represents an important element of identity formation (de Cremer & Tyler, 2005), providing a foundation for involving all societal members. A renaissance in teacher education should enable students' understanding of social justice, recognizing its absence or presence in their lives, and fostering change in its absence. The idea of economic justice closely relates to social justice. An economically just society experiences the fair and equitable distribution of societal resources and respectful behavior toward all societal members (individual and corporate) in their economic behaviors. Understanding both social and economic justice is critical for both modeling related behaviors (see Lucey & Hill-Clarke, in press) and teaching these processes.

At the core of this challenge lie questions of how to prepare teachers who are instruments for social justice. Teaching for social justice represents a goal commonly advocated by social studies and multicultural educators. Literature provides sources (e.g., Banks, 2004; Oakes & Lipton, 2007) that advocate preparing teachers who recognize their obligations as leaders and agents for social change and related struggles. Gay (2000) describes the importance of empowering students by engendering positive identity awareness and critical thinking. In their professional roles, teachers should strive to develop students who understand and counter the social ills occurring through artificial class structures. In order to prepare teachers with positive attitudes toward social justice efforts, preparatory institutions must be aware of the dispositions that their students bring to preparation settings. Building from these understandings, teacher programs may better adapt their curricula to respond to patterns of student dispositions.

While many construe citizenship as a process of following societal expectations, good citizens also have the responsibility to correct societal ills—even those that leaders may not perceive. When laws become the focus, rather than support, of citizens' behaviors, society loses the creativity to change and adapt to new environments.

In education, good citizenship has become synonymous with standards compliance. Standards have become the focus of lesson planning rather than the support for developing lessons. Through classroom conversations about citizenship and its elements, preservice teachers gain opportunities to explore these issues. Structured properly, these conversations engender awareness of existing structural challenges and develop dispositions for equality and social justice.

A tenet of healthy citizenship consists of ongoing critical evaluation of one's society and the effects of its decision-making on members and neighbors. Such efforts require understandings of the society's philosophical, historical, cultural, and economic foundations. Members of a democratic society should defy conditions that prevent full participation, including classism. Challenging these settings requires preparation of teachers who develop critically thinking citizens to distinguish between societal myth and reality. Facilitations of student conversations about economic and social justice issues should investigate the bases for these problematic attitudes and conditions to synthesize appropriate methods of response. Democratic citizenship and social justice are mutually supportive concepts.

This chapter presents data to begin a conceptualization of preservice teachers' dispositions toward tenets of economic and social justice. It begins with a brief summary of literature about the influences on preservice teachers' attitudes before presenting data depicting attitudes of preservice teachers at one institution.

Literature

Evoking processes for social justice requires an appreciation of and sensitivity to societal diversity. Literature indicates that many influences affect preservice teachers' interpretations of diversity. Garmon observes (2004) and posits (2005) that both dispositions and experiences shape preservice teachers' interpretations of diversity. These perceptions are particularly relevant for teaching because of the different interpretations of content that a multicultural classroom contains.

Instructional processes have large bearings on the shaping of students' dispositions. Teacher-centered, fact-dependent classrooms arguably jeopardize the academic and social development of students who come from diverse backgrounds and possess various perspectives of academic content. Textbook dependency particularly aggravates this problem where the teaching of social studies is concerned. Loewen's (1995) widely read criticism of American history textbooks, for example, draws attention to the inaccurate portrayals of national leaders and sanitized depictions of the past, both of which are designed to encourage national pride. When teachers depend on the heroes that textbooks uphold as models for behaviors for student emulation, they ignore the contextual nature of heroism.

The foundations for classroom advocacy of social justice lie within the attitudes of the teacher and his or her dispositions toward the topic. McDonald (2005) provides evidence that teacher preparations concerning social justice emphasize conceptual rather than practical ideals. However, these difficulties also relate to concerns over professional impressions and employment security. Research indicates that preservice teachers are uncomfortable discussing social justice issues for fear of stirring up too much controversy (Lucey & Maxwell, 2005). Also, elementary school teachers tend to engage their students in safe citizenship activities (Stephen, 2006).

To some degree, this situation relates to interpretations of authority. Lucey and Hill-Clarke (2006) interpret reflections of preservice teachers as expressing a range of attitudes toward authority, with general acceptance being expressed in formal structured settings. Preservice teachers may be willing to initiate dialogues about social justice issues *if they are consistent with supervisory permission.* Teachers, either by their own dispositions or out of employment concerns, are reluctant to stimulate classroom conversations about social justice. Lacking guidance, students retain their own biases concerning societal issues, lacking appreciation of others' perspectives and possessing diminished receptivity to new ideas.

Teachers' dispositions toward social justice represent factors in their willingness or unwillingness to affect related classroom conversations. This chapter presents an interpretation of the dispositions toward social justice among enrollees in three sections of a social studies methods course for preservice elementary school teachers at a public Midwestern institution. The results are presented to bring attention to these attitudinal patterns and to stimulate further conversation about their implications for teacher educators.

Methodology

The study occurred during the fall of 2005. The author collected data from volunteer students enrolled in three sections of an undergraduate social studies methods course at a Midwestern institution of higher learning. Two sections met on the institution's main campus and the third section met at a professional development site in an affluent suburb of a large metropolitan setting. The total enrollment for all three sections was 93 (88 female and 5 male) students. Nearly all enrollees were Caucasian.

Instrument

The study employed the *Survey of Social Justice and Music Attitudes,* an instrument revised from Lucey (2007). The instrument contained 58 items with agreement responses formatted using a 5 point Likert-style scale. The items were divided into the following subscales.

- Response to stimulus, 9 items (e.g., Item 1: I generally listen to music like that performed by the artist; Item 3: I enjoyed the musical beat; Item 8: I think that the artist expressed valid ideas that parents should discuss with their children at home.)
- Perception of activity, 5 items (e.g., Item 10: I think this activity was an effective technique to begin classroom discussions about social justice issues; Item 12: I think this is an activity that I will use in my classroom to begin dialogues about social justice issues.)
- Economic justice disposition, 18 items (e.g., Item 16: Credit card issuers should not be regulated because credit cards represent the responsibility of the cardholders; Item 21: Honesty is more important than making a profit; Item 28: Students from lower economic backgrounds typically have fewer educational opportunities than their middle class peers.)
- Social justice disposition, 3 items (e.g., Item 33: Social justice represents an important topic that children should discuss; Item 35: Teachers have a responsibility to discuss social justice issues with their children at school.)
- Self-esteem, 10 items (e.g., Item 36: On the whole, I am satisfied with myself; Item 43: I wish I had more respect for myself.)
- Financial trust, 5 items concerning respondents' enjoyment of different aspects of the stimulus and respondents' agreement with ideas expressed in the lyrics (e.g., Item 47: When it comes to money, you can't be too careful in your dealings with people; Item 49: If you don't watch your finances, someone will take advantage of you.)
- Musical efficacy, 4 items concerning the effectiveness of the activity as an instructional device, including its use of music, employment of cooperative learning, and beginning classroom conversations (e.g., Item 51: I have confidence in my ability to sing; Item 54: I anticipate that I will encourage my students to create their own music in the classroom [aside from music classes].)
- Social justice efficacy, 4 items concerning the respondents' attitudes concerning economic responsibilities and related education philosophies and ideas (e.g., Item 55: I have confidence in my ability to discuss social justice issues with my students; Item 57: I will encourage my students to discuss social justice issues in my classroom.)

The self-esteem subscale consisted of ten items published by Rosenberg (1965). These esteem items were employed by Rubin, West, and Mitchell (2001) and produced a meritorious inter-correlational reliability ($\alpha = .85$). The financial trust subscale consisted of several items modified from Rubin, West, and Mitchell (2001) and two items created by the researcher. The items in Rubin, West, and Mitchell's (2001) study yielded moderate reliability ($\alpha = .65$). The instrument also contained items concerning respondents' developmental contexts and preferred teaching levels. It also collected data about respondents' listening tendencies, using the categories described in Rubin, West, and Mitchell's (2001) study.

This chapter only interprets responses to items associated with the economic justice disposition ($\alpha_{17\ items} = .81$) and social justice disposition ($\alpha_{2\ items} = .90$) subscales. Items within the economic justice disposition subscale were drawn from items associated with Lucey's (2004) Financial Literacy Topic Inventory (Cronach's $\alpha_{Subscale} = .68$), items from Pohan and Aguilar's (2001) Personal Beliefs about Diversity Scale ($\alpha = .78$), and Pohan and Aguilar's (2001) Professional Beliefs about Diversity Scale ($\alpha = .81$). The moderately high alphas indicated that selected items could be generally expected to prompt consistent patterns of responses from respondents. While Lucey's (2004) subscale contained marginal reliability, the items employed for this study related to economic justice rather than behavior expectation.

DATA COLLECTION AND ANALYSIS

Preservice education students completed the survey at the end of a class concerning financial education. The activity-based class was designed to stimulate their awareness of financial education and prompt their thinking about how financially related judgments affect societal relationships. The sessions began with an overview of the financial education areas (income, money management, spending and credit, savings and investment), followed by coverage of inconsistencies between child development and financial education pedagogy (Brenner, 1998), and facilitation of three activities. The first activity was based on Welton's (2005) "Build a Class" activity and illustrated the traits that employers may look for in hiring decisions. The second was Lucey and Hawkins' (2003) "Financial Judgments" activity, which prompted students' awareness of how stereotyping prompts classism.

The final activity connected patterns of decisions associated with the first two activities with the hierarchical nature of societal structures. It also provided a creative device to enable students' safe communication about these topics. It began with the author playing a piece of modern music (Lamm & Van Eps, 1999) that portrayed society as a deliberate process of economic sacrifice. The author distributed lyrics to the students as they listened to the music. The song was selected because its unconventional style and provocative lyrics could take students out of their listening and content comfort zones. For example, the first verse asks the listener to consider his or her economic status, and its relationship to his or her life experiences.

Are you a civilized person?
Is your life form advanced?
Has tragedy avoided you?
This is no accident
We all had our highs
The lows we can't command
Sleeping through insomnia
It is more than you can stand (Lamm & Van Eps, 1999, *Sacrificial Culture*)

After playing the selection, the author encouraged the class to discuss the song and the artists' meanings by asking what it was about, and what selected lyrics meant. In general, the students were unresponsive to questions.

Following the debriefing, the author divided students into groups to develop lyrics that expressed their ideas about the perceived effects of economics on human society. The groups had approximately 10 minutes to develop their songs. To reduce students' anxiety about the activity, the author composed and performed his own impromptu lyrics, after which each group performed its song for the entire class.

Finally, using descriptive analysis, the author interpreted the frequencies of responses to items associated with the economic justice dispositions subscale and the social justice dispositions subscale. Interpretations were limited only to surveys of participants who responded to all of the subscales' items ($N = 75$).

Results/Findings

HIGH NEUTRALITY

The items prompting the highest percentages of neutral responses indicate ignorance, ambiguity, or avoidance toward the responsibilities of businesses, the effects of social structures, and the effects of classroom practice. Respondents expressed the highest rate of neutrality (62.70%) toward an item connecting classroom practice with societal structures (Item 32). Other items concerning social structures and their effects (i.e., Item 24: "Economic structures are facts of life and related to social structures" and Item 30: "People live in poverty because of established patterns in major social systems") prompted slightly lower neutrality percentages (49.30% and 50.70% respectively). Their percentages of agreement (44.00% and 38.70% respectively) indicated an acceptance of economic structures as unchangeable.

The items presenting the second highest degree of neutrality (53.30%) concerned regulation of credit card companies (Item 16: "Credit card issuers should not be regulated because credit cards represent the responsibility of the cardholders") and the comparative importance of learning about social justice (Item 29: "Social justice is less important than reading, writing, arithmetic, and computer literacy"). Concerning Item 16, since credit card debts represent well documented banes of college students, these findings indicate some acceptance of personal fiscal responsibility rather than assignment of blame. However, these findings also appear to express uncertainty about governmental intervention or corporate accountability. Another item concerning corporate responsibility (i.e., Item 20: "Credit card companies should accept responsibility") prompted neutral responses from only 37.30% of respondents, with 45.40% of students agreeing with the statement.

Concerning Item 29 ("Social justice is less important than reading, writing, arithmetic, and computer literacy"), more than one-half (53.30%) of respondents expressed neutrality about the item while 38.70% either disagreed or strongly disagreed. Only 8.00% agreed or strongly agreed with the item. This situation could be explained by a conceptual appreciation for social justice issues; however, this approval involves some tepidity when considering future employment and associated language, math, and technology curricular emphases (see Table 14.1).

LOW NEUTRALITY

The items prompting the lowest percentages of neutral responses related to general social justice goals and dispositions. The items prompting the least neutrality (20.00%) concerned the needs for the rich to understand needs of the poor (Item 19: "Rich people should understand the needs and concerns of poor people") and the diminished chances for success in low economic communities (Item 28: "Students from lower economic backgrounds typically have fewer educational opportunities than their middle class peers"). Respondents were also decisive about parents' responsibilities to discuss social issues at home (Item 34: "Parents have a responsibility to discuss social justice issues with their children at home"—25.30% neutrality) and the equal rights of people experiencing different economic circumstances (Item 17: "People of different economic conditions should have equal rights to basic goods and services, such as health care and education"—26.70% neutrality). In general, this sample of preservice teachers readily took positions on items expressing broad societal ideals and supporting home learning.

Other items involving moderately low (28.00%) neutrality concerned consumer responsibility (i.e., Item 15: "Children should think about how their

Table 14.1 Items Resulting in the Highest Neutrality

	Disagree or Strongly Disagree	Neutral	Agree or Strongly Agree
16. Credit card issuers should not be regulated because credit cards represent the responsibility of the cardholders.	26.70	53.30	20.00
23. Profitability should always represent a business' main objective.	26.70	48.00	25.30
24. Economic structures represent facts of life.	6.70	49.30	44.00
25. The reason that people live in poverty is that they lack motivation to get themselves out of poverty.	38.70	48.00	13.30
29. Social justice is less important than reading, writing, arithmetic, and computer literacy.	38.70	53.30	8.00
30. Many people in society continue to live in poverty because of established patterns in the major social systems.	10.60	50.70	38.70
32. Expectations of school and classroom structure and order tend to preserve patterns of economic order in society.	5.30	62.70	32.00

purchases affect other people"), business integrity (i.e., Item 21: "Honesty is more important than making a profit"), social responsibility (i.e., Item 26: "People should develop meaningful relationships with others from different economic groups"), and teacher sensitivity (i.e., Item 31: "Teachers should be expected to adjust their preferred mode of instruction to accommodate the needs of all students"). These responses indicate that respondents were readily decisive about items concerning social awareness and classroom responses (see Table 14.2).

Discussion

Inferences from this study should be tempered somewhat by the homogeneous nature of the sample. Students of this institution generally originate from upper middle class settings located in suburban communities of a major metropolitan area. Attitudes of preservice teachers from other institutions and backgrounds toward these items may differ.

Nevertheless, as presented in McDonald (2005), opportunities to learn about social justice require "recognition that oppression is a result of institutional constraints" (p. 427). While this tenet has implications for curricular content, it also involves meanings for preparatory education environments. McDonald's examples of experiences with social justice learning primarily involved experiences in ELL classes, discussions of assumptions about learners, and responses to clinical settings. None of these examples went outside the classroom-clinical realm to explore community involvement, service opportunities, or experiences with institutional challenges. Lucey and Hill-Clarke (2006) presented a range of preservice teachers' interpretations of elementary school authority structures and appropriate responses. Additional research must explore methods of providing experiential awareness of the institutional hierarchies and other authority structures that thwart efforts for educational equity.

In a similar vein, it is incumbent upon the teacher education community to examine the structural challenges within our processes that counter these learning processes. Most specially, research needs to consider how the authority structures of teacher education programs affect their curricular directions and relate to their candidates' attitudes toward social justice.

This study found that respondents expressed the most reluctance when taking stances concerning the responsibilities of businesses, the effects of social structures, and the effects of classroom practice. The largely neutral stances indicated the inability, unwillingness, or inability and unwillingness to form judgments about these items. Such findings are particularly relevant since these

Table 14.2 Items Resulting in the Lowest Degree of Neutrality (N = 75)

	Disagree or Strongly Disagree	Neutral	Agree or Strongly Agree
15. Children should think about how their purchases affect other people.	10.70	28.00	61.30
17. People of different economic conditions should have equal rights to basic goods and services, such as health care and education.	6.60	26.70	66.70
19. Rich people should understand the needs and concerns of poor people.	9.30	20.00	70.70
21. Honesty is more important than making a profit.	5.30	28.00	66.70
26. People should develop meaningful relationships with others from different economic groups.	4.00	28.00	68.00
28. Students from lower economic backgrounds typically have fewer educational opportunities than their middle class peers.	6.60	20.00	73.40
31. Teachers should be expected to adjust their preferred mode of instruction to accommodate the needs of all students.	6.70	28.00	65.30
34. Parents have a responsibility to discuss social justice issues at home.	2.60	25.30	72.10

topics are foundational elements in understandings of social studies in particular and education in general.

Concerning business responsibilities, textbooks offer virtually no narratives that stimulate conversations about corporate citizenship obligations until coverage of President Theodore Roosevelt's crusades against corporate abuse of consumers appeared. However, because social studies standards generally limit elementary school coverage of American history to European exploration periods through 1877, elementary school teachers are unlikely to provide meaningful conversations about responsibilities for all citizens (individual and corporate). Although textbooks mention slavery (a citizenship issue involving business motives) as a factor causing the Civil War, Loewen (1995) points out that slavery represented an influential factor in government policy well before regional differences led to this military conflict. Because survey respondents have not been taught to connect corporations or employers with responsibilities of citizenship, they are not prepared to critically evaluate corporate behaviors.

Similarly, social structures lack coverage in social studies textbooks (Loewen, 1995), thus affording learners with limited background information to make judgments about such matters. If honesty represents a desirable virtue, then teachers must be honest with their students about ongoing internal and external social struggles and related patterns of government decision-making. In developing their own sense of identity, students recognize the acceptability of grappling with difficult life choices. Dialogues defining social justice and exploring vehicles for its development represent important foundational discussions.

Respectful teaching builds upon students' diversity to employ instructional techniques that encourage students' experience, interpretation, and dialogue about the different social perspectives to form broad conceptualizations of our societal whole. Conversations about social justice require processes that enable students to step outside of themselves and see the larger societal picture and the inequities requiring their attention.

The items concerning general social justice goals and dispositions yielded the lowest percentages of neutral responses. These items presented general societal goals without providing specific responsibilities of members (groups or individuals). Carpendale and Krebs (1995) found that college students expressed different moral values when surveyed than they demonstrated in their own behaviors; they also determined that accountability represents a vital role in performance of moral behaviors. Respondents in this study seemed to generally understand these items and have well-formed opinions concerning their postures toward them, but how they would actually respond when put in a real-world context remains in question.

Conclusions

This sample of preservice education students expressed more decisiveness about social justice topics of which they had general understandings; however, items concerning particular social responsibilities or theories prompted less certain responses. Teacher preparation programs should consider examining these topics with their students in greater depth. As Lucey and Maxwell (2005) previously observed, teacher candidates are reluctant to discuss social justice topics. This chapter documents a similar reluctance on the part of respondents to take stances on issues relating to social responsibility and social structures. Although additional studies need to confirm or refute the above findings using larger more heterogeneous samples, this study reveals that sampled preservice teachers were reluctant to express opinions about specific issues related to social justice.

Teacher educators need to facilitate the conversations about the difficult social justice topics that their students avoid. Pollock (2001) described the challenges of a school system that denied the presence of and ineffective policies toward bridging a racial achievement gap. Similarly, teacher educators should consider the structures and processes of their preparations and how their natures limit the opportunities for candidates to fully consider social justice issues. If graduates of teacher programs emulate the philosophies of their preparatory environments, and teachers are not prompting dialogues or activities about social justice, then preparatory institutions need to reconsider their commitments toward these issues. If a renaissance in teacher education that significantly impacts society is to be realized, teacher educators must critically examine the patterns of fence sitting that occur in their candidates and respond to the conditions in preparatory institutions that cause them.

References

Banks, J. A. (2004). Multicultural education: Characteristics and goals. In J. A. Banks & C. A. M. Banks (Eds.), *Multicultural education: Issues and perspectives* (5th ed.) (pp. 3–30). Hoboken, NJ: John Wiley & Sons, Inc.

Brenner, M. E. (1998). Meaning and money. *Educational Studies in Mathematics, 36*(2), 123–155.

Carpendale, J. I. M., & Krebs, J. (1995). Variations in the level of moral judgment as a function of type of dilemma and moral choice. *Journal of Personality, 63*(2), 289–313.

de Cremer, D., & Tyler, T. R. (2005). Am I respected or not?: Inclusion and reputation as issues in group membership. *Social Justice Research, 18*(2), 121–153.

Freire, P. (1970). *Pedagogy of the oppressed*. (M. B. Ramos, Trans.) New York: Herder and Herder.

Garmon, M. A. (2004). Changing preservice teachers' attitudes/beliefs about diversity: What are the critical factors? *Journal of Teacher Education, 55*(3), 201–213.

Garmon, M. A. (2005). Six key factors for changing preservice teachers' attitudes/beliefs about diversity. *Educational Studies, 38*(3), 275–286.

Gay, G. (2000). *Culturally responsive teaching: Theory, research and practice*. New York: Teachers College Press.

Lamm, R., & Van Eps, J. (1999). Sacrificial culture. *In my head* [CD]. New York: Mystic Music & Entertainment.

Loewen, J. (1995). *Lies my teacher told me: Everything your American History textbook got wrong*. New York: Touchstone.

Lucey, T. A. (2004). *Assessing character and technology as components of a financial education curriculum for grades K–4: A multicultural interpretation*. Unpublished doctoral dissertation, The University of Memphis, Memphis, Tennessee.

Lucey, T. A. (2007). Beginning conversations about social justice and financial education: Exploring music's role. *Eastern Education Journal, 36*(1), 31–40.

Lucey, T. A., & Hawkins, J. M. (2003, November). *Pre-Colonial East Africa and the Bantu: Lessons for teaching economics in grades K–12*. Paper presented at the annual meeting of the National Association for Multicultural Education, Seattle, Washington.

Lucey, T. A., & Hill-Clarke, K. (2006, August). *Authority structures in public education: Views from below*. Paper presented at the summer meeting of the Association of Teacher Educators, Philadelphia, Pennsylvania.

Lucey, T. A., & Hill-Clarke, K. (in press). Considering teacher empowerment: Why it is moral. *Teacher Education and Practice*.

Lucey, T. A., & Maxwell, S. A. (2005, October). *Pre-service teachers' interpretations of social justice within financial education*. Paper presented at the annual meeting of the National Council for Economic Education, San Antonio, Texas.

McDonald, M. A. (2005). The integration of social justice in teacher education: Dimensions of prospective teachers' opportunities to learn. *Journal of Teacher Education, 56*(5), 418–435.

Oakes, J., & Lipton, M. (2007). *Teaching to change the world* (3rd ed.). New York: McGraw Hill.

Pohan, C. A., & Aguilar, T. E. (2001). Measuring educators' beliefs about diversity in personal and professional contexts. *American Educational Research Journal, 38*(1), 159–182.

Pollock, M. (2001). How the question we ask most about race in education is the very question we most suppress. *Educational Researcher, 30*(9), 2–12.

Rosenburg, M. (1965). *Society and the adolescent self image*. Princeton, NJ: Princeton University Press.

Rubin, A. M., West, D. V., & Mitchell, W. S. (2001). Differences in aggression, attitudes toward women, and distrust as reflected in popular music preferences. *Media Psychology, 3*(1), 25–42.

Stephen, V. P. (2006, February). *The "good" citizen: What teachers are doing to promote participatory citizenship in a global community*. Paper presented at the annual meeting of the Association of Teacher Educators, Atlanta, Georgia.

Tyler, T. R., & Blader, S. L. (2003). The group engagement model: Procedural justice, social identity, and cooperative behavior. *Personality and Social Psychology Review, 7*(4), 349–361.

Welton, D. A. (2005). *Children and their world: Strategies for teaching social studies (instructor's resource manual with test items)* (8th Ed.). Boston: Houghton Mifflin.

CHAPTER 15

The Categories That Bind
CONNECTING TEACHER EDUCATION TO TEACHING PRACTICE

Renée T. Clift
University of Illinois at Urbana-Champaign

Raúl A. Mora
University of Illinois at Urbana-Champaign

Patricia Brady
University of Illinois at Urbana-Champaign

>Renée T. Clift, Ph.D., is a professor in the Department of Curriculum and Instruction at the University of Illinois at Urbana-Champaign. She is the principal investigator on the Crossing Contexts research project and is the Director of the Illinois New Teacher Collaborative. Her research interests include teacher learning and development and the use of technology for preservice and continuing teacher education.
>
>Raúl Alberto Mora, M.A., is a doctoral student in the Department of Curriculum and Instruction at the University of Illinois at Urbana-Champaign. In addition to his research duties in the Crossing Contexts research project, he currently serves as a graduate teaching and research assistant in the Department of Curriculum and Instruction. His research interests include the impact of teacher education programs, literacy development in English teacher education, and the use of media in foreign language instruction.
>
>Patricia Brady, M.Ed., is a doctoral student in the Department of Curriculum and Instruction at the University of Illinois at Urbana-Champaign. She formerly taught English in urban and suburban high schools. Her research interests focus on preparing teachers to meet the needs of diverse students.

ABSTRACT

>Drawing on data from a five-year longitudinal study of thirteen teacher education graduates, this chapter discusses the importance

of abandoning the concept of a renaissance in preservice teacher education *alone*, and, instead, to creating more inclusive and cross-institutional structures for career-long professional education. It argues that a rebirth or reconfiguring of one element of professional education may be blocked or inhibited by other elements that are not changed and that a systemic view is important to any vision of educational reform.

Many people equate teacher education with a set of formal and informal professional experiences that will lead prospective teachers to certification and to employment in a district, school, or classroom. In practice, this definition has often created problematic boundaries within the education profession. For example, instructors in university-based preservice programs in teacher education are often distinguished from instructors in other master's programs, even though many master's programs provide continuing education for certified teachers or provide for a transition from teacher to administrator. The teaching of graduate (non–teacher education) courses, in many institutions, is seen as more prestigious than teaching undergraduate or graduate preservice courses, which then creates status distinctions within and across faculty members and departments.

Field-based practitioners and university-based practitioners engage all too often in negative labeling and distancing—each claiming to be more important in the education of teachers than the other. Advocates for higher education and P–12 education often find themselves competing with policymakers for funding. The list of divisions among educators goes on and on.

At the same time, researchers who study the process of learning to teach over time (e.g., Wilson & Berne, 1999; Darling-Hammond & Bransford, 2005; Flores & Day, 2006); collaborative school leadership (e.g., Clift, Veal, Holland, Johnson, & McCarthy, 1995); or the mentoring of teachers (Feiman-Nemser, 2001) often argue for a unity of purpose and for a conceptualization of teacher education as enabling the lifelong learning of professors, teachers, administrators, professional developers, and policymakers. Accrediting agencies such as the National Council for the Accreditation of Teacher Education (NCATE) call for closer links between preservice and inservice education, complete with feedback mechanisms that will allow for the simultaneous improvement of education and the culture that supports that education.

And so we find ourselves in a conundrum. On the one hand, our institutions, funding agencies, FTE allocations, etc. create the structures in which we work, and our language reinforces and is reinforced by these structures. On the other hand, our knowledge of professional development, learning, and school culture reminds us that, as individuals who want to improve what we do in order to better serve our students and to work together to create equity and excellence in education, we must transcend the structures we have created and the practices that are bounded by these structures. This chapter presents a data-based argument for abandoning the concept of a renaissance in teacher education *alone*, in order to create more inclusive structures and labels for these structures that encourage mutual respect, shared responsibility, and continuous improvement in the education of children, adolescents, and adults.

Crossing Contexts

From fall 2000 until the present, we have had the pleasure of working with thirteen graduates from the University of Illinois at Urbana-Champaign's English teacher preparation program and to study their career development. In this section we describe the teacher education program they completed and provide an overview of the methodology of the study, concentrating on what we have extracted from the data set for this chapter.

THE DEVELOPMENT OF PRACTICE

The work of activity theorists such as Vygotsky (1978) and Leont'ev (1981) introduced the concepts of psychological and technical tools and their relationship to learning and social practice. Vygotsky argued that the process of human development involves the transformation of innate human cognitive functions (he referred to these as "lower mental functions") such as memory and perception to higher mental functions such as cultural knowledge. Vygotsky argued that higher mental functions are distinctly human and employ signs to act as representations for ideas, mental processes, or physical objects. Language, memory, and reasoning are examples of psychological tools that facilitate development within the self. Technical tools, such as pens, the Internet, and books, allow individuals to extend their individual mental processes to a broader social context.

Thus, the process of development occurs when people use psychological and technical tools to transform lower mental functions (innate cognitive processes) into higher mental functions, or culturally or socially constructed knowledge. A developing practice includes the conscious and unconscious appropriation and use of tools. Instruction, we argue, is an intervention that influences appropriation. But instruction does not occur independently of the individual's history or the social setting in which we live and work.

Therefore, we have drawn also on Bourdieu's (1990b) argument that practice is socially constructed, shaped by individual and cultural histories and by the social rules and power relations governing social settings. An individual teacher's history is socially and culturally influenced by past and present interactions with formal and informal teachers and students, living and teaching environments, and so on. Thus, an individual is continuously working within a system of structures and principles that establishes practice within and across individuals, defined as *habitus*. The *habitus* (Bourdieu, 1990a, 1990b) seeks to preserve itself over time and establishes practices in accordance with the social rules known and understood by both the individual and that society to which he or she belongs. These rules not only define acceptable and unacceptable actions, but also describe status and power relations and their effect on individual interactions.

All these rules, power relations, and relationships are situated within social and historical settings known as fields (Bourdieu, 1993; Bourdieu & Wacquant, 1992). The field prescribes socially and historically established norms for behavior, defines roles and relationships, establishes status hierarchies, and identifies sanctions for violating norms. Bourdieu (1990b) argued that practice is conscious and deliberate in part because it is constrained by *habitus* and field. The development of practical sense, or the "feel for the game," involves an understanding of social conventions and rules, as well as strategies for accomplishing goals. A teacher education program such as ours defines a field within a larger field known as a university, and as teachers-to-be move in and out of schools or churches or other settings they move in and out of fields that are not necessarily governed by the same "rules" as a university classroom.

THE TEACHER EDUCATION PROGRAM

In fall 1998, a redesigned secondary teacher education program was implemented at the University of Illinois at Urbana-Champaign. Students in the English education program were required to obtain a major in English that emphasized British and American literature and Western culture, with additional courses in rhetoric. Admission to the cohort-based program, with a minor in education, occurred in the sophomore or junior year and was quite selective. Those who were admitted had high grade point averages and often had much experience working with children and adolescents. The English teacher education minor introduced students to literature from many cultures, emphasizing that issues of race and class permeate the educational system in the United States.

The content-based methods courses were titled "Teaching in a Diverse Society," "Teaching Diverse Middle Grade Students," and "Teaching Diverse High School Students." Each of these courses had associated early field experiences in local middle and high schools in the communities surrounding the university. Most of the field placements were in classrooms populated by racially and economically diverse students. In addition to methods courses, the students also completed coursework in adolescent development, assessment, legal and professional issues, educational technology, and working with students with special needs.

The fourth semester of the program, "Teaching and Assessing Secondary School Students," was a seminar that accompanied student teaching. Most students completed seven-week placements at both a middle school and a high school in Illinois, but a few completed fourteen-week placements at a single high school. Student teaching was book-ended by an intensive week at the university at the beginning and end of the semester.

PARTICIPANTS

The research team, which has changed over time, has included five graduate students (two white, US females; one Korean female; one white, US male; and one Colombian male) and one professor (white, US female). The professor (Renée) was the instructor in the first two methods courses; Patricia was the graduate student who took notes in all of Renée's classes and has been with the project since the beginning. Raúl joined the project in the fall after the participants had graduated. The other team members helped collect and analyze data at various points in the project, but left the project to pursue their own, unrelated work.

The teacher education students, in addition to their outstanding academic college history (all held GPAs over 3.0 and made the Dean's List in their colleges on several occasions), were involved in different leadership positions and organizations across the University of Illinois campus (e.g., leadership in sororities, religious organizations, choral groups, etc.). All thirteen graduated as highly qualified (U.S. Department of Education, 2001) middle school and high school English teachers; they have chosen career paths that included teaching (with or without changing schools) and not teaching. Tables 15.1, 15.2, and 15.3 provide more detailed information about the participants.

DATA COLLECTION

Data collected prior to student teaching included detailed notes on Renée's classes, all course assignments for all methods classes, and a retrospective tran-

Table 15.1 Crossing Contexts Participants Teaching in Same Schools since Graduation

Name and Background	Teaching Position	Graduate Studies
Carrie: married white female	Majority white suburban high school; hired part-time 1st year after graduation, full time	Master's in counseling thereafter (in progress)
Iris: single Vietnamese-American female	Mixed-income, racially mixed (predominantly white and Latino) suburban high school where she had been a student	None
Julia: married white Jewish female	Majority white suburban high school where she had been a student	Master's in English and educational administration
Marie: engaged white female	Majority white suburban high school where she student taught	Master's in reading and learning disabilities
Mimi: married white Christian female	Mixed-income, racially mixed (predominantly African-American and white) middle school in the mid-sized community in which she had been a student	Master's in curriculum and instruction
Rachel: single white Jewish female	Majority white suburban middle school	Master's in reading

script interview covering all university coursework. During student teaching, each participant was observed and interviewed twice. For three years following their graduation from the university, we observed and interviewed all thirteen participants twice a year (whether they were teaching or not). We also took field notes on the participants' work contexts.

Each summer after graduation, we met with the participants and shared our notes and our summaries of the notes. The participants provided feedback on our work and provided additional details about their experiences and reflections. Even though we are not collecting data anymore, we are in contact with each participant at least once a year. As we are now beginning to publish our work,

Table 15.2 Crossing Contexts Participants Who Have Changed Schools since Graduation

Name and Background	Teaching Positions (Years after Graduation)	Graduate Studies
Eldridge: single white Christian male	Year 1: mixed-income, predominantly white high school in a mid-sized community Year 2, semester 1: mixed-income, majority white high school in a mid-sized community Year 3: assistant librarian and coach in a small, mostly white rural community Present: mostly white rural middle school near his hometown	None
Kelly: single white Jewish female	Years 1–2: mixed-income, racially diverse (predominantly white), suburban middle school Year 3: teaching science in a racially-diverse (predominantly African-American and Latino) and primarily low-income urban charter school Present: majority white suburban high school	Master's in reading
Lisa: married Latina	Years 1–3: racially diverse (predominantly white and Latino) high school in a mid-sized community Present: racially diverse (predominantly white and Latino) urban high school with many bilingual students	Master's in educational administration (in progress)
Susan: single white female	Year 1: racially diverse (predominantly white and African-American) high school in a mid-sized community Year 2 to present: mixed-income, racially diverse (majority white and Latino) suburban middle school	Master's in educational administration

15.3 Crossing Contexts Participants Who Chose Not to Teach

Name and Background	When Decided Not to Teach	Positions after Graduation	Graduate Studies
Dexter: single white male	Prior to student teaching	Years 1–2: Peace Corps Year 3 to present: marketing	None
Jenni: married white female	First semester in teacher education program	Years 1–3: law school Present: Attorney General's office, disability rights	Law school
Grace: single white female	During student teaching	Years 1–2: teacher's aide in a residential home for special needs youth Year 3: special education teacher in urban charter school Present: in seminary	Theological studies (in progress)

* Note: Religion is identified when the participants specifically discuss their religious affiliation and how they perceived that it affected their identities.

several of the participants have begun preparing narratives of their own, to be included in a book that is in progress. We are drawing from drafts of their narratives in this chapter.

DATA ANALYSIS

Our analysis of course syllabi identified five major themes within the program (literacy, diversity, pedagogy, student learning and response, and technology), which became our initial categories for analysis. Because our participants were beginning careers, we added a sixth category of career development. These data were summarized by category and shared with the participants once a year in the form of chronological narratives. Across the years, we created charts for each participant in which we noted trends in their reflections and practices over time and across work contexts. The entire remaining research team discussed the charts in preparation for a detailed analysis of participants' career development over time. Following these discussions, Renée then collapsed the data into slightly different categories that corresponded to questions the team identified as important to understanding the participants' developing practice:

- What can we say/infer about influences on the participants' practices prior to entering the teacher education program?
- What opportunities to learn were present during the teacher education program and how did they influence the participants (or not)?
- What opportunities to learn were present during student teaching and how did they influence the participants (or not)?
- What opportunities to learn were present during the first three years following graduation and how did they influence the participants (or not)?

From this analysis, we began to identify what we are learning from our participants. There is a lot of data and the analysis and interpretation of the data comprise far more than the space we are allocated for this chapter. Therefore, the next section focuses only on what we have learned that can inform a rethinking of professional education.

What We Have Learned about Professional Learning Needs

In the information we provided about the teacher education program we noted that our English majors were academically successful students who completed an intensive English major and a four-semester, field-based teacher education program that emphasized working with diverse student populations. We see evidence that the emphasis on diversity created not only an awareness of the importance of working with diverse populations, but provided some psychological and technical tools for doing so. For example, Marie noted that the program was successful "in making me aware of diversity issues that are going to arise in my classroom" (Student teaching interview, spring 2002).

In another example, Lisa's goals for her students were to learn about different cultures through literature by giving them choices in selecting books about cultures with which they were not familiar, and providing "a chance to read something they're interested in, something that they like" (Teaching interview, spring 2003). This strategy was similar to the one employed by her methods instructor in the second year of the program. Carrie used a technique from the first year of the program—constructing an "identity pie"—to have her students explore stereotypes:

> Make a pie chart of different aspects of your identity. . . . Think of anything—could be your culture, school stuff—school takes up a lot of your life." She also asked the class to write about what assumptions do others make about you that are inaccurate. For example, people look at you and because you have blond hair and fair skin, they think you can't be Italian. (Classroom Observation, Fall 2003)

We also saw evidence that the participants became champions for students who were labeled as not being academically successful and for students with special needs. Julia, who began the teacher education program intending to teach honors classes, became committed to working with struggling students while in the teacher education program. During student teaching she worked with a cooperating teacher whom she labeled the "Worksheet King." She reported that she was told to do whatever she wanted with the class because, "you can't mess these kids up anymore than they are." After her first few days, Julia realized that a traditional approach was not working, so she told the students to write what they were interested in. She then designed a curriculum around their interests: "And from that point on, I just loved those kids . . . once they saw that I cared about their opinion and what they wanted to do" (Teaching interview, Fall 2003). In her second year of teaching, Julia requested to be assigned no honors classes and more lower-level classes.

Jenni, the lawyer, chose to complete several internships involving the rights of students with special needs and is now working in the area of disability rights with the State Attorney General's office. In the third year following graduation, her first year of teaching, Grace taught ten 5th and 6th graders who qualified for special education, co-teaching two English and two math classes, and—at the end of the day—supervising homework and teaching reading.

BEYOND THE PRESERVICE PROGRAM

While the teacher education program did prepare students, like Grace, to be sensitive to developing curriculum that provided accommodation for students with special needs it did not, however, prepare them to be *the* special needs teacher for a given school. Our data document several instances in which graduates' major assignments were out of field. There are five cases in addition to Grace that are less dramatic examples of out-of-field assignments. Mimi was assigned to teach social studies in her first year. Iris and Kelly taught speech, despite having had only one college course in that subject. Kelly was hired to teach English, but was moved into a science class in her second teaching assignment—in her third year of teaching. Carrie ran the school newspaper despite having no experience or coursework in journalism. Even Dexter, whose Peace Corps assignment was in Turkmenistan, reported teaching out of field in that he was expected to teach English as a Foreign Language and to teach others about teaching.

Many of the participants also were teaching reading either as an explicit assignment or as a part of their overall English assignment. Kelly, Rachel, and Marie began master's programs in reading and found them to very helpful in their teaching. For example, Kelly reported that her graduate courses helped her develop strategies that enabled students to make connections:

> There are picture books where if you don't look at the pictures, you're not going to understand what's going on. . . . And the kids like it, because it's a picture book. It's harmless. It's benign. It's not scary, it's not like the master anthology—it's *The Cat in the Hat.* (Teaching Interview, Fall 2004)

Marie reported applying information from her master's program in the reading lab, where she was able to help other teachers construct pre-reading activities and other strategies. She also reported that her pacing had slowed, realizing:

> More and more that I need to do more pre-reading, take things slower, spend another day on this, than I did last year, in both my classes, you know, in my sophomore, the "accepting differences" unit, like I said, I taught *The Secret Life of Bees* this year before *To Kill a Mockingbird* and nobody ever did that before, so I created like the entire unit for it [because] there's nothing out there on it so I did all the activities and supplementary stuff. That took a lot of time. (Teaching Interview, Fall 2003)

Rachel, who began her graduate program in the fall of 2004, felt that the graduate program aligned with her teacher education program, but went way beyond as it, "quickly moved into educational research demonstrating how those theories play out in classrooms" and the graduate courses, "focused on specific reading strategies including literature circles, questioning the author, book clubs, and reader's and writer's workshop." She reasoned that, "Maybe because I actually had students to practice on, or because I had real teaching experiences to draw from, both the theory and the methods seemed not only useful and relevant, but also imperative for my continued growth as a teacher" (Narrative Draft, Fall 2006).

Our analyses indicated that while the preservice program laid a foundation for learning, it did not prepare all of the graduates to teach in each situation in which they found themselves. We also learned that while there was variation in the degree to which the practices advocated by the teacher education program and the school contexts in which our participants taught built upon the teacher education program, there were no outright school-based attempts to override the content of the program. For example, Rachel described how her practice and her school culture reinforced ideas from the teacher education program in that she was required to, "Maintain high expectations for all students, and give them all opportunities for success." But she also noted that:

> Revising [papers after receiving feedback] is awesome, but I cannot read the same set of papers that many times. My students have tons of time to have a friend peer edit, or have me look over it for a few key items, but they only get to hand it in for grading once. A multicultural curriculum is not always easy to implement, especially if your school only approves (and owns) certain books. It's something you have to ease your school into gradually (especially when it comes to proposing a new book to be approved by the board! Scary!). (Reflective Writing, Summer 2004)

Susan noted that her second teaching position, "felt a lot like an extension of C & I [Curriculum and Instruction] because they were very up-to-date and encouraged growth." She gave a few specific examples, including goal-setting, classroom management, and technology use:

> The assessment class taught me how to use my objectives in planning tests, which I certainly do and expect the state to do on standardized tests. . . . I remember Renée specifically using examples of how she managed our C & I class—from simple things such as how to pass out papers. This might seem insignificant, but it was the first time I ever thought about the simplest tasks and how they should be executed in a precise manner. . . . Having created my own web-based portfolio, I decided to use Teacherweb as a website for posting class expectations and big projects. (Reflective Writing, Summer 2004)

However, Susan also identified areas in which her teaching and context were inconsistent with the ideals she learned in the teacher education program, such as the details of lesson plans and the limitations of No Child Left Behind.

> The types of lesson plans that we wrote [in the teacher education program] are not reasonable to do on an every day basis. They were far more detailed than my principal expects. . . . While I like to explore different types of literacy . . . No Child [Left] Behind keeps me from really exploring a lot of different types. There is such a push for students to be able to read and immediately spit back what they

read, that I feel some of my class is tailored to those standardized models (when I have to). (Reflective Writing, Summer 2004)

Many of our participants talked about the pressure to produce results on standardized tests. Mimi, for example, mentioned that all classrooms had timers, specifically bought for all 7th and 8th grade teachers for ISAT (Illinois Standards Achievement Test) preparation and that, "Two or three classes made up raps, their own raps that they created and wrote to get pumped up for the ISAT, and we'll see if it all worked when we get the scores back, because last year the scores were really low. So that was just to encourage them and inspire them to do well" (Teaching Interview, Spring 2004). We observed Marie explicitly teaching her high school students how to take a standardized test. She provided handouts on the ACT and discussed questions and strategies for answering: "Go ahead and look at the paragraph that starts on line 80 where it says [reads the line]. If you read that paragraph, it talks about the letter, but it never talks about a note, so even if you weren't positive, by process of elimination you could come up with number two" (Classroom Observation, Spring 2004).

FAMILIARITY WITH THE SCHOOL AND THE STUDENTS

In many cases, the participants who were teaching either began in schools with which they were already familiar or worked their way back to familiar situations. Julia, Rachel, Iris, Mimi, and Carrie began teaching in districts in which they had been students or in similar districts nearby. Lisa, now in her second school, is teaching very near her home community. Kelly, now in her third school, is teaching in a district that is very similar to her home district. Eldridge, who is now in his fourth school, credits knowing the students as one of the factors that led to being rehired—for the first time, ever.

> My familiarity with the communities of Ashel and Charruke [pseudonyms] also helped me get through the past year. It is difficult to explain, but I just feel comfortable in my interactions here. At Diamond Bay, the rich suburb, and LaRue [pseudonyms], the rough river city, I had trouble fitting in. Both towns are in the same state as my rural hometown, but people operated differently there. I compare it to hearing different accents. Listen to someone speak and you can tell if they are from the area or from elsewhere. If the accent is familiar, communication and interaction comes more effortlessly. I think it is the same thing with lifestyle and everyday behavior. For me, when I moved out of farm country, it was more difficult to interact with co-workers, students, and parents. (Narrative Draft, Summer 2006)

Interestingly, however, some of the participants returned to familiar situations with new lenses and a new view of the students in those settings. Julia, as we have mentioned before, realized that there was a whole group of students who deserved better instruction and more chances to be academically successful. Kelly, who, after three years, worked her way into a job in an affluent suburb, noted:

> The first time I sought this job I was a different person with a different agenda. I wanted the job for the prestige and because I thought it was the only job I wanted. But now I was more experienced. I had learned to embrace diversity in my classroom and I wanted an opportunity to expose other students to the world beyond their communities. (Narrative Draft, Fall 2006)

And Iris provides a poignant example of returning to a school, seeing it differently, but not being sure how to proceed based on this new insight.

> One of the biggest problems that I learned about in my coursework and still witness daily is the inequality that the school system perpetuates. Schools perpetuate the inequalities of society by feeding the cycle of inequality through what is taught and how it is taught in the classroom. I am seeing how different classes of students will be taught differently so that their education corresponds with jobs in their social class. For example, working-class students are not taught ideas as much as they are taught to behave and follow directions. This type of education seems to prepare the working-class students for blue-collar jobs like factory work where behaving appropriately and following the orders of the supervisor are key. What results is that working-class students become more resistant to authority because they are not allowed any liberties, only strict rules.
>
> I, personally, feed into this cycle when I handle my lower level students with a firm voice and give them worksheets to keep them quiet. On the other hand, affluent students are taught to be creative, critical, and independent and are given much more freedom because they have been named the "good kids" who have good futures on the horizon. In a similar manner, I know I have given my regular and honors level students many more liberties and a more relaxed style of teaching because I felt they could handle it. Why I didn't believe my low level students could handle such responsibility just demonstrates how easy it is to slip into the cycle that our society has become. (Narrative Draft, Fall 2006)

SUPPORT ACROSS CONTEXTS

Our participants' work contexts sent varied messages about the degree to which new teachers were valued and encouraged to learn. Iris reported that her school provided her with opportunities to go to conferences and in-services to learn new ideas. She said that she got the idea to do a think-aloud in her developmental class from a conference she went to. She had originally heard about "think-alouds" in a methods course, but she never really thought to use them until she heard about it again at the conference (Teaching Interview, Fall 2003). "Think-aloud" is a methodology employed in reading comprehension instruction in order to help learners become more active readers. In a think-aloud, the teacher first models how to engage with the text by making predictions or inferences about the text while thinking out loud. Then, students read short text segments while asking each other questions about what they are thinking about the text they are reading. Think-alouds are usually linked to the development of specific reading strategies. For further information, Kukan and Beck (1997) offer a very thorough historical overview of thinking aloud as a reading comprehension methodology. Rachel reported that she received assistance from her team, the reading specialist, and her principal. Eldridge felt that in his fourth position he finally received specific help from a mentor:

> She welcomed me to any of her materials, and I used a great deal of them. I lifted my entire spelling curriculum and a ten-week research project from her. If I needed a last minute activity, she would have some worksheet I could copy off. She also helped me get wise to all of the school's policies and procedures. (Narrative Draft, Summer 2006)

But perhaps Kelly put it best as she talked about what she perceived as a communal effort to help her succeed:

> SHS gives each new teacher a mentor. They try to seat the new teacher near his or her mentor in the department office as well as make sure the two teachers have at least one common planning period. Although each new teacher is assigned a mentor, it is the community of the school that collectively takes on that role. When a lesson does not work and you want to think it through, many ears are willing to help you reflect. Teachers are open to letting others come in and observe how they teach, not only to help the observing teacher, but also for the observed teacher to gain useful feedback. It is a community where the goal is not to have perfect lessons everyday, but rather to learn how to improve your craft from lessons that do not go well. (Narrative Draft, Fall 2006)

Their experiences emphasize the nature of professional learning as continuous and context dependent. Our own experiences as teacher educators suggest to us that our system(s) of professional education and our thinking do not always promote continued learning that is aligned with the goals and the content of our preservice programs. In other words, we seldom support teachers' learning across years, across students, and across contexts.

CAN WE REDEFINE PROFESSIONAL EDUCATION CATEGORIES?

Words matter (Gee, 1999; Kress, 2003). The questions we raise and the words we use are grounded in the assumptions of the cultures in which we live and work; they also predispose certain answers. In the previous section we presented data that showed the influences and the limitations of preservice instruction. We also suggested that the schools and districts varied widely in their support for new teachers' learning, as did the participants' efforts to continue learning on their own.

Kelly's and Eldridge's cases (both were fired from their first teaching positions and quit their second positions because they perceived a lack of "fit") demonstrate perceptions of career paths across contexts that do not support their learning and promote feelings of doubt and low self-esteem. Kelly worked to learn more through a graduate program; Eldridge did not seek out similar learning opportunities. Marie and Rachel both worked in contexts they perceived as supporting them personally and professionally and that provided people, materials, and ideas to continue their professional development. They not only took advantage of their contexts, but took advantage of additional professional coursework in order to draw on resources beyond the school.

Our participants' experiences suggest that our preservice program was able to foreground the importance of certain practices (and the use of certain tools) but they were unable to link theory, recommended practice, and actual practice until the participants perceived a need for the information. Additional teacher education—professional education—is absolutely necessary to provide tools that can be appropriated and employed in specific contexts.

Furthermore, until we analyzed our data set we were only somewhat aware of the numbers and variations in our participants' out-of-field classroom placements (fifth grade special needs, newspaper, middle school social studies, science, etc.) and after school responsibilities (dance team, tennis team, reading lab, etc.). Our analysis across the entire group, however, led us to realize that a comprehensive program with additions such as fundamentals of coaching, physical conditioning, content preparation in science and social studies, etc. would take years to complete and would be unreasonable, impractical, and completely unworkable. It is impossible, if not absurd, to expect preservice programs to offer courses and field experiences in every possible combination of teaching assignments and school teaching situations. Providing additional support once graduates have begun teaching, however, is something that is crucial.

Finally, as we tracked our participants' moves toward contexts (fields) with which they were familiar and in which they understood a local and particular variation in the "game" of school, we also realized that they needed support for understanding students and school and community cultures, and their own responses to those students, schools, and communities—when they were in the actual settings. The preservice field did not present a challenge to our academically successful participants' *habitus*—they understood how to excel as students. Indeed, they were all accustomed to academic success and had very little familiarity with failure. When confronted with unfamiliar situations in their new role of teacher and when they perceived no assistance with understanding the field and no tools for quickly adapting to their new environment, they acted to move away from relative failure and into situations in which they might succeed.

The reforms promoted by the Carnegie Foundation of New York's Teachers for a New Era Project (Carnegie Foundation of New York, n.d.) call for more support of graduates and the universities supported by this project are using varied methods for doing so. Electronically based projects such as WINGS (Welcoming Interns and Novices with Guidance and Support, n.d.) at the University of Texas at Austin and BRIDGE (Building Resources: Induction and Development for Georgia Educators, n.d.) at the University of Georgia, and e-mentoring programs such as those based at Loyola University of Chicago and Northeastern Illinois University (Klecka, Clift, & Cheng, 2005) seek to keep professors and graduates in touch with one another. While it is too early to evaluate the long-term impact of these efforts, they are noteworthy in that they are beginning to break down the structure that terminates teacher education upon graduation and they lead us to think about how words might be used to help create new ways of talking about professional education and to help create more inclusive structures.

What if we abandoned the phrase, "teacher education"? What would that mean? It would certainly be a threat to many individuals and institutions whose identities depend on that phrase. But it could also be liberating. What if we used technology appropriately to offer a variety of short-term educational experiences for educators who want to learn more about teaching English as a Second Language at times when they need to learn how to better work with their students who represent a rich array of linguistic and cultural backgrounds? What if we created projects in which teachers and those who manage building and personnel were able to work with other educators (the term "higher education" itself is a status marker) on projects targeted to understanding and acting on specific issues in teaching, learning, curriculum, and management? And what if we committed time and resources to enabling those projects to be completed and evaluated?

We are, of course, bound by the social rules and fields we have inherited and perpetuate. Our language, our *habitus*, our hierarchies and power relations constrain us and, at the same time, give us a sense of security because we know the game, even if we do not particularly like it. A rebirth or reconfiguring of one element of professional education may be blocked or inhibited by all those other elements that are not changed, and those who would be reformers must be mindful that developing expertise in education is not synonymous with producing a product called "certified teacher" or "new and improved preservice teacher education program."

We teachers/educators need information and tools when we need them and we need time, space, and support for learning to think and learning to act. We also need to provide for ourselves, for one another, and for skeptics thoughtful and systemic ways to modify social rules, roles, structures, and power relations as we develop new senses of who we are as practitioners and how we learn with and from one another.

Authors' note: This paper is based upon work supported, in part, by the Department of Education (Grant No. P336990042-00A) and by the University of Illinois at Urbana-Champaign Research Board. The government has certain rights in this material. Any opinions, findings, and conclusions or recommendations expressed in this material are those of the author(s) and do not necessarily reflect the views of the Department of Education or the University of Illinois at Urbana-Champaign.

References

Bourdieu, P. (1990a). *In other words: Essays towards a reflexive sociology.* Stanford, CA: Stanford University Press.
Bourdieu, P. (1990b). *The logic of practice.* Stanford, CA: Stanford University Press.
Bourdieu, P. (1993). *The field of cultural production.* New York: Columbia University Press.
Bourdieu, P., & Wacquant, L. (1992). *An invitation to reflexive sociology.* Chicago, IL: The University of Chicago Press.
Building Resources: Induction and Development for Georgia Educators. (n.d.). Retrieved January 22, 2007, from www.coe.uga.edu/gstep/pages/bridge.html
Carnegie Foundation of New York. (n.d.). *Teachers for a new era.* Retrieved January 7, 2007, from www.teachersforanewera.org.
Clift, R. T., Veal, M. L., Holland, P., Johnson, M., & McCarthy, J. (1995). *Collaborative leadership and shared decision making: Teachers, principals, and university professors.* New York: Teachers College Press.

Darling-Hammond, L., & Bransford, J. (Eds.) (2005). *Preparing teachers for a changing world: What teachers should learn and be able to do.* Hoboken, NJ: John Wiley and Sons, Inc.

Feiman-Nemser, S. (2001). From preparation to practice: Designing a continuum to strengthen and sustain teaching. *Teachers College Record, 87,* 1013–1055.

Flores, M. A., & Day, C. (2006). Contexts which shape and reshape new teachers' identities: A multi-perspective study. *Teaching and Teacher Education, 22,* 219–232.

Gee, J. P. (1999). *An introduction to discourse analysis: Theory and method.* London: Routledge.

Klecka, C. L., Clift, R. T., & Cheng, Y. (2005). Are electronic conferences a solution in search of an urban problem? *Urban Education, 40,* 412–429.

Kress, G. (2003). *Literacy in the new media age.* New York: Routledge.

Kukan, L., & Beck, I. L. (1997). Thinking aloud and reading comprehension research: Inquiry, instruction, and social interaction. *Review of Educational Research, 67*(3), 271–299.

Leont'ev, A. N. (1981). *Problems in the development of mind.* Moscow: Progress Publishers.

U.S. Department of Education. (2001). General Provisions: Definitions. In *The Elementary and Secondary Education Act (The No Child Left Behind Act of 2001, Title IX).* Retrieved September 29, 2006, from www.ed.gov/policy/elsec/leg/esea02/pg 107.html.

Vygotsky, L. S. (1978). *Mind in society: The development of higher psychological processes.* Cambridge, MA: Harvard University Press.

Welcoming Interns and Novices with Guidance and Support. (n.d.). Retrieved January 22, 2007, from https://uteach.utexas.edu/wings.

Wilson, S. M., & Berne, J. (1999). Teacher learning and the acquisition of professional knowledge: An examination of research on contemporary professional development. In A. Iran-Nejad & P. D. Pearson (Eds.), *Review of Research in Education, 24* (pp. 173–209). Washington, DC: American Educational Research Association.

CHAPTER 16

Encountering Relational Complexity

ON "THE ARTS OF THE PRACTICAL" IN LEARNING TO TEACH

Margaret Macintyre Latta
University of Nebraska-Lincoln

> Margaret Macintyre Latta, Ph.D., is an associate professor and graduate chair of teaching, learning, and teacher education in the College of Education & Human Sciences at the University of Nebraska-Lincoln. Her work foregrounds the integral role of aesthetic considerations such as attentiveness to participatory thinking, emotional commitment, felt freedom, dialogue and interaction, speculation, and greater consciousness within the acts of teaching and learning. She emphasizes the primacy of teachers in the lives of their students and the long-term impact on the future, contributing to the scholarship regarding teacher education and professional development reform initiatives. She is co-editor of the *International Journal of Education & the Arts* and her recent publications can be found in the *Journal of Teacher Education, Teachers & Teaching: Theory & Practice, Studying Teacher Education, Education & Culture, Teaching Education, Journal of Curriculum Theorizing,* and *Teaching & Teacher Education*.

ABSTRACT

> The notion of practice has been, and continues to be, problematic for the work of teaching and learning. The problems at the crux of practice are revealed in the narrative accounts of three representative prospective teachers' experiences. These narratives grapple with the nature of practice and consider what it means to learn to teach. In particular, the practical effects of these teaching/learning experiences position the reader to confront the role of relational complexities within teaching. Relational complexities are explored as the given particularities of students, teachers, context, and subject matter. Drawing on Schwab's (1970) "arts of the practical" deliberately fos-

tering teacher experimentation with ways to access and attend to the relational complexities of classrooms, the internal goods furthering the work of learning are encountered. Teacher investment in practice demands attention to the relational complexities of classroom life. But, such experimentation and attention is desperately missing in the narrative accounts shared in this paper. The arts of the practical offer a ground for teacher education that acknowledges relational complexities encountered and generated are integral to the practice of teaching. Prospective teachers need to live the language of practice through encountering, negotiating, and articulating the relational complexities of classrooms. The narratives evidence the potential relational complexities hold for understanding the arts of practice and the powerful significances of entrusting/distrusting these arts of practice to teachers and their students.

Introduction

Practice is a contentious phenomenon. Even a cursory review of the literature on teacher education reveals that practice is a site of competing discourses on why, what, how, and to what effects. The kind of practice I am concerned with in this chapter is the practice of learning to teach. I explore prospective teachers' experiences of learning to teach, and more specifically, the practical effects of that experience, what Schwab (1970) called "the arts of the practical," denoting at once, practitioner debate, deliberation, and choice. Shulman (1983), building on Schwab's ideas, insisted (and continues to insist) practice must be necessarily understood as a "complex and demanding art" (p. 36). But, my work as a teacher educator tells me concrete encounters for prospective teachers to experience the arts of practice are far too limited and controlled. As Schwab warned 30 years ago, practice continues to be dangerously undermined.

I am concerned here with the kind of practice that would allow for the formation of the prospective teacher such that they are able to respond to ever more demanding kinds of teaching/learning experiences. I argue that this is fundamental, given the essential difficulty that teachers encounter in the classroom—a phenomenon I call "relational complexity." I use this term to refer to an uncertain and risky process that entails building relationships across self, others, and subject matter through dialogic inquiry. Biesta (2004) construes this as a gap, and names it, after Dewey (1934), as the "location of education" (p. 13). He argues that although this gap cannot be represented in predetermined terms, it is the performative nature of the gap that constitutes the work of educating. Biesta conveys two paths that teachers may take when confronted with the educative gap. Teachers can choose to negate the gap altogether and teach from a prescribed script blind to the particulars of students and context. Or, teachers can attend to the given relational complexities as the means for interaction and communication. The latter "entails both a risk and an opportunity" (p. 22). The risks and opportunities afforded in the gap and the consequences of denying prospective teachers access to this gap are revealed in this chapter.

My aim is to not only restore within practice Schwab's (1970) plea for practice as deliberation that is "complex" and "arduous" (p. 36), but also to outline the formative effects of that practice: the ability to respond sensitively and wisely furthering learning within the demands of given teaching/learning situations. To examine the inherent risks and opportunities encountered within Biesta's educative gap, I draw on the thinking of Connelly and Clandinin (2006), Dewey (1904; 1934), Dunne (2005), Arendt (1958), and Shulman (2004), among others, who attempt to articulate the teaching/learning conditions promoting Schwab's "arts of the practical."

Context

Positioning prospective teachers to delve into Biesta's (2004) gap became my task as a teacher educator. The courses I taught attempted to engage students in exploring teaching practice, not as a thing, but as a process of transformation, as a catalyst for furthering questioning and deliberation, inciting new ways of seeing and being a teacher. Such participation elicits questions that must be continually addressed: What does it mean to learn and to teach? What significances do teachers and learners encounter and how are these significances negotiated? What do the ways these questions are addressed make possible and impossible in terms of practices and understandings? What might teachers and learners become and not become as a result of the thinking and acting in classrooms? These questions assume the relational complexities of classroom life are present as givens and consider the ways in which these givens of the personal, social, contextual, historical, cultural, and political impact the experience of learning to teach. These questions live in the gap between self and other—found between teacher and context, between teacher and students, between students and context, between students and subject matter, between teacher and subject matter, and between students and students.

Casework became the medium for these understandings, designed to enable prospective teachers to concretely consider the nature of learners, learning, teachers, and teaching from multiple perspectives. But, as prospective teachers moved into K–12 practicum situations such opportunities were apt to be thwarted, with questioning and deliberation considered to be what Kessels and Korthagen (1996) term "disturbances" rather than "central" to the practice of learning to teach (p. 21). It is clear to me that this tension was heightened through the intents of teacher education casework purposefully positioning student teachers to thoughtfully engage and elucidate theory/practice relations.

In practicum settings, it seems the role and place of seeing and acting on relational complexities as integral within the practice of teaching were repeatedly misinterpreted and misunderstood. As prospective teachers entered and negotiated practicum experiences alongside partner teachers, students, and university personnel, practice as process was often betrayed. Indeed, the impetus for this chapter grows out of extended interviews I had with 20 student teachers revealing such betrayal. (The data included throughout the chapter is representative of dominant themes resulting from a one year research project alongside 20 students in teacher preparation methods courses and throughout student teaching experiences in two research sites focusing on the elucidation of theory/practice relationships in learning to teach. Data collection included regular taped interviews, written responses to casework taken up in the methods courses, and field journal entries by student teachers documenting their practicum experiences, the researchers' observations of learning to teach out in schools and throughout the coursework, and the research literature situating the inquiry and the traditions inherited and being reconstructed. For a detailed account of the methodological approach and findings please see Macintyre Latta & Field, 2005.)

Narrative Inquiry

Interviews with participating student teachers revealed a common narrative tale. So, my interest turned to the contours of these students' narratives regarding the nature of teaching/learning practice—what struck them as significant, and in the course of exploring that question, what they were invested in, what they had to undergo, and what questions they had about becoming teachers. These contours surfaced intersections, identified by Connelly and Clandinin (2006) as the commonplaces of narrative inquiry: temporality, sociality, and place (p. 479). And, the intersections of the commonplaces positioned prospective teachers at the crossroads described by Biesta (2004) of choosing to see, or disregard, the relational complexities of teaching/learning practice.

For example, temporality revealed itself in the narrative tales that unfolded embodying the unique, personal, humanness of meaning making, with knowledge residing in self-experience of the practice of teaching. But, the act of knowing as entailing "reorganizing or reconstruction of experience" (Dewey, 1934,

p. 76) with past informing present, with implications for the future, was curtailed. This temporal reorganizing/reconstructing process, likened to a dialogue between self and other, was apt to be silenced, or at least, not valued.

A pattern of thought acknowledging the social interplay of context, time, and personal experience that had been fostered through coursework as the necessary link to sense making, suggesting directions for the practice of teaching/learning, was dismissed as peripheral to informing practice. The temporal/social discourse that prospective teachers began to explore as not simply interactive, but entailing dwelling within place, was feared. Thus, the act of creating lived meanings regarding the work of practice as socially motivated, socially embedded, and derived from the personal narratives of place were generally undermined in K–12 practicum settings.

I heard in the voices of participants, narratives forming, expressing the interplay of temporality, sociality, and place. My attention turned to narrative inquiry's demand for "a simultaneous exploration of all three commonplaces" (Connelly & Clandinin, p. 479). Indeed, the relatedness and interdependence across all three commonplaces was present, revealed as narrative tensions within the practice of student teaching. Three student teachers' accounts, Cara, Nathan, and Sharon, were selected to gain insights into these tensions. I urge the reader in attending to the following tensions to read beyond the concrete specifics of each student teacher's narrative, considering what each orients teaching/learning practice toward and away from, what is seen and not seen, and the costs of accepting a version of practice stultifying discovery of the arts of the practical I argue are so integral to learning to teach.

Cara's Narrative of Practice Teaching

One of the dominant notions in teacher education is that teachers "learn best by doing." Cara's narrative revealed a version of doing that encouraged blindness to temporality, sociality, and place. Thus, teacher and student focused their seeing on the efficiency of behavior, and toward the completion of a fully anticipated response. Doing became construed as teacher and student tasks oriented in one direction with no consideration given to what students and context might offer. Cara, a prospective high school science teacher elaborated:

> The pressure was to teach. You have to. What does it entail when they say, "Okay, go in there and teach?" . . . What I think my partner teacher expected was that I would walk into her classroom, look at the curriculum, and know what the students ought to be doing. I would then have lesson plans ready to go. I think she really wanted to see this kind of initiative. But, I kind of felt like I did not

know. How should I? I was looking for guidance and she was looking for performance. (Interview 6/6/00)

The phrase "go in there and teach" assumed that knowledge and curriculum existed in forms wholly divorced from temporality, sociality, and place. Knowledge and curriculum were assumed to be self-contained entities that must be represented in pre-specified "outcomes," "competencies," and "indicators." Expecting the prospective teacher to have "lesson plans ready to go" prior to coming to know the situation, with little sense of the particular relational complexities gathering and intersecting, and no awareness of student prior engagement with the topic, forced the student teacher into an instrumental mode of practice, with a primary focus on what Dewey (1904) refers to as "securing immediate proficiency in teaching" (p. 16). What happened, in the ensuing glare by other(s), was not surprising. Cara wrote:

> I can't say how unskilled and unprepared for teaching I felt this past few weeks. I was completely and utterly under the control of the curriculum. My own knowledge was so weak that to even consider deviating slightly from the standard program of studies was terrifying. (Artifact 4, 28/2/00)

What gets produced in these circumstances is what one of our students described as a "planning frenzy." Prospective teachers tried to out run any opportunities to confront complexity or ambiguity with a series of activities that consumed and monopolized everyone's concern with finishing the race. The absence of attending to situated knowledge disturbed Cara. She explained:

> How do I design an assessment that tells whether or not the students understand the concept of a mold? It is nebulous. What is it that I am exactly looking for? How do I mark this? How do I present it to students so that they know what to do? (Artifact 4, 28/2/00)

Cara considered good questions. But, even entertaining these questions for a few moments was dismissed as a waste of time. Rather, her focus was reoriented to pre-specified measurable outcomes. The evaluation rubric was already in place and the criteria left no room for uncertainties. Through a lens valuing abstract, imposed lesson design, Cara's questions were seen as impossible to address. Part of Cara's dilemma appeared to be generated by her partner teacher's advice that she base her lessons solely on concept notes, itemized out in listlike fashion. But this list of paradigmatic knowledge did not provide her with the social context to find out what her students knew and brought to the learning situation itself. In her attempt to make sense of her teaching she asked, "What do I look for?" The time and space to seek answers was quickly closed. Hidden from her view was a living field of complexities that she might immerse herself in, identify with, and develop a feel for. Absent from her thinking was a concrete sense of place. Her teaching practice assumed an instrumental vision. And, so, what happened to Cara is all too familiar:

> Unfortunately, the thing I dislike is I slid into this lecture style of teaching, which I absolutely hate, but that is exactly what I would end up doing. I thought . . . you present this lecture and they take down notes and you see faces staring at you; nobody is falling asleep, but nobody is jumping up and down going "ah ha" or asking questions either. I kept it to myself, but I continued to wonder, "How on earth do you tell if they got it? How do you know?" (Interview, 6/6/00)

So Cara's questions, though hidden, persisted. How, indeed, would one know when/if students understood? And, what is it that her students came to know? The knowledge Cara was asked to see was free of living referents; fixed and fully formed, amenable to endless repetition without variation. Such practice did not require a learner to be brought into being, and it did not seem to bring learning into being either, deepening senses of wonder, helping participants understand both where and who they are. Cara understood that the instruments of practice, deployed "efficiently" can produce well-orchestrated student and teacher behavior: precisely hit pre-specified learning "targets," exquisitely timed lesson transitions, and neatly completed tasks. Concomitantly, she understood they could cut both student and teacher off from a sense of being "corporeally embedded in a living landscape" (Abrams, 1996, p. 65).

Nathan's Narrative of Practice Teaching

As a teacher educator I asked how is it possible for prospective teachers to experience a fuller sense of practice, negotiating their role within the work of learning, finding what furthers learning within given circumstances and specifics of students, subject matter, and context? How might prospective teachers enter the field and explore textured understandings of teaching practice as productively reciprocal in nature, necessarily at the crossroads of temporality, sociality, and place. Nathan, a student teacher in a grade one classroom, revealed the problem:

> The teacher was basically controlling every movement of the children. I did not know where I fit in. That was disenchanting and unsettling. I did not know what to do. I recall going over to look at some of the children's literature, and my eyes turned away from the

> teacher and right away she said, "Mr. Richard, what are you doing?" I was quaking in my boots. . . . I think what bothered me the most was the teacher centeredness of the classroom. There was little room for children's questions. And, little room for me to be different from her. The way I will put it was her desire to make me in her own image. She saw her role that way. I wanted to learn from her, so, this was partially okay. But, on the other hand, I wanted to explore the teaching role as well; the way I saw it. . . . There was a very rigid curriculum. It was not like curriculum making. There was some interaction, but it was only around filling in a blank, so to speak. I knew these kids had so much to offer. The result was that the kids learned to be passive. . . . I also felt quite stifled and rigid. I could not interact freely and I had to watch my step all the time. I did not want to break one of the rules. . . . I saw so much potential in this classroom—in the materials and in the skills of the teacher. It just seemed there was a fear of stepping beyond the boundaries of what she was used to. . . . It was all about efficiently pacing students through stuff; let's crank it out, we have a lot to get covered instead of stopping midway and going in a new direction . . . so many missed opportunities. (Interview, 8/6/00)

Concretely, Nathan was speaking here of "missed opportunities" to see curriculum with his students in ways permitting something new and different to emerge from interactions. His attempts to approach his practice differently disturbed the orderliness of the classroom and disrupted the image of teacher. In response to this, generic features of practice were emphasized and Nathan was positioned to imitate the teacher subsuming her ways of practice. He explained that:

> Basically, none of the children were allowed to move or speak or anything. It was very tightly controlled. And, if they did they were immediately spoken to . . . the teacher told me that if I let students ask all these questions, it would take you on all these tangents. Well in my view, some of that was where I wanted to go. And she was shutting all that down. And it was in the name of behavior control. That bothered me throughout. The children never really got to ask their questions. (Interview, 8/6/00)

Nathan was aware of a tension between what he thought was worthwhile for teaching and learning and what he saw and was being asked to duplicate. He attempted to expose this tension conveying his awareness of tearing his teaching into unrelated pieces. Nathan clarified:

> Interaction with students is key to teaching and learning. When I stepped into the classroom I would interact with students. In the process, I would step outside myself as best I could and observe who

> I was while I was interacting. Did my perceptions of self fit with how others saw me? Was I reaching the child? Was she/he reaching back to me? Was our interaction around subject matter meaningful? But interaction to the teacher meant so much less than I understood to be necessary. It was like one-way communication that was deemed successful if students appeared to be on task. What I attempted to do was interact with the kids and find ways into the subject matter; get to know the kids . . . the teacher did not understand why at first. I had to start to let the teacher know who I was, what my strengths were and how I saw the classroom and the nature of interaction differently . . . and, not fear to actually share about that. (Interview, 8/6/00)

Nathan desired to risk, assuming the necessary vulnerability in order to perceive the intimacy of relations complicating the classroom. Nathan sought out lesson forms coming into being through engagement with students and subject matter. His teacher preferred to bracket out generic features of teaching and learning to be applied to a pre-determined learning situation. Such imposed imitative features such as lesson pacing, closure, and management routines regulated what lessons ought to look like in advance. In contrast, Nathan tentatively considered what it was that ought to be done on a continual basis given the specific subject matter, the context, the students, and the particularities that surfaced throughout his lessons.

Sharon's Narrative of Practice

Participating prospective teachers had spent time theorizing in university coursework about the nature of learning and teaching, collectively reckoning with many possibilities for teaching practices. But such theorizing was quickly desiccated in the concrete realities of some classrooms. Sharon, another student teacher in a junior high art classroom, explained:

> I was only seeing one teaching theory or method and I was having huge problems with it. For example, I think the constructs behind art would help students understand art. But, I was told that they are not going to be able to get it. They are too young. But, I do not think that is the case. It is up to me to find a way into that conversation. And I did have several moments when I felt artistic theory did come alive in the classroom conversation. I was glad I just pushed forward with my sense of what might work. It was my own confidence in myself as an artist that gave me enough assurance to risk, though. Reading Dewey and Eisner made me curious about what can be done by a teacher to encourage true learning experiences for

> students. I wanted to continue to discover the conditions that are necessary. I was pretty sure the students would enjoy new art techniques and the knowledge I could share with them. The teacher kept saying, "You have all this artistic knowledge, but, what about teaching methods? You know about art, but, you do not know about teaching it to kids." And, I am left thinking; I do not understand why I do not know that. (Interview, 5/6/00)

Sharon's consideration as to how she might hold insights into the teaching situation she encountered, pointed to the persistent problem of splitting theory and practice. Kessels and Korthagen (1996) described how abstract teaching theories often "lack flesh and blood":

> They cannot be seen in action, nor talked to, nor criticized, nor admired. In short, they do not have any perceptual reality; they are just concepts, abstractions. Therefore, they cannot be identified with. (p. 21)

Sharon was deterred from the opportunity to practice the lived "flesh and blood" terms of theory though she deliberately set out to "find a way into conversation" with her students about aspects of art theory. Attempts to see theory/practice relationships through continuing to reckon with possibilities for her teaching practice were thwarted. Theory was not understood as occurring within situations, arising out of the purposes and particularities encountered. Instead, theory was understood as an applied approach or method for teaching. Theorizing was foreign territory, feared as abstract, impractical ideals that could never constitute one's practice as a teacher. Thus, opportunities to see the simultaneous interplay of theory and practice in concrete situations of teaching and learning were limited. And, significantly, this further curtailed the role of seeing self within teaching/learning practice. Sharon desired and struggled with ways to bring her identity into the classroom. She commented:

> I have talked about the nature of art until I am blue in the face. And, I have listened to it, I do not know how many times. But when I was thinking about the nature of art in such a way that I could present it to my students, holy smokes did it make a difference! Like I have read so much art theory and if I get from point A to point B I am done and I just hope the professor does not ask me any questions. But, explaining the nature of art to grade sevens is another thing. They do not have an art vocabulary. How do I begin to get the concept across? I really had to know what I was talking about, so that I could find ways that would make sense. (Interview, 5/6/00)

Sharon searched for theory's agentic potential to concretely negotiate her own practice, thus growing her teaching identity. She longed to become actively and operatively engaged. O'Loughlin's (2006) notion of "implacement" is fitting. An implaced body is neither subject or object but always seeking connections with its surroundings, concomitantly perceiving and receiving. Temporality, sociality, and place rather than being bound commodities are newly experienced as reciprocal, in flux, and situated. Such practice purposefully connects one to place, belonging as much to the other as to self. But Sharon's desires and struggles to bring personal understandings to teaching/learning situations were brushed off as interfering with the task of learning. As she struggled to allow a learning space for individual student understandings to emerge and interact, she was told it complicated and delayed accomplishment of the learning task. She gathered that inviting questions and discussion from students was perceived as a complete waste of time. So, Sharon accepted that her forthcoming attempt to enliven art theory would be futile. She acquired a displaced teaching identity rather than an implaced teaching identity in order to meet with "successful" practice. The message conveyed was that the character of teaching/learning situations, self, and participants, were not worthy of consideration in the "successful" practice of teaching. With focus on predetermined work, skill, and regulated procedures, the inattention to character and genuine action in this classroom provided little, if any, opportunity to see/experience teaching practice in other ways. I emphasize that it is not that there is no need for such norms, but, as Varela (1979) states, unless they:

> Are informed by the wisdom that enables them to be dissolved in the demands of responsivity to the particularities and immediacy of lived situation, the rules become sterile, scholastic hindrances to compassionate action rather than conduits for its manifestation. (p. 74)

Schwab's Crises Persist

In addition to calling for a renaissance in the field of education, Schwab (1970) talked of signs of *flight* that have caused a "crises of principle" in the field of curriculum (p. 19). These signs of flight included a) disregarding practitioner knowledge and turning to external sources for expertise, b) negating the particularities of situation and individuals necessitating theorizing, instead seeking/accepting imposed theoretical models and frameworks, c) delegating and disassociating the work of practice away from the direct concern of the practitioner, d) finding solace and certainty in traditionally accepted and known practices manifested in generally applied techniques, strategies, and methods, and e) competing paradigmatic debates and affiliations that pull, separate, and distort. The crises arise when curricular principles leave little to no room to question current teaching/learning practice or challenge and act on inadequacies and relevancies. The narratives of practice as told in the accounts of Cara, Nathan, and Sharon revealed that Schwab's critique continues to be very fitting today. A "flight from the experience of teaching to representing teaching" permeates much teaching practice, designed to legislate and control responsive teaching and learning (Macintyre Latta & Field, 2005). The tensions experienced by prospective teachers at Connelly and Clandinin's (2006) narrative intersections of temporality, sociality, and place, positioned prospective teachers to flee from or embrace these tensions as the work of teaching practice. And, it is this decision to orient teaching/learning practice toward, or away from these tensions, which is at work within Schwab's crises of principle.

Practices orienting away from the tensions of temporality, sociality, and place produce crises of detachment on the parts of teachers and students. The narrative accounts relayed by Cara, Nathan, and Sharon suggest consequences sustaining detachment through 1) repression of teacher and student self-understandings, 2) disregard for pedagogical tone, and 3) disregard for plurality and natality within learning processes (see also, Macintyre Latta, 2005). The narratives revealed these consequences to restrict and tightly contain ways to know and be in classrooms for both teachers and students, further preserving, binding, and dissecting a teacher's practice. The result is that little attention is given to assimilation, internalization, and integration of teacher/student thought, structuring teaching experiences that compartmentalized knowledge, separating pedagogy from content, knowledge from interests, thus, theory from practice.

Rather, orienting teaching/learning toward embracing the tensions of temporality, sociality, and place, cultivated relational practices as teacher and students found moments within the teaching narratives seeking out the criteria that form and inform the relationality within the teaching situation itself. Therefore, personal investment is assumed on the parts of teachers and students with the particularities of individuals and contexts contributing to teaching/learning practices.

The differing consequences of orienting toward, or away from, the risks and opportunities alive in the teaching/learning gap do matter for the lived practice of teaching. Dunne's (2005) notions of the internal and external goods of practice aptly portray the consequences revealed in the narratives of practice. They elucidate how the external goods, framed by Dunne as a kind of competency aimed at "control defined in terms of optimal effectiveness in achieving ends, and optimal efficiency in realizing most benefit with least cost" (p. 374) can sacrifice the integrity of the internal goods of practice, namely, the capacity to respond to the relational complexity inherent within teaching and learning. The internal goods of relational complexity demand prospective teachers gain access to what Dewey (1904) characterized as "internal attention" (p. 13–14), a capacity to "see" students and learning situations with potential for meaningful engagement with subject matter. Dewey distinguished this from "external attention" (p. 13–14), which disregards this movement of engaged thought focusing on "recognition" entailing labeling and categorizing aimed at efficient management and realized in Dunne's external goods.

The Relational Nature of Teaching/Learning Practice

The reciprocity between self (teacher) and other (students, subject matter, context) that Cara, Nathan, and Sharon sought within each of their narratives of practice, must be an active search, demanding ongoing judgments and embracing transformation. Technique alone was not sufficient to Cara's, Nathan's, and Sharon's practices of teaching/learning. It was not enough to know *how*. A teacher must know *when, how much, why,* and *who* and *what* to involve. Teachers must simultaneously address these demands as the risks and opportunities that must be embraced within Biesta's (2004) teaching/learning gap. Weinsheimer (1985) explains, "The choice that is right cannot be determined in advance or apart from the particular situation, for the situation itself partly determines what is right" (p. 190).

Thus, venturing into the gap means the technical cannot be separated from the role of judgment. Both share the central moment of teaching—application. Action therefore is at the heart of practice. And, action is the problem of the interrelation and interdependence of theory and practice. It cannot be housed with theory alone, or practice alone.

Arendt (1958) distinguishes between action and fabrication. Action needs the presence of others, the constant contact with the world, the web of the acts and the words of others(ness). Fabrication manipulates materials toward a preconceived end. Fabrication can take place in isolation but action is never possible in isolation (p. 188). As Arendt (1958) points out, "Without the disclosure of the agent in the act, action loses specific character and becomes one form of achievement among others" (p. 180).

Cara, Nathan, and Sharon, in varying degrees, explored the gap resisting such disconnect experienced as a separate self performing as teacher, distanced from understandings of self and students, mechanically completing the tasks of teacher. Cara, Nathan, and Sharon were uncomfortable with the fabrication they confronted in their teaching/learning practices and longed to feel and experience genuine action. The internal goods found within action engendered moments of practice for Cara, Nathan, and Sharon that were experienced as purposeful for themselves and for their students. These internal goods included multiplicity of perspectives manifesting divergent learning processes and products.

Noddings (2003) claims this ever enlarging and deepening of understandings of self in relation to the world, for both the practitioner and for students, holds the goods bestowed on teachers and students through relational practice (p. 251). But, it seems making these goods visible and tangible to prospective teachers is a critical undertaking teacher education programs keep avoiding.

The Arts of the Practical

Schwab (1970) summarized his argument for energies to be invested in practice, stating:

> The stuff of theory is abstract or idealized representations of real things. But curriculum in action treats real things: real acts, real teachers, real children, things richer than and different from their theoretical representations. (p. 27)

To invest in practice he called for "arts of the practical" (p. 27) that deliberately fostered teacher experimentation with ways to access and attend to the relational complexities of classrooms, the internal goods furthering the work of learning. Such experimentation was what prospective teachers so desperately missed in the narrative accounts shared in this paper. The arts of the practical offer a ground for teacher education that purposefully and boldly encounters Biesta's (2004) educative gap. There must be room for prospective teachers to concretely risk exploring the terrain, the nature of working conjunctures that allow both theory and practice to better inform, that is, shape from within the teaching/learning situation, what prospective teachers do in classrooms.

Locating such theory/practice conjunctures entails prospective teachers building relationships across self, others, and subject matter given the specifics of temporality, sociality, and place, discovered through participatory inquiry. Opportunities must be created and nurtured to examine the consequences of lived theory/practice relations, alongside the input of other educators, valued as productive for everyone's professional growth. I insist alongside others (e.g. Cochran-Smith, 2001; Dewey, 1904; Dunne, 2005; Noddings, 2003; Raider-Roth, 2005; Shulman, 2004), that gaining access to this educative gap, acknowledging the relational complexities encountered and generated, are integral to the practice of teaching.

Prospective teachers need to live the language of practice through encountering, negotiating, and articulating the relational complexities of classrooms.

The narratives evidenced the potential relational complexities hold for understanding the arts of practice and the powerful significances of entrusting/distrusting these arts of practice to teachers and their students. I conclude that this is the deliberative nature of teaching/learning practice worthy of practitioners and their students.

Shulman (2004) has cautioned for some time that teacher education programs must set out to create such organizational change because, "otherwise, the familiar furniture of the mind will remain in its place, and we will be able to do little to replace it" (p. 183). The narratives of Cara, Nathan, and Sharon document the difficulty and the necessity of replacing this furniture associated with teaching/learning practice. Extensive current work (e.g. Clift & Brady, 2005; Cochran-Smith & Zeichner, 2005; Darling-Hammond & Bransford, 2005; Grant & Gillette, 2005; Shulman, 2004) addresses just this, foregrounding the importance of fostering teachers' capacities to evidence improved educational practices and how the capacity to articulate such knowledge is an urgent need placing practitioner knowledge at the center of concern. I conclude teacher educators and programs must take a long overdue turn to the arts of the practical and delve into the risks and opportunities they offer: much-needed debate, deliberation, and choices for change.

References

Abrams, D. (1996). *The spell of the sensuous: Perception and language in a more than human world.* New York: Pantheon Books.

Arendt, H. (1958). *The human condition.* Chicago: The University of Chicago Press.

Biesta, G. (2004). Mind the gap! In C. Bingham and A. Sidorkin (Eds.), *No education without relation* (pp. 11–22). New York: Peter Lang.

Clift, R. T., & Brady, P. (2005). Research on methods courses and field experiences. In M. Cochran-Smith & K. Zeichner (Eds.), *Studying teacher education: The report of the AERA panel on research and teacher education* (pp. 309–426). Mahwah, NJ: Lawrence Erlbaum.

Cochran-Smith, M. (2001). Constructing outcomes in teacher education: Policy, practice, and pitfalls. *Education Policy Analysis Archives, 9*(11), 1–57.

Cochran-Smith, M., & Zeichner, K. (Eds.). (2005). *Studying teacher education: The report of the AERA panel on research and teacher education.* Mahwah, NJ: Lawrence Erlbaum.

Connelly, F. M., & Clandinin, D. J. (2006). Narrative inquiry. In J. L. Green, G. Camilli, & P. Elmore (Eds.), *Handbook of complementary methods in education research* (3rd ed., pp. 477–487). Mahwah, NJ: Lawrence Erlbaum.

Darling-Hammond, L., & Bransford, J. (2005). *Preparing teachers for a changing world: What teachers should learn and be able to do.* San Francisco, CA: Jossey-Bass.

Dewey, J. (1904). The relation of theory and practice in education. In C. A. McMurry

(Ed.), *The relation of theory to practice in the education of teachers: The third yearbook of the National Society for the Scientific Study of Education* (p. 22). Chicago: University of Chicago Press.

Dewey, J. (1934). *Art as experience.* New York: Capricorn Books.

Dunne, J. (2005). An intricate fabric: Understanding the rationality of practice. *Pedagogy, Culture and Society, 13*(2), 367–389.

Grant, C., & Gillette, M. (2005). *Learning to teach everyone's children: Equity, empowerment, and education that is multicultural.* Wadsworth Publishing.

Kessels, J. P. A. M., & Korthagen, F. A. J. (1996). The relationship between theory and practice: Back to the classics. *Educational Researcher, 25*(3), 17–22.

Macintyre Latta, M. (2005). The role and place of fear in what it means to teach and to learn. *Teaching Education, 16*(3), 183–196.

Macintyre Latta, M., & Field, J. C. (2005). The flight from experience to representation: Seeing relational complexity in teacher education. *Teaching and Teacher Education, 21,* 649–660.

Noddings, N. (2003). Is teaching a practice? *Journal of Philosophy of Education, 37*(2), 241–251.

O'Loughlin, M. (2006). *Embodiment and education: Exploring creatural existence.* Dordrecht, Netherlands: Springer.

Raider-Roth, M. B. (2005). *Trusting what you know: The high stakes of classroom relationships.* San Francisco, CA: Jossey-Bass.

Schwab, J. J. (1970). *The practical: A language for curriculum.* Washington, DC: National Education Association.

Shulman, L. S. (2004). *The wisdom of practice: Essays on teaching, learning, and learning to teach.* San Francisco, CA: Jossey-Bass.

Varela, F. J. (1979). *Principles of biological autonomy.* New York: McGraw-Hill.

Weinsheimer, J. C. (1985). *Gadamer's hermeneutics: A reading of truth and method.* New Haven/London: Yale University Press.

Summary and Implications

Cheryl J. Craig

Louise F. Deretchin

Burke, Cowell, Olwell, and Ostra kicked off Division 4 in a bold manner. They enlisted the aid of secondary preservice teachers to research how the students' expectations of their field-based work compared with the students' lived experiences. To begin, the authors reviewed the literature, including Clift and Brady's (2005) recent handbook chapter and Levine's (2006) *Educating School Teachers* report. Two salient points rose to the fore: the fact that little attention has been given to how individual preservice teachers navigate their teacher education programs (Clift & Brady, 2005) and the fact that well coordinated field experiences form the hallmark of exemplary teacher education programs (Levine, 2006).

Burke et al. recognized that there was an absence of preservice teachers' voices (just as Morgan-Fleming et al. in Chapter 7 noted the absence of public school children's voices) in determining what approaches to teacher education, in this case, field experience, would be in their best interest.

The secondary preservice students in Burke et al.'s alternate cohort uncovered strengths and challenges in their field experiences, both of which they felt could be further improved. These included such considerations as disconnections resulting from overreliance on technology, a desire for more face-to-face contact, and a lack of rhythm and coordination between what was going on in school sites and as a result of their university preparation and associated assignments.

In the end result, the preservice students recommended a series of changes that would improve the educative value of their field experiences, changes without which success in field experiences, in their words, would be "possible, but not probable" due to the complexities involved. Readers leave the chapter with a sense that Burke et al. are ready to address the problematic conditions that their study brought to light.

Lucey's chapter bearing the metaphoric title of "fence sitting" came next. Readers will recall that Lucey explored preservice teachers' attitudes toward economic responsibilities and social justice only to find that the "respondents expressed the most reluctance when taking stances concerning the responsibilities of businesses, the effects of social structures, and the effects of classroom practice." When surveyed, preservice education students were largely neutral where items concerning social responsibilities and social structures were concerned, although a range of high percentage of neutrality and low percentage of neutrality responses were apparent.

Lucey perceived an important role for the teacher education community in addressing the problematic condition his research revealed. He viewed textbooks as perpetuating the problem and teaching methods as adding to it as well. To conclude, Lucey urged that teacher educators address the fence sitting of their candidates and "respond to the conditions in preparatory institutions that cause them." Inclusion of difficult discussions in teacher preparation courses is essential if teachers are to learn to facilitate such conversations in their own classrooms, with their own students, thereby breaking the cycle of avoidance and ignorance. For Lucey, this would assist with bringing about a badly needed renaissance in teacher education on the social justice front.

Clift, Mora, and Brady's chapter, readers will remember, resonated in some ways with elements of Ross and Chan's (Chapter 1) and Burke et al.'s (Chapter 13) contributions. Clift et al.'s work spoke to the unhealthy compartmentalization of teacher education (preservice and in-service) and also to the lack of attention paid to prospective and practicing teachers as they proceed through career. This led to the "crossing contexts" study of which Clift et al.'s chapter is a part.

Since Fall 2000, Clift et al. have worked closely with thirteen graduates of their university to study their career paths and development. The researchers studied their teacher education program as well as the students' grades and determined that all thirteen graduates satisfied U.S. Department of Education criteria and were "highly qualified."

However, as the thirteen graduates of the teacher education program ventured into the world of schools and other places of employment, they did not enter into pure or ideal conditions. The practical situations they encountered were complex and often their job descriptions demanded more of them than their content area specialty provided.

This led Clift et al. to assert that additional support needs to be provided to teachers as their careers unfold in highly individualistic ways. Most notably, the separation between preservice and in-service teaching, a highly problematic condition, needs to be addressed. To Clift et al., teacher education needs to pay careful attention to the career span. Moreover, a renaissance in preservice teacher education cannot be achieved without a concurrent renaissance in in-service education. This is the message that Clift et al.'s chapter made crystal clear.

The final chapter in Division 4 was Latta's discussion of practice as a "contentious phenomenon" that is "dangerously undermined." Noting the neglect of relational complexity in learning to teach as well as students' limited exposure to "arts of the practical" (Schwab, 1970), Latta set out to show what is at stake when the questioning and deliberating of practice is viewed as a "disturbance" (Kessels & Korthagen, 1996) rather than integral to the teaching enterprise.

Through the use of narrative inquiry, the author examined the experiences of three preservice teachers and captured the tensions they encountered in their field experiences. Although the student teachers frequently knew otherwise and recognized "missed opportunities," they frequently "slid" into status quo responses and practices in their school-based situations.

This caused Latta to declare that the crisis in education that Schwab (1970) detected over thirty years ago "persists." For Latta, the signs of flight that have caused "a crisis of principle" (p. 19) include disregarding practitioner knowledge and turning to external sources of expertise, negating the particularity of situations and individuals, delegating and disassociating the work of practice away from the concerns of practitioners, finding solace and certainty in "rhetoric of conclusions," and emphasis placed on paradigmatic debates (e.g., No Child Left Behind, Reading First) that "pull, separate, and distort." Ultimately, as both Schwab and Latta have noted, no space for questioning remains. Thus, Latta's version of a renaissance in teacher education would necessarily pay attention to relational complexity and "the arts of practical." Otherwise, as Shulman (2004) noted and Latta reiterated, "the familiar furniture of the mind will remain in its place, and we will be able to do little to replace it" (p. 183).

Taken together, the group of chapters in Division 4 examined problematic conditions that reduced the potential of what can be accomplished through teacher education as broadly conceived. These included the problematic nature of field experiences, neutral attitudes of preservice teachers, narrow definitions of teaching and teacher education, and the negation of relational complexity and "the arts of the practical" in teaching and learning to teach.

References

Clift, R. T., & Brady, P. (2005). Research on methods courses and field experiences. In Cochran-Smith & Zeichner (Eds.), *Studying teacher education: The report of the AERA panel on research and teacher education.* (pp. 309–424). Washington, DC: American Educational Research Association.

Levine, A. (2006). *Educating school teachers*. Washington, DC: Education Schools Project, Inc.

Schwab, J. J. (1970). *The practical: A language for curriculum*. Washington, DC: National Education Association.

Shulman, L. S. (2004). *The wisdom of practice: Essays on teaching, learning, and learning to teach*. San Francisco, CA: Jossey-Bass.

Division 5
RENAISSANCE IN ACTION

Overview and Framework

Cheryl J. Craig

Louise F. Deretchin

Division 5, Renaissance in Action, consists of six chapters, all of which showcase positive changes in practice. Each describes what may be considered a small renaissance that occurred in a local setting, most frequently involving some form of collaboration.

Chapter 17, "Calling for a Renaissance of Care," tells of how teachers, Tami Burcham and Tara Gordon, with the support of Terri Hebert, a professor at a local university, used action research to examine family involvement and to consider the shaping effects of teacher interaction on student self-esteem.

Chapters 18 and 19 both originate in New York City and involve aesthetic ways of knowing. Authored by Helen Freidus, Chapter 18, "Small Steps: Moving Toward a Renaissance in Teacher Education," centers on a partnership between Bank Street College of Education and the American Museum of National History. Meanwhile, Chapter 19, "A Renaissance of the Arts in Classrooms: A Collaboration between a College, a Public School, and an Arts Institution" tells of the shared work of Lehman College–City University of New York, Public School 304, and the Lincoln Center Institute. The collaboration involved twelve individuals, namely Abigail McNamee, Andrea Zakin, Marietta Saravia-Shore, Alexandria Lawrence Ross, Jeanne Peloso, Nancy Dubetz, Christy Folsom, Victoria Rodriguez, Mia Mercurio, and Juan Morales of Lehman College of the City University of New York in addition to Holly Fairbank of the Lincoln Center Institute and Jaime Porteus Iurato of Public School 304.

Authored by Regina Mistretta, Chapter 20 is "Cultivating Parent-Child Collaboration Concerning Mathematical Learning: A Necessary Objective for Teacher Education Programs." The chapter examines how parents work with their Pre-K through 8th grade children on mathematics tasks. It also involved the evaluation of a model mathematics initiative.

Chapter 21, "Minimizing Barriers in Teacher Diversity Professional Development," is contributed by Earl Thomas and David Lamont Bell. The program evaluation investigates the impact of an approach to diversity professional development and provides insights into the conditions that promote positive change where diversity issues are concerned.

The final chapter of Division 5 is Chapter 22, Margaret Olson's "Valuing Narrative Authority, Collaboration, and Diversity in Revitalizing a Teacher Education Program." In the chapter, Olson describes how one teacher education program ceased to be at the same time as a new version of teacher education was introduced at the same institution. Olson's chapter explores the features and factors that enabled the valuing of narrative authority, collaboration, and diversity as broadly understood within the context of the revised teacher education program.

CHAPTER 17

Calling for a Renaissance of Care

Terri Hebert
University of Central Arkansas

Tami Burcham
University of Central Arkansas

Tara Gordon
University of Central Arkansas

> Terri Hebert, Ed.D., is assistant professor at the University of Central Arkansas. She teaches in the middle level program and serves as co-coordinator of the Advanced Studies in Teaching and Learning program. Dr. Hebert is a graduate of the Secondary Education/Educational Leadership Studies program, Stephen F. Austin State University, Nacogdoches, Texas.
>
> Tami Burcham, M.Ed., currently teaches sixth grade math in Greenbrier, Arkansas. She previously taught first and fourth grades in Valley Springs, Arkansas. Tami graduated with a Masters of Science degree in May 2007 from the Advanced Studies in Teaching and Learning program, offered through the University of Central Arkansas in Conway, Arkansas.
>
> Tara Gordon, B.A., currently teaches preschool in the Little Rock School District. Tara graduated with a Bachelors of Science degree with an early childhood emphasis from the University of Houston. She is currently a graduate student in the Advanced Studies in Teaching and Learning program at the University of Central Arkansas.

ABSTRACT

In schools across the nation, children are being thrust into a stark world where numbers quantify degrees of learning. Increasing stress levels play havoc on self-esteem, on future hopes and dreams, and on the perception of lifelong learning. Yet there remain caring educators who believe that learning is worth pursuing for its own sake and who engage students daily in opportunities of creative and social expression. These same educators understand that progress toward student achievement does not necessarily happen without family and teacher care and support. In this chapter, two graduate students in the field of education (Tami Burcham and Tara Gordon) with the support of their professor (Terri Hebert) use action research to investigate the impact of family involvement on education and the influence of teacher interaction on self-esteem.

> *Each time a man . . . acts to improve the lot of others . . . he sends forth a tiny ripple of hope, and crossing each other from a million different centers of energy and daring, those ripples build a current that can sweep down the mightiest walls.*
>
> —Robert F. Kennedy

Time is an interesting factor. When we are children, time moves slowly. As adults, though, it moves too quickly. Indeed, as individuals we probably do not remember a point in our lives when time proceeded at an appropriate pace. Nevertheless, as human beings, we tend to agree that we move through each phase of life only once, and then our time on this planet ceases to be. Kozol (1992) shares his perspective on the issue when he compares our life years to a sporting event or a movie. The difference, he points out, is in the fact that we cannot rewind and start over again or push the pause button until the answers or the cures emerge. Generally, we are not provided a second chance to correct our actions or to embellish mediocrity. What we must realize is that more often than not, our past silently leads us into our future.

Across the landscape of our nation's schools, children are being thrust into a stark world where numbers quantify degrees of learning. Increasing levels of stress among learners and educators alike play havoc on self-esteem, on future hopes and dreams, and on the perception of lifelong learning. Teachers often find themselves experiencing a juxtaposition of roles. On the one hand, they firmly believe that learning is worth pursuing for its own sake; thus, they strive to insert opportunities for creativity amid stacks of test preparation materials. On the other hand, especially the hand of the young, inexperienced teacher, the temptation to use pre-packaged, drill-and-kill ditto sheets paired with the stress of the current testing movement is almost too great to overcome. Teachers need not lose sight that increased student achievement often leads to increased scores; yet, too often, caring for the student is replaced with categorically analyzing test results.

Progress toward student achievement does not often happen without the encouragement and active involvement of family members and the guidance and support of caring educators. Christle, Jolivette, and Nelson (2005) identified school-based policies and practices that promote academic success. They found that supportive leadership, consistent school-wide behavior management, dedicated and caring faculty and staff members, and effective teaching positively impact student learning. The investigators posit that when these qualities are present in a school environment, delinquent behavior that leads to poor academic performance can be lessened among socioeconomic student populations that typically tend to have a high delinquency rate. Lawrence, Jones, and Smith (1999) interviewed elementary-aged children about what they believe to be school factors important for their academic success. Students identified having someone who truly listens as the number one need, while the second identified need, following closely on the heels of the first, is to have someone's acceptance and unconditional love.

The cry for caring and concerned educators resonates from within our students as an increasing number face challenging situations at home. Unless we move ourselves from behind the podium and step into our students' world, which is often filled with pain, neglect, and abuse, we stand the chance of losing a generation of learners even though we, as educators, frequently see the mandate on pamphlets, conference banners, and presidential documents to leave no child behind.

Caring individuals placed within educational settings have the unique opportunity to reach across societal divisions and extend helping hands to those who are in need. Through purposeful dialogue, deep reflection, and mindful inquiry, one comes to the realization that through the blended practice of caring and teaching, one can advance the learning of all children. Action research conducted by the teacher also can serve as a mechanism to help one understand, on a deeper level, what works and does not work within the confines of his or her classroom. Carr and Kemmis (1986) see action research as a bridge that allows practitioners to cross over into the world of scholars, where personal findings lead to recommendations and result in changed actions. The cyclic nature of action research involves planning, action, and reflection in an effort to improve teacher practice and student learning. As this cyclic model is practiced within the classroom environment, students and teachers alike find common ground from which to grow and change.

The Action Researchers

Two graduate students, Tara and Tami, engaged in the process of action research within their own classrooms in an effort to further understand their actions and the impact that each action had on their students. In both instances, the teachers' choice to demonstrate a greater depth of care resulted in not only an increase in their students' performance, but also a positive change in their students' lives.

Tara sought to investigate the relationship between parental involvement and the early years of student achievement. She hoped to gain knowledge that would lead to an improved level of parent/teacher communication and identify creative opportunities to more frequently involve her students' parents in classroom activities. Tami witnessed firsthand the negative impact that low self-esteem amid extreme poverty can have on a middle level student's life. Already committed to her promise of care, she sought a solution to the student's lackadaisical attitude toward homework assignments. We began with Tara's account, followed by that of Tami.

The Preschool Challenge

Tara is a preschool teacher working with children from predominately low socioeconomic backgrounds and who are members of underrepresented racial populations within Arkansas's largest urban school district. Through her work with these children, Tara has come to realize that her students enter school equipped with a diverse range of knowledge and skills. Over time, she has noticed a relationship between the involvement of parents and the achievement of students. Questions have emerged in Tara's mind about this relationship and have caused her to search for clues on how to strengthen the school/home connection. Tara, learning about action research and its ability to provide possible answers through a systematic approach, decided to conduct her own personal study.

IDENTIFYING AN AREA OF INVESTIGATION

For her first action research project, Tara selected four students from her preschool class to monitor through the coming school year. She chose two of the youngest and two of the oldest children. It is important to note that each of the children fell into the extreme poverty category.

Tara officially began her research with an assessment of each student's incoming, academically related skills and abilities. These assessments were repeated during the course of the school year. In addition to this documentation and throughout her study, Tara recorded the depth and consistency of parental involvement as mothers, grandmothers, and aunties dropped off their children in the mornings and picked them up in the afternoons. She also attended to the contents of each child's backpack, whether notes to parents were initialed and returned or if the child's schoolwork had been removed.

LITERATURE REVIEW: CONNECTING HOME AND SCHOOL FOR PRESCHOOL-AGED CHILDREN

Early intervention research has shown that parental involvement produces positive effects on a child's physical, social, cognitive, and emotional development, in addition to improving language and psychomotor skills (Greifner, 2006; Wagner, Spike, & Linn, 2002). Parental involvement also produces positive gains for parents in their overall sense of personal control and self-efficacy and in their level of satisfaction about their child's school services. Parental, or familial, school involvement is basically defined as the participation and commitment in a child's education demonstrated by parents, grandparents, or other adult guardians (Carlisle, Stanley, & Kemple, 2005).

Greifner (2006) presents compelling evidence of the importance of familial involvement in *The Principals' Partnership*—established by the Omaha, Nebraska-based *Union Pacific Foundation*—in which 62% of the principals who were polled believed that the most important action a family can take to ensure the success of a student is for the family to maintain regular communication with the child's classroom teacher(s) and school administrator(s). From a child's initial introduction into preschool and continuing throughout the elementary, middle, and high school years, parental involvement offers the necessary support and sustenance to help create a well-balanced individual capable of stepping into society armed with all of the required tools to become a successful and productive adult.

Wagner, Spike, and Linn (2002) reviewed the literature on the effects of home-learning environments on preschool children representing high-income versus low-income homes. Their report of national longitudinal data revealed startling facts: compared to children from higher-income families, (a) children from poorer families are 1.3 times more likely to experience learning disabilities and developmental delays (Brooks-Gunn & Duncan, 1997); (b) children from poorer families are more likely to score lower on standardized tests, fail, and eventually drop out of school (Lewit, Terman, & Behrman, 1997; Zill, Moore, Smith, Stief, & Coiro, 1991); and (c) many low-income parents do not know what to do at home to prepare their children for school (Zill et al., 1991). Tara desired to document and analyze the relationship between the selected students' achievement levels and the level of communication between her students' families and school.

TARA'S STUDENTS: NATHAN, SAIGON, NANCE, AND JAMAYAL

For her study, Tara purposefully selected two of her three-year-old students and two of her four-year-old students representing both traditional and nontraditional homes. Nathan is a three-year-old whose parents work outside the home but choose to remain active in his school activities and in his learning. During the times when his parents were busy, Nathan's maternal grandparents took responsibility for his safety and well-being. In addition to maintaining school contact, Nathan's parents and grandparents sought opportunities at home to extend his learning experiences. Chores were assigned to help Nathan understand responsibility and family involvement, and television viewing was supervised closely by all of the adults in his life. Tara noted that, during drop-off and pick-up periods, the parents took the time to speak with her about Nathan. They were encouraged that Nathan continues to improve in his letter recognition.

Saigon, a three-year-old, also comes from a two-parent home; however, the similarities end here. Saigon's parents often worked late into the evening, leaving him three and four days a week in the after-school program. His mother seldom took advantage of opportunities to talk with Tara and learn about her child's progress in school. The materials placed in his backpack, such as notes and student work, were often left untouched for several days. During the school year, Saigon's parents failed to attend the parent/teacher conferences or the monthly parental information meetings. At home, Saigon had no engagement with adults or siblings. He had no chores, and he was at liberty to choose his own television programs.

As for Nance, he and his parents celebrated his fourth birthday in May. Nance's father works late, but his mother is faithful in dropping him off and picking him up from school each day. She is quite interested in Nance's progress and converses frequently with Tara about his schoolwork. Both parents consistently attend all parent/teacher meetings. Nance's mother has requested that each Friday evening Tara place additional work in Nance's backpack so that she and his father can work with him during the weekends. On Monday afternoons, Nance's father joins him in the library to select favorite storybooks to read at home. His parents supervised his activities while Nance was in their care, taking every opportunity to add something of value to his overall learning experience.

Four-year-old Jamayal technically lives in two homes, sharing her time with her divorced parents. During the weekdays, she lives with her mother and stepfather, as well as one older and one younger brother. On the weekends, Jamayal and her siblings live with her biological father. Her home life is somewhat confusing for a young child, having to divide her life between two homes. Rules are inconsistent due to the back-and-forth movement between parents. No chores are required of the children, and selection of television programs was typically left to the dominate child's whims. The work schedules of Jamayal's mother and stepfather do not permit them to attend the parent/teacher conferences or the monthly meetings provided by the school; however, there does remain consistent written communication between Tara and Jamayal's mother and stepfather about her school performance.

OUTCOMES OF TARA'S RESEARCH

After approval was granted by school administrators, parents, and children to conduct the action research project, the following questionnaire was given to the parents of all children in an attempt to prevent identification of research participants by other parents and students and to gain an understanding of the home environment of each child:

Name: _____

1. Name three things you and your child enjoy doing together:

2. What do you expect your child to learn by the end of preschool?

3. Does your child have assigned chores at home? If yes, please describe.

4. Approximately how much television is your child allowed to watch everyday?

5. Does your child have an adult supervising her or his television viewing?

_____

_____

_____

6. Which of the following tasks does your child do by themselves at home? Please circle your choices.

    a. Get dressed (shirt, pants or shorts, shoes)

    b. Brush teeth

    c. Brush hair

    d. Serve food at meals

This questionnaire was given to parents as the children were dropped off or picked up, along with an explanation of Tara's research purpose. The adults were asked to carefully read the document and then to candidly complete each question. They were to return the completed questionnaire to Tara as soon as possible so that she could enter the information and proceed to the analysis phase of the work.

Initially, two assessments were administered to each child to establish a baseline of knowledge for comparison over the course of the school year. The Brigance Screening Assessment, required by the state and given quarterly, consists of eleven categories covering a wide array of skills necessary to verify student growth during the preschool years. The second form of assessment, an informal measure repeated twice during the course of the study, provided information on each child's literacy development. This reading rubric follows:

Subject: Literacy   Grade Level: Preschool

Name: _____

Comprehension
4   Four or more of the facts from the story
3   Three or more facts from the story
2   Two or more facts from the story
1   One fact from the story
0   Cannot recall any facts from the story

Sequencing
4 Three-fourth's of the story
3 One-half of the story
2 Less than one-half of the story
1 First or last step of the story
1 None of the story

Characters
4 All of the characters
3 Three-fourths of the characters
2 One-half of the characters
1 One of the characters
0 Cannot recall any of the characters

Setting
4 Time, place, season, and mood
3 Three of the four
2 Two of the four
1 One of the four
0 None of the four

As results of each assessment were recorded, Tara noted that her findings remained consistent with current research: Children with actively involved parents, with time constraints on television viewing, and with assigned chores at home continued to score higher on each form of assessment than did the children with parents less involved in their child's life, with little or no constraints on television viewing, and with few or no assigned chores at home.

In addition to the aforementioned assessments, Tara maintained a journal of her interactions with and observations of the children. This journal allowed Tara to document the social and emotional aspects of Nathan's, Saigon's, Nance's, and Jamayal's learning. Reflecting on informal discussions with the children about their after-school activities allowed Tara to gain a clearer understanding of each child's home life. Tara's anecdotal writings and observational notes also tracked the receipt of parent/teacher notes and take-home assignments, as evidenced in the transfer and movement of items within the students' backpacks. These entries heightened Tara's awareness of the level of parental/guardian involvement in each child's life. Opportunities to talk with each parent during informal moments, such as during the drop-off and pick-up time, provided Tara additional insights into her students' home environment.

Nathan and Nance scored much higher on the Brigance Screening Assessments and informal literacy profiles provided to all students than did Saigon and Jamayal. As noted previously, Nathan and Nance have parents who remain actively involved in their lives and who are dedicated to educational excellence at home and at school. Souto-Manning and Swick (2006) contend that parental support and informal learning opportunities outside of the classroom advance a child's ability to think and learn, as well as extend his creativity and problem-solving skills. Typically, a child with this type of mental stimulation will perform better in a classroom setting than will his counterparts. The theoretical perspectives uncovered in her literature review and the findings brought forth in Tara's action research study have energized her desire to increase parental/guardian involvement in her students' education, especially in the case of lower income, urban families.

Middle-Level Issues of Self-Esteem

Tami is a sixth-grade math teacher who works in a rural middle school setting that has a student population of 570. She is a veteran teacher with 17 years of experience, assisting children in their conceptual understanding of mathematical processes. Equally important are the many occasions Tami has had to positively impact her students and guide them in their journey toward adulthood.

Early in the fall semester, Tami noticed that one of her sixth grade students seemed uninterested in school and seldom completed his homework assignments. Dallas appeared at first glance to be a bright young man, but his mannerisms reflected his distaste for school and all that was associated with it. Whenever Tami approached him to discuss the absence of his math assignments, Dallas shut down. The communication methods that typically worked with other students failed to work with him. Tami began to search for new strategies for reaching Dallas. She privately questioned whether Dallas even cared about his possible failure of sixth-grade math; yet, Tami remained concerned for him, especially the negative effects failure might have on his seemingly fragile self-esteem.

As the days advanced, Tami found herself observing Dallas's actions outside of the math classroom. Students would move from one class to another, but Dallas walked alone. He rarely smiled at his peers and seldom sought out opportunities to talk with others. He was definitely a loner and did not appear to have any friends. Occasionally, Tami would hear Dallas say in passing to another student, "Quit pushing me," "Leave me alone," or "Stop doing that." Tami's design of the sixth-grade math class, in accordance with the district's math curriculum, relied heavily on cooperative learning and group work. Because of the lack of positive interactions between Dallas and other students, Dallas was placed at a rather large disadvantage. Tami's concern grew for Dallas's academic success, and she chose to reach out to Dallas's previous teachers in an effort to gain further understanding of his past behaviors and learning capabilities. She remained hopeful in finding some type of connection with Dallas.

Tami learned that Dallas's home life was full of instability and pain. His parents were never married, and they eventually moved apart. There was a period of time when Dallas and his father lived in an automobile, not from extreme poverty, but from the father's series of poor choices. The paternal grandparents had attempted to reach out to Dallas; but after watching their son, Dallas's father, repeatedly stumble and fall, and experiencing some violent reactions in Dallas, they withdrew completely. By the fourth grade, Dallas had established himself as a failure to the adults in his life and to himself as a result of continually earning poor grades. His self-esteem deteriorated with each report card.

During the first six weeks of school, Dallas was given his first in-school suspension of the year because of his repeated failure to complete homework assignments in science class. Tami came to the realization that if there was no intervention in Dallas's life, he soon would fall through the cracks, eventually dropping out of school and becoming another dismal failure of the educational system. This all too possible prediction prompted Tami to ask the question: Would the development of an individualized and personalized relationship with Dallas result in his improved academic performance and thus prevent possible failure? She determined that this question would form the basis of her action research project.

LITERATURE REVIEW: AT-RISK CHILDREN AND POSITIVE TEACHER RELATIONSHIPS

As reported in the literature, student academic performance improves significantly when teacher/student relationships are developed and strengthened during the course of a school year (Donovan, 1998; Meissen & Garner, 2003; Peters-Felice, 2003; Rogers, 2003; Strahl, 1999). Rogers (2003) purports:

> Motivation or lack of it is an important factor for these [at-risk] children. Those who have become excited about school are the ones who become successful . . . most [at-risk students] are not excited about school and do not find internal motivation to achieve good grades in their classes. (p. 2)

Bost and Riccomini (2006) report a higher dropout rate for students who have "poor relationships with [their] teachers and peers" (p. 303) and who lack a sense of belonging; findings also reveal that teacher/student relationships improve student motivation, resulting in improved student achievement. Strahl (1999) indicates that much of the literature does, in fact, support one-on-one mentoring as making a difference in a student's social and emotional well-being. For this type of a relationship to be successful, the teacher must prove to the student that he or she is trustworthy and must establish a safe environment from which the teacher/student relationship can develop.

DuFour (2004) describes schools in which intervention strategies for at-risk students are developed and implemented, documenting the overall benefits for the students as well as for the educators, administrators, and community members. In such schools adults do whatever is necessary to ensure that students connect with learning, with one another, with themselves, and with staff, faculty, and administrators. Leone (2002) describes how one teacher's influence impacted his own life simply because she was willing to develop an appropriate and caring relationship with him. He states profoundly, "There has to be a relationship, and then, and only then, can there be performance" (p. 22).

Tami decided to work with Dallas in an attempt to positively influence his life, to alter a possible negative outcome of his decisions not to complete homework assignments, and to assist him in developing positive people skills. To monitor her progress in these endeavors, Tami planned to systematically check Dallas's work in math class, as well as in his other classes. She also devised a check sheet to record how interactions with Dallas and his resulting responses might predict his return rate of homework assignments and improve his self-esteem. Would the successful completion of Dallas's homework increase his attention and participation in math class? Would he be more apt to engage with other students if he felt successful in this one area? These questions invited Tami to seek answers through an action research project.

TAMI'S RESEARCH PROJECT

Like Tara, Tami elected to perform a mixed-methods action research project, combining quantitative and qualitative data. First she obtained a copy of Dallas's most recent progress report where she found his grades to be a D in math, an F in literacy, an F in science, and a C in social studies. Then Tami contacted each of Dallas's teachers and requested a meeting to collaborate with them about possible strategies to strengthen his learning experiences. She shared with her peers the possibility of purposefully developing a closer relationship with Dallas to support the overall goal of moving him out of the at-risk category.

After gaining informed consent from her students and their parents to participate in a study of teacher-pupil interactions, Tami created a log to document the specific types of interactions with Dallas during the school day (see Table 17.1). She then began to note the relationship between those contact times and Dallas's assignment completion in hopes of observing a relationship between the two events. In addition, Tami developed a survey for all students in her math class and engaged them in completing the survey to prevent Dallas from feeling singled out. This survey sought to determine personal feelings about school, as well as a variety of events associated with school (i.e., social activities, homework assignments, and peer interactions).

As Tami learned more about Dallas, she realized that he likely was unaware of his deficiencies in school. In math class, he had only returned three of the assignments since school began which, in turn, produced a homework grade of 30%. These had been turned in during the first two weeks of school. Since that time, he had not submitted any homework papers. Shortly after creating her contact log, Tami pulled Dallas aside privately at the conclusion of class and talked with him about this situation. However, Dallas failed to see the seriousness of his actions. He told Tami that he always completed the assigned work but that he would often forget to place it in his backpack and "just leave it at home."

Throughout the fall semester, Tami continued to chart her interactions with Dallas, to monitor Dallas's grades and number of completed assignments, and to take advantage of every opportunity to show her care and concern about Dallas, the person. Slowly, he began to smile and engage in civil conversations with Tami. Four weeks after beginning the action research, Dallas returned a math homework assignment to school. He searched for Tami in the hallway prior to first period to share the good news with her. Dallas was proud of his accomplishment and was even prouder to have someone to whom he could communicate the good news. During class, his behaviors indicated a difference in self-concept as he eagerly engaged in discussions and volunteered to work math problems on the board. Tami believed that she was witnessing a breakthrough, a turning point in Dallas's attitude and, hopefully, a pattern that would promote his success in school.

As the research project concluded, Tami observed that there was an increase in the overall number of homework assignments returned. If Dallas did not have his homework, his attitude reflected his lowered feelings of self-esteem. There would be a greater enthusiasm demonstrated when assignments were completed on time and returned to school. There would be periods of sulkiness and poutiness when the work was not completed. Tami allowed Dallas to witness the patterns by sharing her interaction chart and anecdotal notes with him in hopes of helping him develop a more intrinsic motivation to succeed.

Table 17.1 Contact Log

Date	Type of Contact	Student's Response	Homework	Comments
9/12	Regular class time	Sulky	No	
9/13	Math class—spoke with him about not returning work	Sullen	No	
9/14	Regular class	Seems to not care	No	
9/15	Regular class—asked why work not done	Said he forgot	No	
9/18	Regular class		No	Progress Report—69%, D Math
9/19	Regular class		No	Discussed him with other 6th grade teachers
9/21	He had ISS for 5 zeros in science		No	
9/22	Stopped him in hall—told him I missed him	Smiled	Yes	Work was done in ISS
9/26	Regular class—called him at home to see if he needed homework help	Acted shy but pleased	No	Began calling on him more in class
9/27	Called him to my class during my prep and helped him redo a test	Frustrated	No	Talked to him about how much I care and want to help
9/28	Regular class—also pulled him at my prep time just to check	Smiled and chatted	No	
9/29	Saw him in hall—he stopped to visit	Big smile!	2 late assignments done in LL	
10/2	Regular class—gave lots of 1-on-1 special attention	Still won't raise hand or participate	No	

Table 17.1 (Continued)

Date	Type of Contact	Student's Response	Homework	Comments
10/3	Regular class—chose new partners for more peer help for him	Seemed more willing to engage	No	Made a B on the check-up quiz
10/4	Did Focus test in class—no HW			Worked had on Focus test—did not give up
10/5	Finished Focus test—no homework	Scored a 3		
10/6	Brought him in 2nd period prep again just to visit	Smiled and gave me a hug when he left	No	Seems to be trusting me but I'm frustrated he still doesn't do HW
10/9	Told him that I nominated him for student of the week	Acted very happy	No	Made a B on Partner Quiz
10/10	Lots of attention in regular class	More interactive in class—participates more	No	
10/11	Regular class—saw in hall and gave big hug and high five	Beginning to initiate contact when he sees me in hall	No	Made a B on unit test!
10/12	Sent home a survey for parent conferences			Pulled during prep
10/13	Regular class—lots of attention and note in locker	Acts very happy in class	Returned survey	Dad indicated he never had homework
10/16	Emailed dad about his response on survey	Sent him to LL to do reflections	No	Talked to him about why dad responded about HW

Table 17.1 (Continued)

Date	Type of Contact	Student's Response	Homework	Comments
10/17	Regular class—visited for a moment before class	Shy but pleased	No	End of 1st 9 weeks
10/18	Very engaged in class, his work was done, raised hand and energetic	He stopped me in hall to tell me that he had HW	Yes	Excited that he knew the answers to HW questions
10/19	Very engaged in class, asked his own questions	Again proud of himself, was anxious to answer questions	Yes	Really bragged on him

As a result of this study, Tami's beliefs have been strengthened concerning the importance of building positive relationships with each of her students, of reaching out to make personal connections, and of seizing every opportunity to challenge and encourage her children. Valenzuela (1999), through her ethnographic approach, points out that our schools often deprive young people of important social and cultural resources and make them vulnerable to possible academic failure. Tami has vowed to truly make a difference, to provide not only academic instruction, but also to provide substantive opportunities for student growth in the socio/emotional arena. She realizes the potential impact such opportunities can have especially in the lives of children who do not have a stable and loving familial support group.

Calling for a Renaissance of Care

Our nation's schools house the energy and imagination necessary to foster dynamic change within our students. To advance this change, however, teachers must move beyond seeing students as merely "visitors" to their classrooms; they must invite them to enter into a place of membership, a place in which students become part of a cohesive learning community. If we expect our students to become active participants in the learning experience we, as educators, must create environments in which students share in the ownership of their learning.

In today's world, students from poverty-stricken and divorced homes face extreme challenges to succeed. School personnel have unique opportunities to identify and demonstrate specific ways in which all students can feel valued and cared for, even if they do not feel those emotions anywhere else. Classroom teachers, in particular, have the choice to operate from a sense of care and authenticity and thus to motivate those students who remain disenfranchised due to situations often out of their control. By teachers' redirecting their energies from simply imparting content knowledge to building positive relationships with and encouraging self-worth among students then, and only then, will one witness the subtle shift from "business as usual" to a learning experience of the head, the heart, and the senses.

Valenzuela (1999) states: "If children do not know who they are or where they are going, then any road will get them there" (p. 269). We, as classroom teachers and professors, cannot willingly accept an "any road" approach to education. Participational opportunities designed through life-enriching moments can render our classrooms transformative places for students, their parents and guardians, and teachers. We must set as a goal the individualization of learning opportunities through preparing meaningful educational experiences for each student's journey through life as we demonstrate care about the welfare of those we teach.

Gould (2003) argues: "What can be more powerful than combining the virtue of a clear goal pursued relentlessly and without compromise, and the flexibility of a wide range of clever and distinct strategies for getting to the appointed place?" (p. 276). Tara and Tami remained persistent in their search to understand care and its impact on their students. All educators stand on common ground as we look beyond the horizon in search of something greater. We each have much to gain as we view the world through a different lens and with a different perspective.

As we renew our sense of what it means to be teachers, our beliefs about the importance of student care and respect will become the learning communities' norm. Educators and students will enjoy collaborating, a higher quality of education will be advanced to every member of society, parents will view the work of the school through a new lens, and trust will open the door to an even larger learning experience in which life and living are connected. When Robert F. Kennedy spoke of actions that seek to improve our fellow human beings' lot, he reminded us of the ripple effect. One tiny ripple of hope extends both outward and inward and creates an energizing response that breaks down the strongest of barriers. Let us become educators who extend hope through our care and respect, and then let us observe the lives of those influenced.

References

Bost, L. W., & Riccomini, P. J. (2006). Effective instruction: An inconspicuous strategy for dropout prevention. *Remedial and Special Education, 27*(5), 301–311.

Brooks-Gunn, J., & Duncan, G. J. (1997). The effects of poverty on children. *The Future of Children, 7,* 55–71.

Carlisle, E., Stanley, L., & Kemple, K. M. (2005). Opening doors: Understanding school and family influences on family involvement. *Early Childhood Education Journal, 33*(3), 155–162.

Carr, W., & Kemmis, S. (1986). *Becoming critical: Education, knowledge, and action research.* Lewes: Falmer.

Christle, C. A., Jolivette, K., & Nelson, C. M. (2005). Breaking the school to prison pipeline: Identifying school risk and protective factors for youth delinquency. *Exceptionality, 13*(2), 69–88.

Donovan, H. J. (1998). *On schools, learning, and becoming ourselves.* Madison, WI: Madison Metropolitan School District Classroom Action Research Report.

DuFour, R., Eaker, R., & Karhanek, G. (2004). *Whatever it takes: How professional learning communities respond when kids don't learn.* Bloomington, IN: National Education Service.

Gould, S. J. (2003). *The hedgehog, the fox, and the magister's pox: Ending the false war between science and the humanities.* New York: Harmony.

Greifner, L. (2006). Family involvement. *Education Week, 25*(43), 20.

Kozol, J. (1992). *Savage inequalities: Children in America's schools.* New York: Harper Perennial.

Lawrence, W., Jones, E., & Smith, F. (1999). Students' perceived needs as identified by students. *Journal of Instructional Psychology, 26*(1), 22–29.

Leone, S., Jr. (2002). Making love in public schools. *Executive Speeches, 16*(6), 17–22.

Lewit, E. M., Terman, D. L., & Behrman, R. E. (1997). Children and poverty: Analysis and recommendations. *The Future of Children, 7,* 4–24.

Meissen, T., & Garner, M. (2003). *Improving relationships in the middle school classrooms: A key to successful learning.* Madison, WI: Madison Metropolitan School District Classroom Action Research Report.

Peters-Felice, M. (2003). *How can I mentor/support my six underachieving female African American students in becoming more successful learners?* Madison, WI: Madison Metropolitan School District Classroom Action Research Report.

Rogers, B. (2003). *Closing the achievement gap: Strategies that work with "at risk" students.* Madison, WI: Madison Metropolitan School District Classroom Action Research Report.

Souto-Manning, M., & Swick, K. J. (2006). Teacher's beliefs about family involvement: Rethinking our family involvement paradigm. *Early Childhood Education Journal, 34*(2), 187–193.

Strahl, J. (1999). *Can mentors make a difference in students' self-esteem?* Madison, WI: Madison Metropolitan School District Classroom Action Research Report.

Valenzuela, A. (1999). *Subtractive schooling: U.S.–Mexican youth and the politics of caring.* Albany, NY: State University of New York Press.

Wagner, M., Spiker, D., & Linn, M. I. (2002). The effectiveness of the parents-as-teachers program with low-income parents and children. *Topics in Early Childhood Special Education, 22*(2), 67–77.

Zill, N., Moore, K. A, Smith, E. W., Stief, T., & Coiro, M. J. (1991). *The life circumstance and development of children in welfare families: A profile based on national survey data.* Washington, DC: Child Trends.

CHAPTER 18

Small Steps
MOVING TOWARD A RENAISSANCE IN TEACHER EDUCATION

Helen Freidus
Bank Street College of Education

> Helen Freidus, Ed.D., is a member of the graduate faculty at Bank Street College in New York City. Her research and teaching foci include literacy development, teacher development, and teaching for social justice. Her latest publication is Nurturing Cognitive Dissonance in New Teachers, in Tidwell and Fitzgerald's *Self-Study and Diversity* (2006).

ABSTRACT

This chapter describes a self-study of an innovation in the content of a graduate course in literacy methods designed to help teachers understand and implement learner-centered pedagogy in an age of accountability. A curriculum module was designed to integrate a workshop at the American Museum of Natural History with assigned readings and class instruction. Teachers learned through their own experiences how to integrate literacy skills and strategies into experience-based units of study. The data sources suggest that a renaissance in teacher education can be supported when experiential models of progressive schools of teacher education are revisited, rearticulated, adapted and enacted to meet today's needs.

> *You must either make a tool of the creature, or a man of him. You cannot make both.*
>
> —Ruskin, 1853, 2004

The editors of this yearbook have called for a renaissance in teacher education, a revisioning of the connections between teacher education and curriculum. Their goal is that the rich resources of educational research and the strengths that teachers, learners, and the communities surrounding them bring to the learning process might be combined in more fruitful ways. In response to this call, this chapter describes a self-study of an innovation in the content of a graduate course in the teaching of literacy methods. This new content is designed to encourage teachers and student teachers to question the mandated curriculum and to see themselves as professionals whose role includes the responsibility for designing instruction to meet the needs of the children they teach. Teachers are encouraged to look beyond the classroom doors in order to better understand and maximize the learning opportunities for young children. They are taught to look recursively at research, their own knowledge base, and the experience and language of their students as rich resources for instruction.

The course, The Teaching of Reading, Writing, and Language Arts, is taught to candidates for a Masters Degree in Education at the Bank Street College of Education in New York City. For the past two years, a curriculum module incorporating a workshop co-designed with Maritza Macdonald, Director of Professional Development at the American Museum of Natural History, has been added. The museum, geographically and philosophically a part of the Bank Street community, has been introduced as a legitimate and powerful resource for teaching children how to read and write. Assigned readings and follow-up instruction helps teachers learn how to incorporate literacy content including but not limited to systematic phonics, word study, comprehension skills, and writing strategies into units of study that are both rigorous and relevant to children's knowledge and interests. The museum experience is viewed not as an enrichment experience but as a piece of core curriculum. Its goal is to enable teachers to better understand the concept of literacy as a language-based learning process that builds on and extends children's understanding of the world.

How can so small an innovation be considered relevant to a discussion of a renaissance in teacher education? Renaissance, according to Dictionary.com Unabridged (v 1.0.1) comes from *renaistre*, a word from the Old French meaning rebirth. It is particularly relevant to a revival in art and learning. The answer, then, is that this innovation is, hopefully, a harbinger of revisiting, rearticulating, and reclaiming models of teacher education that look not only at the curriculum but also at the child and the teacher. Such models acknowledge the complex needs of today's classrooms but, unlike so many of today's prescriptive educational mandates (Pullman, 2003), do so without diminishing or demeaning the teachers and the children within them.

The Context

This renaissance is taking place within the Reading and Literacy Program at Bank Street College of Education in New York City. Bank Street is a small, freestanding graduate school of education, founded in 1916 with a commitment to a progressive vision of education. From the very beginning, Bank Street has been an institution in which the purpose of education has been seen as transformative; social change and social justice have been key concepts. For this to be accomplished, a critical stance is essential. In 1930, Lucy Sprague Mitchell, the founder of Bank Street College, wrote

> Our aim is to help students develop a scientific attitude towards their work and toward life. To us this means an attitude of eager, alert observations, a constant questioning of old procedure in the light of new observations; a use of the world as well as of books as source material; an experimental open-mindedness; and an effort to keep as reliable records as the situation permits in order to base the future upon actual knowledge of the experiences of the past. . . . We are not interested in perpetuation of any special "school of thought." Rather, we are interested in imbuing teachers with an experimental, critical and ardent approach to their work. (Mitchell, in Antler, 1987, p. 309)

Historically, Bank Street faculty and students look at teaching and learning through constructivist (Piaget, 1932; Duckworth, 1987) and, more recently, social constructivist perspectives (Lave & Wenger, 1991; Rogoff, 1990; Vygotsky, 1922, p. 35, p. 78). According to these perspectives, both adults and children learn through experience with people, objects, and places. New understandings emerge through verbal and non-verbal interactions with others. These interactions shape the development of habits of mind and habits of practice as they are framed and reframed within the ongoing context of individual and group experiences. Change and flexibility are both desired and inevitable.

In today's world of literacy education, it can feel as if terms like "experimental," "critical," and "ardent" are far removed from the discourse of teacher practice. The curriculum mandated by No Child Left Behind policies uses terms like replicable, scientifically based, and adequate yearly progress. Student teachers at Bank Street, like those throughout the United States, consistently encounter classrooms that are shaped by these terms. They see little room for the learner-centered practice they are being taught in their Bank Street classes. And yet, they see that despite the presence of scientifically based curriculum models, children still are not achieving. They are frustrated; they do not know how to respond.

In recent years, faculty members have been conflicted. We have felt torn between our own beliefs about what constitutes good education and the frustrations that our students express. We wonder if a greater emphasis on skills-based education is necessary to prepare our students for the workplace. We question whether by teaching the discourse of mandated practice, we are helping teachers to function more effectively or merely to step farther and farther away from the language and practice of learner-centered pedagogy. Now, suddenly it seems that in efforts to hone our instruction and help teachers to develop essential skills, we have inched away from some of the practices that are essential if we are to be true to the mission that frames our work.

Ten or more years ago when faculty began to place more emphasis on the teaching of specific skills and strategies, our students were working in classrooms in which they could observe curriculum models that addressed the strengths, needs, experiences, and interests of a broad range of learners. In that world teachers were viewed as professionals whose role it was to identify students' strengths and needs and to develop curriculum that supported these strengths and needs. Student teaching, at that time, could be construed as an apprenticeship model. Students came to Bank Street because they believed in models of learner-centered education and wanted to develop the knowledge and skills needed to implement them. Field experiences helped them to clarify and operationalize these visions.

However, at that time, classes in the public schools were becoming larger and increasingly more diverse. Resources were being cut. More and more children and teachers were struggling. And so, it seemed appropriate to sharpen our teacher education practice and help our students to focus on developing a more clearly articulated repertoire of strategies for assessment and instruction. It was assumed that with faculty coaching, they would integrate this into an existing model of learner-centered practice.

This perspective of teacher as professional no longer prevails in urban schools. In most schools, teachers are now expected to implement curriculum developed by others. More and more curriculum and instruction is prescribed and paced according to a "generic" script.

Students still come to Bank Street because they believe in learner-centered education, and because they want to make a difference. However, no longer can it be assumed that their fieldwork experiences will give them an opportunity to participate in the kind of educational practice they value. The need for a strong repertoire of assessment and instructional strategies to meet the needs of all students has never been stronger, but the context has changed. The curriculum that prevails in today's schools, especially that which is mandated in the field of literacy, ignores decades of studies from related fields, research that documents how children learn from experience and how this experience differs among individuals and populations (Dewey, 1938; Duckworth, 1987; Owocki, 1999; Cole, Cole, & Lightfoot, 2005). It ignores the entire field of cognitive research that explores and documents the ways in which knowledge is socially constructed rather than simply transmitted (Borko, 2004; Putnam & Borko, 2000; Rogoff,

1990). Teachers who have been taught to look at their students with these concepts in mind are often chastised rather than praised. They are told to toe the mark, to keep their insights to themselves.

Evidence of this can be seen in one teacher's response to a reading on current policy. Having taught successfully in one school for three years, she wrote about a discussion she had with her principal:

> Earlier this year I offered reflective feedback about the curriculum for reading and writing instruction that I have been using for the past two years. It was not all negative, but it was honest and I thought very informed. I was reprimanded and told that we were a College Reading and Writing Process School and that I didn't have a choice but to teach it [as the manual prescribed]. I was also told that Fundations [a systematic approach to phonics] was scientifically based and how could I argue with science? (DS, e-mail communication, 11/07)

And so, it seems that as the realities of life in classrooms have changed, it is time once again to revisit not only what we teach in our teacher education course but also how and why we teach it.

> If the aim of teacher education is a reformed practice that is not readily available, and if there is no reinforcing culture to support such practice, then the basic imagery of apprenticeship seems to break down. . . . [This] creates a puzzle for reform. Through what activities and situations do teachers learn new practices that may not be routinely reinforced in the work situation. (Sykes & Bird in Putnam & Borko, 2000, p. 8)

It is time for a renaissance in teacher education that looks backward to the premises of progressive pedagogy and forward to the integration of specific skills instruction within this pedagogy. This renaissance will enable teachers to understand the importance of practices that they do not routinely see in their work situation. Moreover, it will facilitate their ability to implement these practices in whatever time and space they can negotiate. The alternative, as Pullman (2003) describes, is that well-educated, intelligent teachers will continue to be inspected, nagged, and examined on an ongoing basis. Ultimately, these teachers will leave or submit and become tools of an educational system that requires all teachers to follow the same curriculum and the same lesson plans, regardless of the children who sit in their classrooms. A renaissance in teacher education is not only desirable but also necessary. The unit of study in development of literacy curriculum that is here described is one small step toward this renaissance.

The Innovation

As discussed above, the original content of the course, The Teaching of Reading, Writing, and Language Arts, had been developed based on the assumption that students would be participating in learner-centered practice in their fieldwork. As classrooms in the New York City area have begun to implement more and more models of scripted curriculum, a schism has developed between what student teachers were learning in teacher education classrooms and what they were seeing implemented in the schools. By the fall of 2005, it had become apparent that fewer and fewer graduate students were having opportunities to observe models of integrated curriculum that were responsive to the needs and interests of the children they taught. Faculty talked about the importance of prior knowledge and experience as a basis for learning. Students listened carefully and acknowledged that these concepts made sense, but they did not understand how to weave them into the realities of the classrooms in which they worked.

We could not change the ways in which city classrooms were responding to mandates, but we could change the kinds of experiences our students were having in teacher education classrooms. We could provide them with the kinds of learning experiences that would enable them to understand viscerally as well as cognitively why learning that builds on what individuals know and value is so very powerful (Dewey in Dworkin, 1959). We could not only talk about the importance of authentic learning opportunities, but we could begin to model these experiences. And so, a collaboration with the education department at the American Museum of Natural History was developed.

The Museum Experience

In fall of 2005 and 2006, students were asked to meet at the American Museum of Natural History for the seventh session of their literacy course. Earlier sessions of the course had emphasized the relationship of language and experience to literacy development (Clay, 1991; Holdaway, 1979; Peregoy & Boyle, 2004) and strategies for helping children to make meaning from text (Harvey, 2002; Harvey & Goudvis, 2000; Pinnell & Fountas, 1998). Through the workshop and related class instruction, students would learn how and why integrated curriculum that builds on the knowledge, experiences, and interests of specific learners is an essential framework for the development of academic skills and strategies. As Dewey wrote so long ago:

> Present education fails because it neglects the fundamental principle of the school as a form of community life. It conceives the school as

> a certain place where specific information is to be given, where certain lessons are to be learned.... The value of these is conceived as lying in the remote future; the child must do these things for the sake of something else he is to do; they are mere preparation. As a result, they do not become part of the life experience of the child and so are not truly educative. (Dewey in Dworkin, 1959, p. 24)

The workshop structure was simple in design. The graduate students entered a classroom in the educational wing of the museum. The room was set up with small tables; on each table a variety of shells had been laid out. Students were invited to sit in small groups and explore the objects on the table—touching, looking, using magnifying glasses if desired, observing the shells and sharing their observations with their peers. As students began to engage with the materials, marine biologists from the teaching faculty of the museum circulated among them, answering questions, pointing out interesting aspects of the shells, guiding them to written materials that contained further information about their shell or family of shells.

Following this period of open exploration, students were asked to select one shell and—using a worksheet to guide them—record their observations of and responses to the shell. Specifically they were directed to:

- Use words and pictures to describe the shell they had selected in an objective manner;
- Reflect on their attraction to specific shells, acknowledge the subjectivity of their choices, and describe feelings, memories, thoughts that the selected shells elicited;
- Respond to the question: What do you wonder about this shell?

After students had had time to explore and describe, discuss the shells with their peers, and even do a bit of research in appropriate text sources, the marine biologists gave an overview of the materials, discussing why some of the shells had been selected and how they related to the field of marine life.

At this point, the focus turned back to the students' interests. Leaving the classroom, students were guided to the museum's extensive exhibits of shells. Here they were instructed: "Find something that excites you and that (hypothetically) you would like to continue researching. Record it in a way that will be useful to you." Following this second, more open-ended observation, students were asked to return to the classroom to discuss their experiences from both personal and pedagogical perspectives. Personally, they were invited to share what made the shells they chose of interest to them. Pedagogically, they were asked to identify the instructional components that comprised this workshop, how/why they were effective, how could they/why should they inform their own teaching practice? As the workshop drew to a close, students were asked to make connections between this experience, assigned readings, and practices they were learning in other courses. Finally, each teacher/student teacher was given two free admission tickets to the course. These tickets could be used for their own further learning or to bring a child with whom they were working in a tutorial role for this course to the museum.

GOALS OF THE MUSEUM EXPERIENCE

We hoped that the museum experience would provide an opportunity for students to examine their own learning responses, to recognize how choice and opportunities to build their own prior knowledge and experience could be deeply motivating. We also wanted them to see how much they could learn from and with their colleagues—how shared learning could open new pathways and lead to new understandings, how opportunities for dialogue, along with access to real objects, individuals with expertise in the field, and different forms of text, could create learning opportunities that were authentic and rigorous. In short, we wanted to provide for teachers the kinds of experiences that we hoped they would provide for children and—through experience and reflection on that experience (Dewey, 1938)—enable them to understand how and why many of the tenets of learner-centered pedagogy articulated by Dewey and Mitchell hold true despite all the changes in today's world.

WAS THIS EXPERIENCE EFFECTIVE?

There is a great deal of evidence indicating that the museum experience was successful. The dialogue that emerged during the workshop, the discussion that ensued in class the following week, and written reflections on the experience all indicate that students learned a great deal about teaching and learning. References back to the workshop in written logs documenting students' work with individual children and in the case studies students wrote as a final project for the class indicate that many of them applied this learning to their own work with children. The following themes emerged across the data sources: the importance of linking new learning to prior knowledge, the importance of choice, the value of open exploration, the value of access to multiple ways of gathering information and developing skills (experts in the field, written texts, real objects, peer discussions), the motivating power of sharing ideas and experiences with peers, and the relevance of thinking outside the box when developing literacy curriculum for young children.

WHAT STUDENT TEACHERS SAID

It seems very clear that students understood, consciously and subconsciously, how the workshop process enabled them to activate their prior knowledge and experience. They could see and articulate the ways in which this knowledge and experience provided a powerful catalyst for learning new material. When asked during the workshop to consider and explain their choice of shells, virtually every student made connections to experiences they held dear.

> My father collected shells. This one reminds me of one that I was always attracted to when I was a little girl (CM 10/06).

> I am a deep-sea diver. I chose a shell I had never seen before (AP 10/06).

> I chose a long shell that had one side cut open. I chose it because I could see the spiral structure on the inside, it looked like it would be very strong. I spent a year in Barcelona and was fascinated by the architecture. This shell reminded me of one of Gaudi's buildings because of the waviness on the outside and the strong spiral structure on the inside. I wanted to know more about it. (AG 10/06)

And, when this last student commented, "These memories were part of my learning. Surely experiences like this will influence my students' learning," there were nods of agreement throughout the class.

In the class that followed, students were asked to reflect on the museum experience. Was it worth spending a session of a course on The Teaching of Reading, Writing, and Language Arts in this way? How did it enhance their own learning? How did they anticipate that it would enhance their practice? Should this experience be repeated in future courses? Did the experience offer them new perspectives on teaching and learning?

Responses were submitted anonymously. A request for candor was made; student feedback would play a major role in curriculum modifications for the following year. Once again, responses indicated a new and deeper understanding of the ways in which choice and the opportunity to build on one's own interests and experiences motivated and engaged learners. Students reported that they wanted to know more about these shells and were eager to develop the skills that would facilitate acquisition of greater content knowledge. One student wrote:

> Through our exploration of shells, we were constructing our own understanding and connection with the materials. As I was drawn to what I could relate to, I was also intrigued to learn what I didn't know.

Many described new understanding about the ways in which interactions with objects motivated them:

> The idea of letting us choose an object (from many possibilities) was great. I looked at the shells until I knew just the one to write about. The experience was that much richer because I could connect my own experience to the shell.

Others spoke about the ways in which access to multiple sources of information supported and extended their desire to learn:

> Having the "expert teacher" in the room, available for questions and answers, furthered my discovery and intrigue. It opened up new questions, new predictions, and new observations. Later, observational texts about the object were available. I was motivated to look for more information. Frankly, I was surprised at how much I *wanted* to know about sand dollars.

Many referred to the ways in which the opportunities to share their observations and feelings with their classmates extended the learning process:

> Having such interesting and unusual materials on the table invited me to explore. You couldn't help but touch and examine each shell that was placed in the center. I could see how helpful and supportive it is to be experiencing this process with my classmates. . . . [It showed me why] it is important to let children share their ideas, predictions and observations instead of just doing it on their own.

They identified the importance of both experience and the reflection upon experience in the learning process:

> I appreciated participating in the guided activity. . . . Our discussion in response to the activity brought to light the ways in which personal experience connects to literacy learning. It inspired me to include not only factual texts in my work with students but also objects, manipulatives, and other items students can interact with and research.

Moreover, students were very clear about the ways in which the experience helped them to integrate research, readings about pedagogy, and theory:

> [The trip] was an amazing follow-up to the article on non-fiction reading in classrooms (Harvey, 2002). All we were encouraged and inspired to think of from reading the article came to life during the museum visit. . . . [The trip] was surprisingly closely tied to all we have been learning about the development of literacy.

And more than half the students spoke about their intentions of using similar forms of instruction in their own teaching:

> The trip made me aware of other activities that could be used to engage children in using descriptive language. Already I have begun to think of using what I learned with my child. I have discovered a recent interest in science (in my child) and hope to explore it further, having been inspired by our visit.

APPLICATION OF THE EXPERIENCE

Teachers often leave workshops with new understanding and good intentions. Research in the field describes how all too often these intentions fade as teachers return to their daily routines (Rust & Freidus, 2001). However, this does not seem to be the case in this instance. The course that incorporated the museum experience was, in part, a practicum. Students worked with individual students for six sessions. They documented this work as part of the course requirements. Many students implicitly and explicitly made reference to the museum experience in this documentation. For example, Vivian wrote:

> In preparing for this session [her third instructional session], I reflected on our class trip to the American Museum of Natural History. During that class period we explored tangible objects and later used that knowledge in combination with personal experience to analyze an article of further interest. During the class discussion about this activity a common thread was the use of prior knowledge. In this session, I sought to give Jill (age 6) the opportunity to connect her experience with the exploration of new readings and creative writing. (VW, 11/06)

And Alicia described her instructional plans for her third session with Emma, the child with whom she was working, in the following way:

> After our discussion at the museum, I thought that it would be helpful to take some time to develop Emma's oral language. In this session, I plan to focus on descriptive language. I have noticed that Emma often says, "It is pretty," or "It's not pretty." I would like to help her develop descriptive language by examining and describing real fruit and vegetables.

Since it was October and Emma and Alicia had been reading about pumpkins in earlier sessions, it seemed appropriate to make a trip to a nearby farmers' market. Alicia writes:

> Emma was very excited to leave school and go to the market. Her initial comment for almost every item was, "It is pretty." Or "It is something." I would repeat her comment and add my own, "It is pretty. Look at the green and yellow stripes!" Emma began to adopt and imitate some of my language such as stripes, bumpy, and heavy.... [At the end of the visit to the green market] Emma chose a pumpkin, and we carried it back. As we walked, I asked if she had a pumpkin at home. She told me that she did not and that she had wanted one. She told me that she had never before had a pumpkin.

In the session summary, Alicia reflects on both Emma's learning and her own:

> In context, Emma was able to understand and use new vocabulary to describe objects. Her vocabulary includes limited descriptive language. Still, since she is younger than six and speaks Spanish at home, it seems obvious that she simply needs more exposure, appropriate modeling and more opportunities to use more specific vocabulary [in order to learn].... Walking back, I realized how important this pumpkin was to Emma. Allowing her to make a choice, as we discussed Tuesday night at the museum, allowed her to choose something that she was truly interested and invested in.... This conversation showed me the importance of prior knowledge in understanding the texts. Children with no prior knowledge of pumpkins as plants assume that they come from the market, and the men in the market make them. No wonder Emma had trouble making sense of the story we read about pumpkins last week.

Alicia turned to her own experience at the museum to design a lesson that would support the instructional goals she had set for her student. Finding the child responsive to the instruction, she identifies the importance of providing children with learning opportunities that provide an opportunity for them to demonstrate both what they know and what they would like to know. In addition, she demonstrates ways in which the development of important skills can be woven into this instruction.

Conclusion

In their schools, our students have been immersed in a discourse of accountability. With few exceptions, they work in classrooms that require children to move at an articulated pace and engage in the reading and writing process with little opportunity to engage with objects or make choices that are personally meaningful. In these settings, more often than not, instructional goals focus on improving test scores. Lip service may be paid to lifelong learning, but little effort is made to monitor the consonance between pedagogy and this bigger goal. Students consistently hear this practice defined as effective teaching.

In their teacher education classes, our students read texts that describe a different vision and a different practice. These they frequently interpret as idealistic messages from another time. They respond with the request: "Tell us what to do. Just teach us the right way." And when they are instructed to begin by looking at the child and the community, they often feel that their voices are not being heard, their needs are not being met. For most of the students in this course, the museum experience and ensuing sessions appear to have made a difference. One student writes:

> Working with Ann has been an inspiring experience for me. I went into this practicum thinking it was my job to fill a child with new knowledge. I now see that teaching is a far more complicated and interesting task. A child comes to a teacher filled with ideas and knowledge. It is the teacher's job to inspire a student to motivate him/herself to deepen and expand that knowledge. Simply sitting at a desk and having children write and observe may enable some children to absorb the facts, but I see now that the goal of a good teacher is first to engage the student and then to provide materials and experiences that will aid the teacher in guiding each student to play a powerful role in his/her own education. . . . I have read these ideas over and over. It took the hands-on experience at the museum [and my second trip] with Ann to make this real for me. A child must have an interest in the subject, feel empowered through lessons, and have real, quality materials to be able to relate his or her experiences to previous knowledge and their life at home . . .

The data sources suggest that teacher education pedagogy that models ways of integrating theory with the experience and interests of student teachers and the resources of the community does help students to value and implement learner-centered practice. In so doing, it appears to support teachers in enacting an approach to the classroom that is experimental, critical, and ardent. Thus, it may be considered one small step toward a renaissance in teacher education.

References

Antler, J. (1987). *Lucy Sprague Mitchell.* New Haven: Yale University Press.
Borko, H. (2004). Professional development and teacher learning: Mapping the terrain. *Educational Researcher, 33*(8), 3–15.
Clay, M. (1991). *Becoming literate.* Portsmouth, NH: Heinemann.
Cole, M., Cole, S., & Lightfoot, C. (2005). *The development of children* (5th ed.). New York: Worth Publishers.

Dewey, J. (1938/1997). *Experience and education.* New York: Free Press.
Duckworth, E. (1987). *The having of wonderful ideas.* New York: Teachers College Press.
Dworkin, M. S. (1959). *Dewey on education.* New York: Teachers College Press.
Harvey, S. (2002). Nonfiction inquiry: Using real reading and writing to explore the world. *Language Arts, 80*(1), 12–22.
Harvey, S. & Goudvis, A. (2000). *Strategies that work.* York, ME: Stenhouse.
Holdaway, D. (1979). *The foundations of literacy.* Portsmouth, NH: Heinemann.
Lave, J., and Wenger, E. (1991). *Situated learning: Legitimate peripheral participation.* Cambridge, UK: Cambridge University Press.
Owocki, G. (1999). *Literacy through play.* Portsmouth, NH: Heinemann.
Peregoy, S., and Boyle, O. (2000). *Reading, writing & learning in ESL* (4th ed.). New York: Longman.
Piaget, J. (1932). *The moral judgment of children.* New York: The Free Press.
Pinnell, G., & Fountas, I. (1998). *Word matters.* Portsmouth, NH: Heinemann.
Pullman, P. (2003, April 1). *Isis Speech.* Retrieved January 22, 2007, from Philip Pullman website: www.philip-pullman.com/pages/content/index.asp?PageID=66.
Putnam, R., & Borko, H. (2000). What do new views of knowledge and thinking have to say about research on teacher learning? *Educational Researcher, 29*(1), 4–15.
Renaissance. (n.d.) *The American Heritage Dictionary of the English Language* (4th ed.). Retrieved January 22, 2007, from Dictionary.com website: http://dictionary.reference.com/browse/renaissance.
Rogoff, B. (1990). *Apprenticeship in thinking: Cognitive development in social context.* New York: Oxford University Press.
Ruskin, J. (1853, 2004). *On art and life.* London: Penguin Books.
Rust, F., & Freidus, H. (2001). *Guiding school change.* New York: Teachers College Press.
Vygotsky, L. (1922/1935/1978). *Mind in society: The development of higher psychological processes* (M. Cole, V. John-Steiner, S. Scribner, & E. Souberman, Trans.). Cambridge, MA: Harvard University Press.

CHAPTER 19

A Renaissance of the Arts in Classrooms

A COLLABORATION BETWEEN A COLLEGE, A PUBLIC SCHOOL, AND AN ARTS INSTITUTION

Abigail S. McNamee
Lehman College of the City University of New York

Andrea Zakin
Lehman College of the City University of New York

Marietta Saravia-Shore
Lehman College of the City University of New York

Alexandria Lawrence Ross
Lehman College of the City University of New York

Jeanne M. Peloso
Lehman College of the City University of New York

Nancy E. Dubetz
Lehman College of the City University of New York

Christy Folsom
Lehman College of the City University of New York

Mia L. Mercurio
Lehman College of the City University of New York

Juan Morales-Flores
Lehman College of the City University of New York

Holly Fairbank
Lincoln Center Institute

Jaime Porteus Iurato
Public School 304

Abigail S. McNamee, Ed.D., Ph.D., is chair of the Department of Early Childhood and Childhood Education and professor in the Graduate Early Childhood Program at Lehman College, City University of New York. She has worked with Lincoln Center Institute to integrate aesthetic education in her courses each semester since the program's inception at Lehman College.

Andrea Zakin, Ph.D., is an assistant professor of art education in the Department of Early Childhood and Childhood Education at Lehman College, City University of New York. Her research investigates the connections between art, cognition, and literacy.

Marietta Saravia-Shore, Ph.D., is associate professor in the Department of Early Childhood and Childhood Education at Lehman College, City University of New York. She received her doctorate in Anthropology and Education from Columbia University. She co-edited *Cross-Cultural Literacy: Ethnographies of Communication in Multiethnic Classrooms* (Garland). Her research interest is the outcomes of aesthetic education for teacher candidates.

Alexandria Lawrence Ross, Ed.D, is an associate professor in the Department of Early Childhood and Childhood Education at Lehman College, City University of New York. Her research specializes in the areas of school-university collaborations and teacher preparation.

Jeanne M. Peloso, Ph.D., is an assistant professor in the Department of Early Childhood and Childhood Education at Lehman College, City University of New York. Her research interests center on nurturing the imagination of preservice teachers and the children they teach.

Nancy E. Dubetz, Ed.D., is an associate professor in the Department of Early Childhood and Childhood Education at Lehman College, City University of New York. She is coordinator of the undergraduate Childhood program. Her research interests are Professional Development Schools and the preparation and professional development of teachers working with English language learners.

Christy Folsom, Ed.D., is an assistant professor in the Department of Early Childhood and Childhood Education at Lehman College, City University of New York. Her teaching and research focus on curriculum design that integrates the teaching of thinking skills and social-emotional learning.

Mia L. Mercurio, Ed.D., was formerly an assistant professor in the Department of Early Childhood and Childhood Education at Lehman College, City University of New York. Her research interests include the use of literature to help children deal with many of life's stressors including the death of grandparents, pets, fear of the dark, and bullying.

Juan Morales-Flores, Ph.D., is the professional development network coordinator in the Division of Education at Lehman College, City University of New York. His research interests include the relationship of race, class, gender, and ethnicity to learning. Additionally, he has investigated the role of preservice programs in facilitating teacher candidates' thinking in that area.

Holly Fairbank, M.A., is assistant director of the Teacher Education Collaborative at LCI, overseeing programs at eight campuses. Since 1997, she is the site manager for LCI/Lehman College partnership. Holly has been with LCI as a dance teaching artist since 1985 and was principal choreographer/director of *Holly Fairbank and Dancers*.

Jaime Porteus Iurato, M.S., graduated from Iona College with a B.S. in elementary education. She later completed an M.S. in elementary education at Lehman College, City University of New York. Jaime has worked for the New York City Department of Education since 2000 and is currently teaching third grade at PS 304 in the Bronx.

ABSTRACT

This article describes a program which integrates the arts in teacher education courses as well as in a Professional Development School (PDS), through a collaboration involving a college, Lehman College, The City University of New York; a PDS school, PS 304, the Bronx; and a local arts organization, Lincoln Center Institute. A description of the development of the program, the design of the program, student responses to the program, benefits of the program, on-going concerns related to the program, and ideas about program adaptability to other institutions, are included.

Introduction

A decade ago, Lehman College, a senior college in the City University of New York, began a collaboration with the Lincoln Center Institute (LCI), the educational branch of Lincoln Center in New York City. The primary purpose of the collaboration was to integrate the arts in teacher education courses in the Division of Education, which offers teacher and counselor education programs at the undergraduate and graduate levels. The collaboration was intended to encourage preservice and in-service teachers to integrate the arts into their classrooms, especially during a time when budget cuts are often forcing classes in the arts out of the curriculum. Lehman is not the only college with which LCI works, nor is it the only educational institution. What follows, however, is Lehman's story: a description of the program that resulted in the Department of Early Childhood and Childhood Education (ECCE) from a semester-long faculty aesthetic education workshop in the spring of 1997. Similar programs have developed in other areas of the United States as public schools and colleges work with arts institutions to enrich coursework and students' lives with the arts.

The Participants in the Collaboration

LEHMAN COLLEGE, CITY UNIVERSITY OF NEW YORK

Lehman College, located in the Bronx, is one of the five senior colleges of the City University of New York (CUNY) serving both undergraduate and graduate students in a wide range of programs. It is a public, comprehensive, coeducational liberal arts college with more than 90 undergraduate and graduate degree programs serving over 9,000 students. Lehman was the first of the CUNY schools to achieve national accreditation from the National Council for the Accreditation of Teacher Education (NCATE) in 2002 and the first to be reaccredited in 2007. The student population is diverse reflecting the ethnic groups prevalent in the Bronx and wider metropolitan area. Most of Lehman's students have to work full-time while attending college, and most are first generation college students. For many of Lehman's students, English is a second language. Also, many need academic and psychological support to remain in college, and few complete their undergraduate degree in four years.

THE DIVISION OF EDUCATION AT LEHMAN COLLEGE

The Division of Education consists of three departments: the Department of Early Childhood and Childhood Education, the Department of Middle and High School Education, and the Department of Counseling, Leadership, Literacy, and Special Education. Undergraduate and graduate programs serve both preservice and in-service teachers. Undergraduate students interested in a teacher education major in a New York State approved liberal arts program take required liberal arts coursework for future teachers and begin teacher education coursework in their junior and senior years. Graduate students can select from a wide variety of New York State certification programs to become initially certified or to complete dual certification in a professional program.

Undergraduate and graduate students in the Division of Education generally work full-time, often in schools. They struggle with difficult students, difficult schools/day care centers, difficult standards, and evening after-work programs that extend their day and keep them away from families as they work for New York State Certification. Many rarely leave the Bronx; few have attended performances at Lincoln Center or anywhere else in the greater New York area.

PUBLIC SCHOOL (PS) 304

Lehman College works with PS 304 as a Professional Development School (PDS) in order to improve teacher education programs, strengthen school programs, and stimulate collaborative research. In the spring of 2000, PS 304 was selected to become an elementary PDS site, and the collaboration began immediately in June 2000. The selection process was created to ensure that there was potential for compatibility among partnering institutions before embarking on a collaboration. A full-time Lehman professor works as a liaison with PS 304. The school's organization is composed of three kindergarten classes, three first grade classes, three second grade classes, three third grade classes, three fourth grade classes, and two fifth grade classes. All classes are heterogeneously grouped and supported by a pedagogical staff consisting of 20 classroom teachers. Four of these classroom teachers participate with the Lincoln Center Institute to integrate aesthetic education in coursework.

LINCOLN CENTER INSTITUTE

Lincoln Center Institute (LCI) brings dance, music, theater, architecture, and visual arts from a diversity of cultures into classrooms around the New York metropolitan area and across the nation, enabling students and teachers to learn about and through the arts, a process referred to as "aesthetic education." Founded in 1975, the Institute is the educational cornerstone of Lincoln Center for the Performing Arts, Inc., and a global leader in education and the arts. The Institute offers a wide array of resources including performances of dance, music, and theater as well as experience with the visual arts; 100 + professional artists, trained by LCI for work as "teaching artists" who work with school and college faculty to integrate the arts; and a multi-media library focused on education and the arts.

LCI is a vital force in classrooms and college programs throughout the five boroughs of New York City. LCI's innovative approach to arts and education involves students, teachers, and parents in order to have a lasting impact on young people. Students in grades pre-K through twelve are provided with unique and varied opportunities to learn about the arts through long-term school-based programs that improve learning across the curriculum. Teachers, locally and throughout the United States, as well as teachers-in-training in the New York City area colleges (which work with LCI), attend workshops and courses focused on the arts and integration of the arts with school and college curriculum. These workshops and courses give them the knowledge and skills to implement the arts effectively in their classroom practices. The Institute has developed and recently made public nine "Capacities for Aesthetic Learning" (Lincoln Center Institute for the Performing Arts, Inc., 2005), which are valuable in assessing student experience with the arts. LCI's website provides additional information about LCI's programs (www.lcinstitute.org).

PROFESSIONAL DEVELOPMENT PARTNERSHIP BETWEEN LEHMAN COLLEGE, PS 304, AND LINCOLN CENTER INSTITUTE

The goals of the partnership that was struck were to:

- bring dance, music, theater, architecture, and the visual arts from a diversity of cultures into classrooms enabling students and teachers, teacher candidates and professors, to learn about and through the arts;
- institute programs at every level, from pre-kindergarten through graduate school, utilizing the same basic process: exploring a work of art, designing a curriculum, awakening the imagination (Lincoln Center for the Performing Arts, Inc., 2006).

These goals are consistent with the philosophy of Dr. Maxine Greene, who was largely responsible for the general design of the Institute's program. In Greene's (2001) words,

> 'Aesthetic education' . . . is an intentional undertaking designed to nurture appreciative, reflective, cultural, participatory engagements

with the arts by enabling learners to notice what is there to be noticed, and to lend works of art to their lives in such a way that they can achieve them as variously meaningful. When this happens, new connections are made in experience: new patterns are formed, new vistas opened. Persons see differently, resonate differently. (p. 8)

As mentioned, the partnership between Lehman College and LCI is not the only collaboration of a New York City area college with the Institute. Beyond Lehman, LCI currently collaborates with four other senior colleges within the City University of New York (Brooklyn, City, Hunter, and Queens) and three private colleges as well (Bank Street, St. John's, and Stern College). Each of these partnerships has evolved uniquely; no two partnerships are alike. While education departments throughout CUNY do, in fact, participate with LCI, Lehman's Department of Early Childhood and Childhood Education has made the commitment to integrate and infuse aesthetic education across an entire teacher education program offering arts experiences in disparate courses.

LEHMAN COLLEGE INTRODUCTION TO LINCOLN CENTER INSTITUTE (LCI) AND AESTHETIC EDUCATION

To expand the work of integrating aesthetic education in public school programs, representatives of LCI realized that they needed to work with college teacher education programs in addition to their work in public schools. Lehman was invited to participate in a partnership with LCI which began with an LCI and Lehman co-designed and co-led faculty development in spring 1997. It involved a semester-long, weekly Friday morning workshop series attended by interested liberal arts and teacher education faculty. These workshops, led by an LCI staff member (Holly Fairbank) and a Lehman faculty member (Richard Blot), exposed (or further exposed) faculty to the arts as they might be introduced in college classrooms. Attending faculty reflected on each art form, and how a performance or gallery show might relate to individual course content. This faculty development experience was voluntary on the part of faculty. Five faculty from the Division of Education participated, including the chair of the Department of Early Childhood and Childhood Education.

DEPARTMENT OF EARLY CHILDHOOD AND CHILDHOOD EDUCATION AND THE DIVISION OF EDUCATION

In the Fall of 1997, LCI's work was extended through Lehman's undergraduate and graduate teacher certification programs in the Department of Early Childhood and Childhood Education (ECCE) by the faculty who participated in the Spring faculty development workshop. Programs in ECCE include undergraduate early childhood and childhood education initial certification programs and graduate early childhood and childhood education initial and professional certification programs. Having attended the spring faculty development workshop series, Dr. McNamee, chair of ECCE, began to think not only of the integration of aesthetic education in her own courses, but of this integration through the department as a whole. It was the chair's leadership, supported by the two faculty who had also attended the workshop series, in partnership with LCI that fostered the rooting of aesthetic education in the particular department. Thus, the integration began, and continued through the last decade, shifting from isolated events and courses to a systematic infusion of aesthetic education throughout ECCE. This systematic infusion in the department was due to the faculty of the department's decision to integrate aesthetic education throughout the coursework of each program in two ways: 1) work with LCI teaching artists in selected courses through each program, and 2) link arts courses with other methods courses (e.g., art with math, science with music). The plan was to affect a shift toward aesthetics throughout teacher education in the department. Course change was made easier because the department was about to begin the redesign of each program in response to changes in New York State regulations for teacher education and in preparation for the National Council for Accreditation of Teacher Education (NCATE) assessment of Lehman teacher education programs.

ECCE course redesign began, covering the years of NCATE preparation. Simultaneously, the encouragement of additional faculty participation in aesthetic education began. ECCE faculty met weekly; these meetings began to incorporate faculty development related to aesthetic integration twice monthly, which was planned with LCI staff member Holly Fairbank and aimed at encouraging new faculty participation and, for involved faculty, further development. Faculty development at this time involved on-going exposure to new art forms, work with LCI teaching artists around art forms, presentations by involved faculty of unique attempts to integrate aesthetic education in their courses, discussion of philosophical issues between LCI and Lehman, and program redesign including aesthetic education. As new faculty were interviewed and hired, the department's work and commitment to aesthetic education was communicated.

The infusion of aesthetic education has been more intense in ECCE, but not limited to this department, in the Division of Education. Inclusion of the importance of aesthetic education in the Division of Education's conceptual framework, *Lehman Urban Teacher and Counselor Education* (LUTE) was approved by each department in the division. It became apparent that, for this work to proceed in individual departments, the participation of department chairs was crucial with a gradual accumulation of interested faculty. It is, of course, the department chair who initiates and/or supports programmatic change, initiates and/or supports faculty development, schedules meetings and agendas, and encourages a department pulse or atmosphere. The chair's work in ECCE was made possible because of decisions made years before the LCI partnership began on how we would relate to each other: the decision that the department had to work together better, and the decision that this necessitated faculty members coming to know each other through spending time together. ECCE implemented weekly department meetings, often eating together. These decisions may have been unique to the development of the particular department's partnership with LCI; they have not been replicated by other departments in the Division of Education.

While other department members had participated in the initial 1997 LCI workshop series, no other department chair had. It took an additional seven years for a second education department (The Department of Middle and High School Education), to begin this work in one course and eight years for the third education department (The Department of Counseling, Leadership, Literacy, and Special Education) to begin this work in two courses.

The work in the Division of Education proceeds each semester according to a plan that is addressed and amended at the Core meetings of Lehman and LCI personnel. The progression of aesthetic education work in the Division of Education is outlined in Table 19.1.

PROGRAM DESIGN AT LEHMAN AND PS 304

A faculty member, or teacher in PS 304, who is planning to integrate aesthetic education in coursework selects an art form from the array of art forms scheduled by LCI for the current semester. The professor or teacher is then assigned a teaching artist (TA) with expertise related to the art form by LCI, and next meets with the LCI teaching artist to plan the possible integration of the art form with course content. As is typical of the LCI planning process, this work between the TA and professor, with support from LCI staff, proceeds in six stages prior to the TA coming into the college classroom as described in Table 19.2, Brainstorming Guide for Aesthetic Education Curriculum Plan (Lincoln Center Institute for the Performing Arts, 2006).

For example, if a college professor selected a performance of Hans Christian Anderson's fairy tale, *Snow Queen,* as the semester's art form to integrate in a Teacher as Researcher course, she would meet with the TA assigned by LCI and view a DVD of the performance prior to introducing the work of art to her class. The college professor would gradually move through the six steps outlined

Table 19.1 Crossing Contexts for Participants Who Chose Not to Teach

The Focus	The Procedure
Preparation of faculty	Seminar schedule; reading and discussing an esthetic education (AE)
	Working definition of what AE is, working plan of what AE might be, generally in the setting
	Commitment to collaborative planning decisions on how to work with each other: individuals, couples, teams
General planning among faculty	Who will be on the faculty liaison?
	Who will be on the Core Committee?
	How will AE be included in mission statement?
	How will AE be included in course descriptions?
Specific planning for courses	What faculty/what courses?
	Will courses be grouped (all sections)?
	Decide on the art form for each course
	Preparation with the LCI teaching artist: line of inquiry, relation of art form to course content, overall design of course related to art form, how art form will be addressed, role of teaching artist and instructor
	Explanation of design and purpose to students, how the experience might be of benefit to them
Assessment of AE integration in courses/programs	Determine what level of assessment is desired (individual/course/program)
	Determine how to assess graduated teacher candidates
	Continued implementation of assessment decisions
Assessment of relationship with LCI	Determine what faculty have learned about the process of integrating AE and working with a teaching artist

Table 19.1 (Continued)

The Focus	The Procedure
On-going faculty development	Getting and keeping faculty interest
	Mentoring newly involved faculty
	Continued development for AE experienced faculty
	Attendance at LCI winter and summer seminars
Relationship with partnership schools	Placement of student teachers in LCI partnership schools
	Integration of AE work in PDS schools
Seeking outside funding for program development and assessment	Determine where to look for continued funding
	Determine to how to work with LCI on proposals for funding

in Table 19.2 with the TA. While viewing the DVD with the TA, for instance, she may notice the huge size of the human puppets performing the tale, the unusual costumes of the puppets, their movement while attached to the human actors, and the role of the narrator. Questions might occur to her about how the performance was staged, what was included in Anderson's story and what was left out of the performance, as well as Anderson's themes in the story. The college professor would be asked by the TA to consider contextual connections of the piece perhaps related to Anderson's life and work or the elements of drama. She and the TA would begin to list ways in which the performance

Table 19.2 Brainstorming Guide for Aesthetic Education Curriculum Plan

Step	Procedure
1	Work of Art: List what you noticed about the work of art.
2	Capturing Questions: What questions arise about the work of art?
3	Contextual Connections: Brainstorm the many contexts of the work of art.
4	Touchstones: List ways the work of art connects to the lives of the participants.
5	Activity Ideas: Capture ideas for course activities.
6	Possible Lines of Inquiry: List lines of inquiry as they arise; draft your line of inquiry.

connects to the lives of the students in the professor's course, whether the themes of Anderson's story resonate with her students' lived lives. The professor and TA would then discuss activities to be introduced in the class that would serve as an introduction to this art form and connect it to the content of the course. Finally, lines of inquiry would be drafted and redrafted until one line of inquiry is agreed upon. A question which carefully connects a particular art form with particular course content takes shape. For example, in this case, the question was: Given the performance of Hans Christian Anderson's *Snow Queen*, how do preservice and in-service graduate teacher education candidates develop an understanding of their own and young children's developmental themes as expressed in their own research. The six-stage process was developed by LCI for work with K–12 teachers, and the model has been adapted for work in the colleges.

When this planning work is completed, the TA is ready to come into the college classroom and does so, generally two times, once prior to the performance (to prepare students for what they will see and the connections to course content), and once following the performance (to debrief the experience with the art form and once again connect it to course content). In addition to work with the TA, the professor plans and implements strands of a particular semester's art form throughout a course prior to and following the TA's work in the class. This six-step procedure is basically the same whether an LCI TA is working with college professors or public school teachers.

In addition to Lehman faculty, four teachers from PS 304 have participated in LCI's annual summer session when educators are trained to incorporate the arts into their curriculum using LCI's experiential approach to education. As a result of this training, teachers from the school have worked consistently with an LCI teaching artist to integrate an art form into their syllabi and infuse in some way their course content with aspects of this approach to aesthetic education. Also, under the leadership of a Lehman faculty PDS liaison, faculty at PS 304 selected their work with LCI (integration of the arts and aesthetic education with the support of LCI) as one of three strands of their PDS self-study. The PS 304 steering committee chose the LCI strand for several reasons: 1) The work in the area designated was significant; 2) The work highly correlated to the PDS partnership; 3) The work centered on student learning; 4) The work drove adult learning—teacher candidates, school faculty, and college faculty were all involved in furthering their professional development; 5) The work cut across all four functions of a PDS—teacher preparation, student learning, staff development and inquiry. School faculty, teacher candidates, and K–5 students were involved in learning and furthering their own development through this strand. Hence, research was conducted and professional development was provided for school faculty, college faculty, and teacher candidates. Finally, student work was available for collection.

Financial Support for the Program

Financial support for the partnership between the college and LCI was shared by LCI, The City University central, and Lehman College. Also, finances between LCI and the public school, in this case PS 304, were shared. The joint responsibility for the costs of this program limits the number of schools that participate and, at the college, the courses at the college in which an LCI sponsored art form and a teaching artist can be assigned. ECCE knew that, in addition to the LCI work, it was necessary to extend our work in the arts beyond our work with LCI. In courses without an LCI teaching artist assigned, aesthetic education is also integrated in ECCE's undergraduate and graduate methods courses. For example, two faculty (one specializing in art or music, the other in math or science) work together to design and implement content and teaching method. Each partnership functions uniquely, but the goal is for faculty and students to wrestle with how the two areas of curriculum can be integrated with each other, and with the arts, in their work with children.

Library and Website Support of Implementation

As is true of all partners in LCI's Teacher Education Collaborative, Lehman has a resource collection that is intended to support the study of LCI's featured artworks, its practice, and philosophy, in order to facilitate the inclusion of contextual materials in the exploration of each art form. These collections are co-funded by LCI and Lehman or CUNY. The Lehman College education librarian serves as the collections coordinator. For each art form, a collection called *Window on the Work of Art* (Holzer & Noppe-Brandon, 2005) is available to instructors in the library and through the LCI website. It provides educators with rich information that helps them better understand the historical, cultural, and artistic context in which a work of art is created. The LCI also makes its Heckscher Foundation Resource Center available to faculty and students, offering a specialized collection on the arts.

Evaluation Protocol at Lehman

Evaluation of the aforementioned collaborative program is conducted in a variety of ways at Lehman. For example, students are asked in each aesthetic education integrated course to assess their experience in integrating aesthetic education through a standardized, written, IRB (Institutional Review Board) approved questionnaire. Each instructor working with LCI distributes this questionnaire to students in the instructor's course toward the end of the semester. Also, instructors often include informal oral assessments, as well as written open-ended assessment questions for particular aesthetic education class sessions, or individually designed aesthetic education questions in general course assessments. Students also have the option of referring to the LCI experience on the university-wide assessment of Instructor and Course Effectiveness, feedback from which is shared with instructors, and on the division-wide LUTE assessment distributed at the end of each year.

Education students' responses were noteworthy in their consistency. They responded that the workshop experience stands out for them: because it is working together in groups (as a team to create one idea), learning to listen to each other, expressing ideas creatively, expressing self, and communicating in different ways. They described the performances as giving students a different perspective on life, a way of looking at things and understanding what they are seeing from different points of view, and a desire to listen and seek interpretation. Most described a new and surprising enjoyment of the arts; recognition that college was not what they expected (only books, lectures, sitting) but that learning could occur outside of the classroom walls in an off campus location. They also described the "specialness" of the LCI experience: "It was live and very special, I'll remember it forever. It gave us a chance to realize there's a lot going on in the world and it all relates to our lives . . . it [this program] is a life lesson." Students wrote that they "felt privileged that I got to participate in a program related to the Lincoln Center." Responses to key questions from the in-class written survey are presented as follows (evaluation by students of aesthetic education integration):

#1 Have you ever attended a Lincoln Center performance unrelated to Lehman College? 93% of undergraduate students and 62% of graduate students have never attended a LC performance prior to their experience in the program.

#2 Have you attended other performances unrelated to Lehman College? 85% of undergraduate students and 67% of graduate students have never attended an arts performance prior to their experience in the program.

#6 Did the workshops related to the performance this semester enhance your understanding of the goals of this course? 80% of undergraduate students and 82% of graduate students responded yes.

#7 Did the workshops related to the performance enhance your enjoyment of class time? 85% of undergraduate students and 92% of graduate students responded yes.

#10 Did your experience with the arts, either this semester or previously, increase your interest in attending other performance/museum trips? 70% of undergraduates and 30% of graduate students responded yes. They wrote that they had already visited a museum or had gone to another performance based on this experience; most indicated that they intended to.

#11 What did you like best about your participation in the Lehman/LCI collaboration? There was no difference in the response of undergraduate and graduate students: They like the performances which they described as "eye opening" and "perspective broadening," delightful, the connection to life's struggles; acting out in the workshops which were "new and exciting" (which they sometimes thought weird or uncomfortable at first), the chance to be creative, the opportunity to express thoughts, doing artwork, group interaction, "The TA's know how to get art inside you."

#12 What did you like least about your participation in the Lehman/LCI collaborative? Students who responded to this question listed three main concerns: going to Lincoln Center (travel, time, rushing, bad weather, parking, cost), not understanding program goals and the connection to course content, AE taking too much time.

#13 Have you given thought to some of the ways in which you might incorporate the arts into your own classroom as a teacher? Undergraduate students recognized that the program provided a fun way to teach/learn and encouraged participation, reduced stress, improved thinking skills, offered something many children did not experience. They described that they "would like to" include the arts in their eventual teaching for these reasons but not knowing how, yet, to do so short of taking children to museums, showing videos, drawing, creating hands-on projects. Some recognized that "Art is everywhere."

Graduate students, generally more experienced, described the program giving them "more ideas and a background for working with the arts," fighting for them in their classroom; the need for the arts in children's lives . . . that the arts would always be part of their classroom, that the arts help one "see things deeper," broaden perspective, offer opportunities for more active teaching. Some described specific ways to include the arts: discussing illustrations, creating an arts center, including dance, doing and experiencing art as a way of learning, taking children out of the classroom to performances and museums.

#15 Do you think the Lehman/LCI collaboration is of value to the Department's programs? 76% of undergraduate students and 75% of graduate students responded yes, their responses indicating personal as well as profession value: the program increases interest in the arts, develops critical thinking, makes you see life differently, and it's fun, stress reducing; they learned about a program available to schools, offered ideas for their classroom (real and potential), that "the arts are a good way to reach out to people and children . . . to help them," to make learning more active and interesting.

#16 Would you suggest any changes in the Lehman/LCI collaboration as you have experienced it? 87% of undergraduate students and 80% of graduate students responded no. Suggestion for changes were infrequent but involved offering more experiences with the arts, doing so earlier in the semester when coursework pressures are less, and explaining the connections to coursework clearly. Some responded that the workshops took up too much time; some did not like writing about the performances.

Instructors at Lehman use the variety of student responses to determine how students are responding to experiences in the courses, whether or not to adjust how the work is continued in a course, and whether or not to continue the work in particular courses or at all. Program coordinators assess the aesthetic education work across each program to determine which courses should include the integration, whether students understand the purpose of the integration, and what additional work needs to be done.

The Core Committee of Lehman faculty and LCI personnel undertakes ongoing informal assessment at meetings that take place generally three times per semester. The agenda is co-designed by LCI's program manager and the Lehman College liaison. Issues raised by administrators and faculty are always dealt with based on what is working well, what is not, and what new ideas are introduced for implementation. PDS faculty and the Lehman liaison to PS 304 use the PDS study data to further coordinate and strengthen the partnership among the school, college, and LCI.

Benefits of the Lehman College/Lincoln Center Partnership to the College

The program has significantly changed the Department of Early Childhood and Childhood Education through emphasizing and integrating the arts throughout the program. Additionally, it has stimulated publication and presentation among ECCE faculty and the college librarian. It also brought together liberal arts and teacher education faculty annually in arts performances presented by the LCI and the Division of Education. As well, the program works closely with PS 304, Lehman's PDS, training teachers and integrating the arts in the children's curriculum.

Ongoing and Future Concerns for the Program

Given the feedback received from students and faculty thus far, we know our collaborative journey is far from complete. Areas in need of improvement and/

or expansion include student evaluation, curriculum development, and collaboration.

Printing and distribution of a newly developed brochure are needed to explain the goals of the program to students. Conceptualization and sequencing of student's ongoing development in aesthetic education with each course experience is essential as they move through their college program. Plus, student evaluation can be expanded from the current course evaluation to the end of each program and into their teaching years.

Experimentation with the use of LCI's "Capacities for Aesthetic Learning" (Lincoln Center Institute for the Performing Arts, Inc., 2005) could lead to better means of assessing students' aesthetic education experiences. Continued development and implementation of research questions by participating faculty (in addition to program evaluation) and increased writing and publication on their part are among our list of concerns. Faculty could implement aesthetic education in specific courses throughout a program as well as in each section of these courses, providing all students with the same opportunity to participate in aesthetic education.

Collaborations are another focus of concern. The program desires continued and increased collaboration with PS 304. Encouragement and support should be provided to increase faculty participation in the Department of Middle and Secondary School and the Department of Counseling, Leadership, Literacy and Special Education. Additionally, encouragement will need to be extended to promote collaboration between liberal arts and teacher education faculty at the course level.

Program Adaptability to Other Teacher Education Programs

The Lehman/LCI partnership can be adapted to other teacher education programs. The LCI information can be accessed through its website (www.lcinstitute.org). See the following timeline of implementation for the practical planning of the program:

Spring 1997: Faculty Development Workshops (weekly) throughout the semester (Liberal Arts and Division of Education faculty participate)

Fall 1997: Implementation of aesthetic education by initial faculty in courses in the Department of Early Childhood and Childhood Education (ECCE); Implementation of Core meetings at Lehman with LCI, participating faculty, and college librarian (3X during each semester)

January and Summer 1997 to Present: Selected ECCE faculty participation in January and/or Summer faculty development at LCI

Spring 1998 to Spring 2005: Continued implementation in the Department of ECCE through self-selection of faculty; continuation of Core meetings

Spring 1998 to Spring 2001: Intensified faculty development in the Department of ECCE (every other week during the time designated for department faculty meetings); increase in the number of participating ECCE faculty

Fall 1999: College-wide faculty development seminar on aesthetics and aesthetic education (11 meetings drawing on campus artists)

Spring 2000: Completion of division conceptual framework, Lehman Urban Teacher Education (LUTE) with inclusion of the importance of aesthetic education to the division's work; ECCE decision to officially link arts courses with other methods courses and math and science courses; election of PDS 304 as PDS school and beginning collaboration

Spring 2002: Lehman NCATE accredited; aesthetic education emphasis described in written documents and orally to accreditation team

Fall 2000 to Present: Lehman participation in the LCI cross-campus research group (4X yearly); Lehman College-wide arts presentations/workshops (sponsored by the Division of Education, bringing together liberal arts and teacher education faculty)

Spring 2003: ECCE presentation of aesthetic education program at KNESSET/NYACTE Conference

Fall 2003: Designation of "AE" as part of course section code so that student can select AE courses at registration

Spring 2004: Presentation of ECCE program at AACTE Conference, Chicago; aesthetic education is part of the self-study of one of Lehman's PDS elementary schools (PS 304)

Fall 2004: Decision in the Department of ECCE to sequence specific courses integrating aesthetic education so that program students have the same experience (beginning implementation fall 2005); initial participation of faculty of the Department of Middle and Secondary School

Spring 2005: ECCE presentation on aesthetic education integration at Lehman (International Conference of Educators, Honolulu, Hawaii, January); ECCE presentation on aesthetic education integration at Lehman (AACTE, Washington, D.C., February); college-wide LCI concert: The Blues (February)

Summer 2005: Publication of *Imaginative Connections: Aesthetic Education in the Lives of New Teachers*, Teachers College Press; 3 chapters by Lehman faculty and staff

Fall 2005: Presentation to Lehman of the NYSATE/NYACTE Distinguished Program Award; formation of the Lehman College center for faculty development and research in AE

Spring 2006: Invited ECCE presentation on aesthetic education integration at the NYSATE/NYACTE Spring Conference, Saratoga, New York; beginning planning among faculty experienced in integrating aesthetic education in coursework to continue AE work in their courses independently (without a TA) and to mentor new faculty in AE

Summer 2006: Division faculty participation in a week-long workshop on research and aesthetic education

Based on pragmatist philosopher John Dewey and existential philosophers, the writing of philosopher Maxine Greene was influential in designing LCI's work in aesthetic education at both the public school and college level, and underscores the importance of aesthetic education in her many publications. Many teacher educators base their work on Maxine Greene's philosophy and would be open to aesthetic education as a result. Additionally, the LCI publication with Teachers College Press, *Community in the Making: Lincoln Center Institute, the Arts, and Teacher Education* (Holzer & Noppe-Brandon, 2005) describes its work with the public and private colleges of New York City, of which Lehman is one.

Conclusion

Arts programs have often been devalued or removed from school curricula. Sometimes within college programs, too, the arts are seen as less important than literacy, math, and science. This can result in the elimination of arts courses in teacher education programs, the reduction of credit hours for these courses, as well as a reduction of emphasis on the arts. What is meant by "the arts" when the arts do exist is generally art production or art appreciation. Aesthetic education is not widely understood by teachers, and perhaps, not by college instructors. We return again to Maxine Greene's description of aesthetic education: "We are interested . . . in openings, in unexplored possibilities . . . in new ways of seeing, hearing, feeling, moving . . . the nurture of a special kind of reflectiveness and expressiveness, a reaching out for meanings . . ." (Greene, 2001, p. 7). Engaging teacher candidates, teachers, and school students with the arts in ways that support their ability to notice what there is to be noticed; that support the lending of their life to a work; that support making new connections, experiencing new patterns, opening new vistas, seeing and resonating differently, changing something in their life. . . . Is this not what we aspire to in education at any level?

Authors' note: The collaboration featured in this chapter was the recipient of the 2005 Distinguished Program Award from the New York State Association of Colleges of Teacher Education (NYSATE) and the New York State Association of Teacher Educators (NYACTE).

References

Greene, M. (2001). *Variations on a blue guitar: The Lincoln Center Institute lectures on aesthetic education.* New York: Teachers College Press.

Holzer, M. F., & Noppe-Brandon, S. (Eds.). (2005). *Community in the making: Lincoln-Center Institute, the arts, and teacher education.* New York: Teachers College Press.

Lincoln Center Institute for the Performing Arts, Inc. (2006). *Entering the world of the work of art: A guide for designing an aesthetic education curriculum.* New York: Author.

Lincoln Center Institute for the Performing Arts, Inc. (2005). *Teaching and learning at Lincoln Center Institute.* New York: Author.

CHAPTER 20

Cultivating Parent-Child Collaboration Concerning Mathematical Learning
A NECESSARY OBJECTIVE FOR TEACHER PREPARATION PROGRAMS

Regina M. Mistretta
St. John's University

> Regina M. Mistretta, Ed.D., is an associate professor in the Department of Early Childhood, Childhood, and Adolescent Education of the School of Education, St. John's University, where she strives to help advance the field of mathematics education. Her research includes investigations of geometric understandings, pedagogical practices, student error patterns, and parental issues and perspectives concerning mathematical learning.

ABSTRACT

> There is a critical need for teachers to guide parents on how to support classroom practices so that the goal of students succeeding in mathematics can be achieved. This chapter reports on a study that was undertaken to address this need. The study investigated the extent to which Pre-K through 8th grade parents collaborate with their children on mathematical tasks. It included an evaluation of a model mathematics initiative designed with conditions that sought to cultivate productive collaboration between parents and their children. Findings reveal significant grade level differences in parent-child collaboration, specific parental needs that warrant attention, and favorable feedback on efforts designed to energize the home-school mathematics connection. Findings serve to enhance the content of teacher education programs so that preservice and in-service teachers become knowledgeable of parental needs and sufficiently prepared to nurture parent-child collaboration concerning mathematical learning.

Introduction

Parents who are involved in children's learning of mathematics have a profound effect on those children's ability to learn. Studies have found that consistent parental involvement provides a strong foundation for children's attitudes toward mathematics (Kliman, 1999), promotes mathematics understanding (Kokoski & Downing-Leffler, 1995), and produces higher academic achievement in mathematics (Goldstein & Campbell, 1991). Just the simple act of children engaging in discussion with a parent about their mathematical thinking can improve their achievement (Ford & Crew, 1991; Epstein & Dauber, 1991; Myers, 1985). Unfortunately, though, for most parents the reform efforts affecting today's mathematics classrooms have created a much different learning environment than they experienced as young learners, and fear of the unknown often results in confusion and anxiety about how to help their children (Mistretta, 2004).

This chapter reports on a study that investigated the extent to which Pre-K through 8th grade parents collaborate with their children on mathematical tasks and evaluated a model mathematics initiative designed with conditions that sought to cultivate productive collaboration between parents and their children. Findings reveal significant grade level differences in parent-child collaboration, specific parental needs that warrant attention, and favorable feedback on efforts designed to energize the home-school mathematics connection. References to parents and parental collaboration are meant to be inclusive of all adults who play an active caretaker role in a child's home life.

Purpose

Knowledgeable of the value of parental collaboration, a former president of the National Council of Teachers of Mathematics stated that "we have to help parents bridge their fear and encourage them to join hands in providing a solid mathematics education for all students" (Price, 1996, p. 538). Currently, however, the formal training of educators to nurture parental collaboration in any form is underemphasized in the teacher education programs in the United States (Witmer, 2005). The National Center for Education Statistics (2003) reported that 48% of teachers indicated that their lack of adequate training for effectively involving parents was a significant barrier. Thus, addressing this challenge is congruent with the *ATE Yearbook XVI* calling for a renaissance in teacher education.

To address the critical need for teachers to be better prepared to guide parents on how to reflect classroom practices so that the goal of students succeeding in mathematics can be achieved (Bezuk, Whitehurst-Pane, & Aydelotte, 2000), answers to the following research questions were sought:

- To what extent do parents collaborate with their children about mathematical learning and does this vary across grade level groups?
- What challenges do parents face collaborating with their children about mathematical learning and does this vary across grade level groups? and
- How effectively does a model mathematics initiative cultivate parent-child collaboration in grades Pre-K through 8?

Teacher preparation programs play a vital role in empowering teachers with the necessary skills to cultivate parent-child collaboration. This study serves to energize the content of teacher education programs with findings that highlight both parental needs and field-tested strategies toward nurturing such collaboration in the area of mathematics education. These findings, when included in teacher preparation courses and professional development initiatives, add to the knowledge base and contribute to the preparation of preservice and in-service mathematics teachers.

Theoretical Framework

When the family is viewed as separate from the school, a message that the education of children is the sole responsibility of the schools is likely to form. To convey a more accurate message about the importance of parent-child collaboration concerning academic learning, the theory of overlapping spheres of influence identifies students as the main actors in their education, supported by others at home, at school, and in their communities (Epstein, 1987). The combined efforts of these supporting factors benefit students, strengthen families, and improve schools.

Specific benefits of parental input have been noted in the area of mathematics education. For example, as parents become more involved, their understanding of the changes occurring in school mathematics increases, and they begin to support and enhance their school's efforts to reform mathematics programs (Peressini, 1997). Teachers benefit when families serve as an added resource that supports learning beyond school hours (Epstein & Sanders, 1998), and parents realize that they have opportunities to interact with their children and do mathematics together (Moldavin, 2000).

Effective steps toward cultivating productive collaboration between parents and their children include parents participating in workshops that promote awareness of changes in mathematics education (Sheldon & Epstein, 2001). One such workshop topic is the use of manipulatives in the mathematics classroom. Survey results consistently indicate that parents frequently request hands-on workshops so they can concretely learn how to use the tools their children are using in school (Mistretta, 2004; Orman, 1993; Dauber & Epstein, 1993; Epstein, 1986).

Another important finding is that parents are much more knowledgeable about their children's learning of mathematics at the close of a series of activities where both parents and children engage in mathematical tasks together (Tregaskis, 1991). This form of collaboration, when extended to the home, can, in turn, reflect classroom learning of mathematics (Cathcart, Pothier, Vance, & Bezuk, 2003).

Research reveals the value of parental involvement and the importance of the manner in which educators establish collaboration between parents and their children. The study discussed in this chapter adds to the existing research through efforts that sought to develop an understanding of how parents collaborate with their children, the challenges they face, and the effects of steps taken to cultivate productive collaboration in mathematics education.

Method

PARTICIPANTS

In the study, 977 parents of Pre-K through 8th grade children from seven non-public schools in the metropolitan area of New York participated. Their ethnic backgrounds consisted of 3% Asian, 53% African-American, 23% Caucasian, and 20% Hispanic. Funding requirements guided the selection process to target schools with families of low socioeconomic status and whose children were classified with low mathematics achievement levels based on standardized testing scores. The parents were categorized into three groups: Group 1 (parents of children in grades Pre-K through 2), Group 2 (parents of children in grades 3 through 5), and Group 3 (parents of children in grades 6 though 8). Thirty-two percent (317) of the parents had children in grades Pre-K through 2, while 35% (339) had children in grades 3 through 5, and 33% (321) had children in grades 6 through 8.

PARENT INITIATIVE MODEL

The goal of the parent initiative was to bring life to mathematics education learning at home by exciting both parents and their children about doing mathematics together. It sought to inform, engage, promote reflection, and maintain collaboration between parents and children concerning mathematical learning. The initiative's model framework consisted of six components involving parents and children from grades Pre-K through 8. A mathematics professional development program was being implemented in the same schools by the same facilitator of the parent initiative. This allowed the content and instructional methods of the parent initiative to be consistent with that of the children's mathematics teachers. These teachers attended the parent initiative sessions to allow them to experience the dynamics of the parents and children working together. They also participated in maintaining the connection established by the initiative.

Beginning with the belief that if schools and students reach out and invite parents into a "village of learners," they will come (Guastello, 2004), along with the realization of the importance of creating an atmosphere of consideration and real partnership (De la Cruz, 1999), an invitation to the parents was extended. This first component of the initiative informed parents of the initiative's intent, requested their commitment to participate, and inquired about times that would best suit their busy schedules. To personalize the experience, students designed their own cover for their parents' invitation.

The second component of the initiative was an initial workshop attended by parents only. This component informed them about the importance of their involvement and the rationale behind specific instructional methods used in the mathematics classroom. Topics of discussion consisted of the changes in mathematics teaching through the decades, a constructivist foundation to teaching mathematics, the value of manipulatives (moveable objects) to make abstract concepts concrete, the importance of parental involvement, and productive ways parents can collaborate with their children to support mathematics education reform efforts.

The dynamics of the third component, an engagement workshop, created an active and insightful environment for parents and their children as they explored spatial relationships among tangram pieces (a seven piece set of shapes consisting of 2 big triangles, 1 medium triangle, 2 small triangles, a square, and a parallelogram), and reasoned about ways to solve a mathematics problem relevant to their grade level using tangrams (Adams, 1996). Emphasis was placed on communicating in both written and verbal form so that information and ideas could be gathered and organized, as well as thoughts clarified in a meaningful manner. Parents were advised not to do all of the telling. Rather they were encouraged to communicate and explore their children's thought processes by asking questions such as: Where shall we begin? What do we know that can help us? Can we approach this another way? Why? and How? This workshop concluded with a sharing of solutions in both small and large group settings.

To both reinforce and extend the engagement workshop experience, the fourth component of the initiative consisted of home activities distributed to the parents along with related content information to guide their solutions. These activities reflected activities completed at the engagement workshop. Parents were instructed to collaborate with their children in the same manner they did during the engagement workshop. They were reminded not to do all of the telling, but rather to communicate and explore thought processes together. Most importantly, emphasis was placed on the importance of just having fun at home with mathematics.

The fifth component, a follow-up session, served to promote reflection as a learning community. Families came back to share solutions as well as contribute feedback on the following questions:

- What was your solution and how did you arrive at it?
- Did you and your child approach the problem in the same manner?
- How did you help each other?
- What did you find interesting about working with each other? and
- Would you change anything the next time concerning your method of solution or how you worked together?

To ensure continuity, the sixth and final component of the initiative concerned mechanisms to maintain the collaboration between parents and their children. An interactive homework assignment, classroom follow-up techniques, and an interactive newsletter served to maintain the established home school mathematics connection. The interactive homework assignment required parents and their children to use tangrams once again. The format of the assignment consisted of sections where the parents were invited to work with their child on a mathematics task relevant to their grade level (Adams, 1996). The assignment provided necessary background information, facilitated a cooperative effort between the child and his/her parent, promoted a sense of multiple methods of solution, and provided parents with the opportunity to offer feedback about the assignment.

To maximize the potential of the interactive homework assignment and foster classroom communication among students about learning at home with their parents, the teachers of the students involved in this study allotted classroom time for the students to share their interactive homework assignments with each other and offer feedback.

Students discussed how their solutions were similar and how they were different, as well as the most enjoyable and the most challenging aspects of collaborating with their parents. Such discussion reinforced the students' conceptual understandings and skills with the assignment's task and allowed them to interact as a community of learners who are growing with their parents as partners in their learning of mathematics.

The interactive newsletter served to review the initiative's components. Explanations of what was done at each stage of the initiative were given along with a website corner containing Internet resources involving tangrams, a book corner containing children's literature that incorporate tangrams, and a listing of additional resources concerning the use of tangrams and mathematics in general. A report on classroom events related to the initiative and an area for parents to share their comments were included as well.

MEASURES

Parent Survey

A parent survey consisting of 14 statements requiring 5-point Likert scale responses and one narrative response question was used in this study to investigate the extent of parents' collaboration with their children's learning of mathematics (see Figure 20.1). The statements inquired about actions such as helping with mathematics homework, preparing for mathematics tests, communicating about what is being learned in mathematics class, discussing different ways to solve mathematics problems, communicating with the mathematics teacher about their child's progress, and voicing their concerns. The narrative response question asked the parents to highlight the challenges they face while helping their children with mathematics.

Parent Evaluation Form

An evaluation form consisting of four statements requiring 5-point Likert scale responses and three narrative response questions was used to assess parents' reactions to the initiative. Parents responded with extremely well, very well, adequately well, not very well, or not at all to the following statements:

- This initiative increased my awareness of the need for parental collaboration in mathematical learning.
- This initiative increased my awareness of current forms of mathematics instruction.
- This initiative increased my awareness of the use of tangrams in mathematical learning.
- This initiative increased my awareness of the importance of communication about mathematical thinking.

In their narrative responses, parents shared how the home activities were most helpful, what surprising and/or interesting events occurred at home, and how the entire experience impacted the family.

After each statement, circle the number in each row that corresponds to your response:
1. almost never 2. seldom 3. about half 4. usually 5. almost always

1. I help my child with math.
   1   2   3   4   5
2. I ask my child what he/she is doing in math.
   1   2   3   4   5
3. I help my child prepare for math tests.
   1   2   3   4   5
4. I check to see if my child is finished with his/her math homework.
   1   2   3   4   5
5. I check to see if my child's math homework is correct.
   1   2   3   4   5
6. I ask my child to explain to me how he/she arrived at his/her math solutions.
   1   2   3   4   5
7. I talk with my child about different ways to solve a math problem.
   1   2   3   4   5
8. I help my child correct his/her mistakes on math homework.
   1   2   3   4   5
9. I help my child correct his/her mistakes on math tests.
   1   2   3   4   5
10. I share ideas and talk with my child about math homework/projects.
    1   2   3   4   5
11. I point out to my child how math is used in our everyday lives.
    1   2   3   4   5
12. I provide a quiet setting for my child to do math homework.
    1   2   3   4   5
13. I ask my child's math teacher about his/her progress in math.
    1   2   3   4   5
14. I talk with my child's math teacher about my concerns about mathematical learning.
    1   2   3   4   5

15. **Please respond to the following question in depth. Give specific examples where appropriate.** What challenges do you face helping your child with mathematics?

Figure 20.1 Parent Survey

Student Reflection Form

A reflection form involving two narrative response items was used to assess students' reactions to the initiative. In their responses, students shared the most enjoyable and challenging parts of working with their parent. For students in grades Pre-K through 2 where communication in written form posed a challenge, students were asked to either speak about or draw a picture that depicted their response.

Procedure

The parent survey was administered by the investigator of this study to parents at each of the participating schools. An independent samples t-test was completed to compare the overall mean responses among the three groups of parents. Mean responses to each individual statement were compared within and among the parent groups to note the specific ways parents involve themselves in their children's learning of mathematics. Narrative responses to the question concerning parental challenges were tallied and transformed into percentages to determine the existence of patterns within and among the parent groups.

The rationale for and design of the parent initiative model implemented during this study stemmed from the theory of overlapping spheres of influence, supporting research on parental involvement, best practices advocated by the National Council of Teachers of Mathematics (NCTM, 2000), and the identified needs of the parent population who participated in the study as evidenced from the results of the previously described survey.

After reviewing invitation responses for the most convenient times for the parents to participate, the initiative was facilitated by the investigator of this study with groups of approximately 50 parents and children at a time (from grades Pre-K through 8) at each of the participating schools. Approximately 85% of the parent population at each school participated in the initiative. The rationale for involving such a wide span of grade levels was to build parents' awareness of the incremental power of manipulatives throughout the grades and diminish the possible misunderstanding that manipulatives exist only for use by younger students. Engagement workshops were held two weeks after the initial workshops, and follow-up sessions were held two weeks after the engagement workshops.

Parent evaluations and student reflection forms were completed at the close of the follow-up session. Further evaluation on the part of the investigator of this study was conducted through group discussions with teachers at each school to monitor the implementation of the interactive homework assignment, classroom follow-up techniques, and the interactive newsletter. At these discussions, teachers shared classroom experiences concerning the progress of these strategies to maintain the home-school mathematics connection, and reported on parent feedback gathered from the comment sheets included with the interactive homework assignment and newsletter.

Results

PARENT SURVEY

A reliability analysis was done to determine the reliability of the parent survey. The obtained overall alpha level was .919, indicating high reliability since the alpha level was greater than 0.8. The alpha levels for Groups 1, 2, and 3 were

.905, .888, and .921 respectively, indicating high reliability as well within each group of parents.

Independent samples t-test data concerning the overall mean responses between Groups 1 and 2 (3.9906 and 3.8234), and Groups 2 and 3 (3.8234 and 3.3048) revealed significant declines ($p<.01$) in parental collaboration as grade levels increased (see Tables 20.1 and 20.2). Comparisons of mean responses for each survey statement (see Table 20.3) among each group surfaced the highest mean for Groups 1 and 2 (4.75 and 4.47, respectively) for survey Statement 4, "I check to see if my child is finished with his/her math homework." and the highest mean for Group 3 (4.12) for Statement 12, "I provide a quiet setting for my child to do math homework." The lowest mean for all groups (2.96, 2.84, and 2.63, respectively) was for Statement 14, "I talk with my child's math teacher about my concerns about mathematical learning."

Of the 977 parents who completed the first portion of the survey consisting of the 14 statements, 287 parents completed the portion requiring a narrative response. Noted patterns indicated that the most reported challenge (23% of those responding) especially among parents of Groups 2 and 3, was that "math is taught differently than in my time." This finding should be viewed with caution, though, since not all of the parents responded to this portion of the survey. However, this response is consistent with the findings of a previously conducted study (Mistretta, 2004) where the majority of the 790 parents of children in grades Pre-K through 8 noted this same concern.

PARENT EVALUATION FORM

The responses to the four statements on the parent evaluation form revealed the majority of all three parent groups responding with either extremely well or very

Table 20.1 Independent Samples of T-Test Results for Groups 1 and 2

Group	N	M (SD)	p
1	317	3.9906 (.75)	.004
2	339	3.8234 (.75)	

Table 20.2 Independent Samples of T-Test Results for Groups 2 and 3

Group	N	M (SD)	p
2	339	3.8234 (.75)	.000
3	321	3.3048 (.95)	

Table 20.3 Mean Responses to Survey Statements (S1 to S14)

Group	1	2	3	4	5	6	7	8	9	10	11	12	13	14
1	3.97 (316)	4.28 (315)	3.90 (292)	4.75 (314)	4.68 (311)	3.86 (310)	3.89 (307)	4.41 (313)	3.83 (287)	3.94 (308)	3.76 (309)	4.35 (307)	3.01 (296)	2.96 (293)
2	3.59 (337)	4.26 (339)	3.87 (337)	4.47 (338)	4.20 (339)	3.85 (336)	3.82 (337)	3.97 (339)	3.49 (332)	3.84 (337)	3.92 (329)	4.33 (331)	2.98 (325)	2.84 (322)
3	2.91 (318)	3.97 (320)	3.10 (320)	3.90 (321)	3.32 (320)	3.22 (319)	3.19 (321)	3.21 (321)	3.08 (317)	3.27 (319)	3.45 (314)	4.12 (314)	2.83 (315)	2.63 (310)

well to Statement 1 (90%, 93%, and 88%, for Groups 1, 2, and 3 respectively); Statement 2 (89%, 93%, and 89%, for Groups 1, 2, and 3 respectively), Statement 3 (90%, 93%, and 88%, for Groups 1, 2, and 3 respectively), and Statement 4 (95%, 100%, and 90% for Groups 1, 2, and 3 respectively). Positive feedback was gleaned from all narrative responses concerning the home activities. The most frequently noted feedback among all three parent groups (75%, 83%, and 77%, respectively) concerned their appreciation for the opportunity to work together with their child and share ideas.

STUDENT REFLECTION FORM

Positive feedback was gleaned from all student reflection forms about their collaboration with their parents. The most frequently noted feedback (80% of the students) concerning the best part of working with their parents was their opportunity to share a method of solution that was different from that of the parent. The most frequently noted challenge (82% of the students) was that the parents would not offer the answers but questioned how and why.

Discussion

PARENT SURVEY

Overall mean responses to the parent survey revealed regular levels of collaborative efforts between parents and children of Grades Pre-K through 2 and Grades 3 through 5 concerning mathematical learning, but only a moderate level of collaboration between parents and children of Grades 6 through 8. Further analysis showed that even though collaboration was common among Grades Pre-K through 2 and Grades 3 through 5, parents and children in Grades 3 through 5 were collaborating significantly less than parents and children in Grades Pre-K through 2. This decline in collaborative efforts surfaced again when overall mean responses indicated parents and children in Grades 6 through 8 collaborating significantly less than parents and children in Grades 3 through 5.

Review of mean responses to the individual survey statements indicated that the most common form of collaboration existing between parents and children of Grades Pre-K through 2 and Grades 3 through 5 was parents checking to see if homework was finished with less attention paid to checking whether or not the homework was correct. The most common form of collaboration existing between parents and children in Grades 6 through 8 was parents providing a quiet setting for homework completion with even less attention paid than in Grades Pre-K through 2 and Grades 3 through 5 to checking whether or not the homework was correct. The least common form of collaboration of all groups was parents' talking about their concerns with their child's math teacher.

This last finding may be due to the limited amount of time parents and children spend working together on mathematical tasks as revealed from the parent survey. Survey findings showed parents taking on a role that engages them for the most part in checking that the home allows for assignment completion, and less involvement in sharing ideas about mathematical thinking. Greater emphasis by teachers on parents' role as learning partners may energize parents' interest in voicing their concerns and learning about ways they can better collaborate with their children.

Narrative survey responses depicted parents' feelings of being disconnected from current mathematics instruction. Common responses included "Math is taught differently than in my time," "I don't want to confuse my child," "I don't know how to use manipulatives," and "I need answers to my child's questions about how mathematics applies to the real world." Such concerns voiced by parents need to be heard by teachers so that they can properly service needs, encourage more communication about concerns, and ultimately enrich students' learning experiences.

PARENT EVALUATIONS AND STUDENT REFLECTIONS

Positive parent and student feedback on the initiative was illustrative of the parent evaluation and student reflection forms. Parents indicated being more aware of the need for parental collaboration in mathematical learning, more knowledgeable of current forms of mathematics instruction including the use of manipulatives (specifically tangrams), and better prepared to communicate with their child about mathematical thinking. Narrative responses included "This initiative allowed me to see how my child's mind works," "Now I listen and guide rather than insist on using my way to solve a problem," and "The communication that this initiative fostered among the entire learning community helped demystify mathematics."

Students reported that working with their parents was enjoyable for reasons such as "I got to share my ideas with my mom and she shared hers with me," "We put our thinking together and got a chance to brainstorm," and "I'm happy now because when I go home my parent will know what I'm talking about." Students also reported the experience as challenging for reasons such as "My parent didn't give me the answer," "I had to do a lot of the thinking and explain my answers," and "Looking for different ways to solve the problem made my head hurt."

Conclusions and Recommendations

This study reveals the need for meaningful and consistent parental collaboration in mathematics education in Grades Pre-K through 8 and describes action steps that can effectively cultivate such collaboration. Survey findings shed light on the need for educators to encourage parents to assume tasks that go beyond just checking homework and providing a quiet environment in which to work. Parent and student reactions to the described mathematics initiative surfaced a sense of active engagement in mathematical learning as opposed to being on opposite sides of the fence.

Responsibility for the goal of empowering parents lies in great part with teacher preparation programs. Inclusion of this chapter's findings in preservice and in-service mathematics methods courses as well as in professional development programs can inform preservice and in-service teachers of the importance of attending to parental needs and nurturing productive collaboration between parents and children. Deepened understanding of parental needs and effective actions that cultivate parent-child collaboration allow teacher educators to make informed decisions about teacher education programs and professional development initiatives that will ultimately improve student achievement. Future research should expand upon this study's investigation by involving other academic areas. Such research would help inform a renaissance in teacher preparation.

References

Adams, J. (1996). *Tangrams: The super source.* White Plains, NY: Cuisenaire Company of America.

Bezuk, N.S., Whitehurst-Payne, S., & Aydelotte, J. (2000). Successful collaborations with parents to promote equity in mathematics. In W. G. Secada (Ed.), *Changing the faces of mathematics* (pp. 143–148). Reston, VA: NCTM.

Cathcart, W., Pothier, Y., Vance, J., & Bezuk, N. (2003). *Learning mathematics in elementary and middle schools.* Upper Saddle River, NJ: Pearson Education, Inc.

Dauber, S. L., & Epstein, J. L. (1993). Parents' attitudes and practices of involvement in inner-city elementary and middle schools. In N. Chavkin (Ed.), *Families and schools in a pluralistic society* (pp. 53–71). Albany, NY: SUNY Press.

De la Cruz, Y. (1999). Reversing the trend: Latino families in real partnerships with schools. *Teaching Children Mathematics, 5*(5), 296–300.

Epstein, J. L. (1986). Parents' reactions to teacher practices of parent involvement. *The Elementary School Journal, 86*(3), 277–293.

Epstein, J. L. (1987). Toward a theory of family-school connections: Teacher practices and parental involvement. In K. Hurrelmann, F. Kaufmann, & F. Losel (Eds.), *Social intervention: Potential and constraints*. New York: DeGruyter.

Epstein, J. L., & Sanders, M. (1998). International perspectives on school-family community partnerships. *Childhood Education, 74*(6), 340–341.

Ford, M., & Crew, C. (1991). Table-top mathematics—a home-study program for early childhood. *Arithmetic Teacher, 38*(8), 6–12.

Goldstein, S., & Campbell, F. (1991). Parents: A ready resource. *Arithmetic Teacher, 38*(6), 24–27.

Guastello, E. F. (2004). A village of learners. *Educational Leadership, 61*(8), 79–83.

Kliman, M. (1999). Beyond helping with homework: Parents and children doing mathematics at home. *Teaching Children Mathematics, 6*(3), 140–146.

Kokoski, T., & Downing-Leffler, N. (1995). Boosting your science and math programs in early childhood education: Making the home-school connection. *Young Children, 50*(5), 35–39.

Mistretta, R. M. (2004). Parental issues and perspectives concerning mathematics education at elementary and middle school settings. *Action in Teacher Education, 26*(2), 69–76.

Moldavin, C. (2000). A parent's portfolio: Observing the power of Matt, the mathematician. *Teaching Children Mathematics, 6*(6), 372–375.

Myers, J. (1985). *Involving parents in middle level education*. Columbus, OH: National Middle School Association.

National Center for Education Statistics. (2003). *Parental involvement in children's education: Efforts by public elementary schools*. Retrieved on April 12, 2004, from http://nec.ed.gov/surveys/frss/publications/98032.

National Council of Teachers of Mathematics. (2000). *Principles and standards for school mathematics*. Reston, VA: NCTM.

Orman, S. (1993). Mathematics backpacks: Making the home-school connection. *Arithmetic Teacher, 40*(6), 306–309.

Peressini, D. (1997). Parental involvement in the reform of mathematics education. *The Mathematics Teacher, 90*(6), 421–427.

Price, J. (1996). President's report: Building bridges of mathematical understanding for all children. *Mathematics Teacher, 89*(6), 536–539.

Sheldon, S., & Epstein, J. L. (2001). Focus on math achievement: Effects of family and community involvement. Paper presented at the 2001 annual meeting of the American Sociological Association, Anaheim, California.

Tregaskis, O. (1991). Parents and mathematical games. *Arithmetic Teacher, 38*(7), 14–17.

Witmer, M. (2005). The fourth *r* in education-relationships. *The Clearing House, 78*(5), 224–228.

CHAPTER 21

Minimizing Barriers in Teacher Diversity Professional Development

Earl Thomas
Saint Xavier University

David Lamont Bell
Saint Xavier University

> Earl Thomas, Ed.D., is an assistant professor in the School of Education at Saint Xavier University, Chicago, Illinois. His research interests include teacher practices, diversity, and faculty in higher education. His recent publications include *Collaboration: An Alternative for Mentoring New Faculty* (2006), and *The Adult Learner: Here to Stay* (2005).
>
> David Lamont Bell, Ed.D., is an assistant professor in the School of Education at Saint Xavier University, Chicago, Illinois. His research interest includes diversity professional development of teachers. His recent publications include: *Barriers to Teacher Change* (2005), and *The Impact of a School Uniform Policy* (2006).

ABSTRACT

> This program evaluation documented teacher perceptions of the impact of the first year of a 3-year diversity professional development experience. A survey was administered to 150 Catholic school teachers. The survey documented: 1) teacher identification of strengths and needs (Identification); 2) delivery in a non-threatening and non-judgmental environment (Non-Threatening); 3) supportive opportunities for ongoing reflection (Reflection); and 4) program responsiveness to the needs of the school environment (Program Responsiveness). The results revealed that a professional development experience that allows teachers to identify their needs in a non-threatening and non-judgmental environment, and provides oppor-

tunities for ongoing reflection, is critical in fostering change with respect to issues of diversity.

In recent years there has been a growing interest in serving the needs of diverse learners. Many school districts in responding to this growing interest have launched special in-service programs to educate and train teachers on culturally sensitive teaching approaches for serving diverse students. Often these professional development programs have involved one-time workshops that strive to transform the school environment and teacher practices. Although such efforts have consistently yielded little to no impact on transformation of the school environment and teacher practices, they continue to be the favored teacher professional development model. Nothing has been so frustrating for teachers as the thousands of conducted one-time never to be repeated workshops that have led to no significant change in teacher practices (Fullan, 1991). Consequently, issues of adapting to the changing student demographics persist and remain the greatest challenge for teacher preservice and in-service preparation.

Review of Literature

CHANGING DEMOGRAPHICS

Changing demographics have challenged preservice and in-service programs to prepare teachers, counselors, and administrators to serve a rapidly shifting diverse student community (Klauke, 1989). Embedded in this challenge is understanding how to better address the needs of the diverse experiences children bring with them to school (Klauke, 1989). These may include a wide range of languages, cultures, learning styles, and intelligences that require a variety of models and strategies for meeting the needs of diverse learners in the school environment (Darling-Hammond, Wise, & Klein as cited by Futrell, Gomez, & Bedden, 2003).

Logan (2003) reported that the 2000 Census count found nearly 29 million immigrants living in metropolitan regions throughout the United States—an increase of 10 million since 1990. Most of America's minority racial/ethnic populations are unevenly distributed and concentrated in certain geographical regions and large urban areas (Zhou, 2003). Additionally, immigrant growth in the suburbs has surpassed the growth in the inner city increasing from 3.5 million to 4.8 million immigrants (Logan, 2003). The Census Bureau estimates that by 2050 Whites will make up 53% of the population (García, 2000).The influence of the estimated demographic shift will have a significant impact on the design of the school environment and delivery of instruction. The consistent shift in racial and ethnic demographics presents challenges for schools that wish to employ teachers who possess the knowledge, skills, and dispositions required to understand and teach a diverse student population. A survey conducted by the National Center for Education Statistics revealed 80% of teachers did not feel adequately prepared to understand and teach a diverse population of students, including students with disabilities or limited English proficiency (as cited by Futrell, Gomez, & Bedden, 2003). Teachers have not been adequately prepared nor provided with experiences in school environments that foster teaching culturally diverse students effectively (White-Clark, 2005).

ISSUES OF TEACHER PREPARATION IN STUDENT DIVERSITY

One of the major challenges for teachers is the broad spectrum of student diversity found in American classrooms. In a most basic way, diversity can relate to academic abilities as well as students' cultural identities, ethnicities, and religious beliefs. As a result, issues pertaining to student diversity persist. Teacher preservice and in-service preparation programs struggle to prepare teachers in ways that enable them to support all students of diverse backgrounds (Futrell, Gomez, & Bedden, 2003). However, due to the lack of adequate preservice and in-service teacher preparation in culturally responsive pedagogy, teachers have often implemented ineffective practices to meet the needs of the diverse students in their classrooms (White-Clark, 2005). This means teachers are unprepared to address the substantial diversity of experiences and abilities students bring with them to class each day.

Students' wide ranges of languages, cultures, exceptionalities, learning styles, talents, and intelligences demand an equally wide and varied repertoire of teaching approaches and strategies (Darling-Hammond, Wise, & Klein as cited by Futrell, Gomez, & Bedden, 2003). Teachers not only need preservice teacher education experiences that prepare them in appropriate culturally responsive teaching practices (White-Clark, 2005; Ladson-Billings, 1997), but may well benefit from ongoing professional development experiences that systematically cultivate them to serve an increasingly diverse student population.

BARRIERS FOUND IN IN-SERVICE TEACHER EDUCATION

Fullan (1991) suggested that teacher in-service efforts are likely to fail because they often are delivered as one-time, never to be repeated workshops. These one-time workshops often lack strategies for follow-up and the support needed to ensure the learning transfer of ideas and practices introduced during the workshop. Rarely are teachers' concerns and needs addressed through participation in this type of training.

An additional barrier to teacher change involves the inability to obtain teacher support of diversity reform efforts. Resistance frequently occurs as a response to an interpersonal or organizational change mandate that has the potential of personal impact (Friend & Cook as cited by Janas, 1998). Therefore, teachers often have perceived diversity efforts as activities forced upon them, with little or no teacher voice guiding the change initiative. However, successful teacher professional development experiences are long-term and viewed as a strategy for implementing specific instructional/school-wide change efforts in ways that promote teacher involvement (Fullan, 2000).

TEACHER PROFESSIONAL DEVELOPMENT

Magestro and Stanford-Blair (2000) suggested that the goal of increasing teachers' growth, satisfaction, and motivation demands a staff development model that provides opportunities for teachers to actively construct their own meaning. Fullan (2000) suggested a teacher professional development model must ensure that all participants have a vested interest in the process and outcomes. In effect, participants should engage in activities that build on their strengths but also identify areas needing improvement.

Often professional development experiences are not based on expressed needs but remediation and quick fix approaches (Fiszer, 2004). However, ongoing professional development experiences that involve teachers in diagnosing their learning needs, and designing and implementing the change effort, ultimately yield better outcomes for students with diverse backgrounds (Futrell, Gomez, & Bedden, 2003).

Danielson and McGreal (2000) suggested that the sharing of teacher expertise through dialoguing needs to be embedded in a professional development model. Teachers need to be provided with regular "opportunities to explore, question, and debate in order to integrate new ideas into their repertoires and classroom practices" (Fiszer, 2004, p. 16). Fiszer found that the lack of time for reflection and dialogue could negatively impact ongoing teacher professional development. Further professional development efforts are more likely to produce a non-threatening climate when reflective dialogue and feedback are offered in a non-judgmental way.

Terehoff (2002) believed that when working with teachers, principals need to be aware of the essential elements of adult learning, such as the characteristics that distinguish adult learners from children as learners, and the principles by which the process of adult learning is guided. In essence teacher professional development planners must consider the experiences that teachers bring, their needs, motivation for learning about diversity, and the design of an appropriate learning environment that supports teachers' pre-, during, and post-staff development experience (Knowles, 1980). In addition, there must be awareness that adult learning experiences involve active engagement of all participants in mutual assessment and agreement of learning needs, goals, activities, and the evaluating of learner and program outcomes (Knowles, 1980).

PROGRAM EVALUATION

Program evaluation is defined as a systematic method for collecting, analyzing, and using information to answer basic questions about a program (U.S. Department of Health and Human Services, 1997). Caffarella (2002) suggested a systematic evaluation consists of specifying what is to be judged and formulating evaluation questions. Thus, by answering evaluative questions program planners are able to determine the impact of a program on subunits or whole organizations as well as participant learning. Along these same lines, program evaluation serves as a useful tool for determining the impact of a school improvement effort and the direction for corrective actions (Jason, 2003).

Program evaluation serves two primary organizational functions, that of 1) confirming and 2) diagnosing the impact of the program model and its activities (Jason, 2003). The program evaluation model used to document the impact of particular diversity professional development experience included analysis of quantitative data that was collected at the end of the first year of the project. The purpose of evaluating the impact of the first-year experiences was to understand if the experience was non-threatening, supportive of opportunities for reflection, addressed teachers' strengths and needs, and if the program was responsive to all 10 schools' unique environments.

FIRST YEAR OF THE PROJECT

In the initial phase of the project, principals at 10 Catholic schools identified two teacher leaders who were responsible for facilitating the change process and gaining faculty ownership of the professional development experience. The teacher leaders attended an orientation with the researchers and were provided with an overview of the project's aims and activities. In addition, the researchers outlined the teacher leaders' roles and responsibilities. The teacher leaders were expected to articulate the project's vision to other teachers at their respective schools and to prepare materials for dissemination at the first Diversity Awareness Day seminar experience.

During the second phase of the project, the 200 teachers working within the 10 schools attended the one-day Diversity Awareness Day seminar experience. This experience focused on engaging the participants in activities that stimulated relevant dialogue regarding cultural diversity and the school environment. Each teacher completed the School-Wide Diversity Needs Assessment. The survey instrument documented information about the schools' environment with respect to school organization, student services, and facilities that supported diversity.

In the third phase of the project, the researchers met with the teacher leaders and principals to share the results of data gathered from the School-Wide Diversity Needs Assessment. Teachers and principals analyzed and interpreted the results of their school's report to understand the strengths and areas needing improvement with regard to their school environment.

In the fourth phase of the project, the teacher leaders and their school's teaching faculty interpreted the results of the assessment and developed school action plans. The action plans included specific goals, objectives, strategies, outcomes, and timelines that addressed the interpreted diversity areas needing improvement within the school environment. Researchers then conducted follow-up visits to each school. The purposes of the visits were to monitor and provide technical assistance supportive to each school in the implementation of their action plans.

In phase five of the project, 150 of the 200 teachers who originally attended the Awareness Day seminar participated in an end of the school year exhibition day. The exhibition day provided the opportunity for each school to showcase their progress and achievements toward creating a diversity inclusive environment. Table 21.1 provides a description of the project aims and sketches the project's activities.

Methodology

This program evaluation sought to document teachers' perceptions regarding the impact of the first year of a 3-year diversity professional development experience. The research was conducted in 10 Catholic schools, located on the south side of Chicago. The Program Evaluation survey was administered to 150 Catholic school teachers who voluntarily agreed to participate in this study. The survey included statements followed by a five-point Likert-type scale that allowed participants to report their perception of the professional development

Table 21.1 First-Year Project Aims and Activities

Project Phase	Project Aims	Activities
Phase One	To provide a one-day orientation for teacher leaders to project aims and activities.	Principals identified two teacher leaders who were orientated project aims and activities.
Phase Two	To support the development of teachers in gaining greater self-understanding of other cultural groups	In small groups teachers identified, shared, and examined the strengths of their own unique cultural heritage and ethnic background while learning about others.
Phase Three	To holitistically transform the school environment into a system that reflects cross-cultural diversity and multicultural educational approaches	By completing a Schoolwide Diversity Needs Assessment, teachers distinguished the various cultural and ethnic backgrounds of the students they serve.
Phase Three	To holistically transform the school environment into a system that reflects cross-cultural diversity and multi-cultural educational approaches	By completing a Schoolwide Diversity Needs Assessment, teachers identified culturally sensitive practices that are used in their school to respect and affirm all students, parents, and the community they serve.
Phase Three	To holistically transform the school environment into a system that reflects cross-cultural diversity and multi-cultural educational approaches.	By completing a Schoolwide Diversity Needs Assessment, teachers assessed the school environment to learn about the school's current delivery system and its response to promoting a multicultural environment.
Phase Four	To holistically transform the school environment into a system that reflects cross-cultural diversity and multi-cultural educational approaches	Teachers created and implemented a School-wide Diversity Improvement Action Plan based on the results found in Schoolwide Diversity Needs Assessment.
Phase Five	To support the development of teachers in gaining greater self-understanding of other cultural groups	Teachers discussed and reflected on personal and school environment changes that had occurred.

experience (i.e., 1 = strongly disagree, 2 = disagree, 3 = neutral, 4 = agree, and 5 = strongly agree). For example, teachers were asked to respond to a series of survey questions such as 1) Overall, did the program help me to identify strengths and appreciate cultural groups other than my own? 2) Overall, did the program introduce information about diversity in a non-threatening manner? 3) Overall, was the Awareness Day seminar experience helpful in creating a reflective dialogue amongst teachers? and 4) Overall, was the program responsive to the needs of individual schools?

Demographic data was collected with respect to number of years teaching experience and grade groupings. Teachers were asked to self-report their number of years teaching ranging from 0–5 (New), 6–10 (Intermediate), and 11 or more (Experienced). Additionally teachers self-reported their grade groupings according to the following categories: Pre-K–2nd (Early Childhood), 3rd–5th (Middle Elementary), and 6th–8th (Upper Elementary); and resource teachers, specialists (Other).

INSTRUMENTATION

The survey was developed to understand teachers' perceptions regarding the impact of the first year of a 3-year diversity professional development experience. The 15 items in the survey were based on the literature, which, in general, revealed that professional development program experiences should include: 1) teacher identification of strengths and needs (Identification); 2) delivery in a non-threatening and non-judgmental environment (Non-Threatening); 3) supportive opportunities for ongoing reflection (Reflection); and 4) responsiveness to the needs of the school environment (Program Responsiveness) (Fiszer, 2004; Knowles, 1980). A Cronbach alpha test was conducted to determine the reliability of the items on the survey. Results indicated an alpha level of .96 showing the internal consistency of the items on the survey.

Results

A multivariate analysis of variance (MANOVA) test revealed no significant differences in teachers' perceptions in relationship to teacher grade groupings and years of experience. Next, the collected descriptive data mean scores were analyzed to determine teachers' perceptions of the impact of the first year of the professional development experience. The results revealed that teachers perceived the program favorably with a mean score response ranging from 3.70 to 4.22. With respect to the question theme "Program Responsiveness" in all four grade groupings teachers reported the program was responsive to their needs.

However, "Early Childhood" and "Other" grade groupings demonstrated a higher mean score than "Middle Elementary" and "Upper Elementary" grade groupings. Furthermore, results revealed that all grade groupings agreed that the program provided an environment that was non-threatening. Table 21.2 provides the descriptive statistics of teacher perceptions with respect to grade groupings.

With respect to teachers' perceptions and teachers' years of experience, results revealed that teachers perceived the program favorably with a mean score response ranging from 3.77 to 4.20. Specifically the results suggested that teachers, regardless of years of experience, agreed that the program model offered opportunities for reflection. However, "Experienced" and "Intermediate" teachers demonstrated a higher mean score than "New" teachers. Table 21.3 provides complete detail of descriptive statistics of teachers' perceptions with respect to number of years of teaching experience.

Discussion

This program evaluation sought to document teachers' perceptions regarding the impact of the first year of a 3-year diversity teacher professional development

Table 21.2 Descriptive Statistics of Teacher Perceptions with Respect to Grade Groupings

Question Theme	Grade Group	Mean	SD	n
Identification	Early childhood	4.17	.60	49
	Middle elementary	3.89	.91	39
	Upper elementary	4.03	.69	37
	Other	4.07	.75	25
Non-threatening	Early childhood	4.20	.68	49
	Middle elementary	4.06	.84	39
	Upper elementary	4.07	.71	37
	Other	4.29	.81	25
Reflection	Early childhood	4.16	.70	49
	Middle elementary	3.82	1.07	39
	Upper elementary	3.90	.86	37
	Other	4.10	.88	25
Program responsive	Early childhood	4.22	.66	49
	Middle elementary	3.70	1.12	39
	Upper elementary	3.72	1.01	37
	Other	4.12	.90	25

21.3 Descriptive Statistics of Teacher Perceptions with Respect to Years of Experience

Question Theme	Years of Experience	Mean	SD	N
Identification	New	3.91	.90	34
	Intermediate	4.09	.49	33
	Experienced	4.09	.75	83
Non-threatening	New	4.10	.87	34
	Intermediate	4.15	.53	33
	Experienced	4.20	.78	83
Reflection	New	3.77	1.0	34
	Intermediate	4.08	.56	33
	Experienced	4.06	.89	83
Responsive	New	3.79	1.05	34
	Intermediate	4.03	.57	33
	Experienced	3.98	1.02	83

experience. According to Jason (2003), program evaluation confirms and diagnoses the impact of a program model and its activities. An effective teacher development experience provides teachers with the opportunity to discuss and reflect on their beliefs and practices, be actively involved in assessment of personal learning needs, and participate in the evaluation of the program's impact (Fiszer, 2004; Terehoff, 2002; Knowles, 1980). Fiszer (2004) suggested teacher professional development experiences should be implemented as a large-scale action research project. Through this approach, teachers would be able to engage in meaningful experiences that reflect on their beliefs and practices.

IDENTIFICATION OF NEED

The results of the first-year impact evaluation revealed that, on the whole, teachers generally perceived that the professional development experience helped identify their school strengths and needs. Fiszer (2004) suggested that educators are more motivated to change if they themselves are able to identify the problem or need relative to their school context. Thus teachers in this study were given opportunities for collaborative engagement with respect to identification of the problem or needs specific to their school environments. Futrell, Gomez, and Bedden (2003) believed that it is critical that a professional development experience involve teachers in diagnosing the needs of their school, which can lead to successful change.

LACK OF THREAT

The results of this study indicate that teachers perceived the professional development experience to be non-judgmental and non-threatening. Knowles (1980) believed that education and preparation programs for adults should be delivered in an environment of mutual respect and trust between the adult learner and the learning facilitator. However, long-term sustainable change efforts require creating a non-threatening school climate that motivates teachers to embrace the benefits of change (Hargreaves & Fink, 2003) while minimizing overall resistance to change. Resistance is usually based on participants' knowledge, experience, and comfort level, which often can limit any significant behavioral changes (Huzicker, 2004). Further professional development experiences are more likely to produce a non-threatening climate when reflective dialogue and feedback are supported in a non-judgmental way (Fiszer, 2004).

REFLECTION

Teachers perceived that the experience provided opportunities to reflect on their cultural diversity. The provision of opportunities for reflection is critical for stimulating internal change in values and behaviors (Lindsey, Nuri-Robins, & Terrell, 1999). Cafferella (2002) suggested that effective professional development experiences accommodate participants' individual diversity and cultural differences. These opportunities create environments where participants can engage in ongoing critical reflection as part of their learning. Brookfield (2000) suggested that professional development opportunities must help participants articulate their experiences in dialogic circles and then encourage them to review their experiences through the multiple lenses provided by colleagues in that circle. Thus, knowledge is viewed as malleable, and experience is seen as being open to multiple interpretations. Fiszer (2004) indicated that teachers must constantly assess and reassess their practices in order to meet the needs of the shifting demographics of the student populations they serve. In order to meet the needs of a changing student population, teachers must have sufficient time and follow-up to support the mastery of new strategies along with opportunities for collaboration with other teachers. As is evident, teachers learn best when there are opportunities to collaborate, practice, engage in reflective dialogue, and follow-up (Fiszer, 2004).

PROGRAM RESPONSIVENESS

Finally, results of this study revealed that overall teachers generally perceived the program as being responsive to the needs of their school. Fullan (1991) suggested that teacher in-service efforts are likely to fail because they are often unresponsive to the needs of teachers and the school environment. Thus, one-time, never to be repeated workshops often lack strategies for follow-up and support that ensure the portability of ideas and changes within the school environment and outside of it. Rarely are school and teacher concerns addressed in this approach (Fiszer, 2004).

Conclusion

Based on the findings of this study, we conclude that it is essential that the first year of a 3-year diversity professional development experience be comprehensive in scope and nature. Data analysis revealed no significant differences in teacher response with respect to the number of years teaching or grade grouping. We recommend that the first year of a comprehensive diversity professional development experience consist of the following elements that foster teacher and environmental change:

- The experience must support teachers in the identification of the diversity needs within their school,
- The experience should be responsive to participants and school needs,
- The experience should provide opportunities for ongoing reflection, and
- The experience should be non-threatening and non-judgmental.

We further recommend that, when planning a diversity experience, the design of the program should ensure that participants are not seen as the problem; instead, they must be viewed as equal partners in the diversity initiative. Therefore teachers must be respected at all times. It is also imperative to understand that any reform initiative can lead to teacher resistance. If the magnitude of the resistance is not understood, this may lead to tension that could impact the outcomes of the professional development experience and negate the possibility of a renaissance in teacher education.

In conclusion, the outcome of this program evaluation supports a new perspective that engages teachers. As noted earlier, one of the supreme challenges for teacher education programs is the lack of appropriate preparation in culturally responsive pedagogy (White-Clark, 2005; Ladson-Billings, 1997). Thus, practicing teachers may also lack the knowledge and skills to address the substantial diversity of experiences and abilities students bring to class everyday (Darling-Hammond, Wise, & Klein as cited by Futrell, Gomez, & Bedden, 2003). A renaissance in teacher education demands re-evaluation of preservice and in-service programs in order to ensure diversity professional development experiences are non-threatening, reflective, and responsive to identified needs of the teacher participants and their school environments.

References

Brookfield, S. D. (2000). The concept of critically reflective practice. In A. L. Wilson & E. R. Hayes (Eds.), *Handbook of adult and continuing education*, 33–49. San Francisco: Jossey-Bass.

Caffarella, R. S. (2002). *Planning programs for adult learners* (2nd ed.). San Francisco: Jossey-Bass.

Danielson, C., & McGreal, T. L. (2000). *Teacher evaluation: To enhance professional practice*. Alexandria, VA: ASCD.

Fiszer, E. P. (2004). *How teachers learn best: An ongoing professional development model.* Lanham, MD: Scarecrow Education.

Fullan, M. (1991). *The new meaning of educational change*. New York: Teachers College Press.

Fullan, M. (2000). The three stories of education reform. *Phi Delta Kappan, 81*(8), 581–584.

Futrell, M. H., Gomez, J., & Bedden, D. (2003). Teaching the children of a new America: The challenge of diversity. *Phi Delta Kappan, 84*(5), 381–385.

García, E. (2000). *Student cultural diversity* (3rd ed.). Boston: Houghton Mifflin.

Hargreaves, A., & Fink, D. (2003). Sustaining leadership. *Phi Delta Kappan. 84*(9), 693–700.

Huzicker, J. (2004) The beliefs-behavior connection: Leading teachers toward change. *Principal, 84*(2), 44–46.

Janas, M. (1998). Shhhhhh, the dragon is asleep and its name is resistance. *Journal of Staff Development 19*(3), 13–16.

Jason, M. H. (2003). *Evaluating programs: To increase student achievement.* Glenville, IL: Skylight Professional Development.

Klauke, A. (1989). *Coping with changing demographics.* ERIC Clearinghouse on Educational Management. Retrieved August 20, 2006, from www.ericdigests.org/pre-9214/coping.htm.

Knowles, M. S. (1980). *The modern practice of adult education.* New York: Cambridge University Press.

Ladson-Billings, G. J. (1997). *The dreamkeepers: Successful teachers of African-American children.* San Francisco: Jossey-Bass.

Lindsey, R., Nuri-Robins, K., & Terrell, R. (1999). *Cultural proficiency: A manual for school leaders.* Newbury Park, CA: Corwin Press.

Logan, J. R. (2003). *Americas newcomer.* [Report by the Lewis Mumford Center for Comparative Urban and Regional Research University of Albany]. Retrieved September 2006, from http://mumford.albany.edu/census/NewComersReport/NewComer 01.htm.

Magestro P. V., & Stanford-Blair, N. (2000). A tool for meaningful staff development. *Educational Leadership, 57*(8), 34–35.

Terehoff, I. (2002). Elements of adult learning in teacher professional development. *NASSP Bulletin, 86*, 65–77.

U.S. Department of Health and Human Services (1997). *The program manager's guide to evaluation.* U.S. Government Printing Office.

White-Clark, R. (2005). Training teachers to succeed in a multicultural classroom. *The Education Digest, 70*(8), 23–26.

Zhou, M. (2003). Urban education: Challenges in educating culturally diverse children. *Teacher College Record, 105*(2), 208–225.

CHAPTER 22

Valuing Narrative Authority, Collaboration, and Diversity in Revitalizing a Teacher Education Program

Margaret Olson
St. Francis Xavier University, Canada

> Margaret Olson, Ph.D., is associate professor of education in the School of Education at St. Francis Xavier University in Nova Scotia, Canada. She uses narrative inquiry to better understand the process of learning to teach, and has published several chapters in books and articles in journals including *Curriculum Inquiry, Teaching and Teacher Education*, and *The Canadian Journal of Education*.

ABSTRACT

> This chapter examines the renaissance of a particular teacher education program in Canada through the lens of the author's conceptualization of narrative authority. The chapter begins with a historical overview of the demise and rebirth of the program, describes some of the program's main features, then focuses on one particular course and discusses factors that enable valuing narrative authority, collaboration, and multiple dimensions of diversity in a revitalized and revitalizing teacher education program.

Carse (1986) tells us that "explanation sets the need for further inquiry aside; narrative invites us to rethink what we thought we knew" (p. 125). In this chapter I explore how valuing the narrative authority of individuals has enabled me and others with whom I work to continually revitalize our teacher education program by rethinking what we think we know through collaboration and the valuing of multiple dimensions of diversity. Just over a decade ago I developed a conceptualization of narrative authority which I (Olson, 1995, p. 123) described in the following way:

> Because the narrative version of knowledge construction is transactional, authority comes from experience and is integral as each person both shapes his or her own knowledge and is shaped by the knowledge of others. Knowledge is personally and socially constructed and reconstructed in situations as people share their ideas and stories with others. Since everyone is a knower who deserves to be heard, all voices become authoritative sources. In this version, individuals' narrative authority forms, is informed, and reforms through the continuous and interactive nature of experience. Thus, a person's narrative authority grows through experience where "the principle of continuity of experience means that every experience both takes up something from those which have gone before and modifies in some way the quality of those which come after." (Dewey, 1938, p. 35)

I also outlined what I imagined a teacher education program that valued narrative authority might look like. A brief excerpt from that description follows:

> When we place the narrative authority of the individuals involved at the center of our teacher education curriculum, we begin to provide opportunities to explore not only what we know, but how we know, how we come to know, and why we choose to know in particular ways. We begin to experience ourselves as dynamic learners and as such live rather than only tell a story of lifelong learning. . . . When it is not assumed there is one correct answer or one right way, questions lead to understanding as students and teachers become researchers of their own narrative authority. (Olson, 1995, p. 131)

This particular article received a publication award from the American Association of Colleges of Teacher Education (AATCE) as a piece of scholarship that had the potential to shape the field of teacher education in new ways. However, there appeared to me to be no earth shattering repercussions in the aftermath of the award. Telling a new story and living one are two very different things. Simple terms like "application of knowledge," "implementation," or "dissemination" (Craig, 2006) become incredibly complex in "multistoried" (Olson, 2000a) educational contexts. At that point in my career, I could imagine what a teacher education program that valued the narrative authority of individuals might entail, but I had no experience living such a program. My experiences of teacher preparation had, for the most part, been ones where the transmission of knowledge was valued rather than individual's narrative authority and "when a transmission model remains at the heart of a program, change is ornamental rather than fundamental" (Russell, McPherson, & Martin, 2001, p. 50).

Shortly after writing that article and receiving that award, I began teaching in the university where I have spent the past decade. In this chapter I describe a renaissance, or rebirth, of that teacher education program in which I have been fortunate enough to teach and describe how I, in collaboration with others, have continued to work toward finding ways to live a teacher education program that values many of the things described in my earlier article.

I begin with a historical overview of the demise and rebirth of the program, narrow my view to describe some of the program features, then focus in on one particular course and discuss factors I think enable valuing narrative authority, collaboration, and multiple dimensions of diversity in a revitalized and revitalizing teacher education program.

Historical Overview

In the early 1990s, a review of all nine teacher education programs in Nova Scotia was conducted as part of a governmental "rationalization" project with the purpose of lessening the number of separate programs within the small province, determining which of these should remain open, and lengthening initial teacher preparation programs to two years rather than one. The program at our institution, assessed as out-of-date and too disconnected from the professional field, was one of six recommended for closure. Our university administrators fought hard to justify the need for a teacher education program in our particular area of the province and were eventually given permission to develop a revised program that, if approved in principle, would be implemented on a trial basis. This approval was achieved and, in the fall of 1995, the first year of the newly revised two-year program was brought to life by seven faculty members, four of whom were newly hired. In the summer of 1996, nine more new faculty members were hired; seven to double the original faculty complement in order to serve the doubling of students through the addition of a second year and two to replace faculty who left.

Thus, when I joined the program in 1996 the faculty consisted of 14 members; nine new, four who had been hired the year before, and one who had been hired just before the assessment review threatened closure and was part of the team involved in creating the new program on paper. We were literally in a position to "bring life to the field" (Clandinin & Connelly, 1998, p. 149) in this particular context.

We comprised a diverse group of teacher educators, from those who had worked for many years in other Canadian teacher education institutions to those beginning careers in university settings. We brought a diversity of research interests and methodologies although we had more of a qualitative bent than a quantitative one. We all had experience working in public school systems in a variety of roles and a variety of locations including Canadian urban, rural, First Nations, and Inuit communities as well as schools in Britain, the United States, and Asia. Our diverse narrative authority provided a wealth of experiential knowledge that we were able to draw on to figure out how best to live this new program.

As the 14 of us sat around a table at our first department meeting, questions of how things were normally done here arose. As one of the faculty members hired the year before said, "We have no history," I thought, "But we do. There has been a teacher education program here for decades that local teachers have been familiar with and yet that is not who we are or what this new program is." One of our primary mandates and goals was to develop meaningful links with the professional field. Knowledge about this new program would need to be not only constructed by us but reconstructed by practicing teachers who would be working with preservice teachers in their classrooms during the field experience component of the program. However, while immensely challenging, not having an embedded collective story of "how we do things here" meant that we were free (and bound) to make this new program a success. Its eventual approval (and therefore our continued employment) depended on it. Being in this challenging situation led us to depend and rely on each other in ways that might not have been possible in a more settled, stable context. Christiansen, Goulet, Krentz, and Maeers (1997) echo my understanding of part of what was occurring:

> The context was rich in situations requiring immediate attention. At those times, decisions needed to be made by all members of our group. Some of these decisions were stressful and involved sensitive communication. In collaboration, each individual's work and ideas need to be valued by others. (p. 284)

This culture of figuring things out together has persisted. We are often misunderstood by others who live more hierarchical relationships. We were brought up short a few years ago by new faculty members who expected to have a mentor when we expected everyone to "jump right in" like we had needed to do, easily forgetting our initial query of "how are things done here?" We suddenly realized that there was no way for new faculty to know the story of collaboration we had learned to live together in those first few years unless we made it explicit.

Because our rural location makes it challenging for spouses and partners of faculty members to gain employment, several professors have moved on to larger urban centers. While their diverse expertise are missed, faculty renewal has been an ongoing benefit to our program as each new person brings a fresh perspective that enables us to continually look again at what we are doing and why. Over the years we have gained a wealth of knowledge from seconded and retired school personnel, graduate students, and new tenure track faculty from around the globe including China, Kenya, and Zimbabwe. Each new member brings valuable suggestions that help strengthen our courses and our program as we reconstruct what we know about ourselves and each other. As Clandinin and Connelly (1995) explain:

> The horizons of our knowing shift and change as we awaken to new ways of "seeing" our world, to different ways of seeing ourselves in relation to each other and to the world. We begin to retell our stories with new insights, in new ways. (p. 2)

This collaborative structure of valuing the diverse narrative authority of others has grown over the years to include school board personnel, teachers, teachers union members, students—both undergraduate and graduate, and so on.

Program Features

Because our campus is situated in a small town more than two hours from a larger urban center, it was not possible for all two hundred preservice teachers to do their field experience locally. Therefore, the program was designed to alternate between courses on campus and field experience placements in approximately 70 schools around the province. The two-year program, as written, consisted of four courses on campus and a five- or six-week field experience component in each of the two four-month terms each year. When the program began, students spent four weeks on campus, two weeks in the field, five weeks back on campus, and another three weeks in the field each term. What we faculty thought was a way to help them further develop their narrative authority of good teaching by integrating theory and practice only led to confusion and frustration for most. The technical rational story they and many co-operating teachers implicitly knew of learning enough theory and then implementing it in practice competed with this narrative version of learning through experience. What we thought would lead to integration and reflective praxis instead led to fragmentation of both coursework and field experience.

Through feedback from students and cooperating teachers we decided to "defragment" the program by having students complete nine-week courses on-campus followed by five- or six-week field experiences. This shift provided a better opportunity for students to weave paradigmatic and narrative understandings of teaching into their narrative authority while acknowledging the dominant story in the area. Because all faculty members normally teach on-campus courses and supervise field experience, we are in a position to see first hand the kinds of connections or contradictions students are experiencing. Sharing these with each other enables us to continually make educative adjustments for ourselves and our students. We also shifted our "Reading Week" break to the public schools' Spring Break which brought the rhythm of our program more in line with the field while still fitting into the university calendar's beginning and end of term dates.

The four on-campus courses each term consisted (and still consist) of a core foundations course for elementary and secondary students combined, two curriculum and instruction courses determined by students' teaching focus, (year one students take either elementary or secondary Principles and Practices as a foundational curriculum and instruction course), and an elective course. Thus, the program reflects a commitment to common core foundations courses, specialized curriculum and instruction core courses, and individual choices through electives, which balances program coherence with individual diversity. This combination builds a sense of community through common discourse in the foundation courses that is infused with individual differences of other courses and personal experiences and sets the foundation for future interdisciplinary communication and collaboration rather than compartmentalized isolation. Four threads were identified as grounding the program: a valuing of experience, a commitment to diversity and equity, a focus on professionalism, and recognition of the importance of technology.

This program framework and a faculty that values personal experience as well as diverse expertise has provided an educative context in which narrative authority, collaboration, and the valuing of multiple dimensions of diversity can flourish.

Core Foundations Courses

The four core foundation courses consist of a Sociology course in term one of year one discussed in more detail later, an Inclusion course in term two of year one, a second Inclusion course in term one of year two, and a Contemporary Issues course in the final term. These courses continually evolve based on input from students, practicing teachers, faculty, and shifts in the field of education. For example, the present Inclusion courses have shifted from courses on Exceptional Children and Students with Special Needs to reflect changes in the field. The present Contemporary Issues course evolved out of students' discontent with what they perceived as the irrelevance of the original History and Philosophy course. After several iterations in attempts to make the course content relevant for students, history and philosophy are now more successfully accessed through students' concerns with contemporary issues. The professional issues component of this course is now taught in collaboration with the provincial teachers' union. This year in the Sociology course, based on comments from former students who are now practicing teachers, we have helped students create individual "tool kits"—folders in which they can keep a collection of what they consider to be good teaching practices. However, these are presented through an inquiry mode rather than an apprenticeship one.

The instruction of these courses has also evolved from one or two faculty teaching the three or four sections of 100 students enrolled in the courses to teams of three or four faculty collaborating in the planning and teaching of each course. Thus, while each faculty member has a class list of approximately 25–35 students, because all sections of any one foundations course are now scheduled at the same time, faculty can create flexible groupings for a variety of purposes including team teaching, shared videos, guest speakers, and field trips.

The Sociology Course

I now hone in on the Sociology course I have taught collaboratively with other faculty over the past 10 years to provide more specific examples of how we continue to revitalize our teacher education program and ourselves through valuing the narrative authority of the individuals involved. Valuing narrative authority both enables and requires the valuing of collaboration, and multiple dimensions of diversity. While team members shift over the years, each one brings new ways to revitalize the course based on their unique narrative authority. I begin this section with an overview of the course and then describe two activities that have developed over time through a brief look at the cultural capital auction and a more in-depth look at learning centers focused on poverty.

All first year Bachelor of Education students enroll in Sociology of Education in their first term before their first field experience. Elementary and secondary streams from all program strands are combined together into four heterogeneous sections of this course. Our students, mostly in their mid-20s with an additional 10% returning to school after working or raising families, are predominantly Caucasian (usually of Scottish, English, Irish, or Acadian ethnicity) with a small number of Mi'kmaq First Nations students (5%–10%) and a smaller number of Blacks (under 2%). We deliberately "balance" the classes to ensure that they each have similar proportions of males (20%–30%) and females (70%–80%), elementary (35%) and secondary students (65%), as well as a balance of ages, geographic origin, and "teachables," Math, English, French, Social Studies, Science, and Physical Education being our main curriculum areas. Students are placed in triadic base groups to facilitate the sharing of individuals' diverse narrative authority through a variety of activities (see Craig & Olson, 2002, for a more detailed account). These triads stay together for the nine-week course but also move into a variety of other groupings such as double base groups, jig-saw groups, whole group talking circles, and others. Five major understandings shape this course. Briefly stated they are:

- That inequality exists in society and schools and that the notion of meritocracy is a myth;
- Teachers need to examine the attitudes, values, beliefs, and knowledge they bring into the classroom;
- Teachers/schools can maintain or challenge inequality by examining how, what, and why they teach;
- Teachers need to consider the sociopolitical context in which schools are located;
- Schools can create and be sites of social justice.

Like Clandinin and Connelly (1988), we believe "the more we understand ourselves and can articulate reasons why we are what we are, do what we do, and are headed where we have chosen, the more meaningful our curriculum will be" (p. 11). Therefore, through a variety of readings, class activities, and assignments, students are encouraged to examine three main questions:

1. Who am I as a person and a learner? What are my personal experiences of schooling and how might they be a reflection of privilege and/or disadvantage?
2. What is the sociopolitical context of schooling? Who is advantaged/disadvantaged in schools as they are traditionally set up? Whose interests are served in public schools?
3. What kind of educator do I hope to be and what do I imagine my practice will be as I begin my journey into teaching? What tools do I have that I can use in my classroom? What do I need to think about in terms of teacher knowledge, skills, and attitudes? From whose perspective will I view schooling? As a teacher, what degree of responsibility will I assume for the success of *all* learners in my care? What are practices that are truly educative?

As we continue to revise the activities and the order of them in the course we continue to be reminded by our students, like Santoro and Allard (2005), that "working from the personal to the more general appeared to help these student-teachers gain some insight into the centrality of class and ethnicity within education" (p. 872). For example, while diversity based on race, gender, and socioeconomic class form three key components in this course, we have learned that if we start with race, students often see diversity in terms of skin color alone. They have been taught to see themselves as a generalized homogeneous group.

We now begin by having students look at multiple dimensions of diversity within themselves including gender, ethnicity, language, race, family structure, socio-economic class, geographical origin, religion, abilities, interests, learning styles, multiple intelligences, and so on. Once they understand the multiple dimensions of diversity within themselves and each other, they are less likely to stereotype (Randall, 1995) others and are more open to seeing the complexity of multiple dimensions of diversity within themselves, others, and their future students.

NARRATIVE INQUIRY AS A MODE OF KNOWING

Sfard and Prusak (2005) point out "Lengthy deliberations led us to the decision to *equate identities with stories about persons*. No, no mistake here: We did not say that identities were *finding their expression* in stories—we said they *were* stories" (p. 14). Students entering our program for the most part experience a huge epistemological shift from being expected to be receivers of knowledge (Belenky, Clinchy, Goldberger, & Tarule, 1986) during their undergraduate degrees to being expected to examine the narrative knowledge, the stories, they have constructed and begin to experience a variety of ways to examine and reinterpret these stories—to rethink what they thought they knew.

While the structure of the course and the collaborative nature of the milieu provide fertile ground for the shaping and examination of individuals' narrative authority, having the experience is only the first step and living or telling the story is not yet enough for learning to occur.

> Careful examination and exploration of stories is the essence of narrative enquiry. People often focus on the word *narrative* but skip lightly over the word *enquiry*. Yet it is the enquiry into the stories that creates the educative experience as individuals find new and more expansive ways to interpret their own and others' experience. Thus, narrative enquiry continually opens up new story lines to pursue and new issues to address. (Olson, 2000b, p. 350)

Shields (2005) describes narrative inquiry as a method that "can provide a theoretical and practical framework for (re)interpreting our lived experience" (p. 179). We use a research framework based in Dewey's (1938) epistemology and developed by Clandinin and Connelly (2000) which they describe as a "three-dimensional narrative inquiry space" (p. 49) that "allows our [and our students'] inquiries to travel—inward, outward, backward, forward, and situated within place" (p. 49). Over the nine weeks of the course we create activities in which students, situated in university classrooms, begin to explore their narrative authority by looking inwardly at their own experiences and beliefs about school, outwardly to the experiences and beliefs of others including peers, faculty, readings, guest speakers, videos, and so on, backward to their own experience as students, and forward to their imagined place and practices as teachers. We also agree that traditionally in teacher education programs:

> What is missing is an understanding of knowledge, not so much as something given to people, but as something narratively embodied in how a person stands in the world. Knowledge as attribute can be given; knowledge as narrative cannot. The latter needs to be experienced in context. (Clandinin & Connelly, 1998, p. 157)

The following Principles of Learning, articulated in the Public Schools Programs (Nova Scotia Department of Education, 2003–2004) document of our province, provide a piece of knowledge as attribute that our students are expected to know and implement.

- Learning is a process of actively constructing knowledge;
- Students construct knowledge by making it meaningful in terms of their prior knowledge and experience;
- Learning is enhanced when it takes place in a social and collaborative environment;
- Students need to continue to view learning as an integrated whole;
- Learners must see themselves as capable and successful;
- Learners have different ways of knowing and representing knowledge;
- Reflection is an integral part of learning.

Within the Sociology course we not only continually refer to these in a manner of knowledge as attribute, but try to help students incorporate them into their narrative authority of educative situations. Over the years we have collaboratively developed and revised many activities that enable students to inquire into and challenge taken-for-granted assumptions embedded in their narrative authority about schooling and their place as teachers. Readings, children's literature, individual and collaborative activities, and associated journal writing "enable students to surface and examine unchallenged assumptions embedded in their narrative knowledge about equity and diversity" (Craig & Olson, 2002, p. 188). I now center on two specific examples of activities we have created to enable students to inquire into their narrative experiences and make their narrative authority explicit.

THE CULTURAL CAPITAL AUCTION

One concept we address is that of cultural capital in conjunction with discussions of power and privilege. Our students also read and discuss Peggy MacIntosh's (1990) classic "White Privilege" article at this time. We found that often students' narrative authority was blindly embedded in a position of white middle class privilege seeing others with different kinds of cultural capital as deficient rather than different. This would surface in verbal or written comments about others having less or not enough cultural capital and in suggestions of how as teachers they could help "them" become more like "us." In order to try a different approach to expand their narrative authority, I began to use a simple example of economic capital. I described how our Canadian currency (coins and bills) was accepted anywhere in Canada but, no matter how much of it a person had, the moment they crossed the border into the United States (or any other foreign country), that economic capital was worthless until converted into that particular country's currency (This example does not take into account things like credit cards which seem to work anywhere!). This helped many students develop a better understanding of the cultural capital of others as different rather than deficient. When I shared this in a weekly team planning meeting, other faculty members decided to pick up on the example. The next year, one of my colleagues came back with a cultural capital auction activity to extend the example. This is how she described it in a handout she gave students to put in their "tool kit."

> **Cultural Capital Auction**
> Find as many currencies as you can (Canadian Tire Money, Co-op money, coupons, food [corn, meat, rice], Canadian coins, Euros, monopoly money, and so on). Set the chairs in a circle. Pass out randomly some currency to each person in the group. Give each person a kind of currency—varying amounts. Tell the class you are going to have an auction and find something to auction that will be considered "valuable or interesting" to the class. Tell people that they can act alone or with others—they might consider strategic alliances. Get ready to proceed—ask people to count their money, tell them to use hand signals. Make it as real as possible.
>
> Just before the auction starts tell the group that you forgot to mention that you will only be accepting one kind of currency (you can decide what you want that to be). Continue with the auction. People will be disgruntled, annoyed, frustrated, give up, be happy. Proceed and auction off the item—in spite of the fact that only a very few select individuals or groups can participate.
>
> Debrief the activity using a talking circle. The first time round ask

> people how they felt before, during and after the auction. Ask them to focus on how it "felt" to be in or out! You can chart comments like "it's not fair," "I thought I was going to be in because I had a lot of Canadian coins and then I found it was useless." Be sure to have the person who won the auction talk about what it felt like to have unearned privilege . . .
>
> The second time round connect this to school and how all children come with different currencies which are valued in their home, community. Schools however have historically only recognized a narrow range—Eurocentric, male, straight, English speaking [standard English, not dialects] . . .

My colleague had moved what I was doing from knowledge as acquisition to knowledge as narratively experienced. Students do become confused and then incensed. Many want to drop out of the activity. However, it is in the inquiry about the experience that students are able to articulate shifts in their narrative authority. For example, one student in my class said,

> I was furious. I had to use only what you gave me and when it did not count, I had no power to change it. It made me think how powerless children can be in schools when they have inherited valued cultural capital from their parents that a teacher will not or cannot recognize and they can do nothing to change it.

As Lynn and Smith-Maddox (2007) point out, "Inquiry is a guided experience for preservice teachers to challenge existing beliefs, assumptions, and understandings about teaching and learning while valuing their experiences, knowledge, and voice" (p. 96).

LEARNING CENTERS ON POVERTY

A few years ago, when students were learning in other courses about advantages of using learning centers to meet their students' diverse learning strengths and needs, we began to notice, based on students' and faculty's comments, that secondary students seemed to think learning centers were for "young children" and could not be used for "serious" teaching. There also appeared to be a perception that while learning centers looked like "fun" they were far removed from essential curricular outcomes and there would be no time for such "frills" in the "real" world. We decided to create a variety of learning centers in the Sociology course around the topic of poverty in relation to the theme of socioeconomic class.

Using the theme of poverty as the subject matter, we wanted students to see, through experiencing learning centers, that learning centers: (1) can be easy to prepare and organize, (2) can be used to examine difficult, complex, and challenging topics, (3) can meet provincially determined curriculum outcomes, (4) can facilitate the Principles of Learning, (5) can provide for learning through Multiple Intelligences, and (6) can address visual, auditory, and kinesthetic learning modalities.

We began with 12 learning centers which have now grown to nearly 20, some having different variations. Students have the opportunity to do these centers in their own classroom as well as in the classrooms of the three other sections. All centers have information about poverty provided in a variety of forms including video documentary, audiocassette, magazines, websites, research articles, cartoons, statistical data, and so on. During four hours spread over two classes, students have the opportunity to participate in three or four learning centers each class by choosing from ones that include: magnetic poetry on youth and gambling, write/read/respond to the gender of poverty article, critical thinking sentence strip, chart points on community/school approaches to poverty, video documentary, *Zoned for Slavery*, painting center depicting gap between rich and poor, food bank debate center, computer search for websites on poverty, graphing data on poverty, and play dough to depict equity. We have now added a Design Your Own center in which students can describe a center they would like to see incorporated.

After participating in the learning centers, students are asked to comment on the following questions:

- Which centers did you find the most engaging? Why?
- What Principles of Learning did you experience at the centers?
- What essential graduation learnings did you experience at the centers?
- What learning modalities did the centers enable you to use?
- What Multiple Intelligences did the centers enable you to use?
- What did you learn about yourself as a learner?
- What did you learn about poverty?
- How might you use centers in your classroom to provide for diverse learners?

These prompts provide students with some direction for burrowing into their experience in educative (Dewey, 1938) ways. The following excerpts from students' responses offer a glimpse of how they were making sense of their experiences by looking inward, outward, backward, and forward to examine what they now felt they knew about themselves, possible others, the sociopolitical context, and their imagined future as teachers. The first excerpt shows all these dimensions; the others show various combinations or a clear focus on one. It is interesting to see the epistemological shift these students make in such a short time from the detached writing they were expected to do before entering our program to the narrative mode where they are encouraged to put themselves at the center.

> Although there were many centers set up from which to choose, I find it very interesting that I chose the centers that best suited my preferred mode of learning, which is visual. I always, to some degree, knew that I was most comfortable writing, reading, and drawing to make sense of the world. However, it was not until I really began to think about the activities I chose to participate in during the learning centers workshop that I realized I have a distinct preference for certain modes of learning and that throughout my learning process I have actually consciously chosen to refrain from other types, such as logical/mathematical and bodily kinesthetic when possible. I have also come to the realization that I am very much an interpersonal-type learner. I like having the opinions of others and I generally feel more comfortable in performing academically or otherwise by having support and feedback from others. For instance, while painting the gap between the rich and the poor and while designing the advertisement, I frequently consulted with my peers as to what their opinion was regarding the issue of poverty and how it affects their thinking. I find this quite interesting because it gives me some explanation as to why I tend to get very anxious and nervous while writing tests—it is the isolation and the individual expectations that I find bothersome. In summation, I feel that the centers really gave me the opportunity to more fully understand my own modes of learning and subsequently made me more understanding and sensitive to the fact that other people, as well, have their own personal modes and ways of learning/knowing. I believe that this is a very important quality to have in terms of my role as a teacher because I need to be flexible in addressing the learning modalities of all my students, while being careful not to focus solely on my own modality strength.

The following three responses discuss which centers these students found most engaging and why.

> As a student who just finished a chemistry major and math minor, I was immediately drawn to the graphing station. Once there, I found the task too easy and it soon became boring and disengaging. This station appealed to my learning style but I clearly needed more of a challenge. I have never really enjoyed poetry, as the teachers were obsessed with analyzing what poets had secretly written, and I was not expecting to enjoy [the magnetic poetry] station. However, sorting through the magnetic pieces, looking for key words was a great way to start the poetry writing process. This center was not like sitting down with a blank paper and pen and trying to figure out what word to use; the words were provided and it was up to me to organize them in a rational and logical fashion. For me, this center took the

> most thought and was the most thought provoking. Although the poem will never be ranked high in literary circles, writing it was an accomplishment for me. Perhaps the challenge and sense of accomplishment was the reason I found this center the most engaging.

The magnetic poetry center always creates a lot of discussion. Students seem to either love it or hate it. Those like the above student are grateful to have the words as a scaffold to assist them in an area in which they do not feel confident. Others become extremely frustrated when they have a poem in their heads and cannot find the magnetic words to express it. This provides a wonderful opportunity for pointing out yet again the diverse ways in which we learn. I usually ask, "So what would it be like if this was the main activity you did every day in school?" Students are quick to see how essential it is to have diversity in the activities and assignments they create for their students if they want to provide for student engagement and success.

> The center that engaged me the most was the center on Food Banks. I was always the type of person who felt that by giving to the food bank, I was helping the poor with the poverty issue. I saw parents from the day care center I worked at utilize this service, and it made me feel good to know they were able to feed their children. I hadn't really thought very long about the whole concept of food banks or considered that it only provides a "band-aid" for the real issue. I haven't stopped analyzing this in my mind since I completed the center.

The food bank center leads students to rethink what they thought they knew about ways to help those who live in poverty. Students develop a much more critical understanding and learn to see past individual acts of kindness (or racism) to larger systemic issues that perpetuate poverty.

> The centers I participated in involved me making connections between the life I live and what is going on outside of my comfort zone. The video involved the named brand clothing I wear and where it all comes from. I wear it everyday yet had no idea what was going on behind the scenes.

The *Zoned for Slavery* video also always leaves a powerful impression that students link to themselves personally. Students often become enraged that they did not know about this sooner and often borrow the video to show to their students during field experience. The question of engagement is essential for students to achieve and articulate shifts in their own narrative authority as new experiential knowledge leads to reforms in their ways of thinking—what Dewey (1938) would call educative experience.

The following was a response to the question "What did you learn about yourself as a learner?"

> I very much enjoyed the learning centers because they let me express my views on poverty in a variety of different ways. I learned that I am more engaged in tasks when they do not take a long time. I also enjoyed being able to move around the classrooms. It showed me that I am more of a kinesthetic learner than I thought. I was naturally drawn towards the Equity learning center where we used play-dough. I like to work with my hands, which is a common trait of kinesthetic learners. I tended to avoid centers where there were long articles to read. I enjoy writing but reading must be short to keep my attention. I also learned that I am not very intrapersonal. I consider myself to be an independent person, but I am also very social. The learning centers were a good balance because I was able to independently voice my own opinions about poverty but I was also able to converse with my classmates.

This question, like the others, leads students to an experience of reflexive praxis where they think carefully about what they have experienced. As students discuss their responses to these questions with each other, their understanding of the diverse complexity of individuals as learners is enhanced. Thus, they both learn more about themselves and about each other. Each experience is intended to enhance this understanding and appreciation of the immense diversity percolating below the surface of what might at first glance appear to be a homogeneous group. The final two excerpts are responses to how they might use learning centers in their own future classrooms.

> I believe that learning centers are valuable tools for accommodating a classroom population of diverse learners. By using learning centers that provide children with the opportunity for hands-on, active learning, I believe that they will be more prone to learn and understand new material than they would be if you were to continuously drill and indoctrinate. Learning centers provide children with the opportunity to learn through a variety of approaches and enables students to see different viewpoints which further challenges them to think critically about their own position as well as the thoughts and feelings of others. Learning centers also provide enough variety for all students to experience success because they are set up to accommodate multiple intelligences and different learning modalities.

And . . .

> In my math classes, learning centers will be useful in introducing or finishing a unit. They can also be used to relate "real world" topics to math. Students cannot usually see math outside of the classroom and I think learning centers would make it more concrete for them.

> Kinesthetic learners often have trouble with math because classes are usually very instructional and there is little or no movement. Learning centers would provide all types of learners with concrete examples so that they could construct knowledge.

It is interesting to note that as students imagine a future situation, the contextual narrative detail that was present in the previous examples gives way to more abstract musings of what might be. This is one reason it is important to provide students with opportunities to revisit their experiences after each field experience. This revisiting of their stories also gives us as faculty members another opportunity to reassess and restory the ways in which we teach.

Revitalization as Educative Evolution

I believe we, as individuals and as a teacher education program, are in a process of educative evolution rather than revolution. Reform is not now something that is presented to us from outside, as a version of best practice from other places that everyone should conform to or an ultimatum preceding impending closure as was the impetus for change in the past. Rather, our best practice is continuously informed, inspired, and reformed through valuing the evolving narrative authority of each individual. This narrative authority is informed by diverse sources including theoretical sources as well as narrative ones. Program review and revitalization is an ongoing part of our practice rather than only determined by outside agencies' timelines. This process of ongoing assessment and renewal can only occur in a collaborative context that values the multiple dimensions of diversity that individuals bring and share with each other. It is the response to diversity, shared in collaboration that continues to intrigue, inspire, and challenge new ways of seeing and thinking to evolve. This is not an easy road nor is it often comfortable. However, it is a freeing and challenging one that has become a vital component of what we do.

References

Belenky, M., Clinchy, B., Goldberger, N., & Tarule, J. (1986). *Women's ways of knowing: The development of self, voice, and mind.* New York: Basic Books.

Carse, J. (1986). *Finite and infinite games: A vision of life as play and possibility.* New York: Ballantine Books.

Christiansen, H., Goulet, L., Krentz, C., & Maeers, M. (1997). *Recreating relationships: Collaboration and educational reform.* New York: SUNY Press.

Clandinin, D. J., & Connelly, F. M. (1995). *Teachers' professional knowledge landscapes.* New York: Teachers College Press.

Clandinin, D. J., & Connelly, F. M. (1998). Stories to live by: Narrative understandings of school reform. *Curriculum Inquiry, 28*(20), 149–164.

Clandinin, D. J., & Connelly, F. M. (2000). *Narrative inquiry: Experience and story in qualitative research.* San Francisco: Jossey-Bass.

Connelly, F. M., & Clandinin, D. J. (1988). *Teachers as curriculum planners: Narratives of experience.* New York: Teachers College Press.

Craig, C. (2006). Why is dissemination so difficult? The nature of teacher knowledge and the spread of curriculum reform. *American Educational Research Journal, 43*(2), 257–293.

Craig, C., & Olson, M. (2002). The development of teachers' narrative authority in knowledge communities: A narrative approach to teacher learning. In N. Lyons & V. K. LaBoskey (Eds.), *Narrative inquiry in practice: Advancing the knowledge of teaching* (pp. 115–132). New York: Teachers College Press.

Dewey, J. (1938). *Experience and education.* London: Macmillan.

Lynn, M., & Smith-Maddox, R. (2007). Preservice teacher inquiry: Creating a space to dialogue about becoming a social justice educator. *Teaching and Teacher Education, 23,* 94–105.

Nova Scotia Department of Education (2003–2004). *Public School Programs.* Nova Scotia Department of Education.

Olson, M. (1995). Conceptualizing narrative authority: Implications for teacher education. *Teaching and Teacher Education, 11*(2), 119–135.

Olson, M. (2000a). Curriculum as a multistoried process. *Canadian Journal of Education, 25*(3), 169–187.

Olson, M. (2000b). Where the story leads: A response to Cheryl Craig. *Canadian Journal of Education, 25*(4), 349–352.

Randall, W. L. (1995). *The stories we are: An essay on self-creation.* Toronto: University of Toronto Press.

Russell, T., McPherson, S., & Martin, A. (2001). Coherence and collaboration in teacher education reform. *Canadian Journal of Education, 26*(1), 37–55.

Santoro, N., & Allard, A. (2005). (Re)Examining identities: Working with diversity in the preservice teaching experience. *Teaching and Teacher Education, 21,* 863–873.

Sfard, A., & Prusak, A. (2005). Telling identities: In search of an analytic tool for investigating learning as a culturally shaped activity. *Educational Researcher, 34*(4), 14–22.

Shields, C. (2005). Using narrative inquiry to inform and guide our (re)interpretations of lived experience. *McGill Journal of Education, 40,* 179–188.

Additional Sources

Garen, M., & Carlton, M. (Producers), & National Labor Committee (Director). (1995). *Zoned for slavery: The child behind the label* [Motion picture]. (Available from Resource Center of the Americas.org, www.americas.org/bookstore.)

MacIntosh, P. (1990). White privilege: Unpacking the invisible knapsack. *Independent School, 49*(2), 31–35.

Summary and Implications

Cheryl J. Craig

Louise F. Deretchin

Hebert, Burchan, and Gordon began Division 5 by introducing some of the harsh realities that students live, some of which resonate with those described in Voltz et al.'s Division 1 chapter. Given those realities, Burchan and Gordon, who are teachers and graduate students, teamed up with Hebert, a professor, to conduct action research projects that examined family involvement and the influence of teacher interaction on self-esteem.

Gordon presented a preschool challenge having to do with parent involvement and the early years of student achievement whereas Burchan addressed a middle school case and documented issues relating to a student's self-esteem. Each educator embarked on person-centered inquiries where they focused on how actions and interactions with students influenced their academic growth and esteem.

In the end result, Hebert, Burchan, and Gordon suggested that classroom teachers redirect their energies from a focus on core content knowledge to building positive relationships and promoting self-worth in children. This way learning experiences would involve, in the authors' words, "the head, the heart, and the senses." For Hebert, Burchan, and Gordon, like McBee and Wescott in Chapter 3, caring was a prerequisite for a renaissance in teacher education that significantly affected students.

Helen Freidus's "Small Steps: Moving Toward a Renaissance in Teacher Education" showed, through self-study, how a teacher educator addressed a known disconnect between what students are taught about literacy learning in their preservice education classes and the literacy instruction they witness in real-life classrooms bounded by accountability demands and deeply affected by the literacy wars. In this situation, Freidus and her colleagues, like other teacher educators, wrestled with alternatives and felt very conflicted. The perennial question of "What to do?" inevitably emerged.

In response, Freidus drew on history and geography to resolve the dilemma: the historical fact that Bank Street College is "not interested in perpetuation of any special school of thought" and the geographical proximity of the American Museum of National History to Bank Street College. By forging a partnership and developing shared purpose, Freidus and her collaborators created an activity that enabled the preservice education students to experience a learner-centered literacy practice. More importantly, the preservice education students were not just told about the practice or simply shown what to do. Rather, they actively lived it. This experience had a sustained impact on the students' understanding of the impact of learner-centered literacy practices. But the experience also influenced Freidus, who came to know that a renaissance in teacher education "would look backward to the premises of progressive pedagogy and forward to the integration of specific skills instruction within this pedagogy."

A second renaissance in teacher education also involved a museum and an institution of higher learning in New York City in addition to a public school. Written by McNamee and her ten coauthors, the chapter featured Lehman College's story of working with the Lincoln Center Institute and Public School 304 to improve Lehman's teacher education program, to strengthen Public School 304's program, and to stimulate collaborative research among all parties involved.

Throughout the chapter, a wide variety of exchanges and resources were shared so that aesthetic education could shape the fabric and tenor of the teacher education program as well as the curricular experiences afforded the students at Public School 304. Particularly useful in this chapter were the concrete details of what each partner contributed to the collaboration and how the collaboration gained momentum over time. Also helpful was the outline of the different evaluation protocols used.

To conclude, McNamee et al. discussed how the three-party collaboration addressed the devaluing and removal of the arts from both public school and preservice education classrooms. Concurrently, the collaborators enacted Maxine Greene's vision of aesthetic education as a "special kind of reflectiveness and expressiveness, a reaching out for meanings . . . (Greene, 2001, p. 8)." For this group of educators, the experience represented a renaissance in action, an aesthetic pathway they would recommend to others.

Mistretta's chapter came next. It approached the boilerplate issues of parent-child collaborations, mathematics learning, and teacher preparation in an interrelated way. The inquiry was framed by the following research questions: (1) To what extent do parents collaborate with their children about mathematical learning and does this vary across grade level groups (Pre-K–2, 3–5, 6–8)? (2) What challenges do parents face collaborating with their children about mathematical learning and does this vary across grade level groups (Pre-K–2,

3–5, 6–8)? (3) How effectively does a model mathematics initiative cultivate parent-child collaboration in grades Pre-K through 8?

One of the many findings of Mistretta's research was the extent to which parents felt disconnected from the method in which mathematics is currently taught and how this sense of disconnection increases as students' grade levels and mathematics rigor increases. Another interesting observation was how parents and children discussing mathematics through questioning appeared to improve their relationships with one another as well as the students' academic achievement.

Mistretta concluded her essay with a far-reaching conclusion: teacher education programs have a role to play in teaching preservice teachers about collaboration and how to develop parents' and caretakers' knowledge of mathematics. Such a focus, in Mistretta's view, would do much to inform a renaissance concerning how preservice teacher education could be improved.

While Mistretta's chapter took readers on a journey that pondered mathematics learning and parent-child collaborations, Thomas and Bell's chapter, which appeared next, educated readers concerning what it might take to minimize barriers in teacher diversity professional development. The chapter began with a literature review that established the need for teachers to experience diversity professional development in order to understand what culturally sensitive pedagogy entails. This literature review resonated with the one presented earlier by Voltz et al.

Thomas and Bell's program evaluation addressed the barriers to teacher professional development historically found in the literature. These included the "one time, never to be repeated" workshop syndrome as well as administrative fiats that impose training sessions on teachers, both of which contribute to teacher resistance and lack of change in attitude and actions.

The project Thomas and Bell described depended on teacher leaders to facilitate the change process and to grow faculty support for the change effort. The five-phase project culminated with an Awareness Day seminar attended by 200 teachers in which faculty members from the participating Catholic schools highlighted the progress they had made in creating a diversity inclusive environment in their classrooms and schools.

The participating teachers were then administered a survey by Thomas and Bell. In the first phase of the project, the authors determined that the particular professional development experience helped identify school strengths and needs in a non-judgmental, non-threatening manner. Additionally, the diversity professional development allowed teachers to reflect on their individual cultural diversity and how it shaped perspectives and interactions. Furthermore, the diversity professional development was deemed to be responsive to the needs present in the school contexts where the teachers taught.

In the final analysis, Thomas and Bell emphasized the importance of not approaching teachers as problems but engaging them as equal partners to be respected throughout the multiphased project. Through this approach, culturally responsive pedagogy was modeled and teacher resistance was avoided. This enabled a local educational renaissance around matters of diversity professional development to be achieved.

As readers will recall, the final chapter in Division 5 was authored by Olson. In contrast to Thomas and Bell who defined diversity as racial and cultural diversity, Olson dealt with narrative authority, collaboration, and diversity in her essay, with diversity pertaining to all matters of human difference.

To begin, Olson told of a piece of scholarship she contributed to the literature that received an American Association of Colleges of Teacher Education (AATE) award for its potential to impact the field of education. Unfortunately, the essay did not bring about change in the manner anticipated because, as Olson keenly observed, "telling a new story and living one are two very different things."

However, as her career unfolded, Olson found herself part of a university that had phased out its previous education program and was re-creating a new one. At this time, Olson and her thirteen colleagues were given an opportunity to live a new story of teacher education, although the old story, as Olson aptly informed us, never disappeared because it remained a part of human memory.

Olson next shared with readers many of the decision points and challenges of creating and living a new story of teacher education in the small town where her university is located. One of the changes involved coordinating the school district and university calendars. Another had to do with bringing teachers' association representatives into the university classroom to discuss rights and responsibilities of teachers in the local schools. A further highlight was professors choosing to collaboratively plan and teach courses.

The main focus of Olson's chapter, however, was the Sociology of Education course she has taught in conjunction with her colleagues in which the valuing of narrative authority, the subject of her award-winning essay earlier mentioned, became part of the very fabric of the program offering and lived in the activities and experiences afforded preservice education students. Here, readers learned of how the five underpinnings of the course, all pertaining to social justice, became enacted through the process of narrative inquiry and the enactment of narrative teaching practices. Of particular note were the Cultural Capital Auction and the Learning Centers on Poverty, which were both activities that arose from faculty collaboration and served to stretch preservice students' boundaries of how they narratively conceived of different aspects of human diversity.

Olson concluded her chapter by associating revitalization (or renaissance, for that matter) with educational evolution. She particularly discussed reform as not being imposed from the outside and best practice as not being etched in stone. Rather, both, in Olson's view, are "continuously informed, inspired, and reformed through valuing the evolving narrative authority of the individual."

In summary, then, the six chapters in Division 5—beginning with Hebert, Burchan, and Gordon and ending with Olson—presented different renaissances in teacher education enacted in local settings, frequently involving partnerships and collaborations. Each offered a different purview of how significant changes are taking place in teacher education programs in North America and throughout the world.

Reference

Greene, M. (2001). *Variations on a blue guitar: The Lincoln Center Institute lectures on aesthetic education.* New York: Teachers College Press.

Division 6
LESSONS LEARNED

Overview and Framework

Cheryl J. Craig

Louise F. Deretchin

Imagining a Renaissance in Teacher Education: Teacher Education Yearbook XVI concludes with Division 6, Lessons Learned. In this section, two chapters are featured: one, international; the other, national.

Chapter 23 centers on a chapter co-authored by prominent teacher educators from Australia, The Netherlands, and Canada. Written by John Loughran, Fred Korthagen, and Tom Russell, "Teacher Education that Makes a Difference: Developing Foundational Principles of Practice" presents a set of foundational principles emanating from three teacher education programs in three different countries; indeed, three different continents. The authors assert that these principles are integral to cultivating responsive teacher education programs and initiating a teacher education renaissance.

Chapter 24 is authored by Stefinee Pinnegar and Lynnette Erickson. Appropriately titled "Questioning What We Know About Teacher Education," the authors maintain that all teacher education practices need to be held open to question. When teacher education programs and pedagogy are treated as ongoing objects of inquiry, high quality teacher education is more likely to be achieved. In Pinnegar and Erickson's view, this is the way that stagnation can be avoided and a growth orientation can be embraced.

CHAPTER 23

Teacher Education that Makes a Difference
DEVELOPING FOUNDATIONAL PRINCIPLES OF PRACTICE

John Loughran
Monash University, Australia

Fred Korthagen
Utrecht University & Vrije Universiteit, The Netherlands

Tom Russell
Queen's University, Canada

> John Loughran, Ph.D., is the Foundation Chair in Curriculum & Professional Practice in the Faculty of Education, Monash University, and Associate Dean. His research has spanned both science education and the related fields of professional knowledge, reflective practice, and teacher research. John is the co-editor of *Studying Teacher Education* and his recent books include: *Developing a Pedagogy of Teacher Education: Understanding teaching and learning about teaching* (2006), Routledge; *Understanding and Developing Science Teachers Pedagogical Content Knowledge* (Loughran, Berry, & Mulhall, 2006), Sense Publishers; *The International Handbook of Self-Study of Teaching and Teacher Education Practices* (Loughran, et al., 2004), Kluwer.
>
> Fred Korthagen, Prof.Dr., is a professor of education at the Vrije Universiteit in Amsterdam and at Utrecht University where he serves as chair of the Pedagogy of Teacher Education. He has published many research articles on teachers' professional development, and is the author of the book *Linking Practice and Theory in Teacher Education*. In 2000 and in 2006, he received the Exemplary Research Award from Division K (Teaching and Teacher Education) of the American Educational Research Association.
>
> Tom Russell, Ph.D., is a professor in the Faculty of Education and holds a chair in Teaching and Learning at Queen's University. He teaches preservice physics teachers and supervises the school practicum, and his re-

search focuses on how people learn to teach. He is co-editor of a number of books and of *Studying Teacher Education*, a Routledge journal.

ABSTRACT

Teacher education has long been criticized for having little apparent impact on practice. Despite the fact that the teacher education literature is replete with examples of alternative or restructured programs designed to better align teacher education practices with the anticipated demands and expectations of school teaching, principles of practice seem strangely absent. Principles of practice for teacher education programs must be at the heart of any attempt to construct a meaningful and relevant program that might realistically respond to the expectations, needs, and practices of student teachers. In this chapter, the authors develop a set of foundational principles based on teacher education programs in Australia, Canada, and the Netherlands, in order to initiate a renaissance of teacher education based on fundamental principles to guide the development of responsive teacher education programs that genuinely make a difference.

Claims that traditional teacher preparation programs do not adequately prepare beginning teachers for teaching have long been familiar in the research literature, as are calls for change (Lanier & Little, 1986). Responding productively has been difficult, not least because teacher educators themselves have had little voice in the literature in comparison to university researchers, lawmakers, and policy analysts (Fenstermacher, 1997). Consider how difficult it must be to determine how to respond constructively and coherently to issues as broad and complex as the perceived mismatch between teacher preparation and the reality of schools (Barone, Berliner, Blanchard, Casanova, & McGowan, 1996; Sandlin, Young, & Karge, 1992), the fragmented nature of teacher preparation programs (Bullough & Gitlin, 2001), over-reliance on theory transfer through lectures despite obvious limitations and inadequacies (Ben-Peretz, 1995; Carlson, 1999; Clandinin, 1995), the persistence of teacher education practices that are generally counterproductive to teacher learning (Wideen, Mayer-Smith, & Moon, 1998), and traditionally trained teachers becoming teachers who teach in a traditional manner (Stofflett & Stoddart, 1994).

For many teacher educators, these challenges are very real in their daily work. Recognizing and acknowledging the difficulties is one thing, but responding is quite another; many of the authors noted above hoped to create an agenda for change within the community of teacher educators of which they themselves were members. As the report by Cochran-Smith and Zeichner (2005) makes clear, part of the problem involves the complex methodological issues associated with trying to establish an empirical basis for effective teacher education. We need a serious rethinking of the nature of teaching about teaching that is encapsulated in views about, and approaches to, a pedagogy of teacher education (Korthagen, 2001; Loughran, 2006; Russell & Loughran, 2007).

With the emergence of self-study of teacher education practices (Hamilton, Pinnegar, Russell, Loughran, & LaBoskey, 1998; Kosnick, Beck, Freese, & Samaras, 2006; Loughran, Hamilton, LaBoskey, & Russell, 2004; Samaras, 2006), a productive avenue for such rethinking has become available. Self-study of teacher education practices has allowed teacher educators to begin to demonstrate their individual responses to the dilemmas, issues, and concerns of teacher education by highlighting in detail the complex nature of teaching and learning about teaching that is rarely apparent to those not involved on a day-to-day basis. A growing range of self-study reports illustrate how teacher educators have been working to address these concerns in their own practice, their programs, and their institutions (Loughran, 2005).

The field of self-study represents one positive way of beginning to create more coherent, meaningful, and applicable responses to the vagaries and contradictions of teacher preparation and has led to new ways of teacher educators beginning to share their attempts at developing a pedagogy of teacher education. However, without a strong foundation from which to build a pedagogy of teacher education, the deeper understandings of practice necessary to achieve genuine educational change may still not be fully grasped. To better capture the opportunities created through the research outcomes of self-study and other teacher education research, we propose seven foundational principles that can improve the quality of teacher education practices, programs, and structures.

A Basis for Principles

Teacher education programs are embedded in institutional contexts that are important in shaping not only what happens, but also why and how. In the three institutional contexts through which our understanding of principles has emerged (Monash University in Australia, IVLOS in the Netherlands, and Queen's University in Canada), we conceptualized our teacher education programs as case studies. The three cases from three different continents were interrogated with the question: What central principles are apparent that are intended to respond to the expectations, needs, and practices of teacher educators and student teachers?

As this research question suggests, our attempt to see beyond specific contexts is one way of creating possibilities for generalizing across the three programs in ways that allow our research efforts to speak to one another in meaningful ways. The three programs lend themselves to comparison because each has had an end-on model (post-graduate teacher preparation) for a considerable period of time, originally with the common organizational features of curriculum method subjects, educational foundational subjects, and school teaching practicum.

Each of the programs has been extensively researched (Brouwer & Korthagen, 2005; Hermans, Créton, & Korthagen, 1993; Kessels & Korthagen, 1996; Koetsier & Wubbels, 1995; Koetsier, Wubbels, & Korthagen, 1997; Korthagen, 1985; Korthagen & Kessels, 1999; Korthagen & Russell, 1995; Korthagen, Kessels, Koster, Lagerwerf, & Wubbels, 2001; Loughran, 1996, 1997, 2002; Loughran & Russell, 1997; Northfield & Gunstone, 1983, 1997; Russell, 1995, 2002; Upitis, 2000; Vedder, 1984; Vedder & Bannink, 1987) and our meta-analysis of these research studies combined with our analysis of a variety of program documents generated a strong base from which to extract underlying program features that might lead to principles of practice. Our criteria for constructing a principle were three:

1. On the basis of the materials under study, it was evident that the staff of the teacher education program considered the principle to be fundamental, in the sense that without this principle the program would lose its essential nature.
2. The principle could not be considered as self-evident. The principle should differentiate the approach followed in the program from several others in the world.
3. The principle could be recognized in many practices throughout the entire program.

It is not the intention of this chapter to fully outline the methodology and individual program features and contexts from which the underlying principles were derived (see Korthagen, Loughran, & Russell, 2006). The principles presented here were developed by focusing on paradigmatic examples (Freudenthal, 1978) of good practice. One feature that gave direction to our method was the notion of *naturalistic generalizability* (Stake & Trumbull, 1982), which means that an aim of our study was to support the transfer of our findings to other contexts, such that they might also contribute to *catalytic validity,* i.e., the degree to which the research can lead to transformations of practice (Lather, 1991).

Articulating Principles of Practice for Teacher Education

From our meta-analyses of the three cases we derived seven principles of student teacher learning and program change that we consider fundamental and foundational to teacher education practices. Central to these principles is the importance of creating real opportunities for learning from experience, for student teachers and teacher educators alike. We briefly outline each of the principles below and conclude the chapter with a discussion of several implications of applying such principles in teacher education more generally.

1. Learning about teaching involves continuously conflicting and competing demands. Teacher education is inevitably inadequate (Northfield & Gunstone, 1997) and cannot fully prepare teachers for their entire careers. In accord with views of professional learning, teacher education needs to focus explicitly on encouraging participants to learn through experience in ways that help them build their professional knowledge. In so doing, there is a need to recognize and respond to a range of conflicting and competing demands. Those learning to teach inevitably struggle with the need to be both learners of learning and learners of teaching at the same time. What students experience as learners of teaching can dramatically shape their understanding of practice. Teacher education practices must continually make explicit the dual roles of learning about learning and learning about teaching so that both perspectives are always at the forefront of students' analysis of their experiences.

As Lortie (1975) pointed out, the *apprenticeship of observation* has a lasting impact on students' understanding of practice and certainly maintains a strong influence on students' learning about teaching. This is hardly surprising, for students rarely have access to the pedagogical reasoning of their teachers and what they construct as images of teaching unwittingly carries little about the underlying thinking that shapes the teaching and learning experienced. Hence teaching will appear simple and straightforward rather than driven by a multitude of questions, choices, and decisions that collectively make teaching highly problematic. Because of the competing demands of learning about learning and learning about teaching, the apprenticeship of observation can easily "spill over" into teacher education (as Goodlad [1990] suggested) and mask the complexity of "good practice."

Creating opportunities for student teachers to recognize and respond to the competing demands in their learning to teach is one way of helping them to learn in meaningful ways through experience and to see that the better they manage these competing demands, the more likely they are to develop richer understandings of the complex nature of teaching and learning.

2. Learning about teaching requires a view of knowledge as a subject to be created rather than as a created subject. Teaching as telling has had a lasting influence on both teachers and teacher educators and partly explains the perceived "unhelpfulness" linked to approaches to teaching about teaching in many schools of education (Russell, 1999). The practice of teaching as telling, whether performed intentionally or not, also detracts from and discounts the significance of experience in learning. An outcome of teaching as telling is that theory is imparted to student teachers in an "unquestioned manner," generally ignoring issues about the nature of theory and the way it is developed in teachers.

Like Freudenthal (1978), we see knowledge as a subject to be created by learners themselves which can be facilitated through a process of guided reinvention. This means that theory development as a consequence of student teachers' learning from their own situations has greater individual significance. Also, developing personal knowledge offers a vision for ongoing professional growth and autonomy in practice. One way that this approach to knowledge creation can be encouraged in teacher education is through the one-to-one (Korthagen et al., 2001, p. 73-75) which gives student teachers opportunities to learn on the basis of their own experiences and the concerns they develop through such experiences. They learn not so much by being taught by their teacher educators but by structured reflection on their experiences and discussions with peers. Thus student teachers begin to create their own professional knowledge as their learning through experience is overtly supported and valued, but not made complicated through issues such as maintaining order in the classroom.

3. Learning about teaching requires a shift in focus from the curriculum to the learner. Teacher educators teach teaching. If student teachers are to "see into" teaching in sophisticated ways and to be better informed about the nature of practice, then they need to better understand the dynamics of a teaching situation—what is involved in planning the teaching, doing the teaching, and reflecting on the teaching. One way of doing this is through student teachers experiencing teaching practice being both constructed and deconstructed so that their learning about teaching is purposefully linked to their experiences of learning and teaching (Segall, 2002).

Principle 3 builds on principle 2 and challenges the assumption in teacher education that the university-based components concentrate almost solely on the theoretical underpinnings of teaching while the school practicum is the site in which teaching is practiced. When we teach teaching there is a constant need to "not tell the class" about an issue but to make the issue a part of the teaching episode itself. It is not hard to see how "teaching as telling" can create major problems in terms of mixed messages about teaching and learning that can detract from developing deeper understandings of practice. This issue establishes why it is so important to teach the students, not the curriculum, and how crucial it is to link theory and practice through experience. The learning of student teachers is obviously considerably more meaningful when it is *embedded in their experiences* of learning to teach. Teacher educators need to be actively creating situations where this can occur as a natural part of teacher preparation.

4. Learning about teaching is enhanced through (student) teacher research. Principles 2 and 3 create an impetus for principle 4, which depends on challenging traditional practices and trusting that student teachers can not only learn about practice through their own experiences, but also do so by researching their own practice. Just as teacher research and practitioner inquiry (Cochran-Smith & Lytle, 1990, 2004; Lytle & Cochran-Smith, 1991; Zeichner & Noffke, 2001) have been important in encouraging teachers to learn about, and better value, their knowledge of practice, so they are important in learning about teaching.

By embarking on formalized processes in researching practice, student teachers are better able to grasp issues surrounding the perceived distinctions between theory and practice that so often confront them in their emerging roles as beginning teachers. In one sense, by adopting a student teacher–as–researcher stance, there is the overt expectation that student teachers will actively seek out, and therefore more whole-heartedly explore, problems of practice that are rooted in their needs, their concerns, and their expectations for their own professional learning. By actively researching their own practice, they are more likely to come to "see into" pedagogic situations differently and reframe (Schön, 1983) their practice.

Trusting student teachers to adopt a student teacher–as–researcher stance is one way of giving permission for them to place more faith in the development of the authority of their own experiences (Munby & Russell, 1994), which contrasts starkly with teacher educators or school practicum supervisors telling them what their problems are, how to resolve them, and what their practice should look like. Establishing a student-teacher-as-researcher expectation in teacher education is important for creating a sense of ownership in learning about teaching that goes beyond the technical aspects of practice alone. When student teachers purposefully collect and analyze data from their own experiences, the outcomes are twofold. Firstly, the individual learning for the student-teacher-researcher is often powerful in its own right. Secondly, that which they choose to document and share with their peers is more likely to influence their colleagues' learning because of the added value of identifying with similar issues, concerns, and practices. Being in a similar situation makes a major difference to the nature of the learning that results. Student teachers learning by researching their own practice is a crucial component in learning about teaching and offers an explicit way to counterbalance the tendency in traditional teacher education programs to accentuate the gap between research-based knowledge and practice.

5. Learning about teaching requires an emphasis on those learning to teach working closely with their peers. Research literature draws attention to the importance of collegiality as a crucial factor in shaping teachers' understandings of classroom practice (Hagger, Burn, & McIntyre, 1993). Putnam and Borko (1997) capture the essence of the need for a focus on collegiality.

> Just as students need to learn new ways of reasoning, communicating, and thinking, and to acquire dispositions of inquiry and sense-making through their participation in classroom discourse communities, teachers need to construct their complex new roles and ways of thinking about their teaching practice within the context of supportive learning communities. (p. 1247)

Learning about teaching is enhanced by explicitly collaborative and collegial approaches to "unpacking" teaching and learning. The school practicum is clearly a time when this may be most advantageous, but such an approach need not be limited to schoolteaching experience. One aspect of collaboration that can accentuate learning about practice involves the way that standing back from experience and looking for patterns in accounts of teaching experience can be used as a catalyst for learning from and through experience.

By working closely with their peers, student teachers have direct access to others' perspectives on the process of learning to teach. This matters because almost everywhere else they turn, they see teaching as an individual and isolated process. They rarely see two teachers at work in the same room at the same time, yet they are well aware that learning is enhanced through sharing and collaboration. Hence learning about teaching can create a "clash of identities" as the expectations of individualism and isolation confront the experiences of collaboration and collegiality. Creating serious prospects for learning about teaching to be viewed as "optimal" through collaboration is then a platform from which views of learning about teaching more generally might be challenged to enhance approaches to articulating professional knowledge of practice.

Peer-supported learning (Tigchelaar & Melief, 2000) is a mechanism for student teachers to not only structure their own reflection, but also to help each other reflect. Through the process of learning how to support each other's reflection, student teachers can gain insights into their own practices and into the process of reflection. When student teachers develop their skills of peer-supported learning, benefits can extend to their guidance of their own students in school. This fifth principle shifts the emphasis in learning to teach from the traditional reliance on *vertical* relationships to endorsing and valuing *horizontal* relationships (Galesloot, Koetsier, & Wubbels, 1997).

6. Learning about teaching requires meaningful relationships between schools, universities, and student teachers. Northfield and Gunstone (1997, p. 49) remind us that "teacher educators should maintain close connections with schools and the teaching profession." Although it is difficult to disagree with this view, the worlds of school and university can be very different and distinct places. Yet in teacher education, each relies heavily on the other for support, and cooperation is crucial. One major difference between the work of schoolteachers and the work of teacher educators can complicate understandings and expectations of each institution. Teachers are mainly concerned with the intricacies of *teaching itself,* which is both similar to and different from *teaching about teaching,* and it can be argued that these similarities and differences are not always fully grasped by both and can play out in unusual ways in student teachers' learning about teaching.

The type of close cooperation necessary to support quality learning about teaching requires recognition of three different perspectives: (1) the individual learning to teach, (2) the teacher in the school setting, and (3) the teacher educator in the university setting. Each requires careful consideration in constructing the relationships central to teacher education programming. Despite their naturally different perspectives, experienced teachers in schools and teacher educators in universities will have occasions to discuss the development and progress of the student teachers for whom they are responsible, yet it would seldom be the case that conversations about the experiences and expectations of learning to teach would involve all three together. Unfortunately, both experienced teachers and teacher educators tend to respond to the need for school-university relationships as being driven by their own program needs and concerns and student teachers' voices are strangely mute.

Student teachers' perspectives need to be sought actively and responded to positively in building up the relationships so crucial to quality in learning to teach (Goodlad, 1990). Cook-Sather (2002) captures this point and builds a strong link to principle 5 when she argues that student teachers' voices must be attended to in order to provoke a "conceptualization of teaching, learning, and the ways we study them as more collaborative processes" (p. 3). We maintain that the issues inherent in learning about teaching cannot be understood appropriately if a student teacher perspective is not adequately represented by student teachers themselves.

> Close cooperation is needed, not only in the sense of school-university partnerships, but also in three-way cooperation among teachers in schools, teacher educators in universities, and those who

are learning to teach. While school-university cooperation is often seen as the broad goal, it is easy to overlook the teacher candidate who is passing through the program structure en route to a classroom of her or his own. Ironically, if we were to view the temporarily present teacher candidate as the one with the most to gain from closer cooperation, that goal might be much more readily achieved. The problems that teacher education has faced for a long time, may be well due to the fact that this sixth principle has only recently been taken seriously in the organization of teacher education programs. (Korthagen, Loughran, & Russell, 2006, p. 1035)

7. Learning about teaching is enhanced when the teaching and learning approaches advocated in the program are modeled by the teacher educators in their own practice. Segall's (2002) analysis of the experiences of social studies methods course students at a Canadian university provides compelling evidence of the importance of modeling in teacher education. Segall highlighted the importance of breaking away from a technical-rational approach to teaching about teaching based on the "how to," the "what works," and the mastering of the "best" teaching methods (Aronowitz & Giroux, 1985, cited in Segall, 2002, p. 13). What Segall made abundantly clear was that for student teachers' deeply held views and assumptions about teaching to be challenged adequately, and for them to consider alternative approaches and be able to contextualize theory within practice and practice within theory, modeling pedagogical episodes that foster such challenges is crucial. Such modeling is not common in teacher education (Lunenberg, Korthagen, & Swennen, in press). In the absence of such challenges, it seems unrealistic to expect a transformation of teaching practices in schools.

It is not unusual to hear stories about teacher educators who advocate innovative practices to their student teachers but fail to model those innovative practices. Russell (1999) boldly questions this situation by asserting that "universities generally, and university-based teacher educators particularly, have no right to recommend to teachers any teaching practices that they have not themselves used successfully at the university" (p. 220).

Student teachers need opportunities to experience and learn about how experienced teachers and teacher educators take risks and develop new teaching approaches in their own practice as a fundamental form of modeling the development of pedagogical understanding: "Making the pedagogical reasoning for practice clear, explicit and understandable for student teachers is an important aspect of modeling teaching in teacher education" (Korthagen et al., 2006, p. 1036). However, although modeling offers ways of looking into practice, it should not be confused with attempts to simply demonstrate particular teaching procedures. Everything done in teacher education models something—the intended and the unintended.

> [Modeling needs to be] conceptualized as embracing the possibilities for critique and interrogation in learning about teaching experiences, no matter how they arise; be they planned or unplanned. Modeling of this form means that teaching itself is continually being questioned so that both the subtleties and complexities of practice might be viewed and reviewed in order to shed light on pedagogical reasoning, thoughts and actions. This view of modeling carries with it the hope that as students of teaching see their teacher educators teach in this way that they will be encouraged to risk doing the same. As a consequence, there is a greater likelihood that the holistic, nonlinear and personal nature of teaching might be better illuminated while at the same time the notion that knowledge of practice must inevitably be tacit may be challenged. (Loughran, 2006, pp. 39–40; see also Lunenberg et al., in press)

This approach to modeling offers student teachers a variety of ways of seeing for themselves the complexity of teaching while capturing the essence of teaching as a problematic activity, something that needs to be experienced to be understood and something that goes hand in hand with the confidence necessary to manage the uncertainty of practice.

Conclusion: Principles Working Together

In their exhaustive analysis of North American research on the effectiveness of teacher education, Cochran-Smith and Zeichner (2005) find no clear evidence that certain approaches in teacher education are more effective than others. However, Brouwer and Korthagen (2005) offer an alternative view of that conclusion:

> [Our research results] present empirical evidence that more specific principles guiding the practices within a program may lead to clear and positive outcomes in the graduates of such a program. This suggests an urgent need for identifying such principles, especially principles that support the link between experience and theory in ways that are responsive to the expectations, needs and practices of teacher educators and student teachers.

The seven principles we offer in this chapter resonate in many ways with teacher education programs across the globe. We believe that the principles fit together in such a way that their sum matters more than the individual principles alone and that, in considering the development of teacher education from a principled base, some of the concerns and issues raised by Cochran-Smith and Zeichner (2005) can be addressed.

The principles proposed in this chapter have a necessary interconnection that is illustrated in Figure 23.1. The principles can be grouped into three elements that we see as fundamental to teacher education: (1) views of knowledge and learning that direct the practices of the teacher educators, (2) program structures and specific practices, and (3) the quality of staff and organization.

This perspective on the seven principles acknowledges that simply changing a principle in one component without simultaneously addressing the other components reduces the power and effectiveness of the principles as a whole.

> For example, if teacher educators make the important step from building on *episteme* to developing *phronesis*, as when they start to see knowledge about teaching as a subject to be created instead of an already created subject (principle 2), this will require helping student teachers to become a strong community of learners in which they work and learn closely together (principle 5). This in turn has consequences for the way teaching practices are organized, which points towards the importance of principle 6. In other words, we believe it is the coherence across the three components . . . that will make a difference. (Korthagen et al., 2006, p. 1037)

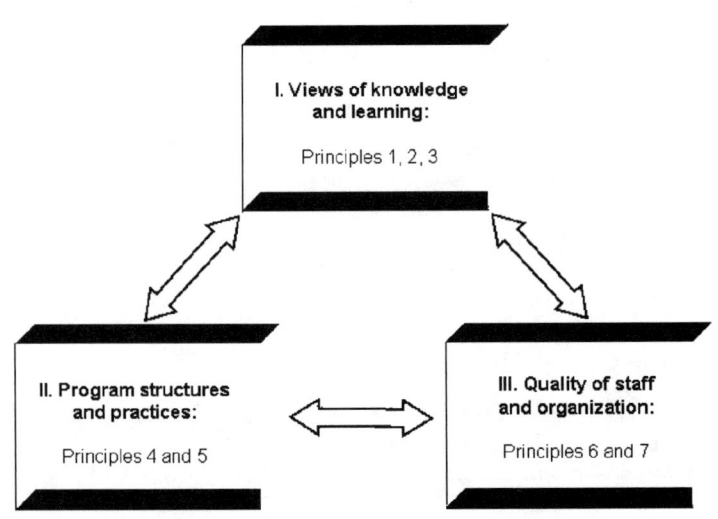

Figure 23.1 Clustering Seven Principles into Elements of Programs and Program Change

In working from this position about the principles and the manner in which they relate to one another, it becomes clear that program change in teacher education must be viewed as an in-depth process that does not happen in a meaningful way overnight. As Russell (1999, p. 221) reminds us, "it is far too easy to propose early changes that fail to give the innovation a clear chance." In contrast, considerable progress was made in the 15-year approach to bridging the gap between theory and practice played out in the IVLOS program in The Netherlands (see Korthagen & Kessels, 1999; Brouwer & Korthagen, 2005).

For program structures and practices to change, both how we think about teacher education and how we practice teacher education must change. Without such changes, the structures may look different and the way the constituent parts of teacher education are put together may be new, but the essence of student teachers' experiences of teaching and learning about teaching will still be traditional. Change is a long-term process, and at the heart of such change is the development of a pedagogy of teacher education driven by and constructed as a result of teacher educators accepting more responsibility for the nature of the total teacher education program experience.

The three aspects of Figure 23.1 are often viewed in isolation. This diminishes the likelihood that teacher education programs and practices can be genuinely responsive to the needs, concerns, and expectations of those learning to teach. Considering change in the holistic manner suggested by the seven principles and their inter-relationships is one way of more fully embracing a pedagogy of teacher education. The principles we offer here indicate one way of focusing attention on the place of experience in learning about teaching. The seven principles also provide a way of considering what a common language for the development of a pedagogy of teacher education might entail. The principles can act as guidelines and possibilities for all those teacher educators keen to work toward reconstructing teacher education from within. For teacher educators, it may be helpful to reflect on two questions: "How can I work with the principles in my own teacher education program?" and "What do the principles mean for my personal teacher education practices?"

References

Aronowitz, S., & Giroux, H. (1985). *Education under siege: The conservative, liberal, and radical debate over schooling.* South Hadley, MA: Bergin & Garvey.

Barone, T., Berliner, D. C., Blanchard, J., Casanova, U., & McGowan, T. (1996). A future for teacher education. In J. Sikula, T. Buttery, & E. Guyton (Eds.), *Handbook of research on teacher education* (2nd ed., pp. 1108–1149). New York: Macmillan.

Ben-Peretz, M. (1995). Curriculum of teacher education programs. In L. W. Anderson

(Ed.), *International encyclopedia of teaching and teacher education* (pp. 543–547). Oxford: Elsevier Science/Pergamon.

Brouwer, N., & Korthagen, F. (2005). Can teacher education make a difference? *American Educational Research Journal, 42*(1), 153–224.

Bullough, R. V., Jr., & Gitlin, A. (2001). *Becoming a student of teaching: Linking knowledge production and practice* (2nd ed.). London: RoutledgeFalmer.

Carlson, H. L. (1999). From practice to theory: A social constructivist approach to teacher education. *Teachers and Teaching: Theory and Practice, 5*(2), 203–218.

Clandinin, D. J. (1995). Still learning to teach. In T. Russell & F. Korthagen (Eds.), *Teachers who teach teachers* (pp. 25–31). London: Falmer Press.

Cochran-Smith, M., & Lytle, S. (1990). Research on teaching and teacher research: The issues that divide. *Educational Researcher, 19*(2), 2–11.

Cochran-Smith, M., & Lytle, S. (2004). Practitioner inquiry, knowledge, and university culture. In J. J. Loughran, M. L. Hamilton, V. K. LaBoskey, & T. Russell (Eds.), *International handbook of self-study of teaching and teacher education practices* (Vol. 1, pp. 601–649). Dordrecht: Kluwer Academic Press.

Cochran-Smith, M., & Zeichner, K. M. (Eds.) (2005). *Studying teacher education: The report of the AERA panel on research and teacher education*. Mahwah, NJ: Lawrence Erlbaum.

Cook-Sather, A. (2002). Authorizing students' perspectives: Toward trust, dialogue, and change in education. *Educational Researcher, 31*(4), 3–14.

Fenstermacher, G. D. (1997). Foreword. In J. Loughran & T. Russell (Eds.), *Teaching about teaching: Purpose, passion and pedagogy in teacher education* (pp. viii–xiii). London: Falmer Press.

Freudenthal, H. (1978). *Weeding and sowing: Preface to a science of mathematical education*. Dordrecht: Reidel.

Galesloot, L. J., Koetsier, C. P., & Wubbels, T. (1997). Handelingsaspecten bij wederzijds leren van ervaren docenten [Aspects of acting in reciprocal learning of experienced teachers]. *Pedagogische Studiën, 74*, 249–260.

Goodlad, J. I. (1990). *Teachers for our nation's schools*. San Francisco: Jossey-Bass.

Hagger, H., Burn, K., & McIntyre, D. (1993). *The school mentor handbook*. London: Kogan Page.

Hamilton, M. L., with Pinnegar, S., Russell, T., Loughran, J., & LaBoskey, V. (Eds.) (1998). *Reconceptualizing teaching practice: Self-study in teacher education*. London: Falmer Press.

Hermans, J. J., Créton, H. A., & Korthagen, F. A. J. (1993). Reducing the gap between theory and practice in teacher education. In J. T. Voorbach (Ed.), *Teacher Education 9, Research and developments on teacher education in the Netherlands* (pp. 111–120). De Lier: Academisch Boeken Centrum.

Kessels, J. P. A. M., & Korthagen, F. A. (1996). The relationship between theory and practice: Back to the classics. *Educational Researcher, 25*(3), 17–22.

Koetsier, C. P., & Wubbels, T. (1995). Bridging the gap between teacher training and teacher induction. *Journal of Education for Teaching, 21*(3), 333–345.

Koetsier, C. P., Wubbels, T., & Korthagen, F. A. J. (1997). Learning from practice: The case of a Dutch post-graduate teacher education programme. In M. I. Fuller & A. J. Rosie (Eds.), *Teacher education and school partnerships* (pp. 113–132). New York: Edwin Mellen Press.

Korthagen, F. A. J. (1985). Reflective teaching and preservice teacher education in the Netherlands. *Journal of Teacher Education, 36*(5), 11–15.

Korthagen, F. A. J. (2001). Building a realistic teacher education program. In F. A. J. Korthagen, with J. Kessels, B. Koster, B. Langerwarf, & T. Wubbels (Eds.), *Linking practice and theory: The pedagogy of realistic teacher education* (pp. 69–87). Mahwah, NJ: Lawrence Erlbaum Associates.

Korthagen, F. A. J., & Kessels, J. (1999). Linking theory and practice: Changing the pedagogy of teacher education. *Educational Researcher, 28*(4), 4–17.

Korthagen, F. A. J., Kessels, J., Koster, B., Lagerwerf, B., & Wubbels, T. (2001). *Linking practice and theory: The pedagogy of realistic teacher education.* Mahwah, NJ: Lawrence Erlbaum Associates.

Korthagen, F. A. J., Loughran, J. J., & Russell, T. (2006). Developing fundamental principles for teacher education programs and practices. *Teaching and Teacher Education, 22*(8), 1020–1041.

Korthagen, F., & Russell, T. (1995). Teachers who teach teachers: Some final considerations. In T. Russell & F. Korthagen (Eds.), *Teachers who teach teachers: Reflections on teacher education* (pp. 187–192). London: Falmer Press.

Kosnick, C., Beck, C., Freese, A., & Samaras, A. (Eds.) (2006). *Making a difference in teacher education through self-study: Studies of personal, professional, and program renewal.* Dordrecht: Springer.

Lanier, J., & Little, J. (1986). Research on teacher education. In M. Wittrock (Ed.), *Handbook of research on teaching* (3rd ed., pp. 527–569). New York: Macmillan.

Lather, P. (1991). *Getting smart: Feminist research and pedagogy within the postmodern.* New York: Routledge.

Lortie, D. C. (1975). *Schoolteacher.* Chicago: University of Chicago Press.

Loughran, J. (1996). *Developing reflective practice: Learning about teaching and learning through modelling.* London: Falmer Press.

Loughran, J. (1997). Teaching about teaching: Principles and practice. In J. Loughran & T. Russell (Eds.), *Teaching about teaching: Purpose, passion and pedagogy in teacher education* (pp. 57–69). London: Falmer Press.

Loughran, J. (2002). Effective reflective practice: In search of meaning in learning about teaching. *Journal of Teacher Education, 53*, 33–43.

Loughran, J. J. (2005). Knowledge construction and learning to teach about teaching. In D. Beijaard, P. C. Meijer, G. Morine-Dershimer & H. Tillema (Eds.), *New directions in teachers' working and learning environment* (pp. 27–41). Dordrecht: Springer.

Loughran, J. J. (2006). *Developing a pedagogy of teacher education: Understanding teaching and learning about teaching.* London: Routledge.

Loughran, J. J., Hamilton, M. L., LaBoskey, V. K., & Russell, T. (Eds.) (2004). *International handbook of self-study of teaching and teacher education practices.* Dordrecht: Kluwer Academic Publishers.

Loughran, J., & Russell, T. (Eds.) (1997). *Purpose, passion and pedagogy in teacher education.* London: Falmer Press.

Lunenberg, M., Korthagen, F., & Swennen, A. (in press). The teacher educator as a role model. *Teaching and Teacher Education.*

Lytle, S., & Cochran-Smith, M. (1991). Teacher research as a way of knowing. *Harvard Educational Review, 62*(4), 447–474.

Munby, H., & Russell, T. (1994). The authority of experience in learning to teach: Messages from a physics method class. *Journal of Teacher Education, 4*(2), 86–95.

Northfield, J. R., & Gunstone, R. F. (1983). Research on alternative frameworks: Implications for science teacher education. *Research in Science Education, 13,* 185–192.

Northfield, J. R., & Gunstone, R. F. (1997). Teacher education as a process of developing teacher knowledge. In J. Loughran & T. Russell (Eds.), *Teaching about teaching: Purpose, passion and pedagogy in teacher education* (pp. 48–56). London: Falmer Press.

Putnam, R. T., & Borko, H. (1997). Teacher learning: Implications of new views of cognition. In B. J. Biddle, T. L. Good, & I. F. Goodson (Eds.), *International handbook of teachers and teaching* (pp. 1223–1296). Dordrecht: Kluwer Academic Publishers.

Russell, T. (1995). Returning to the physics classroom to re-think how one learns to teach physics. In T. Russell & F. Korthagen (Eds.), *Teachers who teach teachers* (pp. 95–109). London: Falmer Press.

Russell, T. (1999). The challenge of change in teaching and teacher education. In J. R. Baird (Ed.), *Reflecting, teaching, learning: Perspectives on educational improvement* (pp. 219–238). Cheltenham, Victoria, Australia: Hawker Brownlow Education.

Russell, T. (2002). Guiding new teachers' learning from classroom to experience: Self-study of the faculty liaison role. In J. Loughran & T. Russell (Eds.), *Improving teacher education practices through self-study* (pp. 73–87). London: RoutledgeFalmer.

Russell, T., & Loughran, J. (Eds.) (2007). *Enacting a pedagogy of teacher education: Values, relationships and practices.* London: Routledge.

Samaras, A. (2006). *Self-study of teaching practices.* New York: Peter Lang.

Sandlin, R. A., Young, B. L., & Karge, B. D. (1992). Regularly and alternatively credentialed beginning teachers: Comparison and contrast of their development. *Action in Teacher Education, 14*(4), 16–23.

Schön, D. A. (1983). *The reflective practitioner: How professionals think in action.* New York: Basic Books.

Segall, A. (2002). *Disturbing practice: Reading teacher education as text.* New York: Peter Lang.

Stake, R. E., & Trumbull, D. (1982). Naturalistic generalisations. *Review Journal of Philosophy and Social Science, 7*(1&2), 1–12.

Stofflett, R. T., & Stoddart, T. (1994). The ability to understand and use conceptual change pedagogy as a function of prior content learning experience. *Journal of Research in Science Teaching, 31,* 31–51.

Tigchelaar, A., & Melief, K. (2000). Peer supported learning for students on paid practice: Student teachers learn to supervise one another. In G. M. Willems, J. H. J. Stakenborg, & W. Veugelers (Eds.), *Trends in Dutch teacher education* (pp. 185–195). Apeldoorn (The Netherlands)/Leuven (Belgium): Garant/VELON.

Upitis, R. (Ed.) (2000). *Who will teach? A case study of teacher education reform.* San Francisco: Caddo Gap Press.

Vedder, J. (1984). *Oriëntatie op het beroep van leraar* [Orientation towards the teaching profession]. Lisse: Swets & Zeitlinger.

Vedder, J., & Bannink, P. (1987). *The development of practical skills and reflection at the beginning of teacher training.* Paper presented at the meeting of the Association of Teacher Education in Europe, Berlin.

Wideen, M., Mayer-Smith, J., & Moon, B. (1998). A critical analysis of the research on learning to teach: Making the case for an ecological perspective on inquiry. *Review of Educational Research, 68*(2), 130–178.

Zeichner, K. M., & Noffke, S. (2001). Practitioner research. In V. Richardson (Ed.), *Handbook of research on teaching* (4th ed., pp. 298–330). Washington, DC: American Educational Research Association.

CHAPTER 24

Questioning What We Know About Teacher Education

Stefinee Pinnegar
Brigham Young University

Lynnette B. Erickson
Brigham Young University

> Stefinee Pinnegar, Ph.D., is an associate professor of Teacher Education in the McKay School of Education at Brigham Young University. Stefinee's research focuses on self-study of teaching practices and preservice and inservice teacher development.
>
> Lynnette B. Erickson, Ph.D., is an associate professor of Teacher Education in the McKay School of Education at Brigham Young University. Lynnette's research concentrates on preservice teacher education and elementary social studies education.

ABSTRACT

Traditionally, research and practices in the field of teacher education have mirrored the fluctuating educational expectations of society. Public dissatisfaction with education has led to deepening critiques of teacher education accompanied by increased control of it. Imposed accountability and uniformity are based on a perceived knowledge base. Indeed, many in the field advocate that research in teacher education should be a continuing investigation into the efficacy of what is currently accepted in teacher preparation, rather than a philosophical reconsideration. This chapter asserts that to avoid vigilance in asking questions leads to stagnation in the quality and depth of our understanding of teacher preparation and development. A renaissance in inquiry about teacher education could position us to ask better, more strategic, and more relevant questions about teaching and the preparation of teachers. Such inquiry would support teacher educators in designing programs and experiences that allow for the development of the kind of teachers we want to emerge from teacher education programs.

When we look at periods of renaissance in history (e.g., Harlem Renaissance, 12th Century Renaissance, Bengal Renaissance), they usually emerge from times of control, imposition, and turbulence. Teacher education is currently in such a season brought on by demands for reform in teacher education in general and processes for certification more specifically. Since the mid-1980s, teacher education has crossed the threshold of one reform cycle after another. In that time period, individuals and groups representing a variety of educational views have posited the claim, "We know a lot about teaching," or "We know a lot about teacher education." From these claims there typically emerge either prescriptive absolute directions for how teacher education should be or laments concerning its perceived failures.

An early example of this is the now fairly well known debate between Kagan and Grossman in which Kagan (1992) asserted that research on beliefs demonstrated that reflective teacher education and other such attempts to change preservice teachers' beliefs about the processes and purposes of teaching had little impact. She argued that instead of attempting to focus on developing reflective practice, teacher education programs should take a more pragmatic focus and give preservice teachers what they wanted—prescriptions for practice. In rebuttal, Grossman (1992) identified specific studies that demonstrated the impact of particular programs on preservice candidates' beliefs. She also highlighted research on teacher thinking and teacher belief that provided insight into how programs might proceed. These conflicting arguments were both built on the premise that we actually know a lot about teaching and how to promote teacher development.

Knowing and knowledge position (Harre & van Langenhove, 1999) us to further inquire and prompt us to ask valuable questions. The verbal or implied assertion, "we know a lot about teaching and teacher development and therefore we should do X" ignores the questioning cycle that allows us to identify what is not known and proceed to greater understanding and knowledge that then results in further questioning. Indeed, Eleanor Duckworth (1987) argues it is only when we know a lot that we're able to identify what we don't know. We are then able to ask difficult questions and move knowledge and understanding forward. Knowing then, instead of just providing answers, becomes the key to questioning leading to further knowledge, action, and efficacy.

This is demonstrated using the example of infants as they develop the concept of faces (Shaffer, 1995). Initially they look intently at the periphery of the face and at the obvious distinctions and contours. It is only when they develop skill in looking that they become able to carefully and critically examine the small triangle that includes the spaces and relationships between eyes, nose, and mouth that they develop the skill necessary for differentiating one face from every other face. Berliner (1986) reports research on the development of expertise in dog judges, which documents similar skill development among those who become experts in judging dog shows.

Assuming that knowledge is stagnate stifles questioning and limits understanding. We learn from Kuhn (1970) that the kinds of scholarship that result in paradigm change occur when we ask the questions that those engaged in "normal" science at the time considered answered, or when questions once considered to be non-questions were asked regardless of the currently accepted knowledge promoted in the field. Individuals who engage in questioning of current knowledge position themselves to juxtapose inquiry in ways that open up old avenues for new investigation.

In this chapter, we proceed from the perspective not that we know a lot about teacher education and teacher development but that we now know enough to both ask more relevant questions and to re-ask some of the questions people quit asking long ago. We wonder again about the problematics of fragmentation in the preservice teacher's education. We wonder again about the relationship between teaching and teacher belief. We wonder once more about the relationship of theory, practice, and experience. We question what impact institutional roles and relationships have on a potential teacher's development (Wideen, Mayer-Smith, & Moon, 1998). Finally, we ask what difference does any of this make for teacher education.

The Fragmented Influence of Teacher Education Programs

While the supposed failure of American teachers is laid squarely at the door of Teacher Education, teacher education programs account for a fairly small percentage of a future teacher's education. Although not commonly acknowledged, competing influences account for the development and creation of a final product that will ultimately bear the label of "teacher." This fragmentation of the teacher preparation process and knowledge building begs the question of what this does to teachers before, during, and after the formal preparation process.

Teacher education coursework represents a limited portion of the teacher candidates' preparation for teaching. Indeed, in some fields such as secondary teacher education, the proportion of teacher education coursework contributed by colleges of education toward the certification and licensure of a secondary teacher might be less than ten percent of their total course hours. Even in elementary education programs only about half of the coursework that prepares a teacher is centered in colleges of education.

Prior to the university experience, participation in elementary and secondary schools has provided years of subliminal professional development, or inculcation, for candidates entering the teaching profession. Students enter university preparation programs having spent the majority of their lifetimes in schools subconsciously absorbing the methodology and pedagogy of a host of teachers prior to even making application to a teacher education program. In addition, quality teaching pedagogy is usually not a requirement for teaching university courses, leaving the potential teacher exposed over and over to poor examples of teaching. The beliefs and dispositions teacher candidates hold as they enter the university are often affirmed and strengthened by their college experiences in general education and program related coursework.

Included in the teacher preparation coursework are the clinical experience components provided by and supervised by public schools. Preservice teachers routinely identify their clinical experiences as the most valuable part of their teacher education experience. They argue that they learned more from their supervising teachers than they did in any of their university coursework. Teacher candidates consistently report their mentor teachers' admonitions to them to "forget everything you learned at the university" (Russell, 1997), inferring that the real world found within the classroom requires knowledge and practices not taught or learned in teacher education programs.

There is a long history of disrespect for the value and complexity of teacher education coursework (Clifford & Guthrie, 1988). The irony is that teacher educators control a small portion of the total coursework and yet, both partners in the venture of educating teachers—university colleagues outside the college of education and public school teachers—encourage preservice candidates to discount what they learn in the coursework teacher education does control. Indeed teacher educators' ability to impact what candidates take from their coursework in teacher education depends on whether they believe that what is taught has value and how much moral authority they grant teacher educators in shaping their identity as teachers (Pinnegar, 2005).

Fragmentation, Alienation, and Isolation in the Education of Teacher Candidates

In exploring the missing links in teacher education, Hoban (2005) argues that one of the difficulties faced is supporting students in crossing the boundaries of general education, university courses, teacher education courses, and clinical experiences in order to develop identity as a teacher. Since teacher candidates must participate in general education and take numerous courses outside of teacher education, they face the same difficulties in learning that confront all first year college students: fragmentation, alienation, and isolation.

While universities in recent years have taken steps to respond to such challenges (Learning Communities National Resource Center, www.evergreen.edu/washcenter/project.asp?pid=73), fragmentation is still the norm at most colleges and universities. During their early college years, students are enrolled in super-sized classes that give them little contact with faculty who utilize lecture and multiple choice testing methods as their only interactions with students.

Experiences like these make students feel alienated and they rarely have an opportunity to develop relationships with their professors in the early years of their university educations. When students get into upper-division courses this experience could change. However, at this juncture, the routines, rituals, and practices (Wenger, 1998) of being part of a college community are already in place. By the time preservice teachers enter teacher preparation programs, proximity, small class size, and shared specialization could alleviate some issues of fragmentation and alienation. It does not compensate for their learned sense of what it means to "do college," study and learn from coursework, and participate as a student in a college education.

In addition, in their early years at the university, students' educational experience is fraught with competition, which leads to feelings of isolation. They are encouraged to work independently and to consider facts and content as isolated from each other. Future teachers, particularly elementary teachers, must rely on these fragmented, alienating, and isolating learning experiences to develop the content knowledge they will use to teach their future students. In their large biology course students are usually taught science content through a lecture/test method. They are learning not just the content of biology, but indirectly they are learning the rituals, routines, and practices that constitute what it means to be a teacher and learner of biology. Implicitly, this experience instructs them in how biology or even science in general should be taught (Wenger, 1998).

Teacher candidates also come to value the lecture-test approach as the highest level of teaching, even if they themselves feel alienated by it. Furthermore, in these kinds of courses teacher candidates are unlikely to develop deep content knowledge that they can draw on in developing elementary grade level science-learning experiences and encouraging the deeper understandings of their young students.

As a result of this kind of education most preservice teachers assume what Tagg (2003) calls a "surface approach" to learning. In this approach students focus more on jumping hoops, rote memorization, and focus on details rather than big ideas. In other words, they may not develop deep content knowledge in courses where a surface approach to learning is employed.

Students who take a surface approach to learning place responsibility for their learning on others. Tagg places the surface orientation against a deep orientation to learning, one in which students learn to learn, seek to find connections, and focus on overarching ideas. Students who take a deep approach take control and become interested in learning to learn and in guiding and developing their understanding. Research shows that the more years students spend at the university the more pervasive and entrenched a surface approach becomes (Tagg, 2003).

How individuals approach learning from one of these two orientations is significant for those entering the field of teaching. Teachers are responsible for selecting the content and designing learning experiences for their own students. If, as learners, teachers have a deep orientation to learning, they are more likely to create curriculum that positions their students as lifelong learners who know how to guide their own learning, apply school content to real life, and seek new opportunities to grow and develop.

Teacher candidates who have a deep orientation to learning potentially develop deeper content knowledge. Researchers in the content areas have demonstrated how an important consideration in curriculum design is the depth of students' content knowledge. For example, students who perceive math as a series of courses in which you learn to utilize only algorithms to solve math problems have few resources for using a math standards–based approach to teaching (Ball, 2001). In English education, preservice teachers whose understandings of theory, interpretation, and criticism are shallow generally use a superficial reader-response approach to teaching literature. Under this approach, a student's opinion reigns supreme and the teacher provides little or no education in multiple readings of text, the relationship of texts to their historical context, or even guidance in using literary terms to support a particular interpretation (Holt-Reynolds, 1999).

The criticisms of surface approaches to learning are exactly the same issues raised by those concerned about the learning and development of public school students. For example in learning to read students will fail to become proficient readers if they don't move from the position of learning to read to taking a position of reading to learn. Teachers educated in situations where their own experiences led them to embrace a surface approach to learning and where experiences in learning are fragmented, alienating, and isolating are the ones who will design the learning experiences the next generation of students will engage in.

Thus, we continue to wonder how teacher education programs can support teacher candidates in overcoming the fragmentation, alienation, and isolation inherent to the early college experience and often in their K–12 education. How do teacher education programs support teacher candidates in learning to become lifelong learners who develop similar outcomes for their own students?

Teacher Belief and Teacher Education

Teacher education as a field has accepted the fact that how teachers practice is related to what they believe about what it means to be a teacher and what it means to teach. Richardson (1996) laid to rest the fierce debate about the relationship between teacher belief and teacher practice. She maintained that there was a relationship but the relationship was not a straightforward one. She further (Richardson & Placier, 2001) argued that we needed to pay attention to preservice teachers' beliefs and that systematic ongoing exploration of beliefs about teaching and schooling should form a core of their experiences in teacher education coursework.

Bullough, Knowles, and Crowe (1991) demonstrated fairly clearly that preservice teachers' metaphors for teaching had an impact on their ability to succeed as teachers. They argued that while some metaphors might, in the long term, be more helpful than others to guide ongoing development as a teacher, what appeared to be more important was the depth of the development of an individual's metaphor for teaching. In their study, they followed six teachers, three who had well-developed metaphors for teaching and three who had quite shallow metaphors. The three teachers with well-developed metaphors were much more successful as teachers than those whose metaphors were shallow. Indeed, they argued that the preservice teacher needed to understand what they called "the dark-side" as well as the positive side of their metaphor—it was the depth and complexity of their metaphors that allowed them to manage and respond to the complexity of becoming a teacher.

Sprinthall, Reiman, and Thies-Sprinthall (1996) further demonstrated that one of the most important predictors of success in teaching was the teacher's own cognitive complexity. Holt-Reynolds's (1999) study of a content area reading course showed that students can demonstrate the use of content from education coursework that runs counter to their beliefs about and plotlines for teaching while enrolled in the course; but they simply do not incorporate or utilize that knowledge. After a course is over, any of the strategies, theories, or concepts taught that run counter to their belief simply do not become part of the knowledge they use to guide their teaching. In fact, multicultural education charts a long history of research where in spite of numerous attempts to overcome teacher beliefs about poverty and race, preservice teachers leave teacher education with the same concepts about race, class, and gender that they brought with them to teacher education (Cochran-Smith, Davis, & Fries, 2003).

In *Practice Makes Practice*, Britzman (1991) uses two case studies to reveal how the past experience of students emerges in their own work as teachers. Jamie Owl and Jack August, two undergraduate teacher education students, were studied as they attempted to implement university course teachings in their own high school student teaching practica. Though they had successfully learned information, methods, and strategies for how to conduct and manage students and content, during student teaching they found that actual classroom application was quite different.

Issues such as comparable experiences in school and schooling between teacher and students, personal identity, and expectations of self and others all influence the work of teachers and in these two cases resulted in failure on the part of both of these student teachers. These rituals of practice from their sixteen plus years of education formed a powerful apprenticeship of what counted as teaching and hindered their ability as teachers to enact practices that ran counter to their experiences.

Theory, Practice, Experience, and Teacher Education

In teacher education we usually separate theory and practice. We often suggest that universities own theories and public school teachers hold practice and that our responsibility at the university is to teach preservice teachers how to use theory to guide their practice. In contrast, Fenstermacher (1994) (as well as others) argues that theoretical knowledge and practical knowledge are different ways of knowing. Whereas theoretical knowledge ends in propositions, practical knowledge ends in action. Fenstermacher (1986) argues that one way to unpack practical knowledge is to look at practice and then engage teachers in unpacking their reasonings present in the practice.

As a teacher, Morgan-Fleming (1999) used a practical knowledge approach to explore her teaching around an issue where her actions were in opposition to ideas she held as fundamental beliefs. She explores an incident in which she kept students in from recess to read (thus punishing students with reading) when she had such a fervent belief in the importance of literature and engaging students with it in ways that promoted it. As a result of her careful analysis, she finds another way to meet competing demands and yet support student literacy development. What her analysis reveals is not so much that her beliefs were in collision but that her experience and her beliefs collided with each other. Preservice teachers have a difficult time bringing their theories or ours into practice. The complexity of classroom life and its dimensions (Doyle, 1986) mitigate against their ability to bring theory into practice.

However, what the simple dichotomy between theory and practice brings into relief is the fact that personal theory is embedded in our practice. Thus, both theory and practice are theoretic constructs and both guide our experiences in classrooms. As the saying goes, there is nothing more theoretical than a good practice and there is nothing more practical than a good theory. We wonder if a critical key in supporting preservice teachers is not in trying to transform theory into practice but to support them in exploring their experiences as a lens for examining and using both theory and practice.

Currently in teacher education a consequential debate rages which is another stage in the debate about professionalism. Essentially, two groups of teacher educator policy voices are pitted against each other, those who believe that anyone who is bright and has a desire should be able to be employed as a teacher and those who believe that teacher education makes a difference in the quality of teachers. The outcome of this debate may, in fact, result in the demise of teacher education. It will certainly result in the further fragmentation of educational responses to the preparation of teachers.

The Abell Foundation (Walsh, 2002; MacIver, Vaughn, & Katz, 2005) and Darling-Hammond (1994, 2000, 2002; Darling-Hammond, Berry, & Thorenson, 2001) squared off early in this most recent incarnation of the debate (remember the alternative certification debate in the 1980s and the establishment of Teach for America). Marilyn Cochran-Smith's voice as the editor of the *Journal of Teacher Education* often led. While the Abell Foundation/Darling-Hammond discussion centers on whether or not there is a research base for the claim that teacher education makes a difference in the education of children, Cochran-Smith has provided insightful analysis of the positions, politics, and potential policy outcomes of the debate (e.g. Cochran-Smith & Fries, 2001).

Many teacher educators currently feel somewhat blindsided by this debate and the furor surrounding it. They may wonder, "Why didn't I see this coming?" Fenstermacher (2002), in responding to Cochran-Smith and Fries' (2001) analysis, articulates the critical reason why so many teacher educators might have been caught off-guard. He posits the existence of differences in the ways these two groups define the "educational-space" representing the tension between teaching and learning. He argues that the deregulators in the debate define this space more simplistically than those who would professionalize teaching. The issue this raises is an interesting one for teacher educators, "What is the educational space of teacher education?"

While Fenstermacher's characterization asserts that this is an important difference in the debate between the two groups, it posits a rather straightforward relationship between teaching and learning as the basis for teacher education. As teacher educators, many have not only a different view about the complexity of the relationship between teaching and learning than those who would deregulate teacher education, but they actually view the relationship from a different standpoint.

Many teacher educators see the policy debate between professionalism and deregulation as exactly the terrain to be negotiated in the education of every teacher. In this chapter, we have explored this terrain in our concern about fragmentation and the relationship between belief and practice in the learning to teach process. One of the reasons for the debate between the two groups is that most preservice students come to teacher preparation programs believing they already know how to teach by virtue of the fact that they have been the recipients of teaching pedagogy throughout their formal educations.

Most legislators, presidents, and judges take the same view of teaching as many teacher candidates. Britzman (1991) argues that preservice teachers have been watching teaching for years without knowing the preparation behind the teaching acts and what is not known is not valued. Many policymakers agree with a well-known researcher in teacher knowledge, who once argued that while we can say whatever we want about the complexity of teaching, "it can't be that hard if people do it effortlessly all the time." Furthermore, those who might be our advocates in the public schools fail to recognize that they are part of the teacher education process and often undercut their university training as "theoretical" in favor of more "practical" school experiences.

Many of us in teacher education are not focused on the bar of accountability established by external agencies, because any of us that have been teacher educators for long recognize that if we choose not to admit a student into teacher education and they want to be a teacher, they will simply find another way. They may relocate to cities with severe teacher shortages, become long-time permanent substitutes, and through alternative routes to licensure become teachers. They may graduate from a university with a high G.P.A. in a major not related to education and join Teach for America. They may even found a charter or private school.

Instead, we focus on the students admitted to our program. We work to craft programs that move them from being students to being competent teachers of students. Of course, the research identified earlier has supported us in these efforts. We have focused on the educational space, which represents the tension between learning and teaching from the standpoint of how learners become teachers and how they negotiate the tensions between their own theories of teaching and learning and those represented by the institution of schooling.

Bullough has artfully and empirically established that this educational space begins in who students are as people (Bullough & Baughman, 1997; Bullough & Gitlin, 2001; Bullough, Knowles, & Crowe, 1991). Who we are as teachers emerges from who we are as people. Naturally then, a student's experiences as a learner, a student in schools, and his/her judgments and beliefs about those experiences creates a personal identity as teacher and learner. This is the subtext of learning to teach. The funds of knowledge of the preservice teacher, what they learned in math, history, English, extracurricular activities, on their own or in their family and what they learned about people and how to interact with them becomes an important basis for their education as teachers.

The path to becoming a teacher also begins in the beliefs or metaphors students have about learning, the role of teachers and the act of teaching and how they are connected (Bullough, Knowles, & Crowe, 1991). This plays out, as Holt-Reynolds (1999) argues, in decisions students make in teacher education about whether what they are learning is being learned as a student jumping the hoops of a college degree or as a teacher who will one day be confronted by a classroom full of students.

The path starts in their decision to teach: Why do they want to be a teacher? Have they come to teaching because that's what girls do until they get married? Have they come to teaching because they like being a student themselves? Have they come to teaching because they feel more comfortable with adolescents or children than with other adults? Have they come to teaching because they can't think of anything else to do? Have they come to teaching because teachers have easier lives than construction or factory workers (Lay, Pinnegar, Reed, Wheeler, & Wilkes, 2005)? Have they come to teaching because they have had a spiritual witness that teaching is their life work (Bullough, Patterson, & Mayes, 2002)? The path also begins where they are in their own human development process—as young adults, as middle-aged professionals from other fields, as disenchanted doctors, lawyers, as mothers with older children who want to contribute to the world in additional ways.

The educational space that Fenstermacher referred to is a human space and as a human space, it is a space located in Bahktin's (Holquist, 1981) zone of maximal contact, where a person's past life experience and knowledge come in contact with their present decision to teach and progress toward an indeterminate future. In other words it is located in a space of great inconclusivity where potential for good is both most vital and most vulnerable.

The space of teacher education is not just about conceptions of teaching and learning and the tension between them, it is also about educating one generation to care for, nurture, and educate another, and another, and another. Clandinin and Connelly (1996) marked this as a sacred space. This space is not inconsequential not only in the history but also in the future of teacher education. Current policy debates in teacher education feel like the fight between artifact hunters and governments over the ownership of Native American artifacts found in sacred burial grounds, because the voice of the human and tender concern about the vulnerability of this future space is hammered over as contested territory without a very clear articulation of what it is the fight is about (Appiah, 2007).

What Difference Does Any of This Make for Teacher Education?

From this time of turbulence, imposition, and control over research on and processes for teacher education, we have an opportunity for an educational renaissance. Such a time could lead us to reimagine the teacher preparation based in inquiry and new understandings of teaching and teacher development. We claim that we know a lot about teacher education, and in fact, we do know some things.

If we believe that knowledge truly allows further questioning and learning, then we will use what we know to examine our practices, build stronger programs, and ask more questions that broaden our horizons of teacher education beyond tradition and the boundaries of the obvious. Such questioning should lead us to value teacher education as an enterprise. We must look at institutional and environmental influences on those who choose to enter the field of education as potential teachers of children. We must attend to how these individuals are positioned prior to, during, and after teacher preparation so that they can create teaching plotlines that reflect deep understandings about students, subject matter, the cultural context, and what it means to be a teacher.

Knowing what we know about teacher education leads us to argue that we still must learn more if we are to design teacher education that educates teachers to meet the current and future demands of teaching today's students. The deficits in our current knowledge make us vulnerable, not only when we attempt to design teacher education programs, but also in any debates about policies and requirements for licensure. Claims that we know a lot about teacher education and teaching have been made most strongly in defending teacher education programs against simplified paths to alternative licensure and governmentally imposed prescriptions for teaching practice.

We need to explore how fragmentation, alienation, and isolation in previous educational experiences of preservice teachers affect teaching practices, what kinds of clinical and coursework experiences can respond most appropriately to those effects, and how we build on whatever teacher candidates bring to position them as the potentially good teacher they might become. We need to continue to explore the relationships between theory, practice, and experience. We need to question further how teachers develop and utilize their knowledge and understanding of content to develop curriculum that engages their students.

How do we and can we marshal theory, practice, experience, and beliefs to develop this terrain in ways that are most productive for the context where they are being constructed? How do we educate people not only to be teachers but also to educate other teachers? How do we help teacher candidates develop their identity as a teacher so that it will lead them to construct healthy, productive classrooms? When we look at students in teacher education courses, we cannot focus on a generic view of what we would like all teachers to be. Instead, we focus on the individual, who they could be as a teacher, and what we need to do to orchestrate their learning experiences in teacher education so that they can flourish.

We value the effort of our colleagues deeply engaged in research to demonstrate that teacher education as presently constituted makes a significant difference in the learning of public school students. We realize that they may consider our focus on questioning and exploring teacher education at this point to be politically naïve. We assure them we are concerned about the impact of the results of this dispute over licensure on this vulnerable educational space—the space in which we educate teacher candidates to move from their role as students to their roles as teachers.

Clearly this conversation in the field sidesteps what some would consider the more important issues—the issues that remain hidden when the focus of the field of teacher education research centers on defending current practice, rather than further questioning. What we assert here is that instead of merely arguing that we know a lot, we need to reconsider what we know in terms of what kind of teaching we value and what kind of teachers we want to emerge from teacher education programs. As a result this question rises to the fore: What would and does it take to support the development of individuals as teachers in ways that lead them to create the kind of classrooms we desire our children and grandchildren to be educated in?

References

Appiah, K. A. (2007). *Cosmopolitanism: Ethics in a world of strangers*. New York: WW Norton.
Ball, D. L. (2001). Teaching, with respect to mathematics and students. In T. Wood, B. S. Nelson, & J. Warfield (Eds.), *Beyond classical pedagogy: Teaching elementary school mathematics* (pp. 11–22). Mahwah, NJ: Lawrence Erlbaum Associates.
Berliner, D. (1986). In pursuit of the expert pedagogue. *Educational Researcher, 15*(7), 5–13.

Britzman, D. P. (1991). *Practice makes practice: A critical study of learning to teach.* Albany: SUNY Press.
Bullough, R. V., Jr., & Baughman, K. (1997). *First year teacher eight years later: An inquiry into teacher development.* New York: Teachers College Press.
Bullough, R. V., Jr., & Gitlin, A. (2001). *Becoming a student of teaching: Linking knowledge, production and practice* (2nd ed.). New York: RoutledgeFalmer.
Bullough, R. V., Jr., Knowles, G., & Crowe, N. A. (1991). *Emerging as a teacher.* London: Falmer.
Bullough, R. V., Jr., Patterson, R. S., & Mayes, C. T. (2002). Teaching as prophecy. *Curriculum Inquiry, 32*(3), 311–330.
Clandinin, D. J., & Connelly, F. M. (1996). Teachers' professional knowledge landscapes: Teacher stories. Stories of teachers. School stories. Stories of schools. *Educational Researcher, 25*(3), 24–30.
Clifford, G. J., & Guthrie, J. W. (1988). *Ed school: A brief for professional education.* Chicago: University of Chicago Press.
Cochran-Smith, M., Davis, D., & Fries, K. (2003). Multicultural teacher education: Research, practice, and policy. In J. Banks & C. Banks (Eds.), *Handbook of Multicultural Education* (2nd Edition, pp. 931–975). New York: Macmillan.
Cochran-Smith, M., & Fries, M. (2001). Sticks, stones, and ideology: The discourse of reform in teacher education. *Educational Researcher, 30*(8), 3–15.
Darling-Hammond, L. (1994). Who will speak for the children? How Teach For America hurts urban schools and students. *Phi Delta Kappan, 76*(1), 21–34.
Darling-Hammond, L. (2000). Reforming teacher preparation and licensing: Debating the evidence. *Teachers College Record, 102*(1), 28–56.
Darling-Hammond, L. (2002). Research and rhetoric on teacher certification: A response to "Teacher Certification Reconsidered." *Education Policy Analysis Archives, 10*(36). Retrieved March 23, 2007, from http://epaa.asu.edu/epaa/v10n36.html.
Darling-Hammond, L., Berry, B., & Thorenson, A. (2001). Does teaching certification matter? Evaluating the evidence. *Educational Evaluation and Policy Analysis, 23*(1), 57–78.
Doyle, W. (1986). Classroom organization and management. In M. C. Wittrock (Ed.), *Handbook of research on teaching* (3rd ed., pp. 392–432). New York: Macmillan.
Duckworth, E. (1987). *"The having of wonderful ideas" and other essays on teaching and learning.* New York: Teachers College Press.
Fenstermacher, G. D. (2002). Reconsidering the teacher education reform debate: A commentary on Cochran-Smith and Fries. *Educational Researcher, 31*(6), 20–22.
Fenstermacher, G. D. (1994). The Knower and the known: The nature of knowledge in research on teaching. *Review of Research in Education, 20,* 3–56.
Fenstermacher, G. D. (1986). Philosophy of research on teaching: Three aspects. In Wittrock, M. C. (Ed.), *Handbook of research on teaching* (3rd ed., pp. 37–49). New York: Macmillan Publishing Company.
Grossman, P. (1992). Why models matter: An alternate view of professional growth in teaching. *Review of Educational Research, 62*(2), 171–179.
Harre, R., & van Langenhove, L. (1999). *Positioning theory: Moral contexts of intentional actions.* Malden, MA: Blackwell Publishers.
Hoban, G. (Ed.) (2005). *The missing links in teacher education design: Developing a conceptual framework.* Netherlands: Springer.

Holt-Reynolds, D. (1999). Good readers, good teachers? Subject matter expertise as a challenge in learning to teach. *Harvard Educational Review, 69*(1), 29–50.

Holquist, M. (Ed.) (1981). *The dialogic imagination: Four essays by M. M. Bakhtin.* (C. Emerson & M. Holquist, Trans.). Austin: University of Texas Press.

Kagan, D. M. (1992). Professional growth among preservice and beginning teachers. *Review of Educational Research, 62*(2), 129–169.

Kuhn, T. S. (1970). *The structure of scientific revolutions* (2nd ed.). Chicago: University of Chicago Press.

Lay, C. D., Pinnegar, S., Reed, M., Wheeler, E. Y., & Wilkes, C. (2005). The positioning of preservice teacher candidates entering teacher education. In J. Brophy & S. Pinnegar (Eds.), *Learning from research on teaching: Perspective, methodology, and representation* (Vol. 11, pp. 237–254). Amsterdam: Elsevier.

Learning communities national resource center. Evergreen State College, Olympia, Washington. Retrieved March 23, 2007, from www.evergreen.edu/washcenter/project.asp?pid=73.

MacIver, M. A., Vaughn, E. S., & Katz, G. (2005, September). *A teacher for every classroom: New teachers in the Baltimore City public schools, 1999–2004.* Retrieved March 23, 2007, from www.abell.org/publications/detail.asp?ID=107.

Morgan-Fleming, B. (1999). Teaching as performance: Connections between folklore and education. *Curriculum Inquiry, 29*(3), 273–291.

Pinnegar, S. (2005). Identity development, moral authority and the teacher educator. In G. Hoban (Ed.), *The missing links in teacher education design: Developing a conceptual framework* (pp. 259–279). Netherlands: Springer.

Richardson, V. (1996). The role of attitudes and beliefs in learning to teach. In J. Sikula (Ed.), *Handbook of research on teacher education,* (2nd ed., pp. 102–119). New York: Macmillan.

Richardson, V., & Placier, M. (2001). Teacher change. In V. Richardson (Ed.), *Handbook of research on teaching,* (4th ed., pp. 905–947). Washington, DC: American Educational Research Association.

Russell, T. (1997). Teaching teachers: How I teach is the message. In J. Loughran & R. Russell (Eds.), *Teaching about teaching: Purpose, passion and pedagogy in teacher education* (pp. 32–47). London: Falmer Press.

Shaffer, D. R. (1995). *Developmental psychology: Childhood and adolescence* (5th ed.). Belmont, CA: Thomson Brooks/Cole.

Sprinthall, N. A., Reiman, A. J., & Thies-Sprinthall, L. (1996). Teacher professional development. In J. Sikula (Ed.), *Handbook of research on teacher education* (2nd ed., pp. 666–703). New York: Macmillan.

Tagg, J. (2003). *The learning paradigm college.* Bolton, MA: Anker Publishing Company, Inc.

Walsh, K. (2001). *Teacher certification reconsidered: Stumbling for quality.* Retrieved March 23, 2007, from www.abellfoundation.org.

Wenger, E. (1998). *Communities of practice: Learning, meaning, and identity.* Cambridge, United Kingdom: Cambridge University Press.

Wideen, M., Mayer-Smith, J., & Moon, B. (1998). A critical analysis of the research on learning to teach: Making the case for an ecological perspective on inquiry. *Review of Educational Research, 68*(2), 130–178.

Summary and Implications

Cheryl J. Craig

Louise F. Deretchin

In Division 6, the Loughran, Korthagen, and Russell chapter articulated seven principles of practice that are, in the authors' words, "fundamental and foundational to teacher education practices." Arising from sustained research of their respective programs dotted around the globe, the principles rose to the surface when three predetermined criteria were applied: the staff of the particular teacher education program considered the criteria to be fundamental, the principle differentiated the particular teacher education program from others in the world, and the principle was evident in many practices threaded throughout the program. Contrary to the *Studying Teacher Education* report in which Cochran-Smith and Zeichner (2005) stated that they found no clear evidence that certain approaches in teacher education were more effective than others, Loughran, Korthagen, and Russell argued that the principles they identified, particularly when approached holistically, "resonate in many ways with teacher education around the world." The authors furthermore maintained that paying close attention to the principles (summarized below for readers' benefit) would do much to address the concerns and issues that Cochran-Smith and Zeichner raised:

- Learning about teaching involves continuously conflicting and competing demands;
- Learning about teaching requires a view of knowledge as a subject to be created rather than as a created subject;
- Learning about teaching requires a shift in focus from the curriculum to the learner;
- Learning about teaching is enhanced through (student) teacher research;
- Learning about teaching requires an emphasis on those learning to teach working closely with their peers;

- Learning about teaching requires meaningful relationships between schools, universities, and student teachers;
- Learning about teaching is enhanced when the teaching and learning approaches advocated in the program are modeled by the teacher educators in their own practice.

Loughran, Korthagen, and Russell ultimately recommended that the principles be used to develop a common language for the development of teacher education pedagogy and as guidelines and possibilities for renewing teacher education from within. Furthermore, the authors suggested teacher educators actively employ the following inquiry questions to frame their use of the principles: "How can I work with the principles in my own teacher education program?" and "What do the principles mean for my personal teaching practice?"

Taken together, the principles and the inquiry questions are instructive and deeply connected to practice. This forms a stark contrast to "rhetoric[s] of conclusions" disconnected from the policy contexts that produced them, which are not only critical of research in teaching and teacher education in the United States but, by virtue of shared membership in organizations, such as the American Educational Research Association, throughout the world.

The inquiry questions that Loughran, Korthagen, and Russell used to conclude their chapter created an apt segue to Pinnegar and Erickson's "Questioning What We Know About Teacher Education" chapter, the final one in the yearbook. In their chapter, Pinnegar and Erickson reminded readers that periods of renaissance historically have arisen on the heels of periods of control and imposition. They then focused on a number of relevant wonders and ponders: the fragmented influence of teacher education programs, the fragmentation, alienation, and isolation in the education of teacher candidates, the relationship between teacher belief and teacher education, and the complexities associated with theory, practice, experience, and teacher education.

After providing insightful discussion concerning the conflicting ways that educational space is understood differently by different parties, the authors brought to public view an evaded question that pertained not only to their chapter, but to all chapters in this issue of the yearbook. It was this: "What difference does any of this make to teacher education?" While Pinnegar and Erickson did not directly respond to their own query, they keenly observed that "from time[s] of turbulence, imposition, and control over research on and processes for teacher education [comes] the opportunity for an educational renaissance . . ." The authors then reflectively threw themselves and their readers back on all that is known in the field of education which needs to be revisited and all that is not known which needs to be investigated through the framing of sharper questions and use of new and different modes of inquiry. Only this kind of approach, Pinnegar and Erickson declared, would extend "the horizons of teacher education beyond tradition and the boundaries of the obvious." Only through rigorous, sustained inquiry would the timeless query, "What would and does it take to support the development of individuals as teachers in ways that lead them to create the kind of classrooms in which we desire our children and grandchildren to be educated?" be embraced. Only then would we ignite a renaissance in teacher education that would profoundly touch lives.

Afterword

Cheryl J. Craig

Louise F. Deretchin

Six divisions, twenty-four chapters, fifty-nine authors, seven countries, and six regions of the United States. Teachers, teacher educators, graduate students, children, and even a humorist with a deep devotion to teaching brought multiple imaginings of a teacher education renaissance to this research enterprise. *Teacher Education Yearbook XVI* offers a multiplicity of ideas to wonder and ponder; a plethora of potential actions to provoke change with children's best interests ultimately held in view.